SHAREHOLDERS AND STAKEHOLDERS

This book explores the evolution of the shareholder in post-war Britain within the context of changing legal, political, economic and social conditions. It examines how the post-war transformation of the shareholder body influenced relationships amongst stakeholders, impacting corporate behaviour and the legal and political efforts to govern industry and financial markets.

The book addresses a number of themes, including: 1) how the movements for democratisation influenced the treatment of shareholder interests and the calls for stakeholder representation; 2) how the rhetoric of change created a narrative that deflected from the lack of systemic legal reforms and protected the status quo; 3) how, in the post-war consensus environment, political positions on equity ownership de-radicalised, but that proved unsustainable against a background of increasing political polarisation and industrial unrest; and 4) how the institutionalisation of the post-war shareholder body had profound effects on industry, the financial markets and the economy.

With these themes as a foundation, the evolutionary arch of the post-war shareholder is examined, focusing on developments that influenced the treatment and perception of shareholder and stakeholder interests, including nationalisations, shareholder democracy, corporate purpose and industrial democracy. The book further considers how these post-war changes contribute to the post-1979 legal treatment of shareholder and stakeholder interests, including subsequent changes to the Companies Act and the development of corporate governance codes. Parallels to contemporary movements for stakeholder capitalism, corporate purpose and ESG are drawn.

The historical analysis of the post-war shareholder provides a framework for considering current questions on shareholder primacy and the demands for systemic legal reforms. These missed opportunities for meaningful changes to the treatment of shareholder interests in UK company law serve as useful precedents for evaluating subsequent periods.

CONTEMPORARY STUDIES IN CORPORATE LAW

Series editors: Marc Moore, Christopher Bruner

Corporate law scholarship has a relatively recent history despite the fact that corporations have existed and been subject to legal regulation for three centuries. The modern flourishing of corporate law scholarship has been matched by some broadening of the field of study to embrace insolvency, corporate finance, corporate governance and regulation of the financial markets. At the same time the intersection between other branches of law such as, for example, labour, contract, criminal law, competition, and intellectual property law and the introduction of new inter-disciplinary methodologies affords new possibilities for studying the corporation. This series seeks to foster intellectually diverse approaches to thinking about the law and its role, scope and effectiveness in the context of corporate activity. In so doing the series aims to publish works of high intellectual content and theoretical rigour.

Titles in this series

The Foundations and Anatomy of Shareholder Activism
Iris H-Y Chiu

Corporate Governance in the Shadow of the State
Marc T Moore

Reconceptualising Corporate Compliance
Anna Donovan

Corporate Opportunities: A Law and Economics Analysis
Marco Claudio Corradi

The Making of the Modern Company
Susan Watson

Court-Supervised Restructuring of Large Distressed Companies in Asia: Law and Policy
Wai Yee Wan

Activist Shareholders in Corporate Governance: The Australian Experience and its Comparative Implications
Tim Bowley

Investment Management, Stewardship and Sustainability: Transformation and Challenges in Law and Regulation
Edited by Iris H–Y Chiu and Hans-Christopher Hirt

Diversity. Merit and Power in the C-Suite
Eleanore Hickman

Shareholders and Stakeholders

The Unrealised Promise of Company Law Reform in Post-War Britain

Joanne F Sonin

•HART•

OXFORD • LONDON • NEW YORK • NEW DELHI • SYDNEY

HART PUBLISHING

Bloomsbury Publishing Plc

Kemp House, Chawley Park, Cumnor Hill, Oxford, OX2 9PH, UK

1385 Broadway, New York, NY 10018, USA

29 Earlsfort Terrace, Dublin 2, Ireland

HART PUBLISHING, the Hart/Stag logo, BLOOMSBURY and the Diana logo are trademarks of Bloomsbury Publishing Plc

First published in Great Britain 2023

A catalogue record for this book is available from the British Library.

A catalogue record for this book is available from the Library of Congress.

ISBN: HB: 978-1-50996-680-6
ePDF: 978-1-50996-682-0
ePub: 978-1-50996-681-3

Typeset by Compuscript Ltd, Shannon

For my parents, Avi and Helena

Acknowledgements

IT IS WITH sincere gratitude that I would like to acknowledge those whose help and support allowed me to pursue this research project, which began as a doctoral thesis in law at the London School of Economics and Political Science (LSE). I am very grateful to my thesis supervisors, Professor David Kershaw and Mr Edmund Schuster, for giving me the opportunity to take a 'deep dive' into the research topics that are at the core of my professional and academic interests. The support that I have received from David and Edmund has been invaluable and I am profoundly thankful for their encouragement, guidance and critique. In addition, I would like to thank Professor Marc Moore and Professor Michael Lobban, my dissertation examiners, for their diligent, supportive and insightful comments on my PhD thesis. I would also like to thank the many other colleagues and peers at the LSE for their input and encouragement, and in particular Professor Jo Braithwaite and Professor Sarah Paterson. Of course, any errors in my work are wholly my own.

The LSE provided me with a rigorous academic environment and an unparalleled platform from which to undertake research, both as a PhD student and subsequently as a Visiting Fellow at the Law School. I am particularly grateful for the LSE library, and especially the team working in the Special Archives Collection, for its critical help accessing archival documents during the many disrupted and difficult months of the COVID-19 pandemic that profoundly impacted all aspects of life.

I would like to thank Professor Paul Cartledge of the University of Cambridge to whom I owe the debt of planting the seed for the idea of pursuing a PhD in law, as well as for his endless encouragement. In what seems like a lifetime ago, Paul supervised my PhD in classics, and just as his guidance was pivotal then, so it remains today. His enduring friendship is greatly cherished.

For the many friends and family who have encouraged and supported me, I am thankful, and especially my parents, my sister and my exceptional grandmother. Finally, I am grateful for Bella and Hattie, in whose company I have done much of my best work and clearest thinking, and who are my much-loved companions.

Joanne F Sonin
Exmoor
March 2023

Contents

Table of Legislation

UK Legislation, Regulation and Statutory Instruments

Command Papers, Reports, and Official Documents

1

Introduction

THE PRINCIPLE OF shareholder primacy is central to the modern debate on the purpose of the corporation and how shareholder and stakeholder interests are treated in company law, as well as how that treatment is perceived more broadly. This book focuses on the historical progression of this debate in post-war Britain, examining the evolution of the relationships amongst shareholders and other stakeholders, and how, despite profound changes in British society and in the political landscape, and notwithstanding the campaigns of the post-war movements that posed meaningful challenges to the prioritisation of shareholders, the doctrine of shareholder primacy remains a foundational principle in UK company law.[1] It is through the examination of these post-war developments that context is provided for the consideration of subsequent and current challenges to, and defences of, shareholder primacy in UK company law, as well as being relevant points of reference for the ongoing and varied calls for changes in corporate behaviour and for the elevation of stakeholder interests. This work is a historical examination of shareholder and stakeholder interests in the post-war period and how the gestures of change and the calls for reform to core company law remained, ultimately, unrealised. Through the lens of history, and more specifically legal history and the history of law, it considers and addresses these issues, shedding light on the law, the society that it governs, and the political, economic and social environments in which it exists and from which it develops.

The current initiatives for stakeholder capitalism unfolding today reflect vivid historical precedents from the post-war period, which culminated in the industrial-democracy movement that reached its apex in the 1970s. This book seeks to advance the understanding of the contemporary debates on shareholder primacy and stakeholder capitalism by offering considered analysis of their antecedents. It also highlights the parallels that exist amongst the various attempts at legal reform, using historical examples both as a guide for better understanding the motivations of various constituents and as a means to identify attempts at deflection and distraction by entrenched interests invested in preserving the status quo. The legal treatment of shareholders and other stakeholders, and more specifically of directors' duties bound to the primacy of shareholders,

[1] See Moore (2018) 144.

has implications for corporate behaviour, governance norms, financial market efficiencies, economic performance, and societal engagement and acceptance, prompting strong arguments from all sides of the shareholder primacy debate. Notably, the post-war evolution of shareholder and stakeholder interests, and the associated struggle between those seeking to disrupt the existing system and those determined to preserve it, demonstrate that, even when there is political will, public support and mounting momentum, legal reforms can be stubbornly difficult to realise.

The investigation of the post-war period reveals insights into the arguments for, and against, preserving a system based on shareholder primacy that are presented in the ongoing contemporary debate, often as new approaches to recurring issues. Whereas today's challenges to shareholder primacy reflect the circumstances and conditions of the current period, there are lessons that can be learnt from considering prior attempts to realise similar systemic changes and, importantly, why these were not achieved. In the post-war period, entrenched participants effectively resisted and deflected attempts by different constituents, from the trade unions to the advocates for property-owning democracy, to introduce legal reform, successfully preserving the principle of shareholder primacy that continues to underpin UK company law. Grasping the nuances of these developments, the motivations of the different parties, and the tensions that existed between and amongst them provides a framework from which to consider the legal treatment of shareholder and stakeholder interests, giving perspective both for those seeking change and for those favouring the protection of the status quo. The post-war period, although in many ways fundamentally different from the current era, also displays notable similarities with how the modern debates on UK company law, as well as the broader questions on the purpose of the company, the relationships amongst stakeholders and the shape of British capitalism, are deliberated and viewed.

I. THE POST-WAR ERA

The post-war era from 1945 to 1979 spans the transformational decades from peacetime reconstruction immediately following the Second World War through to the end of the post-war political consensus that allowed for the emergence of a modern Britain that became the foundations on which subsequent economic and financial market policies were built. The systemic recalibrations of the 1980s that were the hallmark of Prime Minister Margaret Thatcher's policies and that are associated with the tenets of Thatcherism, and that are often embedded in the current debates on the legal treatment of shareholder and stakeholder interests, as well as on the roles and responsibilities of the financial markets and their participants, cannot be separated from their post-war origins and the political, economic and social conditions from which they emerged. The post-1979 free-market approaches to state ownership of industry, shareholder and stakeholder interests, industrial relations and property-owning democracy, to give a few examples, are part of a historical continuum that is inseparable from the policies of the post-war consensus that preceded it and that are the focus of this book. This examination of post-war shareholder and stakeholder interests contrasts the received narrative of change that accompanies the attempts at reform with the static nature of the core company laws that govern shareholder interests and that remain mostly unchanged, veiled by the rhetorical positioning of interested constituents, including law-makers, policy-makers, leaders of industry and other incumbents. The principle of shareholder primacy has resisted, and continues to resist, decades of proposed legal reforms and efforts by different movements to elevate the position of non-shareholder stakeholders. To gain a deeper understanding of the endurance and persistence of shareholder primacy in UK company law, it is necessary to look to the period that pre-dates the 'Big Bang' and the Thatcher reforms of the 1980s, and to delve into the historical events and currents of the often-underconsidered post-war era of 1945–79, including the movements for shareholder democracy and industrial democracy, which inform the post-1979 legal discourse on shareholder primacy and stakeholder capitalism.

This book focuses on the interests of the equity shareholder, who occupies a central position amongst the participants in the financial markets and whose primacy amongst stakeholders is a core concept in UK company law.[2] The composition and evolution of the shareholder body are key elements in evaluating corporate behaviour, stakeholder interactions, industrial development and legal frameworks, and changes in political, economic, and social conditions are reflected in how shareholders are perceived and treated, including in relation to questions of law and legal reform.[3] This work considers the rights and interests of shareholders and other stakeholders in the context of Britain's post-war era, spanning from reconstruction and the post-war consensus through to the advent of Thatcherism, and examines how, in conditions of volatility and societal change, established systems were put under pressure and the status quo was questioned.[4] During this historical period, the identity of the equity shareholder underwent a transformation that reflects the changes in society that were shaped by the ebbs and flows of political policies and economic conditions, which influenced how the shareholder was perceived, characterised and treated by various influential constituents, such as the main political parties, the trade unions and industry representatives.

Following the historical arc of the post-war period, the consideration of the evolution of the shareholder body sheds light on the relationships amongst the various interested parties and provides insights into how the financial markets

[2] See, for example, Hansmann and Kraakman (2001) 440; Deakin (2005) 11; Moore (2018) 145ff.
[3] Cheffins (2008) 86.
[4] Fox (1985) 375ff.

and industry shaped (and were shaped by) the shifting circumstances, and how this was reflected in company law. The broad ideological conflicts of the post-war period, and the evolution of the political mood from the consensus at the beginning of the era to the breakdown of the settlement by the late 1970s, informed the debates on such questions as shareholder primacy, the purpose of the company and the reform of company law.[5] In particular, the nationalisation policies introduced following the end of the Second World War were fundamental to post-war reconstruction and were of critical importance to equity shareholders, contributing to the trajectory of the development of shareholder democracy and industrial democracy as means to address the tensions between capital and labour and capitalism and socialism. The post-war treatment of shareholder interests and of the demands for company law reform provide context for understanding how the principle of shareholder primacy remains embedded in the existing system and how it was (and still is) central to many of the movements for change, including, for example, corporate social responsibility, stakeholder capitalism and corporate purpose, as well as the varied manifestations of environmental, social and governance (ESG) initiatives. During the three-and-a-half decades of the post-war era, the composition of the shareholder body fundamentally changed, with political, economic and social reverberations for the next stage in Britain's economic and regulatory cycle that began in the 1980s and that lay the foundations for the global financial crisis of 2007–08 that gave rise to today's contemporary considerations of corporate behaviour, governance and the need for systemic changes that have a strikingly familiar resonance.[6]

II. THEMATIC OUTLINE

This study of the shareholder body is underpinned by several key interconnecting themes that weave through the historical narrative and analysis. The first of these themes is the utilisation of the framework of democracy to consider shareholder and stakeholder interests. Democratisation was a key factor to the development of post-war Britain, and the language of democracy was increasingly used by industrialists, trade unionists and politicians who sought to engage with the public to position themselves favourably within the changing political landscape.[7] Within the historical context of the clash between the political left and right, the equity shareholder was a useful avatar for those attacking, as well as those defending, the existing system.[8] The different manifestations of 'democracy', be it shareholder, corporate or industrial, were used to fortify

[5] Kavanagh (1992) 186.
[6] Poole (1982) 193.
[7] Hennessy (2007) 360; Jefferys (2007) 89; Moss et al (2016) 443.
[8] Morgan (1992) 29.

claims of legitimacy and strengthen political positioning across the spectrum, ranging from socialism to capitalism, nationalisations to privatisations, and shareholder primacy to stakeholder capitalism.

The second theme considers how rhetoric and communications devices were used as a means of deflection to protect and preserve the status quo, creating a narrative of reform that masked the lack of meaningful systemic change.[9] Through public statements and gestures, the entrenched parties, as well as the outsiders who were drawn into working within the established system, went through the motions of change, seeming to respond to the calls for the recalibration of shareholder and stakeholder interests and for addressing the existing inequalities, while failing to implement core reforms.[10] The post-war period exemplifies this type of deflection behaviour, demonstrating how, despite what appeared to be irreversible momentum to restructure company law to create a system that empowers non-shareholder stakeholders, and more specifically workers, change was not forthcoming even when backed by public support.[11]

The third main theme is how the political deradicalisation brought about by the post-war consensus influenced the treatment of shareholder and stakeholder interests, a trend that faded by the end of the post-war period, which witnessed a reversion to more polarised politics.[12] Although the political rhetoric of the various parties remained mostly consistent with the traditional positions of the main parties – for example, the anti-capitalist Labour Party and the free-market Conservative Party – the bipartisan cooperation of the post-war consensus required a pragmatism that had implications for the treatment of shareholders and stakeholders.[13] As part of the post-war consensus, both the Labour Party and the Conservative Party accepted the policies of a mixed economy and compromised on issues such as the terms and scope of nationalisations, the handling of shareholder rights and the expansion of shareholder democracy, and addressing industrial relations and the implementation of industrial democracy.[14] The examination of the trajectory of the treatment of shareholder and stakeholder interests in the post-war period shows how, on the one hand, the outsiders and reformers, when faced with the task of governing and administrating, metamorphosised into insiders functioning within the established system, and, on the other hand, how the establishment, to preserve its entrenched position, adapted its approach while resisting systemic changes.[15]

The final key theme that connects all the chapters of this book is the institutionalisation of the post-war shareholder body that reached a critical inflection

[9] Bainbridge (2021) 317.
[10] Fairfax (2006) 706.
[11] Clift, Gamble and Harris (2000) 80; Moore (2018) 159; Pollak (2013) 105.
[12] Middlemas (1991) 178; Davies (2017) 13.
[13] Kavanagh (1992) 177; Dutton (1997) 30ff.
[14] Dutton (1997) 51.
[15] Dutton (1997) 31, 35; Kavanagh (1992) 183.

point in the post-war period, during which it transitioned from mostly dispersed, often apathetic, individual investors to more concentrated, occasionally more active and almost always more sophisticated institutional equity owners.[16] This change in shareholder identity impacted the relationships amongst the various interested constituents and had transformational implications for the distribution of power amongst them.[17] The increasing dominance of the institutions influenced how the democratisation of investing was understood, that is, a refocusing from direct to indirect equity ownership, and underpinned the phenomena of deflection and deradicalisation as the capital markets were fortified by the financial institutions.[18] With this fundamental shift in the shareholder base, the role of the equity owner altered, impacting how the interests of the company, and its shareholders, were interpreted; by the 1970s, the forces seeking to upset the shareholder primacy-based system faced a significantly different target from the small shareholders that had dominated equity ownership at the beginning of the post-war era.[19]

III. STRUCTURAL OUTLINE

With these central themes as signposts, this book considers how the shareholder fits into the political and social discourses and trends of the post-war period, how the concept of the shareholder and the idea of share ownership were used by political actors and were reflected in the law, how the centrality and importance of shareholders (in their different forms) fluctuated depending on the mood of the nation, the state of the financial markets, the stage of the economic cycle and the attitudes towards equity share ownership, and, finally, how these post-war developments impact subsequent eras. Chapter 2 focuses on post-war nationalisations, which provide the historical bedrock on which the understanding of the period's treatment of shareholders should be built. The implementation of the Labour Party's programme to place British industry in the hands of the state was a radical move, although one that was quickly mitigated by operational realities.[20] The post-war equity shareholder faced profound challenges, although fared better than initially feared in light of Labour's ambitious nationalisation programme and, in some cases, even benefited from the state's intervention in failing companies.[21] Already by the 1950s, however, the public's support for nationalisations was wilting and the ways in which state expropriations were implemented and managed became progressively less radical, contributing to the

[16] Cheffins (2008) 345.
[17] Cheffins (2008) 87.
[18] Davies (2017) 215; Cheffins (2008) 350.
[19] Littlewood (1998) 257.
[20] Morgan (1992) 34.
[21] Kavanagh and Morris (1989) 20.

ongoing debate on the roles and responsibilities of companies and their equity owners, as well as their relationships to the state and to the British people.[22]

Chapter 3 addresses the consequences of the post-war nationalisation policies, which created the conditions for shareholder democracy, seen as an alternative way to address inequalities and as a less radical means of including average British working men and women in the burgeoning property-owning democracy.[23] Shareholder democracy was partly a reaction to the socialist and nationalisation policies of the immediate post-war years by attempting to make more individuals direct owners of shares in British industry and resisting the growing dominance of the institutional investors.[24] To understand the support for shareholder democracy, this chapter provides an overview of the types of post-war shareholders and how the shareholder body changed during the period, examining how the perception of the shareholder, whether accurate or not, was integral to the debate on shareholder rights and interests. It also considers how the changes in the make-up of the shareholder body impacted investor behaviour and governance norms. Despite its efforts, however, the post-war shareholder democracy movement failed to gain widespread acceptance, facing the significant obstacles of nationalisations and a lack of broad engagement by UK-listed companies, while also being outpaced by the growing momentum of industrial democracy, which faced its own challenges to achieving systemic reforms.[25]

Chapter 4 examines the interplay between the changes in the shareholder body and corporate purpose, including the doctrine of shareholder primacy, and how these developments influenced both conduct and expectations. The disconnect between company law and corporate behaviour is considered in relation to the development of post-war attitudes to shareholder and stakeholder interests, and how they were addressed in the public debate by various constituents.[26] There were tensions between the accepted shareholder primacy norm and 'enlightened' approaches to what it meant for directors to act in the best interests of the company, contributing to the post-war calls for company law reform.[27] The impetus for broadening corporate purpose beyond shareholder interests was increasingly evident in how directors communicated with their equity owners, as well as with other stakeholders, revealing expectations of increased inclusivity that were not reflected in core company law.[28] The shareholder-primacy debates of the 1970s, set against the backdrop of Britain's economic and political challenges, helped lay the foundations for the

[22] Barry (1965) 379; Shonfield (1958) 170.
[23] Davenport (1961b) 376; Edwards (2016) 108; Francis (2012) 280.
[24] Davenport (1961a) 341; Edwards (2016) 109; Francis (2012) 288.
[25] Rutterford and Sotiropoulos (2017) 529.
[26] Ireland (1996) 300.
[27] Shenfield (1971) 162; Smith (1998) 280.
[28] Fairfax (2006) 697.

financialisaton of the 1980s, which continue to define the terms of the discussion today.[29]

Chapters 5, 6 and 7 address the overreaching topic of industrial democracy. With the sputtering of shareholder democracy, and building on the achievements of the nationalisation policies, industrial democracy became the focus of those seeking to reform British industry, as well as to consolidate their power in the struggle between labour and capital.[30] Chapter 5 considers the worker shareholder, that is, workers as equity owners of the companies for which they were employed. Worker share ownership affects the debate on industrial democracy from two main perspectives: first, that of worker becoming an equity owner and not just the provider of labour; and, second, how the interests of the existing equity shareholders are impacted. The post-war movement for worker shareholders was promoted as a means of addressing the inequalities of British society, while also using equity ownership to integrate labour into the capitalist system as owners and not just as workers.[31] In addition, worker share ownership was part of the more general push for increasing saving and investing by average men and women, occurring at a time when the entrenched British class structure was under pressure from the political empowerment of the working class and the power of the trade unions, as well as from growing industrial unrest.[32] Whereas there was muted enthusiasm by workers for direct share ownership, a result of practical considerations and a lack of interest, it was in the post-war period that growing numbers of workers became indirect owners through pensions and other retirement and investment schemes offered by the financial institutions.[33] This indirect equity ownership by workers might not be the industrial democracy envisioned by its architects, but the ambition of achieving widespread direct ownership of British industry by workers was unattainable.[34]

Chapter 6 on industrial democracy examines the post-war movement for worker representation on company boards, which became the main focus of the industrial democracy movement in the late 1960s and early 1970s, with the promise of legislative reforms that would elevate the interests of employees in company law.[35] Initially, worker directors were associated primarily with the nationalised industries and were separated from the broader idea of worker control through ownership. The demands for worker representation on company boards, however, spilled over from state-owned industries to include all companies and became the central focus of the post-war industrial democracy movement, pushing the calls for worker shareholders further to the margins.[36]

[29] Oren and Blyth (2019) 606.
[30] Cottrell (1978) 58; Gumbrell-McCormick and Hyman (2019) 92.
[31] Goss (1973) 19.
[32] Grout (1987b) 13.
[33] Copeman and Rumble (1972) 33; Plender (1982) 14.
[34] Whiting (2004) 105.
[35] Elliott (1984) 139ff.
[36] Trades Union Congress (1944) 19.

This chapter looks at the role played by trade unions, and the Trades Union Congress (TUC) as the organised representative of workers, and how their expanding power influenced industrial democracy policies. In the mid-1970s the TUC, as the representative of many (but not all) trade unions, finally amended its position and put its support behind the statutory requirement for worker directors, placing itself in the role of gatekeeper to labour, thereby accepting the framework of the existing system for its industrial democracy platform.[37] The potential introduction of worker directors on company boards had implications for the rights and interests of existing equity shareholders, as well as for the responsibilities of all board members, raising issues that challenged the legal status quo.[38] Against this backdrop, an emboldened political left believed that statutory reforms were forthcoming and almost inevitable; however, what seemed like unstoppable momentum to codify the principles of industrial democracy was not nearly as certain as its supporters assumed.[39]

Chapter 7, which also addresses industrial democracy, is an examination of the Bullock Committee and its Report, and considers how, despite conditions that seemed primed for reform, the core company laws that underpinned the principle of shareholder primacy remained mostly unchanged.[40] By the time of the Committee and the Report in the mid-1970s, the post-war consensus was unravelling and the political cooperation of the prior decades was no longer in evidence, with the major political parties reverting to their traditional moorings and the industrial democracy movement becoming a major battleground in the struggle between capital and labour, a dynamic that was made clear in the evidence given to the Bullock Committee and by the partisan positions taken by its members.[41] This chapter looks at the intentions of the Bullock Committee and how its recommendations, and subsequent failed attempts at industrial democracy legislation, exposed the movement's vulnerability to the fluctuating fortunes, and changes in the leadership, of its political patron, the Labour Party.[42] The weakened Labour Party governing during these years of political, economic and social instability produced diluted goals and delivered inadequate results; the Conservatives' return to power in 1979 on the back of the industrial unrest and public dissatisfaction exemplified during the 'winter of discontent' exposed the Bullock Report as a paper tiger.[43] The Report, for all its initial ambition and the excitement it created amongst its supporters, and alarm for its opponents, was first weakened by compromises and then discarded, relegated to a

[37] Trades Union Congress (1974) 37.
[38] City Company Law Committee and Great Britain Committee of Inquiry on Industrial Democracy (1977) 10.
[39] Elliott (1984) 294.
[40] Gamble and Kelly (2001) 112.
[41] Middlemas (1991) 180.
[42] Confederation of British Industry (1977) 13.
[43] Elliott (1984) 294.

footnote in history as a failed attempt to introduce statutory industrial democracy reforms that would transform the capitalist system of post-war Britain.[44]

Chapter 8 examines the historical period that bridges the end of the post-war era with the enactment of the Companies Act 2006, the legislation that currently governs company law and the treatment of shareholder and stakeholder interests. This chapter is not a comprehensive analysis comparable to the detailed study of the post-war period in the preceding chapters, but a selective examination of legislative and regulatory events that follow from the topics explored in these earlier chapters, in particular how shareholder primacy and the movements for stakeholderism advanced after the end of the post-war settlement. This chapter calls attention to the key threads of the prior chapters and their continued development in the relevant aspects of company law and corporate governance in the subsequent post-1979 period. The pattern of there being the semblance of reform, accompanied by persuasive rhetoric and effective deflection while the established shareholder-primacy-based legal system remained mostly unchanged, persisted despite the profound transformations in British society during the decades of the post-war era and those that followed. As in the post-war period that preceded it, the political, economic and social backdrop changed dramatically from 1979 to 2006, whereas the primacy of the shareholder, the prioritisation of shareholder interests and the creation of shareholder value remained virtually unmolested throughout.

The concluding Chapter 9 considers how this analysis of the events from the British post-war period is relevant to the contemporary debate on shareholder primacy and the continued evolution of the shareholder body. This final chapter emphasises the parallels between the issues examined in the book and what has occurred since the global financial collapse of 2007–08 that was the eventual result of the free-market capitalism and deregulation policies of the 1980s.[45] Events that pre-date the Thatcher era do not seem to attract sufficient attention from leaders of industry, commerce, finance and politics, and the lessons that could (and should) be learnt from the post-war period are mostly lost, despite some remarkable similarities in tone and tenor.[46] The post-war shareholder existed in a fundamentally different political and economic environment from today's equity investor, yet much of the debate on shareholder and stakeholder interests remains notably similar, as does the shareholder primacy doctrine in UK company law on which they depend.[47] The groundswells of enthusiasm for

[44] Morgan (1992) 430. At the same time in the US, the Corporate Democracy Act of 1980 was introduced to Congress by Representative BS Rosenthal, with eight co-sponsors and the support of an alliance consisting of labour, consumer, religious, and environmental groups, as well as the national figure and presidential candidate, Ralph Nader. The bill did not succeed and no further action was taken after it was referred to committee. For a summary, see Kolb (2008) 465; for a contemporaneous discussion, see Keim, Baysinger and Meiners (1981).

[45] Oren and Blyth (2019) 618.

[46] On Labour's lessons from Bullock, see Pollak (2013).

[47] Kershaw and Schuster (2019) 31.

an array of movements for corporate purpose and stakeholder capitalism recycle many of the same promises of their post-war predecessors, seeming to achieve similar results of rhetorical deflection and distraction that draw attention away from core legal reform.[48] The close analysis of the post-war period sheds light on both the systemic entrenchment of shareholder primacy in UK company law and the cyclical nature of how various constituents react to those laws; for all the clamouring for reforms, both now, in the post-war period and in the decades in between, these core legal changes prove elusive.[49] This final chapter offers some concluding insights on the intersection between the modern debate and the (often underestimated) lessons of history.

This book addresses the post-war treatment of shareholder and stakeholder interests in UK company law through historical methodologies and approaches and is neither a defence nor an attack on the principle of shareholder primacy or on the movements seeking to prioritise non-shareholder stakeholders. Rather, it is a study of how different constituents sought to advance their interests within the historical and political contexts of their time, examining the specifics of the era, as well as any identifiable patterns and possible lessons that can inform later observers seeking to address comparable or related questions. The history of the legal treatment of shareholder and stakeholder interests is more than just the study of the law itself, but also includes an analysis of the conditions in which the law exists, the pressures both to reform and preserve it, and the actions and reactions of the parties whose interests, both directly and indirectly, were impacted by legal developments. The result is a layered, sometimes contradictory and often equivocal investigation of this aspect of the post-war history of UK company law and the society and constituents that it governed. This book seeks to contribute to the broader understanding of the modern debate on the legal treatment of shareholder and stakeholder interests, bolstering the historical foundation on which contemporary analyses can be built.

[48] Bainbridge (2021) 312; Bebchuk and Tallarita (2020a) 98.
[49] Coulter (2020) 535.

2

Nationalisations and the Post-war Shareholder

I. THE POST-WAR CONSENSUS

Modern UK financial markets did not begin in 1986 with the 'Big Bang', despite the creationist implications of the name, and the decades of the post-war period that preceded it provide rich historical context for understanding how the UK evolved from being an embattled post-war economy to becoming one of the main financial centres in the world.[1] The post-war period, which spans from the end of the Second World War to the late 1970s and is often described as the 'post-war consensus' or 'post-war settlement', was a period of Keynesian-managed capitalism, which led to the liberalisation and deregulation of the 1980s that brought about fundamental changes in UK financial institutions and markets.[2] It is within this context that the post-war evolution of the shareholder body – and how it was perceived and treated – is considered, with the nationalisations of the period being instrumental in understanding the relationship amongst the participants and the attempts to rebalance the relationship between shareholders and stakeholders. Post-war nationalisations were vital to creating the setting in which the treatment of shareholder and stakeholder interests developed.

The recalibration of British industry to a peacetime economy, which included nationalisations, was a central aspect of this repositioning, with consequences for existing equity shareholders. At the end of the Second World War, the British public was demanding increased inclusivity and opportunity within industry, holding politicians to their wartime promises of greater prosperity and equality.[3] The war, said to be fought for the common man, had ruthlessly disrupted civilian society and rocked the established class structure, which further strengthened the demands for a more egalitarian Britain. It demonstrated how the state can mobilise for the benefit of the nation as a whole,

[1] Littlewood (1998) 428.
[2] Konzelmann, Chic and Fovargue-Davies (2021) 610.
[3] Dutton (1997) 12.

an idea that was at the ideological foundations of the post-war consensus, propagating the belief that the state could (and should) reduce social injustice and, through economic growth, create a better life for all. The war showed that there were alternatives to the status quo and there was no desire by the British public to give up on these changes following its end.[4] In the volatile and demanding economic conditions of the immediate post-war era, bold policies were required to rebuild Britain's economy and to support the societal changes that the country was undergoing, which encouraged popular calls for systemic reforms that evoked responses from some politicians and leaders that threatened – or promised, depending on one's view – to disrupt the established system.[5]

During the war and as part of the wartime coalition government led by Prime Minister Winston Churchill, all major parties committed to a bold reconstruction programme that included plans for social insurance, education, the national health service, state housing and full employment.[6] Many of the national programmes that were at the foundation of Britain's post-war reconstruction were derived from these wartime policies, bolstering the political consensus and contributing to the muted tones of the opposition to the new Labour government's policies, even though the post-war settlement deviated from the Conservative Party's historical and interwar platforms, and included aspects that were firmly rejected by many party members.[7] In contrast to its Conservative rival, Attlee's Labour Party not only campaigned on the interventionist merits of the reconstruction programmes, but also promised to go further than the post-war agreement, including nationalising key industries, including coal, transportation and steel, as well as giving more power to organised labour, building on policies that were already part of the Labour's platform before the war.[8]

Labour's emphatic victory in 1945 with 47.8 per cent of the vote (compared to the Conservatives' 39.6 per cent) and the surprising defeat of Winston Churchill were regarded as an endorsement of the Labour Party's socialist mandate and of the plan to continue implementing and augmenting the gains of wartime cooperation, a testament to the British electorate's readiness for change and willingness to express its political will and expectations for social progress.[9] Labour's surprise victory was a transformational historical event, as described by the historian David Edgerton: 'The capitalist country with the largest organized working class in the world (now well unionized) had put a workers' party into office with a majority for the first time.'[10]

[4] Dutton (1997) 14.
[5] Dorey (1995) 5.
[6] Addison (1985) 18; Barry (1965) 370.
[7] Eatwell (1979) 158.
[8] Addison (1985) 19; Dutton (1997) 35.
[9] Dutton (1997) 11, 28; Middlemas (1986) 112.
[10] Edgerton (2018) 217.

II. SUPPORT FOR RADICAL REFORM OR CYCLICAL CHANGE?

The election results in 1945 were a watershed event, with the British electorate giving a majority, for the first time, to the Labour politicians whose policies promised to raise the standard of living for all citizens, creating a new post-war Britain of increased equality and greater opportunities based on socialist principles. The constituents that supported the Labour Party in 1945 were, however, much more varied and unexpected than a socialist political platform would suggest, including voters from commuter towns, suburban neighbourhoods and cathedral cities, as the broader British public sought assurance that the unemployment, stagnation and despair of the interwar period did not return.[11] Although the support for Labour reached far beyond its socialist base, the ideological basis for its political programme was clear. As the Labour Party made explicit when delineating its industrial programme in its 1945 election manifesto:

> The Labour Party is a Socialist Party, and proud of it. Its ultimate purpose at home is the establishment of the Socialist Commonwealth of Great Britain – free, democratic, efficient, progressive, public-spirited, its material resources organised in the service of the British people.[12]

Within this context, the welfare of British workers and the prioritisation of full employment, as well the willingness to oppose the business community, were key elements of Labour's political platform and important priorities for many of its supporters, including the trade unions:

> They [Labour's opponents] say 'Full employment. Yes! If we can get it without interfering too much with private industry'. We say 'Full employment in any case, and if we need to keep a firm hand on industry in order to get jobs for all, very well. No more dole queues, in order to let the Czars of Big Business remain kings in their castles. The price of so-called "economic freedom" for the few is too high if it is bought at the cost of idleness and misery for millions.'[13]

Working-class voters were instrumental to the Labour Party's victory:

> [A] culmination of the growth of class consciousness, a class consciousness reflecting a variety of factors, including the growth of socialism, but more generally a negative rejection of, in Mass Observation's [a social research firm] words, the '"Them" who make vast profits', and belief that 'we' could have a better life.[14]

The Labour victory should not be interpreted, however, as a popular embrace of radical reform, even if it was a move to the ideological left and an electoral upset; in his report on the election, the Secretary of the Labour Party described

[11] Morgan (1992) 27.
[12] Labour Party (1945); Dale (2000b) 55.
[13] Labour Party (1945); Dale (2000b) 54.
[14] Eatwell (1979) 43.

the electoral victory in negative terms, noting that: 'There was a tidal wave of popular discontent which submerged the Tories.'[15] The election results were as much a vote against the Conservatives as they were for Labour, and although this meant an acceptance of more socialist policies, 'overall this was hardly a reforming consensus; a rejecting consensus might be more apposite'.[16] The post-war election of a political party that used the language of socialist ideology did not reflect a conversion to socialism by a large portion of the British public, but a decision by many voters to reject the Conservative Party and its political agenda in favour of change.

Class identity was an important aspect of how an individual voted in the elections following the end of the war.[17] The voting public's support of Labour in 1945 was partly a result of the party's new appeal to the middle class, with Labour gaining 21 per cent of the middle-class vote (compared to 54 per cent for the Conservatives), but, more significantly, capturing the votes of those who identified as working class; of those polled by Mass Observation, 43 per cent gave working-class identity as their specified reason for voting Labour, with the next reason given, behind by a large margin at 6 per cent, being support for nationalisations.[18] By the 1950 general election, voters' class consciousness was still strong and their identification with the Labour Party strengthened, with Mass Observation finding that 47 per cent of Labour voters identified class as the reason for their choice, up from 43 per cent in 1945. Tellingly, no other specific factor was identified as having a meaningful influence on their preferences.[19]

A survey conducted by the polling company Gallup after the 1945 election asked respondents whether they thought that the victory reflected the electorate's desire for Labour to govern along existing lines or to implement more radical changes, such as nationalisations; 56 per cent saw it as a choice for radical change, compared to 30 per cent for staying on the existing course, and both Gallup and Mass Observation found general support for changes rather than for specific legislation.[20] At the same time, there were some voters who hoped that the social change brought in by the new government would be a way to preserve order and stability:

> The presence of Clement Attlee in Downing Street, a far more conventional figure in social philosophy and personal tastes than the romantic, swashbuckling Tory who had preceded him, testified to the sense of national contradiction or perhaps self-deception.[21]

[15] Eatwell (1979) 43.
[16] Eatwell (1979) 44; Kynaston (2007) 80.
[17] Eatwell (1979) 129.
[18] Edgerton (2018) 42; Eatwell (1979) 42.
[19] Eatwell (1979) 130.
[20] Eatwell (1979) 43.
[21] Morgan (1992) 28.

The election of Attlee's Labour Party was not a cry for revolution, with the Labour leaders themselves not seeking to tear down the existing system and replace it with a socialist alternative, but to work within the established system to implement the Party's programme of post-war reconstruction and reforms.[22]

With the Labour Party in government, the Conservatives were jarred into reconsidering their political positions, creating conditions that allowed for the compromises required by the post-war consensus and for the deradicalisation of both parties.[23] The geopolitical context of 1945 Britain was one that pre-dates the decline of communism and one in which the hegemony of capitalism was by no means assured in the struggle between these two major ideological camps, with the promoters of socialism in Britain making earnest promises of a better future. The Labour Party's 1945 manifesto, *Let Us Face the Future*, proclaimed ambitiously that:

> The nation needs a tremendous overhaul, a great programme of modernisation and re-equipment of its homes, its factories and machinery, its schools, its social services … [T]he Labour Party is prepared to achieve it by drastic policies and keeping a firm constructive hand on our whole productive machinery; the Labour Party will put the community first and the sectional interests of business after.[24]

In this manifesto, Labour presented nationalisations as a step on the path towards the eventual Socialist Commonwealth of Great Britain.[25] Despite the emphatic language of the manifesto, and against the realities of the post-war political landscape, ideological dogma gave way to the practicalities and pragmatism of rebuilding the nation, and the Attlee government, building on the policies of the wartime coalition, undertook the task of reconstruction within the framework of a mixed economy; although socialist ideology informed Attlee's policies and governing decisions, including the nationalisations of elements of British industry, it did not lead to profound systemic transformation.[26]

III. NATIONALISATIONS AND THE FOUR LEVERS OF THE BRITISH ECONOMY

The post-war nationalisations are central to understanding the shifts in assumptions about shareholders and industry that jolted the established market players. Clement Attlee's post-war Labour government introduced programmes that were part of the Party's domestic platform that pre-dates the Second World War, but had hitherto been relegated to theory, including the sweeping nationalisation of British industry that sought to take control of the four levers –

[22] Middlemas (1986) 109.
[23] Dutton (1997) 48.
[24] Labour Party (1945); Dale (2000b) 53; Eatwell (1979) 34.
[25] Labour Party (1945); Dale (2000b) 55; Dutton (1997) 36.
[26] Dutton (1997) 32; Middlemas (1986) 164.

finance, land, transport, and coal and power – of the British economy.[27] The new Labour government had an unprecedented numbers of Members of Parliament (MPs) that came from the working and middle classes rather than from the ruling or cultural elite, which further contributed to the advancement of policies that led to the recalibration of the relationships amongst the leaders of industry, the financial sector, the providers of capital and various other stakeholders, including organised labour and workers.[28] Once introduced, the nationalisations cast a long shadow over British industry, viewed by some as welcome shade and by others as darkened obscuration, and that, despite later changes in governments, proved to be persistently sticky until eventually dislodged by the upheavals of Margaret Thatcher's privatisations in the 1980s.[29]

The newly elected Attlee government was committed to implementing the Labour Party's policy of nationalising British industry, a central political objective alongside the establishment of the modern welfare state.[30] Labour was clear in its intentions regarding state interventions and expropriations, and the post-war nationalisation policies, based on the party's pre-war plans, were ambitiously carried out.[31] As part of the post-war consensus, the plan for reconstruction included state control of certain industries, with Labour embracing these policies fully, leading to the most comprehensive nationalisation programme in British history.[32] The political left had advocated for nationalisations and promoted the principles of industrial democracy since the nineteenth century, and the Labour Party, now in government, was finally in a position to implement these economic policies.[33]

In 1918, the Labour Party adopted as part of its constitution what was to become known as Clause IV:

> [T]o secure for the producers, by hand or by brain, the full fruits of their industry and the most equitable distribution thereof that may be possible upon the basis of common ownership of the means of production, and the best obtainable system of popular administration and control of each industry or service.[34]

Although the Labour Party had long advocated for the nationalisation of private industry, its victory in 1945 meant that, for the first time, it needed to devise mechanisms for implementation, with the Attlee government establishing a Ministerial Committee on the Socialisation of Industries tasked with examining the logistics of nationalisations, including issues of shareholder

[27] Harris (1995) 137.
[28] Edgerton (2018) 41.
[29] Kavanagh (1992) 188.
[30] Harris (1995) 317.
[31] Barry (1965) 372.
[32] Addison (1985) 177; Chester (1975) 38; Eatwell (1979) 159.
[33] Chester (1975) 2. Sir Norman Chester's work on the nationalisation of British industry from 1945 to 1951 was a government publication, published by Her Majesty's Stationery Office; Sir Norman is recognised as the foremost authority on the subject of post-war British nationalisations.
[34] Webb (1918) 3; Barry (1965) 200; Coates (1995) on Clause IV and the Labour Party.

compensation, finance and organisation.[35] The gap between political ideals and administrative execution needed to be bridged by the new government, which had a mandate to lead a nation in need of extensive rebuilding, but which had limited hands-on experience.[36] There was no detailed blueprint or draft legislation for many elements of Labour's expansive programmes, including nationalisations, despite the wartime coalition's significant planning for post-war reconstruction.[37] The business of passing legislation to implement Labour's platform needed to be addressed, and bills, which were the responsibilities of different ministries depending on the industry, had to be drafted and then presented to Parliament for approval, a process that subjected political dogma to the arduously practical demands of implementation.[38] Despite its ideological commitment, the new government was unprepared for the upheaval that nationalisations would have on the British economy, which was heavily dependent on the private sector; Labour's original programme was to nationalise 'the lot', even though private industry was responsible for 80 per cent of national output.[39]

A. National Service and Efficiency

The Attlee government maintained that its nationalisation programme was for the good of the nation and that 'each industry must have applied to it the test of national service. If it serves the nation, well and good; if it is inefficient and falls down on its job, the nation must see that things are put right'.[40] Invoking managerial and operational efficiencies, as well as the fair distribution of national assets and wealth, the government proceeded to transfer the ownership of companies and industries from private to public hands.[41] In the five years following the end of the Second World War, the Bank of England (1946), coal (1946), telecommunications (1946), civil aviation (1946), electricity (1947), railways (1947), canals (1947), long-distance road haulage (1947), gas (1948), and iron and steel (1949) were all nationalised by the Labour government, adding more than two million employees to the public sector and accounting for roughly one-fifth of all economic activity.[42]

The Labour Party promoted nationalisations:

> [A]s means of organizing industry more efficiently (cutting out 'wasteful' competition, controlling basic industries and making private monopolies public); more justly

[35] Chester (1975) 41.
[36] Chester (1975) 22; Edgerton (2018) 217.
[37] Eatwell (1979) 49; Edgerton (2018) 218.
[38] For a detailed study of the parliamentary procedures and the processes, see Chester (1975).
[39] Shonfield (1958) 160.
[40] Labour Party (1945); Dale (2000b) 55.
[41] Dutton (1997) 36.
[42] Addison (1985) 177; Chester (1975) 39; Barry (1965) 372.

> (profit for private assets would not take precedence over the interests of workers); and more democratically (workers would have more direct and indirect representation in the enterprises in which they are employed).[43]

Companies and industries that were flailing or failing were the targets of plans to save them in the name of the national interest, with supporters of nationalisations arguing that the state could manage and operate companies (and even whole industries) more effectively and more fairly than the private sector, as was evidenced by the management failures and public controversies that led to the state expropriation of industries in need of intervention.[44] With the expropriations, the nationalised companies became the time-consuming responsibilities of Whitehall, with politicians and civil servants tasked with managing industries.[45]

Although it was hoped that by taking ownership from shareholders and control from directors, the nationalised companies would become examples of scientific management and good industrial relations, in most cases, these ambitions were not realised and the state-run companies failed to become profitable.[46] Writing in 1965, the historian and journalist Anthony Sampson observed:

> In retrospect, perhaps the most surprising fact about the nationalisations was how, in spite of all the theorising and discussion that preceded it, hardly any of the nationalisers had any idea of how large corporations could, or should, be run; this was part of the price of the divorce between parliament and the world of management.[47]

The 1950 Labour Party manifesto, *Let Us Win Through Together*, reflecting the tone of a party seeking re-election, set a more accommodating tone for industry, addressing the concerns of those decrying the inefficiencies and inadequacies of state-run companies. It stated that:

> Labour will not be content until each public enterprise is a model of efficiency and of social responsibility. The Government must be free to take all necessary steps to that end. The initiative and public spirit of the individual manager must be fostered. New leadership should be given its chance to emerge.[48]

These are not the words of socialist revolutionaries, but of a Labour Party faced with the practicalities of governing and the need to promote economic growth that required compromises and cooperation with industry.

The threat of nationalisation presented a dilemma for existing shareholders, often with stakes in underperforming companies; in the immediate post-war period, the shareholder body was still made up mostly of small individual direct investors whose position was typically weak relative to directors

[43] Shenfield (1971) 12.
[44] Chester (1975) 9.
[45] Kynaston (2007) 444.
[46] Middlemas (1979) 412.
[47] Sampson (1965) 572; Sampson (1971) 616.
[48] Labour Party (1950); Dale (2000b) 66; Chester (1975) 39.

and management, although the threat of nationalisation introduced a new dynamic to this relationship as the basis of equity ownership was challenged.[49] When faced with the government's nationalisation policies, many managers and directors sought to secure their own position, often at the expense of their shareholders; the industrialists appeared to be more concerned with confirming their position of the 'managerial elite' and its right to manage British industry than with protecting the rights of the owners (that is, the shareholders) of these companies.[50] Nationalisations were a protracted process during which the companies in question often remained under the control of the existing directors and managers, impacting how these companies were run and for whose benefit.[51] Under these circumstances – that is, state intervention in the running of companies and industries – the disconnect between ownership and control was amplified.

B. Support of the Trade Unions

As part of its nationalisation platform, the Labour Party promoted increased worker participation through the instruments of industrial democracy, working with its natural partners, organised labour.[52] By 1945, the commitment to the requirement for workers' control of public companies was relaxed and '[t]he responsibility of actual management was, however, to rest with full-time professional administrators personally accountable to their superiors and selected solely on the basis of technical and administrative competence'.[53] Instead of becoming examples of state-controlled excellence, the nationalised companies were increasingly independent from the state, with many being managed by individuals from private industry, although performance and operational gaps remained. As Anthony Sampson observed:

> The running of the nationalised industries still presents an unsolved problem to both political parties. They have not reached the comfortable confidence of private industry – self-perpetuating, self-financing, self-admiring. The relations between Whitehall and the state industries – the largest of all parental problems – is still unhappy.[54]

Alongside the nationalisations, the commitment to full-employment and a competitive labour market contributed to the strengthening of the trade unions, which represented a more organised, demanding and confident post-war working class.[55] The unions supported Labour in its plans for the widespread nationalisations of British industry, with the TUC stating in its 1944 Interim

[49] See ch 3, section II.A of this volume for a more detailed discussion of individual shareholders.
[50] Middlemas (1986) 142.
[51] Chester (1975) 333.
[52] See chs 5 and 6 of this volume on industrial democracy.
[53] Coates and Topham (1975c) 54.
[54] Sampson (1965) 593.
[55] Fox (2017) 211.

Report on post-war reconstruction, which details its recommendations for public ownership, that:

> It is not only the Trade Union Movement, however, which recognises the importance of establishing some measure of public control over industry and trade. Full employment; price stability; the protection of the people, either as workers or consumers, against exploitation; the equitable distribution of income and economic opportunity, and the promotion of national development and national security are all aims widely acknowledged to be a responsibility of government which demand some measure of planning, regulation and control if they are to be fulfilled.[56]

And that:

> A controlled economic system is a modern necessity in advanced industrial communities. The choice before us is not between control or no control, but, in principle, between control by public authority responsible to the community, or control by private groups and persons owing a final responsibility to themselves alone and, in detail, between degrees of control and types of control.[57]

The TUC, whose Interim Report was endorsed by the Labour Party, was instrumental in the development of the nationalisation policies and an important player in the post-war movement for industrial democracy, supported the expropriation of British industry as a way of creating a more equitable system for the benefit of British workers and the wider community.[58]

The promotion of nationalisations as benefiting the working class and workers did not, however, address the possibility that these same individuals might also be shareholders in the targeted companies, either directly or through pension plans or other investment schemes that were part of the burgeoning post-war industrial democracy movement; in the post-war period, the number of workers enrolled in schemes rose substantially, from 1.5 million in 1936 to 6.3 million in 1953 and 11.8 million in 1979 (51 per cent of the total workforce).[59] For the worker, there was not necessarily a direct awareness of how the government's nationalisation policies impacted the schemes in which they might be invested, a new experience for much of the working class that was now more likely to be (indirect) equity shareholders.[60] As the lines between the providers of capital and of labour blurred, so the effects of nationalisations on the individual became more complex.

C. Nationalisations as Industrial Democracy

The political upheaval that brought Clement Attlee to power was the setting within which post-war industrial democracy developed – that is, a groundbreaking

[56] Trades Union Congress (1944) 7.
[57] Trades Union Congress (1944) 8.
[58] Barry (1965) 372.
[59] Davies (2019) 83; see ch 5 of this volume for more detailed discussion of the worker shareholder.
[60] Davies (2019) 100.

majority Labour government committed to social and economic changes, including the growth of the welfare state and the recalibration of British industry through nationalisations and worker empowerment.[61] The movements for industrial democracy not only represented the recognition of the increase in the power of workers and their representatives in the trade unions, but also became the means by which elements of the establishment sought to incorporate workers into the existing system that, in many cases, labour claimed to oppose. The Labour Party's nationalisation programme is an example of how radical industrial policies – in the 18 months following the 1945 election, over 20 per cent of the economy was either taken into public ownership or was in the process towards that end – created opportunities to increase the power of workers and to implement a sweeping industrial democracy programme, although, with the exception of the nationalisations, many of these reforms remained largely unrealised.[62]

Whereas nationalisations were promoted as a means to create a fairer and more equal Britain, the policy of expropriation that was pursued vigorously by the Labour government was not demanded by the workers themselves and was seen as a middle-class idea, be it utilitarian or Fabian, rather than one that came from the workers.[63] Furthermore, the nationalisation programme was viewed as a missed opportunity by the industrial democracy movement because of the government's failure to link workers' control with public ownership of industry, the result of a mitigated ideological commitment that pre-empted Labour's defeat in 1951.[64] Labour's post-war nationalisations did not give workers control of industry and were considered incomplete measures that did not address the inequalities in British society, with the nationalisations being viewed by the political left and those leading the struggle for workers' rights as a form of 'business men's syndicalism' and the product of a capitalist state and society based on the principles of private property and market dynamics.[65] Attlee's nationalisation programme functioned within the boundaries of the existing capitalist system, with critics accusing Labour of cooperating with the established industrial powerbase rather than delivering the promised socialist reforms, let alone revolution.[66]

IV. NATIONALISATIONS AND EQUITY SHAREHOLDERS

Even with its limitations, post-war nationalisations were embraced by supporters, and repudiated by opponents, as a systemic restructuring of British

[61] Morgan (1992) 29.
[62] Morgan (1992) 29.
[63] Morgan (1992) 36; Kynaston (2007) 140.
[64] Eatwell (1979) 162; Kynaston (2007) 140.
[65] Coates and Topham (1968a) 227; Runciman (1966) 133.
[66] Eatwell (1979) 162.

industry, with implications for the company, shareholders and stakeholders; the newly nationalised companies took the form of independent public corporations, a structure derived from pre-industrial semi-public corporations and trusts rather than from the private joint stock company.[67] The nationalisation policies highlighted basic legal questions about how the rights of existing shareholders, as described in the companies' memorandum and articles of association, were impacted and, importantly, how to compensate shareholders fairly for the loss of their equity.[68] The government was taking ownership of companies from their shareholders using legislation, the Acts of Nationalisation, to bring British industry under state control, although the manner in which this was done was not viewed as remarkable or as a challenge to the existing capitalist system.[69]

A. Compensating Shareholders

The interests of the shareholders in the companies targeted for nationalisations were not the priority for those authoring the political manifestos and devising governmental policies, and it was only when the logistical questions of how state expropriations would work in practice were addressed that shareholders entered the discussions in a more meaningful way, and even then as a hurdle to overcome and a constituent to pacify.[70] The questions of how to value the expropriated companies and how to compensate the equity owners were of paramount importance to the implementation of the nationalisation programme.[71] Compensation was a central issue and there was an acceptance by the Labour government that nationalisations without fair treatment of existing equity owners was untenable.[72] The way in which the Labour government approached how (and whether) compensation should be paid for nationalised industries illuminates how the existing owners of private industry (that is, shareholders) were seen as being separate from the British people on whose behalf the state was nationalising companies – that equity shareholders, in most cases, *were* the British people was not addressed. In his 1975 definitive work *The Nationalisation of British Industry 1945–1951*, Sir Norman Chester quoted Herbert Morrison, the Labour Minister of Transport at the time of the London Passenger Transport Bill in 1931 and the principal designer of the post-war nationalisations, on the need for fair treatment:

> [T]he Labour Party and public opinion generally favoured the policy of compensation for dispossession; that both the owners of the undertaking which were to

[67] Cornish et al (2019) 264; Fox (1985) 364; Eatwell (1979) 57; Barry (1965) 372.
[68] Chester (1975) 371.
[69] Barry (1965) 369, 372.
[70] See Chester (1975) for a detailed account of the process of nationalisations.
[71] Chester (1975) 217.
[72] Eatwell (1979) 58.

be taken over and the public which was going to take them over were entitled to a fair deal.[73]

Of course, what was considered to be 'fair' was not uncontested.

Along these lines, the Attlee government accepted the principle of fair and equitable treatment, and, in most cases, the existing owners of nationalised industries were considered well compensated for their losses.[74] As a result, the early post-war nationalisations were relatively straightforward, partly due to the very generous terms offered to existing shareholders, even in the cases of companies in distressed industries such as coal.[75] For certain industries, like coal and railways, many shareholders recognised that exiting investments in companies that were in need of vast capital expenditure and that faced new competitive challenges in a post-war economy by accepting fair values through nationalisations was not a bad strategy, and in other industries, like gas, electricity, telecommunications, and civil aviation, where there was already an acknowledgement of the need for state responsibility, there was also little resistance as shareholders were bought out of their positions.[76]

State expropriations not only offered generous compensation to equity owners but also benefited other stakeholders, like workers whose jobs were saved.[77] The trade unions approved of the use of fair compensation in the transfer of companies from private to public ownership, which had the additional benefit of creating taxable income for the private shareholders, generating an effective clawback for the government.[78] Shareholders were not the powerless victims of a socialist revolution stripping them of their valuable assets, but were in most cases constituents who were considered to be fairly compensated by a Labour government that recognised the importance of stability in British industry and the need to preserve trust in British markets.

i. Compensation Stock

For each industry, the government needed to decide what sort of compensation structure would be used, dealing with the issues that arose from the different options depending on the type of shareholder that was being compensated (that is, individuals or institutions) as well as the type of shares (for example, ordinary or preference), as well as the market performance of the companies

[73] Chester (1975) 218; Kynaston (2007) 139. It should be noted that the term 'fair compensation' in relation to the nationalisations of industry was dropped from the nationalisation sections in the Labour Party manifestos after 1950; Labour Party (1945); Labour Party (1950); Dale (2000b) 56, 67.

[74] Edgerton (2018) 124.

[75] Morgan (1992) 34.

[76] Barry (1965) 375.

[77] Kavanagh and Morris (1989) 20, 26.

[78] Trades Union Congress (1944) 11; a discussion of valuation methodologies is included in the report, which concludes that Reasonable Net Maintainable Revenue be applied.

being nationalised.[79] Cash, equity stock and some form of fixed-income securities were all considered possible forms of compensation, with each nationalised industry given a bespoke solution depending on its characteristics and circumstances, although cash and equity were mostly ruled out as viable options.[80] The distribution of cash to existing investors was considered disruptive because it required the state to raise large amounts to distribute to shareholders, as well as from the impact of its reinvestment or, possibly, its use for immediate consumption; the government did not want to be seen as encouraging small investors to take out investment savings to spend immediately.[81] Equity as compensation was also considered inconsistent with the *ethos* of nationalisations and the structures of the new public entities; it would leave shareholders with neither control nor influence while they continued to bear the risks, as well as creating misaligned incentives from those of the greater community that the nationalised industries were designed to serve.[82] Because of these factors, compensation stock was typically used.[83]

Whereas compensation eased the losses to shareholders, there was a need to balance the fair treatment of shareholders with the amount of debt that the government was willing to endure to pay for British industries.[84] Furthermore, even with shareholders receiving what the government valued as full compensation, this did not mean that equity owners were not penalised by nationalisations; when equity shares were replaced by fixed-interest compensation stock, it deprived the original shareholder of future capital appreciation, giving the benefits of any post-nationalisation growth to the state.[85] Furthermore, during a period of inflation and rising interest rates, many holders sold to reinvest in equities, resulting in a discount to value that typically increased; because of the terms of the compensation stock, dispossessed equity shareholders often found themselves with less income than before.[86] The shareholder who took the risk of the initial investment in a pre-nationalisation company was being forced out of his or her position, with no regard to investment basis, timeline or hurdle, and forfeiting any further gains from share appreciation that might have been part of an original investment thesis. The inverse was equally applicable to nationalised companies, with the risk, but not the income, being removed from shareholders and re-allocated to the state, resulting in companies with deteriorating performance and in unprofitable industries becoming its burdens.[87]

[79] Chester (1975) 373.
[80] Chester (1975) 234.
[81] Chester (1975) 243.
[82] Chester (1975) 235.
[83] Kelf-Cohen (1958) 179.
[84] Chester (1975) 221.
[85] Labour Party (1956) 28.
[86] Kelf-Cohen (1958) 180.
[87] Edgerton (2018) 124.

For the industries that were facing operational and financial challenges, with some facing liquidation and collapse, the reward for being relieved of the risk would have outweighed the potential lost upside, although for more stable industries (for example, iron and steel, which were the most contested nationalisations), existing shareholders did not necessarily benefit from this trade-off. The iron and steel industry, which was growing and profitable, was nationalised by the Labour government in 1949 with the Iron and Steel Act.[88] Whereas for certain industries there was only muted opposition to nationalisations, even by the companies themselves, with some industrialists endorsing the reorganisations of struggling industries, although not necessarily going as far as full nationalisations, for performing industries like iron and steel, there was strong resistance.[89] For the Labour government, however, the nationalisation programme was not driven only by performance metrics but was also underpinned by socialist ideology, which sought wider political, economic and social gains.[90]

In 1967, the chairman of the United Steel Companies warned that the compensation offered by the government for the assets in no way reflected their real value and that they, alongside the British Iron and Steel Federation, were taking every step to mitigate the harm being done to individual companies, to the industry and, by extension, to their shareholders.[91] That the government would nationalise functioning companies that were not in need of rescuing caused grave concerns for British industry, which was already critical of the government's policies.[92] Nationalisations that were not factored into original investment theses upended the fundamental assumption that equity investment risks have a counterbalancing return for the shareholder who provided the risk capital that financed the opportunities for the company to succeed, grow and create employment and other economic benefits.[93] Regardless of the strength of the arguments for or against nationalisations, they resulted in equity shareholders being deprived of their investments in companies, even if fairly compensated, drawing criticism of the state for disregarding shareholder ownership rights and removing their economic power.[94]

a. The Net Maintainable Revenue Formula

For the early nationalisations, shareholders were mostly compensated in government stock based on the Net Maintainable Revenue (NMR) formula, a valuation methodology for compensation stock that was based on share prices and not on

[88] Addison (1985) 193.
[89] Addison (1985) 178; Barry (1965) 377.
[90] Kynaston (2007) 140.
[91] Peech (1967) 359.
[92] Addison (1985) 193.
[93] Kellett (1962) 37.
[94] Pint (1990) 272; Edgerton (2018) 124.

asset value that was developed by Labour politicians in the 1930s.[95] The nationalisation of the Bank of England used a variation of NMR, as did the Coal Industry Nationalisation Bill, although reaching a resolution for the latter was much more complicated than the former.[96] Later nationalisations (for example, railways and road haulage) dropped this formula because of the difficulties in determining 'true' value, with shareholders arguing that the share value on the chosen vesting date did not reflect full value and that the market was undervaluing the shares, as companies under the threat of nationalisation would inevitably be trading at discounts to their book values.[97] The challenges of putting a value on a whole industry and not just a single firm, as well as where a nationalised industry had multiple firms of varying sizes and structures, requiring the valuers to make judgements on competitive dynamics, future performance and profitability trends, and then to distribute that sum to the different individual shareholders, were virtually insurmountable and: 'In the final analysis, compensation is paid not for an industry nor even for a particular firm but for the capital and income which each and every shareholder is losing.'[98]

ii. The Bank of England

The Bank of England, because of its charter and special status, was uniquely placed amongst nationalised companies, as its value depended heavily on its global role and reputation as a financial institution, which the government wished to preserve with as little disruption as possible. For the Bank of England, the goal of nationalisation was to replace existing equity shareholders with public owners, but to otherwise leave the workings of the bank undisturbed.[99] With this decision, the Labour government left the beating heart of the British capitalist system intact, offering very favourable terms to the existing owners by not paying market value for the shares, but instead preserving the revenue that they generated, which had been virtually unchanged at 12 per cent for the prior 23 years. A mechanism was devised for the Bank of England to be bought for new government 3 per cent stock, terms that the Chancellor deemed 'fair to the shareholders ... and undoubtedly a good bargain for the State', and to which the market responded favourably, giving a small bonus to existing shareholders.[100] This first example of the post-war Labour government's nationalisation programme was, upon implementation, not hostile to shareholders, with terms that kept the share price high, the markets relatively calm and opponents subdued.[101]

[95] On the origins of this valuation methodology, see Chester (1975) 217; Eatwell (1979) 58. For a detailed discussion on compensation for all nationalised industries, see Chester (1975) ch 3.
[96] Chester (1975) 225.
[97] Eatwell (1979) 95.
[98] Chester (1975) 1015.
[99] Chester (1975) 237; Kynaston (2001) 12.
[100] Chester (1975) 239.
[101] Wall Street Journal London Bureau (1946) 4.

iii. Other Industries

Unlike the Bank of England, other industries could not rely on such a clear and relatively unproblematic solution to the questions of valuation and compensation for the shareholders of nationalised companies. There was no set compensation framework and in some industries there were hundreds of different companies, each with its own capital structures, financial arrangements and diverse stakeholders, including shareholders, trade unions, customers, local authorities and other connected companies elsewhere in the supply chain, that were all impacted by nationalisations and had stakes in the outcomes.[102] In addition, the compensation in one industry influenced those of others, be it coal, transport, civil aviation, gas, electricity, iron and steel, or cable and wireless, informing the participants' negotiating strategies and providing precedents, adapting their approaches to address the uniqueness of each case.[103] As a result, each nationalised industry was dealt with separately, and existing equity shareholders were subjected to different waiting periods and processes while the government and its committees determined the fate of their investments.[104] The Attlee government was in unchartered territory with its implementations of widespread nationalisations, and the valuations were highly subjective and often left all sides feeling unjustly treated, be it the shareholders who felt cheated of the true value of their investments or the state representatives who took on the responsibility of often unprofitable, poorly managed and unviable (yet essential) companies and industries, each with its own attributes and history.[105]

V. REACTIONS TO POST-WAR NATIONALISATIONS

A. Conservatives in Opposition

During the Second World War, there was cross-party support for increases in state control of industry for wartime purposes, but in the 1945 general election campaign the Conservatives opposed the policies of nationalisations endorsed by Labour, promising in their manifesto:

> We will not allow drastic changes of ownership to be forced upon industries on no evidence except a political theory, and with no practical regard to the results they may bring. To us the tests will always be – what will conduce most to efficiency, and what will render the greatest service to the community. This is the policy we shall apply, whether it be coal, cotton or the heavy industries. As against the advocates of State ownership and control, we stand for the fullest opportunity for go and push in all ranks throughout the whole nation. This quality is part of the genius of the

[102] Pollard (1992) 215.
[103] Chester (1975) 237.
[104] Chester (1975) 366ff.
[105] Sampson (1971) 615.

> British people, who mean to be free to use their own judgment and never intend to be State serfs, nor always to wait for official orders before they can act.[106]

Stressing the need for efficiency and to serve the community, arguments that mirror those used by Labour in support of state control, the Conservatives were committed to free-market policies, opposing the sweeping state expropriations promised by Labour, which they considered beyond the compromises of the wartime coalition.[107]

After the Conservatives' 1945 defeat, and despite their campaign rhetoric, when the first post-war nationalisations were undertaken by the new Labour majority, no serious objections were raised and no anti-nationalisation campaigns were organised, and it was only in 1949, with the Labour government weakening and nationalisations expanding to include the iron and steel industry, that the Conservatives became decidedly less cooperative.[108] Already by the late 1940s, and leading into Labour's electoral defeat in 1951, nationalisations were falling out of favour with the British public and there was little enthusiasm for the government's plans to expand state expropriation of companies to additional industries, which included industrial assurance, cement, sugar refining and the wholesale meat trade. The ideologies that underpinned the government's nationalisation programme were increasingly unpopular and the business community and the Federation of British Industries (FBI), the organisation representing employers and businesses and the forerunner to the Confederation of British Industry (CBI), openly campaigned against it.[109] The positions taken on nationalisations were reflected in the reaction to post-war industrial democracy and in attitudes to shareholder interests, and whereas the FBI's position was critical of Labour's fiscal and industrial policies, it was unwilling to risk an outright breach with the government, leaving the targeted industries to defend themselves, although with the support of free-enterprise organisations, such as the Economic League and the Aims of Industry.[110]

The Conservative's 1950 election policy paper, *This is the Road*, states unequivocally: 'We shall bring Nationalisation to a full stop here and now. Thereby we shall save all those industries, such as cement, sugar, meat distribution, chemicals, water and insurance which are now under threat by the Socialists.'[111] With public confidence in the post-war economy increasing and the tolerance for state control declining, there was a shift in popular thinking that aligned with Conservative orthodoxy.[112] In contrast to Labour's platform of expanding nationalisations to more companies and new industries, the Conservatives promised that for certain industries (for example, transportation),

[106] Churchill (1945) 12.
[107] Lowe (1990) 168.
[108] Barry (1965) 375.
[109] Kynaston (2007) 536; Beer (1982) 190; Addison (1985) 205.
[110] Middlemas (1986) 163.
[111] Conservative Central Office (1950) 10.
[112] Barry (1965) 379; Seldon (1994a) 511.

expropriation would not only be halted but also that those companies already nationalised would be offered back to their former owners, including to the private sector.[113] Labour won the 1950 election with a greatly reduced majority and in October 1951 British voters removed them from government, hobbling the expansion of their nationalisation programme.[114]

In opposing the Labour government and its policies, the language of the Conservative campaigns was emphatic in its criticism of the incumbents:

> Britain already knows to her cost that the state monopolies created by nationalisation are rigid, awkward, wasteful and inefficient. Large losses have been made. Monopoly powers are being used to force higher prices on the consumers, who have no effective redress. Responsible initiative is crushed by centralised authority. Frustration and cynicism prevail among the staffs. The power of trade unions to protect their members is being undermined and the freedom of choice of consumer and worker alike is being narrowed. If nationalisation is extended, the creeping paralysis of state monopoly will spread over ever wider sections of industry until the Socialists have carried out their declared aim to nationalise all the means of production, distribution and exchange.[115]

The Conservatives presented their opposition to Labour's nationalisations in broad terms, and not just as a defence of free-market economics under socialist threat, calling for the protection of multiple stakeholders, including customers, trade unions and workers, which were important constituents with whom voters identified.

B. Shifting Public Opinion

In the 1950 general election campaign, Labour's promotion of nationalisations was less urgent than it had been in 1945, possibly due to a mistaken assumption that state ownership was accepted as inescapable.[116] Labour's nationalisation programme was increasingly unpopular and became a central issue of the campaign, with 22 per cent of voters stating that they considered nationalisation as the most important issue in the 1950 election, up from just 6 cent in 1945, with many of these voters hostile to further nationalisations; this was in contrast to the situation in 1945, when the policy had been generally supported, if not particularly influential.[117] The tripod of goals on which the mixed economy of the political settlement was balanced – that is, full employment, rising living standards and stable prices – was under growing pressure by the shifting values of post-war Britain, with full employment being the most vulnerable of the three.[118]

[113] Conservative Central Office (1950) 10.
[114] Morgan (1992) 113.
[115] Conservative Central Office (1950) 9.
[116] Barry (1965) 379.
[117] Eatwell (1979) 128.
[118] Middlemas (1979) 463.

The voting public, having spent the previous five years witnessing the challenges of implementing nationalisation policies, was turning against state expropriation of British companies.[119] Heading into the 1951 general election, whereas many working-class voters continued to support Labour out of fear that a Conservative victory would mean a return to pre-war conditions, the middle classes rejected Labour's socialist platform and nationalisation policies.[120] In an attempt to address this shift, in the 1951 election Labour put less emphasis on nationalisations as a policy issue in their (unsuccessful) campaign.[121] Reflecting this change in voter attitudes, an October 1951 poll found that only 24 per cent of those surveyed approved of the nationalisation of the iron and steel industry, with 54 per cent disapproving.[122] With Labour's defeat in 1951 and the return of the Conservatives to power for the next 13 years, the momentum that powered the post-war nationalisations of British industry from 1945 to 1950 was lost.

The Conservatives' policy position was to oppose nationalisations, although their actions were less clear, which contributed to an uncertain environment for business leaders and market participants; the Conservative platform included generalised condemnations of state expropriation as well as a pledge to repeal the Iron and Steel Act, although when they returned to power in 1951, there were no blanket reversals of Labour's nationalisations.[123] The post-war Conservative Party was experiencing a period of transformation, with an intake of new, young MPs, many of whom supported changes to the Party's approach to economics and governance, putting full employment and controlling inflation at its centre and supporting government intervention in the economy, which included nationalising certain industries, such as mines, railways and the Bank of England.[124] These reforming forces within the Party, although by no means representative of all its members, embraced increased regulations and continued state involvement in the management of certain key industries.[125]

When the Conservatives returned to government in 1951, the programmes implemented by Attlee's government were not easily overturned.[126] For the leaders of industry, their investors and the City of London (hereinafter 'the City'), there remained a persistent overhang from the economic and financial consequences of nationalisations, as well as the ever-present threat of additional expropriations by the state. To the disappointment of industry and the City, only the iron and steel industry, and parts of the road transport industry, were eventually privatised in 1953.[127] Most nationalised industries remained under

[119] Beer (1982) 217.
[120] Pinto-Duschinsky (1970) 71.
[121] Eatwell (1979) 149.
[122] Eatwell (1979) 152.
[123] Conservative Central Office (1950) 10; Churchill (1951); Dale (2000a) 98.
[124] Dutton (1997) 50.
[125] Dutton (1997) 21.
[126] Hennessy (2007) 8; Pint (1990) 277.
[127] Dutton (1997) 58; Seldon (1994b) 47.

state control, with the Conservatives, under the leadership of relative moderates Anthony Eden and Harold Macmillan, limiting their efforts to halting the expansion of the policy and to making promises of increased efficiencies, improved commercial standards of operations and reduced centralisation of state-controlled industries.[128] In most cases, the nationalisations were preserved.

C. The Deradicalisation of Labour's Nationalisation Policies

After the bitterly contested 1951 snap general election, the Labour Party, back in opposition, continued to endorse the nationalisation of British industry, embedded as Clause IV in its political programme, and to advocate for the expansion of state expropriations to additional industries beyond those already affected.[129] In its 1953 annual statement, Labour declared:

> The Labour Government was right to insist that the major basic industries – coal, electricity, gas, steel and transport – should become the property of the nation. Our standard of living, the jobs we do, the expansion of our industry, agriculture, and trade, all depend on the output and efficiency of our basic industries. In every industry output has gone up and services have been expanded and improved since nationalisation. Now, further expansion is called for.[130]

At the same time, Labour encouraged the broadening of participation in the financial markets as it sought to attract voters whose support for state expropriations was waning; in this same 1953 annual statement, the Party encouraged individual savers and called for increased investments in the 'big sector of the economy that will remain in private hands', with incentives given to private industry 'to venture capital in risky projects'.[131]

Despite the less radical direction of the Party, the 1955 Labour manifesto still promoted a platform that promised an expansion of nationalisations to additional sectors, specifically parts of the chemical and machine tool industries.[132] The selection of Hugh Gaitskell as Labour Party leader in 1955 was, however, a step away from the legacy 'cloth-cap' image of British socialism and towards creating a more moderate modern national party.[133] The gradual softening

[128] Conservative Party (1955); Conservative Party (1959); Conservative Party (1964); Conservative Unionist Party (1970); Dale (2000a) 115, 133, 148, 185; Seldon (1994b) 50.

[129] Dutton (1997) 66; Webb (1918) 3. After the 1959 election, which returned the fourth consecutive Conservative government and signalled, amongst other things, the rejection by British voters of Labour's platform supporting nationalisations, certain factions of the party, under the leadership of Hugh Gaitskell, tried unsuccessfully to amend Clause IV, which called for the common ownership of industry; Jobson (2013). It was only in 1995, under the leadership of Tony Blair, that Clause IV was (contentiously) reformed by the Labour Party; see Riddell (1997); Coates (1995).

[130] Labour Party National Executive Committee (1953) 9.

[131] Labour Party National Executive Committee (1953) 19.

[132] Labour Party (1955); Dale (2000b) 85.

[133] Foote (1986) 189; Morgan (1992) 183.

of Labour's commitment to the socialist principles underpinning post-war nationalisations led to new ideas on how British industry could be more equitable, including selectively buying equity in companies, which was addressed in the 1957 policy paper *Industry and Society*: 'We would emphasise, however, that it is not our intention that the Government should indulge in a wildly inflationary scramble for shares: both the timing and occasion for acquiring shares will need careful consideration.'[134] The Labour Party of the mid-1950s adapted its approach to public ownership, moving away from outright expropriations to working within the existing market frameworks, including equity share ownership.[135] Reflecting the mood of the British public, the policy of nationalising large parts of British industry was dropped from Labour's programme in 1957, which adopted a more measured approach of cooperating with private industry.[136]

Under Gaitskell's more moderate leadership of the Party, the left-wing faction, which was still influential, continued to support expanding nationalisations across industries and was able to prevent the removal of Clause IV from the Party's constitution.[137] Even when it was clear that further nationalisations were neither politically popular nor economically effective, the Labour Party, honouring Clause IV, remained committed to the policy, although by the late 1950s it was an increasingly marginalised part of its platform.[138] The Labour Party continued on its path of deradicalisation and following another Conservative victory in 1955, it responded with a definitive position on state expropriations, stating explicitly in its 1959 manifesto that it had no plans for further nationalisations, although reserving the right to take public control of industries that were failing the nation, as well as seeking to benefit from the profits of private industry by investing in shares through public investment agencies.[139] In a shift in position towards private industry, the state as shareholder was seen as a being potentially more effective, and politically popular, than the state as manager.

D. Nationalisations in the Stabilising Post-war Economy

As the British post-war economy strengthened and stabilised, the market forces that existed in normal peacetime conditions, most notably competition, returned.[140] By the end of the 1950s, the economic and social conditions

[134] Dutton (1997) 67; Labour Party (1957) 40, 57.
[135] Kelf-Cohen (1958) 269.
[136] Shonfield (1958) 170.
[137] Foote (1986) 225; Middlemas (1986) 331; Coates (1995). 'When Gaitskell tried to root out the famous "Clause Four" of the party's constitution prescribing wholesale nationalisation, [Harold] Wilson complained "it was like telling the Salvation Army there was no salvation"' (Sampson (1971) 44).
[138] Edgerton (2018) 371; Bogdanor (1970) 81.
[139] Labour Party (1959); Dale (2000b) 96.
[140] Sampson (1965) 576.

in Britain were materially different from those of the immediate post-war period, influencing the attitudes of politicians, and the voting public, towards the nationalisations of British companies and industries.[141] Labour took a more flexible approach, acknowledging the need to work within the system that had private industry at its core, reaffirming in their 1960 annual party statement the principles of industrial democracy, as described by the Labour politician and commentator Ken Coates:

> It [the Labour Party] stands for democracy in industry, and for the right of workers both in the public and private sectors to full consultation in all the vital decisions of management, especially those affecting conditions of work ... It is convinced that these social and economic objectives can be achieved only through an expansion of common power over the commanding heights of the economy. Common ownership takes varying forms, including state-owned industries and firms, producer and consumer co-operation, municipal ownership and public participation in private concerns. Recognising that both public and private enterprise have a place in the economy it believes that further extension of common ownership should be decided from time to time in the light of these objectives and according to circumstances, with the due regard for the views of the workers and consumers concerned.[142]

This position accepted that nationalisations were not the only means by which the societal benefits of ownership could be realised, conceding an acceptance of the capitalist system and private enterprise, although the interests of shareholders, unlike those of the other stakeholders identified (that is, workers and consumers), were not addressed directly.

The Labour Party's 1964 platform, on which it returned to government, took a more market-friendly stance on public ownership:

> Major expansion programmes will be needed in the existing nationalised industries, and they will be encouraged, with the removal of the present restrictions placed upon them, to diversify and move into new fields: for example, the railways' workshops will be free to seek export markets, and the National Coal Board to manufacture the machinery and equipment it needs. Private monopoly in steel will be replaced by public ownership and control. The water supply industry, most of which is already owned by the community, will be reorganised under full public ownership.[143]

[141] Kynaston (2007) 536.

[142] Coates (1995) 43. See section III.C of this chapter on industrial democracy and nationalisations.

[143] Labour Party (1964); Dale (2000b) 110. The British water industry is an example of nationalisations penalising the constituents that they were meant to benefit, as the largest existing equity shareholders were the local authority superannuation funds, whose beneficiaries were local workers, as well as small individual investors in the form of residents investing in local companies that they knew, putting their savings in the companies supplying them with water. The water companies faced years of downward pressure on their shares that negatively impacted individual savings and left existing shareholders languishing in uncertainty. The predicament of these investors exemplifies the complexity of characterising shareholders, in this case public entities and small savers. After years of enduring a nationalisation overhang on share prices, in 1973 the Conservatives' Water Act nationalised the local authority water supply companies in England and Wales. Prior to the Water Bill's implementation on 1 April 1974, when water management became the responsibility of 10 multi-purpose Regional Water Authorities, the water supply had been controlled and managed

The new government under Harold Wilson, following 13 years of the Conservatives in power, during which the nationalisations of British industry remained mostly static, took a more moderate approach to the state's role in private industry than that of the last Labour government.[144] Labour's political platform in the 1960s was still committed to state ownership of British industries, although it was no longer pushing policies for widespread nationalisations and refrained from taking a dogmatic approach that could upset its hard-won political gains, which were held with a small and delicate majority.[145] Labour's approach to expanding state control was based less on a radical ideological imperative and more on the need for an economic transformation of a country that was under threat of falling behind other developed nations in terms of productivity and industrial output.[146] Although Labour's nationalisation policy had evolved and deradicalised, it had not been abandoned, and shareholder interests remained vulnerable.

E. The Industrial Reorganisation Corporation

In the 1960s, despite the Westminster politicians' lack of industrial expertise, the Wilson government sought to make British industries more efficient and effective through state control.[147] In 1966, following the publication of a White Paper outlining the government's plan, a Bill was presented to Parliament that led to an Act that established the Industrial Reorganisation Corporation (IRC): 'the object of the Bill is to set up a statutory body, to be called the Industrial Reorganisation Corporation, with the function of stimulating and assisting industrial concentration, rationalisation and development'.[148] The IRC was active between 1966 and 1970 (it was formally abolished in 1971) and was partially developed in response to the increase in merger activity in the UK, which escalated materially in the early 1960s.[149] This vehicle of state intervention was far removed from the socialist policies of the earlier post-war Labour government, acting as a pragmatic organisation that worked 'to promote industrial aims rather than to further political objectives'.[150]

by 198 separate statutory water supply undertakings, including 33 private companies (as well as 64 local authorities and 101 joint water boards of groups of local authorities). The Conservatives were not adverse to state intervention when there were clear efficiencies and rationalisations, particularly in an industry already mostly owned by state institutions ('Takeover without Tears?' (1965) 1426; Jordan, Richardson and Kimber (1977) 317).

[144] Hague and Wilkinson (1983) 4.

[145] Seldon (1994b) 50.

[146] Hague and Wilkinson (1983) 4.

[147] Sampson (1971) 616.

[148] Industrial Reorganisation Corporation Bill 1966. See also *Industrial Reorganisation Corporation* (Cmnd 2889, 1966) and the Industrial Reorganisation Corporation Act 1966.

[149] Hague and Wilkinson (1983) 7.

[150] Hague and Wilkinson (1983) 16.

The IRC was designed to function within the existing system and to '"beat the capitalists" at their own game', and despite initial protests from the City, it was soon run by it.[151] As described in the White Paper that led to its formation:

> The corporation will seek the fullest co-operation from industry and existing financial institutions, and schemes which it initiates will, whenever possible, be put into effect either through the normal machinery of the market or in close collaboration with the market. It will be able to acquire a stake in the ownership of new groupings or enterprises it helps to create or expand. It will not, however, act as a general holding company and will be able to dispose of its investments when the profits of rationalisation have been assured and it can do so to advantage. The faster it turns over capital, the greater will be its capacity to promote the objects for which it is being set up.[152]

This approach to state involvement relied on the cooperation of existing shareholders in the companies involved, which needed to be convinced of the fairness of the terms of a transaction to gain their support, which the IRC actively pursued, including through public statements and comments in the press to try to influence a proposed transaction.[153] The result was that shareholders were not stripped of their assets in return for compensation determined by the state, as they were in earlier nationalisations, but retained their power as equity owners to determine the fate of their companies.

The IRC was intended as a form of 'state merchant bank', promoting mergers, lending capital and taking equity in companies, although ultimately it was responsible for only around 4 per cent of total mergers during the four years that it was active before being abolished by Edward Heath's Conservatives.[154] Of the 61 situations in which it became involved, many were deemed to have benefited from its intervention, although they also included some of the most notorious industrial failures of the period, including British Leyland, Nuclear Enterprises, Rolls-Royce, Hadfields and Cambridge Instruments.[155] With the establishment of the IRC, the government passed legislation that gave a mandate to the state to support and assist British companies; however, it was unable to establish itself as an effective vehicle before becoming a casualty of the change in governments, with the Conservatives repealing the Industrial Reorganisation Corporation Act 1966 and dissolving the IRC, as well as terminating the power to make industrial investment schemes under the Industrial Expansion Act 1968.[156] Yet, the demise of the IRC was not the end of state intervention in industry as the Conservatives continued to use public funds to help companies in need of

[151] Hague and Wilkinson (1983) 16; Kynaston (2001) 315.

[152] Hague and Wilkinson (1983) 16; for the full text of the White Paper on the Industrial Reorganisation Corporation, see also 17.

[153] Hague and Wilkinson (1983) 43.

[154] 'The State as Shareholder' (1978) 93.

[155] Middlemas (1990) 168.

[156] Industry Bill 1970; Kavanagh and Morris (1989) 26.

support, lending more money to the private sector under the 1972 Industry Act than the IRC had under Labour, with the Act giving ministers four times the discretionary spending power than Labour had made available.[157]

VI. THE FINANCIAL AND ECONOMIC IMPLICATIONS OF NATIONALISATIONS

A. The Ongoing Threat-of-Nationalisation Overhang

The knowledge that a government is willing and capable of nationalisations was a perceived dampener on investing, introducing additional uncertainty and volatility to markets already dealing with meaningful post-war challenges. The overhangs created by the possibility of nationalisation impacted share prices, disruptions that continued well into the 1960s and reasserted themselves whenever governments (or shadow governments) proclaimed or suggested that state expropriations are a viable option to solve industrial and/or corporate challenges.[158] As S Paul Chambers, Deputy Chairman of Imperial Chemical Industries (ICI), argued in 'The Climate for Capitalism', presented in 1958 as a Conservative Political Centre lecture:

> [T]hreats of nationalisation in one form or another discourage the proper investment of savings. The most obvious example is the steel industry which has become almost a shuttlecock between political Parties in this country. Nothing can be worse for capitalism than the feeling of uncertainty which must exist in the minds of those trying to form capital in an important industry such as the steel industry when they do not know whether the industry will be renationalised if there is a Labour Government, or whether if renationalised, the next Conservative Government will again denationalise.[159]

Share prices of impacted companies were depressed, in some cases at less than half of book value, trading at large discounts relative to unthreatened industries, thereby lessening value for shareholders, making it more difficult for companies to invest in development and impacting the valuations given when nationalisations did occur. To give an example, at the end of January 1958, ordinary shares in United Steel Companies, which was under threat of renationalisation, were trading at 20 shillings or less compared to 43 shillings book value.[160] Nationalisations not only impacted the companies and industries taken into state control; with complete sectors removed from the market, investment options narrowed, putting more pressure on the remaining private sectors as capital was funnelled there.[161] The impact of nationalisations was directly felt

[157] Dutton (1997) 97.
[158] Chester (1975) 270.
[159] Lord Hailsham of St Marylebone (1958) 22.
[160] 'Shareholders Oppose State Steel' (1958) 8.
[161] Kynaston (2001) 9.

by shareholders who, after the expropriations of the immediate post-war period and the ongoing uncertainty, were vulnerable to the increased risks associated with equity investing and the implications for the value of their holdings.

i. Iron and Steel

The uncertainty caused by nationalisations was particularly prevalent for the managers of the iron and steel industry, which was subjected to the worst of the policy changes and reversals. At its annual general meeting (AGM) in 1960, the chairman of Stewarts and Lloyds Ltd, one of the iron and steel companies struggling against expropriation, expressed the view that the British electorate, with its repeated support of Conservative governments, had rejected nationalisations as an 'unjustified and ruinous doctrine'.[162] Although in the 1960s nationalisations had become less of a threat than they had been in the immediate post-war period, the possibility remained highly topical for directors, managers and their financial advisers, particularly for the industries that were targeted for nationalisation or, like for iron and steel, renationalisation. As the more recent debates on state intervention and ownership demonstrate, nationalisations remain a tool that governments, both Conservative and Labour, wield when seeking to address industrial and economic challenges, often with seemingly little concern for the impact on equity shareholders.[163]

The threat of the government expanding the scale and scope of nationalisations subsided during the Conservative governments of the 1950s and early 1960s, although by the time of the 1964 general election, most nationalised industries were still in the hands of the state.[164] Despite the changing economic conditions and shifting political climate that were more favourable to the interests of industry and commerce, when in government the Conservatives did not change the underlying legal framework of the nationalised industries, stating in 1961 that: 'The Government takes the view that there would be no advantage in altering the basic financial and economic principles which the statutes require the nationalized industries to observe.'[165] The Conservatives, however, expected the nationalised industries to function as commercial entities. The Chancellor of the Exchequer, Selwyn Lloyd, in *The Financial and Economic Obligation of the Nationalised Industries*, a White Paper presented to Parliament in 1961, stated that 'although the industries have obligations of a national and non-commercial

[162] 'Stewarts and Lloyds Ltd' (1960) 660.

[163] Examples include the nationalisation of parts of the banking industry following the global financial crisis of 2007–08, the proposed nationalisations of the utilities industry by Labour (sitting in opposition) in 2019 and the Conservative government's renationalisation of Northern Rail in 2020. In July 2021, Boris Johnson's Conservative government announced plans to nationalise the steel company Sheffield Forgemasters in a £2.6 million deal with the Ministry of Defence. See www.bbc.co.uk/news/uk-england-south-yorkshire-57997858.

[164] Kelf-Cohen (1958) 280.

[165] *The Financial and Economic Obligations of the Nationalised Industries* (Cmnd 1337, 1961) para 17.

kind, they are not, and ought not, to be regarded as social service absolved from economic and commercial justification'.[166] Even under state control and freed from the demands of private sector shareholders, companies were expected to be profitable and efficient, a view that the Labour Party also endorsed in its promotion of its nationalisation policies.[167]

With Labour's return to power in 1964 under Wilson on a 'national-productivist' platform, there were renewed worries of state expropriation for the iron and steel industry, as well as more broadly.[168] The Labour Party was elected in 1964 on the economic platform of its ambitious National Plan, adding to British industry's distrust of the new socialist government, about which it continued to appeal to its shareholders.[169] At the United Steel Companies meeting in 1966, on the eve of its renationalisation, the chairman, offering a broad-based rebuttal to the government's claim that nationalisations were for the benefit of the British nation, listed all the reasons why the threat of nationalisation was an impediment to companies – that is, it diverted the attention of management from running the company, upset employees, made recruitment difficult and raising capital much more challenging, with an overriding message that nationalisations were against not only the interests of the shareholders but also other stakeholders (that is, employees, customers and the country itself).[170] In 1967, the year that the British Steel Corporation was renationalised, the chairman of the United Steel Companies again addressed the threat of nationalisation at the company's AGM, conceding his willingness to accept rationalisation, but strongly opposing nationalisation on the grounds that it would reduce the effectiveness of the industry.[171] These arguments against state expropriations, which were made against the backdrop of the broader post-war industrial democracy debate, were focused not on the legal rights of shareholders, but on the business and commercial needs of British industry.

With the return of Labour to government in the mid-1960s, there was unease amongst the business and financial communities, and not without justification. Although it took until 1967, the Labour government fulfilled its promise to renationalise the iron and steel industry, beginning the next chapter of the British Steel Corporation, whose plight was described by Anthony Sampson in 1971: 'For the last forty years steel has been a political shuttlecock, nationalised, denationalised, renationalised and now threatened with redenationalisation at its edges.'[172] The years of back-and-forth nationalisation policies created conditions that made it more challenging for companies to raise permanent capital

[166] *The Financial and Economic Obligations of the Nationalised Industries* (Cmnd 1337, 1961) para 2; Sampson (1965) 576.
[167] Dutton (1997) 36.
[168] Edgerton (2018) 371.
[169] On Labour's National Plan, see Morgan (1992) 245.
[170] Peech (1966) 133.
[171] Peech (1967) 359.
[172] Sampson (1971) 622. For a similar badminton metaphor, see n 159.

and more expensive to borrow, contributing to the challenges faced by post-war industrial leaders, as well as a lack of clarity for all equity investors.

VII. THE IMPACT OF NATIONALISATION ON THE RELATIONSHIP BETWEEN SHAREHOLDERS AND DIRECTORS

When faced with the threat of state expropriation, the leaders of British industry turned to their shareholders for support; company boards, regularly accused of not consulting shareholders on issues that affect their interests and of withholding relevant company information, appealed to them for their help.[173] During the Attlee period, the mining company Henry Briggs Son & Co, for example, distributed a circular to shareholders asking for their views on the future operations of the company once the nationalisation of the coal industry was complete, as 'the directors feel that they must be fortified by representative views of the shareholders'.[174] When confronted with nationalisations, directors looked to their shareholders – in whose interests they were managing the company – for affirmation.

The appeals to shareholders occurred across British industry and continued into the 1950s and 1960s as companies tried to avoid state expropriation, although some nationalisations were welcomed by equity owners, who saw the state as a buyer of last resort of failing companies.[175] The leaders of the iron and steel industry, impacted for decades by the volatility and uncertainty introduced by the conflicting promises of nationalisations and privatisations, made similar requests to their equity owners, asking shareholders for support to protect their interests and to fight nationalisations by all means possible.[176] Directors, concerned for their own positions, regularly sought the backing of their shareholders; for example, the board of the steel company Stewarts & Lloyds Ltd presented a resolution to its shareholders at the 1958 AGM seeking their support to take any steps 'necessary and desirable' to fight nationalisation, which it presented as a dangerous advance towards 'Totalitarian Government' and communism in Britain.[177] At the 1960 AGM,

[173] Barry (1965) 379. The complaint that publicly traded companies do not provide enough disclosure has existed since the creation of the joint stock company. On the post-war discussion on disclosure, see the 1945 Cohen Committee Report on the protection of shareholders and the need for more information: 'we have included a number of proposals to ensure that as much information as is reasonably required shall be made available both to the shareholders and creditors of the companies concerned and the general public' (Mr Justice Cohen, *Report of the Committee on Company Law Amendment* (Cmnd 6659, 1945) 8; see also Naylor (1960) 20, 37). The Companies Act 1948 added the basic requirements of a Consolidated Profit & Loss Account and a Balance Sheet. See Jervis (1966) 47, 56; Kellett (1962) 47.

[174] 'Future of Henry Briggs Son & Co' (1946) 1. See also, for example, 'C & W Ltd 1946 Div' (1946) 1; 'Tate & Lyle, Limited' (1949) 6.

[175] See section IV.A in this chapter on the compensation for nationalising failing companies.

[176] For example, see 'Shareholders Oppose State Steel' (1958) 8.

[177] 'Stewarts and Lloyds, Limited' (1958) 10.

the chairman of Stewarts & Lloyds Ltd thanked the company's shareholders and other supporters, who in many cases were also voters, for keeping the issue of nationalisations a priority and for fighting against it.[178] Labour's post-war nationalisation policies created an existential crisis for many of the leaders of British industry, which was evident in how they addressed their shareholders, who they called upon as allies in the fight against state expropriations.

This strategy used by embattled directors of appealing to shareholders as voters in their fight against nationalisations often employed targeted political pleas against the pro-nationalisation Labour Party and in support of the Conservatives.[179] The AGMs in the period leading up to the 1964 general election are examples of how this platform was used by directors and chairmen to call upon their shareholders to try to save their companies from nationalisations.[180] In 1964, *The Economist* reported that remarks made by chairmen and directors criticising Labour's nationalisation policies often had the most time devoted to them of any agenda item; Stewarts & Lloyds Ltd, for example, was reported to have spent 17 minutes of its AGM attacking nationalisations, in comparison to only five minutes for all formal business and only one minute outlining trading projects.[181] Dorman Long, another iron and steel company, went further than just making speeches, with shareholders unanimously passing a resolution condemning the proposed renationalisation of the iron and steel industry and empowering directors to take all practicable steps to oppose renationalisation.[182]

By introducing a resolution, the directors were signalling the importance of a formal expression of shareholder support, as well as the desire to engage their shareholders as directly as possible in their strategies and actions, thereby making management's struggle also that of its equity owners.[183] Other companies held shareholder votes to approve actions in the fight against nationalisations and related policies; in 1968, for example, the automotive parts manufacturer Associated Engineering asked shareholders for permission to donate £5,000 to the Conservative Party, with the stated aim of protecting the private sector from damaging governmental interference, excess taxation, the removal of incentives, the lack of the encouragement to save, and attacks on the principles of free enterprise.[184] These initiatives to engage shareholders are in contrast to the

[178] 'Stewarts and Lloyds Ltd' (1960) 660.

[179] 'Meeting the Shareholders' (1964) 646; Financial Times Reporter (1968) 2. Despite these efforts, in the UK there was not the same level of shareholder organisation for political purposes as in the US (Rutterford (2012) 134).

[180] Meeting the Shareholders (1964) 646.

[181] Meeting the Shareholders (1964) 646.

[182] Meeting the Shareholders (1964) 646.

[183] For a contemporary comparison, this approach is in stark contrast to the signatories of the 2019 Business Roundtable statement on the purpose of the corporation (see ch 9, section II of this volume), whose commitments were, in most cases, not brought to shareholders' votes (Bebchuk and Tallarita (2020b) A15; Bebchuk and Tallarita (2021) A17).

[184] Financial Times Reporter (1968) 2.

common assumptions about shareholder apathy, suggesting a more nuanced perception of the shareholder body, as well as its strategic use in the rhetorical campaigns against nationalisations and other related policies.[185]

VIII. INSTITUTIONAL INVESTORS AND NATIONALISATIONS

A. The Threat Posed by Nationalisation to Financial Institutions

The post-war nationalisations occurred at the same time as the shareholder base was undergoing systemic change with the shift from individual to institutional investors.[186] Like the individual shareholders, the institutional investors were concerned with the nationalisations of their investee companies, but they had the additional worry that their institutions would also be the targets of expropriation as additional industries came into the crosshairs of the politicians looking to expand state ownership, fuelling concerns for self-preservation that provided incentives for investment managers to keep a low profile.[187] The financial institutions felt the effects of the threats of nationalisations and government scrutiny, and there was a particular focus on the banks, which were targeted for governmental intervention not, like with some industries, because they were failing, but because of Labour's objections to how they operated, with implications for stakeholders beyond equity shareholders.[188] The first nationalisation by the post-war Labour governments was of the Bank of England in 1946, and the expropriation of other financial institutions remained a possibility into the 1970s, in particular when the City was accused of not acting in the best interests of British industry and stakeholders.[189] In 1973, Ron Hayward, the General Secretary of the Labour Party, announced that the nationalisations of the banks and insurance companies 'was no longer "whether" but "how"'.[190] This statement was followed by the promise in Labour's October 1974 manifesto that: 'We shall bring forward early proposals to ensure that banking and insurance make a better contribution to the national economy.'[191]

As part of its broader interventionist programme, the Labour Party supported expanding public ownership of banks and insurance companies, criticising

[185] See ch 3, section I.D of this volume on shareholder apathy.
[186] See ch 3 of this volume for a more detailed discussion of the changing shareholder base.
[187] Sampson (1971) 526.
[188] Kynaston (2001) 472.
[189] Kynaston (2001) 467, 478.
[190] Kynaston (2001) 466. During the financial crisis of 2007–08, the nationalisation of certain financial institutions (eg, Royal Bank of Scotland, Lloyds Banking Group and Northern Rock) became necessary to stabilise the global economy rather than being the implementation of a socialist political programme. See Mor, F, *Bank Rescues 2007–2009: Outcomes and Costs* (House of Commons Library Briefing Paper 5748, 8 October 2018).
[191] Labour Party (1974b); Dale (2000b) 202.

financial institutions for not lending enough capital to industry for it to grow.[192] In 1976, the Labour Party conference voted in favour of motions supporting nationalising the four main clearing banks and the seven largest insurance companies.[193] The chairman of Clydesdale Bank responded at his company's AGM, blaming the lack of demand for bank financing on high interest rates and the poor returns resulting from high inflation, and warned his shareholders of the damage that nationalisations and political interference would do to British banks both at home and abroad.[194] The nationalisations of British companies had important consequences for all shareholders, both direct and indirect, and the individuals who invested their savings with financial institutions were called upon to view the expropriations with suspicion and not to trust any government, but especially a Labour government, from keeping non-economic considerations from dominating their decisions.[195]

IX. THE FALTERING POST-WAR CONSENSUS AND STATE INTERVENTIONS

By the time Edward Heath became Prime Minister and the Conservatives returned to power in 1970, Britain was a full generation after the end of the Second World War and the ideological urgency of the post-war consensus was giving way to the pragmatism and individualism of the 1970s.[196] As stated in the 1970 Conservative Party manifesto: 'This election is about Britain's tomorrow. The choice of a Government for the next five years will go far to determine the future of our country right through the seventies and beyond.'[197] The political compromises and moderation of both major parties were breaking down, with an increase in the polarisation of the public debate on both the political right and the political left that compromised the 'liberal, pluralistic and elitist' conventions that underpinned the post-war consensus.[198]

Nationalisations were associated with Labour policies and governments, but they were not alone in supporting state involvement in British industry, and during the 1970s the state increased its control over large sectors of the economy before the final breakdown of what remained of the post-war consensus and the advent of a decidedly new era under Margaret Thatcher that oversaw an extensive and steady privatisation programme of major British public corporations

[192] Labour Party (1976) 20. A similar refrain was heard from critics of the financial system in the recessionary period following the global financial crisis of 2007–08; see de Haas and van Horen (2013).
[193] Labour Party (1976) 21–36; Dutton (1997) 106.
[194] 'Report & Accounts' (1977) 130.
[195] Wincott (1967) 14.
[196] Dutton (1997) 90; Kavanagh (1992) 185; Middlemas (1990) 290.
[197] Conservative Unionist Party (1970); Dale (2000a) 178.
[198] Middlemas (1991) 178.

and companies.[199] During the Heath government of 1970–74, state interventions, when necessary, were accepted as part of the Conservative platform.[200] After the Conservatives' defeat in 1974, and signalling the decline of the ideological compromises that upheld the political cooperation that sustained the post-war consensus, the Party recommitted itself to its core principles, including free-market capitalism, a reduction in state control and limiting the power of the trade unions.[201] The move away from the compromises of the post-war consensus reflected a Britain that was poised for the political changes that led to the 'Big Bang' and the re-emergence of a more classical form of capitalism.

X. THE FINANCIAL CRASH, EQUITY SHAREHOLDERS AND NATIONALISATIONS

The concerns by investors and existing shareholders caused by the uncertainty of nationalisations, which varied depending on the political climate and the changing policies of the sitting government, continued into the 1970s. This was at a time when shareholders faced confidence-shaking economic challenges, with 1974 experiencing the steepest financial crash yet recorded in Britain, fuelled by the oil crisis and spiking inflation.[202] Against this backdrop of economic volatility and with the breakdown of the post-war consensus, the Labour Party moved more to the ideological left under the leadership of Harold Wilson, with Tony Benn as party chairman, making a renewed commitment to public ownership and nationalisations that targeted different industries and sectors.[203] As with the economic difficulties faced immediately after the Second World War, the crises of the 1970s were an opportunity for the more ideologically radical wing of the Labour Party to assert itself.[204]

The October 1974 general election, which closely followed the February 1974 election that resulted in a hung Parliament and the resignation of Heath, returned Labour to power, albeit with a slim majority of only three seats; the Labour Party ran, and won, on a platform that promised to address inequalities and to grow the welfare state, as well as a renewed pledge to increase state ownership of British industry.[205] In its manifesto, the Party declared:

> We do not accept the negative policies adopted by the previous Tory Government towards the nationalised industries. We shall restore to our public enterprises the assets and licences which the Tory Government took away from them and will encourage and help them diversify into new industries.[206]

[199] Kavanagh (1992) 188.
[200] Middlemas (1990) 314.
[201] Kavanagh (1992) 188.
[202] Kavanagh (1992), 188; Gleeson (1981) 116.
[203] Dutton (1997) 98.
[204] Edgerton (2018) 404.
[205] Dutton (1997) 100.
[206] Labour Party (1974b); Dale (2000b) 202.

Facing the possibility of a Labour government, company directors, destabilised by the acute economic challenges and political volatility, spoke out publicly against nationalisations. Sir Val Duncan, the chairman and CEO of the metals and mining company Rio Tinto-Zinc, pleaded in May 1974: 'I implore the country to be very careful of further nationalisation. This is highly dangerous for Britain's future economic prosperity.'[207]

The Conservatives, for their part, increased their opposition to nationalisations in their campaign against Labour, stating in their February 1974 manifesto, *Firm Action for a Fair Britain*, that:

> Labour's policy for industry is one of massive nationalisation on an unprecedented scale. In addition to taking over a number of named industries, Labour is pledged to nationalise key firms in other industries and threatens to take over any profitable firm throughout manufacturing industry. In what would remain of private industry, it is explicitly committed to taking power to issue arbitrary State 'directives' to any company and, if it sees fit, to put in a Government 'trustee' to run the firm. It has also talked glibly of nationalising banks, building societies and insurance companies – which would mean taking over the savings of the people.[208]

By the mid-1970s, shareholders featured explicitly in the Conservatives' political programme and in the October 1974 general election manifesto, which built on the platform from the February campaign, they claimed that: 'There is no majority for a massive extension of nationalisation. There is no majority for the continued harrying of private enterprise. There is no majority for penalising those who save, own property or make profits.'[209] The Conservatives lost the election, suggesting that the electorate still had an appetite for the nationalisations and interventions promised by Labour, although by the end of the decade these were abandoned in favour of Thatcherite capitalism.

A. The National Enterprise Board

In 1974, with the stock market in steep decline and repeatedly hitting new lows, the new Labour government, again under the leadership of Harold Wilson, was primed to 'initiate its programme of radical socialist policies'.[210] In the White Paper *The Regeneration of British Industry*, the Secretary of State for Industry, Tony Benn, embraced planning agreements with British companies and the establishment of the National Enterprise Board (NEB).[211] According to Benn, the NEB was 'the instrument by which the Government ensures the nation's resources' and was a 'substantial expansion of public ownership into profitable manufacturing industry', putting not just the shareholders of struggling

[207] 'RTZ' (1974) 42.
[208] Conservative Unionist Party (1974a); Dale (2000a) 226.
[209] Conservative Unionist Party (1974b); Dale (2000a) 233.
[210] Benn (1989) 113.
[211] Kynaston (2001) 505.

industries in the crosshairs of state expropriation but also those owning equities in sectors that were performing well under private ownership.[212] The NEB was introduced in 1975 to increase public ownership of industry with what was essentially a state-owned merchant bank, whose mandate was 'to provide new jobs and new investment; and to give a major boost to exports and to import substitution … [T]he NEB would need to control a successful, leading company in each of the main sectors in industry and commerce'.[213] Unlike the earlier, short-lived IRC, the NEB was a more active vehicle and by 1978, it had acquired ownership of over 15 companies, including British Leyland and Rolls-Royce.[214]

The Labour government, attempting to deal with the urgent economic challenges of high unemployment and inflation, appeared to adopt conflicting policies – for example, both increasing and reducing state involvement in British industry, and expanding and shrinking public investment simultaneously.[215] As with some earlier nationalisations, equity shareholders in distressed companies could benefit from state intervention; for the bailout of British Leyland, for example, existing legislation did not allow the government to issue new shares (whether straight or convertible) at less than the nominal value without shareholder approval, and any bid for the shares on the open market needed to be done at a premium, giving existing shareholders a windfall profit.[216] In this iteration of Labour's nationalisation policy, the shareholder was involved, protected and even rewarded.

Although many British long-term shareholders were impacted by post-war nationalisations and the loss of their equity positions, there were also investors that opportunistically bought shares in failing companies on the hopes of a rescue, thereby profiting from state intervention, which in turn aroused the ire of those who opposed the NEB's cooperation with the City and industry.[217] Those that hoped that the post-war consensus and the application of the socialist principles underpinning the nationalisation of British industry would, as observed

[212] Benn (1989) 213.

[213] Labour Party National Executive Committee (1975) 6.

[214] 'The State as Shareholder' (1978) 93; Kynaston (2001), 493. Under the auspices of the NEB, in 1975 the Wilson government intervened to save British Leyland, a collapsing industrial icon of British manufacturing, taking an initial £50 million stake (a sum that would reach £580 million by 1979). This was an investment by the state in a company that had approximately 165,000 employees and £500 million a year in exports, which was designed to preserve jobs and help stabilise the British economy – £50 million in 1975 is worth approximately £536 million in 2023, and £580 million in 1979 is worth approximately £3.8 billion in 2023 (www.officialdata.org/UK-inflation; see also Middlemas (1991) 84; McDonald (1978) 108; Kynaston (2001)) 510). See Sir D Ryder, *British Leyland: the Next Decade an Abridged Version of a Report Presented to the Secretary of State for Industry by a Team of Inquiry led by Sir Don Ryder* (HC342, 23 April 1975) for a detail account of the House of Common committee's assessment of British Leyland. Under Margaret Thatcher, the NEB began to lose its power, eventually morphing into the British Technology Group, which was sold to the private sector in 1992 and listed on the London Stock Exchange in 1995.

[215] Morgan (1992) 381.

[216] 'Should British Leyland Have More Worker-Shareholders?' (1974) 91.

[217] Middlemas (1991) 61.

by the economic historian Sidney Pollard, 'usher in a regime of better industrial relations, a motivation of unselfishness and a social purpose in industry, were soon disappointed. Instead, there was an amalgam of social and commercial objectives'.[218] The government's decision to salvage failing industries with an infusion of public capital benefited both long-term and short-term shareholders, to the dismay of those who saw state intervention as a way to reform the entrenched capitalist system, not to reward risk-taking and speculation.

i. The NEB and Institutional Investors

In addition to the NEB's mandate to invest in British companies, the Chancellor Denis Healey also sought to compel pension funds, investment funds and insurance companies to channel a designated percentage of new funds to the NEB and other public enterprises, as well as for the NEB to become more involved in banking activities more generally.[219] The intention of the Labour government was not only to nationalise British companies and industries, but also to dictate, at least to a degree, where certain institutional investors were allocating their capital, policies that were strongly resisted.[220] This idea, embraced by the Labour government and by the trade unions, that the state would have a say in how and where these institutions invested their assets under management was rebuffed by the financial institutions, which dismissed the notion that they had additional obligations beyond those of any equity owner.[221] The financial institutions insisted that capital allocation decisions should be made solely on investment criteria and that if British industry required more financing from private sector institutional investors, it needed to make its shares attractive by improving productivity and increasing distributions.[222]

With each act in the drama of nationalisations, directors of British companies came to realise that institutional shareholders were their allies in resisting the interventionist plans of governments.[223] For their part, institutional shareholders, who were reluctant to be told where to invest their funds, needed to work with the government (and the NEB where it had a stake in a company) to preserve and create shareholder value and to forge a path to independence from state control.[224] Furthermore, it was in the interests of the institutional shareholders to limit the extent to which the NEB penetrated industries; that is, keeping the state from investing in a company in the first place was preferable

[218] Pollard (1992) 261.
[219] Kynaston (2001) 533; Labour Party National Executive Committee (1975) 7.
[220] Davies (2019) 91; Sampson (1971) 528.
[221] Kynaston (2001) 534.
[222] Davies (2019) 91.
[223] Fleming (1975) 16.
[224] Kynaston (2001) 534.

to having to work alongside it afterwards. The delicacy needed to balance their duties to their beneficial investors with the requirements to cooperate with the government was further complicated because of the nationalisation threats that these financial institutions were facing themselves.[225]

B. Nationalisations and Stakeholderism

As the 1970s progressed and the two main political parties became increasingly removed from the compromises of the post-war consensus and reverted back to their ideological homes, the Labour Party, back in government from 1974 and with a renewed sense of confidence, remained committed to nationalisation policies and the ideological foundations of socialism and state control.[226] The National Executive Committee published *Labour's Programme for 1976*, which called for the implementation of the Party's economic plan, including sweeping nationalisations of the leading companies in all British industries.[227] The Labour Party's renewed calls for the expansion of nationalisations left company boards, as well as their equity shareholders and other participants in the financial markets, apprehensive.[228]

Labour's assertion that industry was failing the British public was supported by the recurring argument that equity shareholders were not stewarding companies adequately and that state interventions and nationalisations were a means by which to transform the existing system to meet the needs of all stakeholders, including workers and the community.[229] British shareholders, both institutions and individuals, were seen as neglecting their governance responsibilities of overseeing management; the frustration in the face of the economic struggles and industrial unrest of the 1970s fed the belief that if shareholders remain complacent and inactive, 'there are plenty of people in government ready to do their job for them'.[230] Labour's nationalisations policies assumed that the state would do a better job at managing companies, leading to reforms in the existing system that would promote economic growth, the redistribution of wealth and the elevation of stakeholder interests.[231] Despite Labour's policy commitments to the expansion of industrial democracy for the benefit of British workers, their return to government in 1974 failed to fulfil the promises of systemic and statutory reforms.

[225] Labour Party (1974b) 11. See also section VIII.A in this chapter.
[226] Kavanagh and Morris (1989) 29.
[227] Labour Party (1976) 21–36; Dutton (1997) 106.
[228] Dutton (1997) 106.
[229] Foote (1986) 321.
[230] 'Zzzzz' (1976) 138.
[231] Dutton (1997) 100; Foote (1986) 321.

XI. BRITAIN'S PIVOT TO THATCHERISM

The election of Margaret Thatcher in 1979 was a milestone in British economic and social history, and signalled the end of the post-war consensus, demarking it from the preceding decades that followed the end of the Second World War.[232] By the late 1970s, the post-war consensus had broken down and the assumptions on which it was based – full employment, industrial progress and the mixed economy – were abandoned, to be replaced in the 1980s with Thatcherism and the ideals of monetarism, deregulation and privatisation.[233] In 1979, the Conservatives regained power after five years in opposition from where they witnessed a more radical Labour Party implementing policies that were increasingly out of step with a nation experiencing the economic disruptions and industrial unrest of the 1970s.[234]

Responding to changes in public opinion, the Conservative 1979 manifesto attacked Labour's nationalisation policies:

> The British people strongly oppose Labour's plans to nationalise yet more firms and industries such as building, banking, insurance, pharmaceuticals and road haulage. More nationalisation would further impoverish us and further undermine our freedom. We will offer to sell back to private ownership the recently nationalised aerospace and shipbuilding concerns, giving their employees the opportunity to purchase shares.[235]

The Conservatives promised not just to halt nationalisations and privatise industries but to do so in ways that supported the Conservatives' preferred manifestation of industrial democracy, that is, worker shareholding, which was a prominent policy issue at the time.[236]

The 1979 Conservative manifesto also addressed the NEB and the Industry Act, stating that:

> Even where Labour have not nationalised they interfere too much. We shall therefore amend the 1975 Industry Act and restrict the powers of the National Enterprise Board solely to the administration of the Government's temporary shareholdings, to be sold off as circumstances permit. We want to see those industries that remain nationalised running more successfully and we will therefore interfere less with their management and set them a clearer financial discipline in which to work.[237]

Ultimately, it was the Conservative's victory and the subsequent privatisation of the nationalised industries in the 1980s that led to widespread shareholder

[232] Dutton (1997) 110.
[233] Bogdanor (1994) 359.
[234] Dorey (1995) 165; Dutton (1997) 110.
[235] Conservative Unionist Party (1979); Dale (2000a) 272.
[236] See ch 5 of this volume on industrial democracy and the worker shareholder.
[237] Conservative Unionist Party (1979); Dale (2000a) 272.

democracy in Britain, with the British public becoming owners of the shares in these newly privatised companies.[238]

Nationalisations were a prominent fixture of the post-war period from 1945 to 1979, impacting how the British economy was reconstructed and influencing financial markets and industrial development. During this period, Labour sought to use nationalisations to redistribute wealth, increase state control and recalibrate the existing system, although both main political parties implemented policies to support struggling companies and protect the interests of shareholders and other stakeholders. Nationalisation and interventionist policies were wrapped in different ideological justifications, and the implementations took various forms, but for the equity shareholders, the result was both a loss of ownership in investee companies and forfeiture of the potential future rewards for investing their risk capital. For some shareholders, however, nationalisations were a lifeline that saved them from partial or complete losses of their equity investments in failing companies.

By the end of the post-war era, the Conservatives were vocally opposing nationalisations, a position that helped return them to government under Thatcher. In their 1979 manifesto, the Conservatives claimed that:

> Threats of nationalisation have destroyed confidence. It is time to call a halt to these immensely damaging policies. Above all, we must recognise that in a mixed economy like ours, economic success depends very largely on private enterprise. One of the most valuable things we could do for industry would be to assure it that for several years ahead, there would be no threat of new nationalisation or more state direction.[239]

With the advent of Thatcherism, Britain entered a privatisation stage in the economic cycle, with nationalisations falling out of favour while free-market capitalism was embraced and financial institutions deregulated, creating the conditions that eventually led to the 2007–08 global financial crisis and its aftermath, and to a subsequent reconsideration of the benefits of regulation, legislation, governance and intervention.[240]

[238] Pollard (1992) 408. See also Edgerton (2018) 455 on the details of Thatcher's policy of privatisations and an analysis of its transformative implications.

[239] Conservative Unionist Party (1974b); Dale (2000a) 236.

[240] Oren and Blyth (2019) 618.

3

The Post-war Shareholder Body and Shareholder Democracy

Following the end of the Second World War, Britain faced acute political re-adjustments in which the roles of the individual and of the state were reassessed and redefined; as equity owners and corporate leaders faced the implications of widespread state expropriation of private industries, shareholder interests became part of that recalibration. The post-war evolution of the shareholder body occurred against the backdrop of increased state intervention and the widespread nationalisations of British industry, which profoundly influenced the relationships amongst companies, their equity owners and other stakeholders. Considering how shareholders were perceived, and how they were deployed in the political struggles of the post-war period, contributes to the broader understanding of the post-war developments in British industry and the pressures surrounding the calls for company law reforms. With its one-share-one-vote structure, the equity shareholder was a manifestation of democracy, yet in the post-war political atmosphere imbued with aspirations for increased democratisation and inclusiveness, shareholder democracy failed to achieve its goals.[1]

Changes in the shareholder body, and the acknowledgement of those changes, had consequences for industry – that is, the institutionalisation of the shareholder transferred power from dispersed individual investors to the more concentrated and sophisticated financial institutions.[2] Shareholders were part of the political discourse of the period, with shareholder democracy promoted as a way to address the inequalities and as an addition (or alternative) to nationalisations and socialism. Shareholder democracy was a means by which to empower the shareholder body in its role as equity owner, with the goal of that empowerment variable and often ideologically anchored. Whereas the individual shareholder was virtually powerless on his or her own, working in concert with other shareholders represented the potential to influence corporate decisions of investee companies. HG Manne, a founder of the law and economics movement, suggested in his 2007 article on the 20- to 30-year cycles of shareholder democracy, published just months before the global financial crisis,

[1] Konzelmann et al (2018) 28.
[2] Cheffins (2008) 345.

that: 'Perhaps many of the advocates of shareholder democracy actually have a hidden agenda, most usually either a greater degree of government control over private enterprises, or more power to unions via their control of pension funds.'[3]

I. POST-WAR PERCEPTIONS OF THE SHAREHOLDER

Against the transformative post-war backdrop, and subject to the altering views on the role of industry and its relationship with public and private ownership, the identity of the equity shareholder was used as a symbol by different groups and actors across the political spectrum. The identity of the British shareholder was complicated, including both the honest 'everyman' and the reviled speculator; depending on the situation, the shareholder could be the diligent worker saving his or her wages to invest in British industry and a better future or the financial opportunist making profits off the back of labour and at the expense of a recovering post-war Britain. The post-war shareholder had many different identities, ranging from lone penny-pinching individuals to powerful financial institutions, with a growing investing middle class becoming increasingly relevant.[4]

A. The Shareholder as Greedy Capitalist

The anti-capitalist portrayal of the shareholder depicted him or her as representing sordid laissez-faire greed and of the privileged classes drawing unearned income by exploiting labour.[5] In the 1945 general election, when socialist policies and the nationalisation of British industry were central to the Labour Party's political agenda, the Party ran on a platform that attacked profiteers, the antagonists of the ordinary British voter, claiming that:

> [A]nti-controllers and anti-planners desire to sweep away public controls, simply in order to give profiteering interests and the privileged rich an entirely free hand to plunder the rest of the nation as shamelessly as they did in the nineteen-twenties.

[3] Manne (2007) A.23. The principle of shareholder primacy – ie, profit maximisation for the benefit of the shareholder – was promoted by Manne in the 1960s when he argued that it was necessary to achieve corporate efficiencies and that shareholder primacy was incompatible with considering the interests of any other stakeholders (Manne (1962) 415). The perceived identity of the shareholder had evolved from that of Adolf A Berle's doctrine of shareholder primacy: 'For Berle of the 1920s and 1930s, shareholders were the middle- and working-class "Everyman" … For Manne of the 1960s, shareholders were much different; they were rational actors whose constructed intentions could be used to ascertain and justify market functions' (Stewart (2011) 1457). On shareholder primacy and shareholder democracy see ch 4, section I of this volume.

[4] Davenport (1961a) 341; Hill (2015) 53ff.

[5] 'New Basis for Markets?' (1951) 759. See also Edgerton (2018) 106 on the 'functionless rich' living off 'unearned income'. For the Labour Party constitution of 1918, which introduced Clause IV and refers to 'the unoccupied and unproductive recipients of rents and dividends – the so-called "idle rich" – whom it is interesting to find "The Times" editorially declaring to be of no use to the community' (Webb (1918) 3). See ch 2 of this volume on nationalisations.

> Does freedom from the profiteer mean freedom for the ordinary man and woman, whether they be wage-earners or small business or professional men or housewives? ... Freedom is not an abstract thing. To be real it must be won, it must be worked for.[6]

This vilification of the beneficiaries of investment income continued with Clement Attlee's election and was useful in Labour's push for nationalisations. As described in the *Financial Times*: 'The owner of industry – namely, the investor – has been virtually helpless against an anti-capitalist Government majority.'[7] It was widely believed that shares were owned almost exclusively by the privileged elite, although this assumption was challenged in the 1949 research by AG Ellinger and CF Carter, which showed that large holdings worth greater than £10,000 (that is, those belonging to the wealthy) accounted for only 30.7 per cent:

> [A] long way from having a controlling voting interest in British Industry, Ltd. That, incidentally, disproves the Socialist assumption (which millions of people accepted without compelling evidence) that the industry is owned and controlled by plutocratic people.[8]

The depiction of the equity shareholder as the capitalist opportunist predates (and outlasts) the post-war period, a common trope used by socialists and anti-capitalists to whip up support for their causes by demonising their antagonist – that is, the faceless investor – portraying him (or her) as the representative of exploitive capital and the enemy of the common labourer.[9] The attacks on shareholders and what was perceived as unearned investment income came from proponents of political, economic and social reforms, who targeted the 'functionless' shareholder as a scapegoat for many of the ills and inequities of the economy and society.[10] The average British working man/working woman had little or no exposure to equity investing and the shareholder was a

[6] Labour Party (1945); Dale (2000b) 52.

[7] 'An Association of Investors?' (1949a) 4.

[8] 'An Association of Investors?' (1949b) 2. In this research, 'British Industry, Ltd' is defined as a cross-section of 30 British companies; this research identifies the anatomy of share ownership based on £318 million nominal of industrial capital (a representative sample) as 29.2% small holdings up to £500 and 40.1% medium holdings from £500 to £10,000 (£500 in 1949 is worth approximately £22,606 and £10,000 in 1949 is worth approximately £452,110 in 2023; see www.officialdata.org/UK-inflation). This statement assumes the link between ownership and control, which was central to the debate on shareholder primacy. On the agency problem and ownership and control, see Fama (1980); Fama and Jensen (1983).

[9] Edgerton (2018) 107.

[10] Kellett (1962) 10. John Maynard Keynes, writing between the wars, explains: 'I see, therefore, the rentier aspect of capitalism as a transitional phase which will disappear when it has done its work. And with the disappearance of its rentier aspect much else in it besides will suffer a sea-change. It will be, moreover, a great advantage of the order of events which I am advocating, that the euthanasia of the rentier, of the functionless investor, will be nothing sudden, merely a gradual but prolonged continuance of what we have seen recently in Great Britain, and will need no revolution' (Keynes (1936) ch 24, ii). See also Konzelmann, Chic and Fovargue-Davies (2021).

convenient target on which to focus the frustrations of a section of the population with limited economic security.[11]

The depictions of the greedy profiteer were consistent with the vilification of equity investors that were believed to put profit before all other considerations, including the interests of fellow shareholders and other stakeholders.[12] In the post-war period, the perception of the typical equity investor was often that he or she was removed from the average British citizen – that is, a profiteering opportunist taking rents from the honest worker and becoming rich off of immoral investments. As explained in a 1973 pamphlet on employee participation published by the Bow Group, a conservative think tank founded in the 1950s:

> [A]n employee who puts his money on deposit at a bank still tends to think of industrial financiers as 'they'. The security of investment (and of the return on it) and the fact that he has no concern with the bank's application of the funds means that he feels no involvement with the 'capitalistic' side of industry at all. This certainly applied to his investment in a pension fund.[13]

The post-war worker, even if he or she might be an indirect shareholder, did not identify with the providers of capital that were associated with share ownership. Harold Wilson, a strong advocate for expanding state control of industries, when speaking to the Labour Party in 1973, exemplified the political left's portrayals of the greedy investor that threatens workers with redundancy:

> As like as not it was the result of a smart deal, where some very slick young man saw a chance of buying mixed enterprise; with perhaps millions more pounds to make – for him, not the community, not for the national welfare – by developing and rack-renting the property value, than by keeping even a viable factory going.[14]

This stereotype of the merciless capitalist proved resilient and remained prevalent in the public discourse on the societal roles and responsibilities of the various stakeholders, including shareholders, in financial markets. If the shareholder is the speculator who cares only for profits and distributions, it is easier for politicians and law-makers to sacrifice him or her in favour of the interests of other stakeholders, such as employees, consumers, or the community. That there were many average men and women invested, both directly and indirectly,

[11] See Shonfield (1958) 170 on Labour's ideology that 'capitalists were functionless and evil, fit only for ultimate destruction'.

[12] In the 1945 general election, the Labour Party ran on a platform that attacked profiteers, and the party that they supported, the Conservatives, claiming that 'anti-controllers and anti-planners desire to sweep away public controls, simply in order to give profiteering interests and the privileged rich an entirely free hand to plunder the rest of the nation as shamelessly as they did in the nineteen-twenties. Does freedom from the profiteer mean freedom for the ordinary man and woman, whether they be wage-earners or small business or professional men or housewives? … Freedom is not an abstract thing. To be Real it must be won, it must be worked for'. Labour Party (1945); Dale (2000b) 52.

[13] Goss (1973) 19.

[14] Wilson (1973) 5.

in the shares of British companies seemed inconsequential to the peddlers of political rhetoric who identified 'the shareholder' with the monied classes and made the term synonymous with profiteers and speculators.[15] As the movements for industrial democracy gained more traction, and especially the support for worker shareholders, the simplistic negative characterisations of shareholders became more complicated.[16] The antagonism towards the 'investment class', which was often used for political populist ends, was stubbornly persistent and easily identifiable in the pre- and post-war periods; the depictions of the greedy profiteer endures with the negative portrayals of activists, private equity and other types of investors believed to put profit before all other considerations, including fellow shareholders and other stakeholders.[17]

B. The Shareholder as a Symbol of Inequality

During the Labour government of 1945–51, equity shareholders were targeted more than other types of investors in the capitalist system, a consequence of the hostility of the political left towards the equity shareholders of listed companies that resulted from the post-war position that share ownership and the distribution of profits to equity owners were immoral.[18] As colourfully expressed in the *Financial Times* in 1949:

> Under a Socialist regime, capital ownership is a depressed interest, and the minimum rights to which British people are accustomed are systematically denied to investors as such. They pay their full taxes as members of the community, and are mulcted, additionally and discriminately, qua, investors. As in Dante's Inferno, there are separate degrees and circles of infamy in being an investor. The company shareholder appears to rank lower in the Socialist scale than the Government bondholder, and the owner of 'risk capital' – Ordinary shares – ranks lowest of all.[19]

For the governing Labour Party, the equity shareholder embodied the inequities against which it, and its supporters, struggled, as well as being an identifiable antagonist on which to focus its outrage.

Labour, both in government and in opposition, raised ideological objections to the private ownership of industry, supporting instead nationalisations and public ownership, which 'would substantially reduce unearned income, unjustifiable inequalities of wealth and the division of society into privileged and under-privileged classes'.[20] The Party's 1957 policy paper, *Industry and Society*,

[15] Kellett (1962) 9. For working-class attitudes on shareholders, see Naylor (1968) 46. For Keynesian theory on attitudes on speculation and related economic theory, see Keynes (1936) ch 12, vi.

[16] See ch 5 of this volume on the worker shareholder.

[17] Edmans (2020a) 291. See Hill (2015) on the development of the image of the shareholder.

[18] Munro (2012) 766.

[19] 'An Association of Investors?' (1949d) 2.

[20] Labour Party (1957) 7.

promoted the need to reform share ownership, even while acknowledging the limited influence of individual shareholders: '[I]f share ownership has become relatively unimportant economically, nevertheless its importance as a continuing cause of inequality of wealth remains undiminished'.[21] Even when direct equity ownership by individuals was shrinking and institutional investors were increasingly able to meet British industry's demands for equity funding, Labour objected to equity ownership in industrial companies, which was still more concentrated than any other form of property and remained the largest component of private wealth.[22]

C. The Shareholder as 'Everyman'

The derogatory perception of greedy shareholders was not completely ubiquitous and did not suit all political narratives. In their resistance to systemic reforms to the financial markets, the capitalists and free-market anti-interventionists, while often critical of equity owners as having limited influence and even less engagement, characterised the small shareholders as the representative of the average man (or woman), diligently saving his or her pennies to invest stoically and patriotically in British industry, and carrying more than his or her share of the economic burden of rebuilding Britain while being vilified and victimised for his or her role as an investor.[23] In this guise, the shareholder was not the opportunistic financier or member of the plutocracy, but the average British citizen, encouraged to save and invest by political leaders seeking alternatives to the proposed dismantling of British capitalism.[24] The support for broadening the investor base and for shareholder democracy was a way to reinforce a system of shareholder interests, purposefully identifying the small shareholder with the average man or woman, and building on the idea that the social and societal barriers to investing should be dismantled.

Despite these directed efforts to depict shareholders positively, they were often disparaged and taken for granted by industrial leaders, required for their capital but without having any real individual influence, given attention only when they were needed as a funding source, to strengthen an ideological argument or for political expediency, as was exemplified by British industry's fight against nationalisations.[25] Whereas company directors could be dismissive of their shareholders, there were also expressions of support from boards, particularly when industries were under threat or companies were in need of equity

[21] Labour Party (1957) 34.

[22] Labour Party (1957) 32.

[23] See, for example, the letters to the editor of the *Financial Times*, written by small shareholders expressing this view; 'Shareholders and Dividend Restraint' (1951) 4; Singer (1950) 4.

[24] Kellett (1962) 17; Acton Society Trust (1959) 4ff.

[25] See, for example, 'An Association of Investors?' (1949a) 4; 'An Association of Investors?' (1949b) 2; 'An Association of Investors?' (1949c) 4. See also ch 2 of this volume on nationalisations.

capital, as described, somewhat idealistically, by H Reddish, Chairman and Managing Director of Rugby Portland Cement, in 1952:

> Let us be quite clear who the ordinary shareholders are. In the main – and the same is true of most of the public companies in this country – they are men and women who out of their savings have decided to invest money in the industries of this country, taking with their eyes open the risk of losing their money if things go badly, and, in all fairness, being entitled to the profits if things go well.[26]

Stereotypes were sticky, however, with the *Financial Times* reporting in 1968 that shareholders were still seen as 'chaps in armchairs in their club' and not as the average saver who is placing his or her savings in insurance companies and pension funds.[27] Although there were working-class shareholders who invested directly in the equity markets, and a growing number that invested indirectly through financial vehicles and pensions, these shareholders were not 'the solution to the tensions in modern capitalism', which was the hope of those encouraging the advance of shareholder democracy.[28]

D. The Apathetic Shareholder

The characterisation of shareholders as complacent and apathetic was, and continues to be, enduring and was the default assumption for many of those commenting on the financial markets in the post-war period.[29] Accepting the premise of the separation of ownership and control, shareholder 'passivity was seen as an inevitable result of the scale of modern industrial enterprise and of the collective action problems that face shareholders, each of whom owns only a small fraction of a large firm's shares'.[30] Shareholder apathy, a normative assumption in financial theory, was a target of criticism in a society with changing expectations of citizen participation, influencing how shareholders were perceived and how they perceived themselves.[31] The 'genuine investor' was viewed as being passive and apathetic, taking action only when the board fell short on distributions and, even then, it was rare for an individual investor to have sufficient incentives to expend the resources needed to become actively involved in 'their company'.[32]

The apathy of which individual shareholders were accused, no matter how rational its justification, was understood as an under-utilisation of existing shareholder rights and weakened the arguments supporting corporate and

26 'Rugby Portland Cement' (1952) 2.
27 Wincott (1968) 12.
28 'Who Owns What?' (1972) 73.
29 Black (1990) 524.
30 Black and Coffee (1994) 1999; Berle and Means (1967) (originally published in 1932).
31 On 'the normal apathy of the small stockholder', see, for example, Berle and Means (1967) 76. On shareholder apathy as normative, see Fairfax (2019) 1310ff.
32 'The Modern Shareholder' (1949) 256; Black (1990) 527.

shareholder democracy; if shareholders were not exercising the rights that they have now, why give them more? With consistently low attendance at AGMs and few attempts to engage with company boards on a regular basis, shareholders were viewed as ineffective stewards and, in the eyes of some, had lost their right to the primacy that they are afforded under the law.[33] As expressed by one reader of *The Economist* in 1959: 'We must once and for all accept the relationship of equity shareholder to company for no more than it is – the same as that of a punter to racehorse.'[34] Thus, the shareholder was reduced to a gambler and the income derived from his or her investments no better than that won on the track.[35]

The Economist, in its regular reporting on company AGMs, provided examples of under-attended shareholder meetings at which few, if any, questions were asked by those who were there.[36] For example, at the 1963 AGM of the Reed Paper Group, only 50 shareholders attended the meeting, asking only one unsatisfying question, no questions about board changes and a new chairman, no comments on a change of company name, and not even a vote of thanks to the outgoing chairman who was leaving the company after 18 years on the board; although it is possible that the shareholders were unaware of the changes listed above, of which they had not been informed directly, as speculated by *The Economist*, it was more likely that they were simply not interested.[37] Reporting in 1964 on the steel industry's AGMs, *The Economist* described the lack of shareholder participation and the seeming indifference to the threats of nationalisation that their companies faced – for example, of all the AGMs, the highest attendance was just 75 shareholders at the meeting for South Durham and Steel Company of Wales, with the other companies having only between 14 and 50 shareholders in attendance.[38] Even when equity

[33] Rose (1989) 155ff. See also Hill (2015) 65 on shareholders as corporate stewards.

[34] Swift and Fagan (1959) 680. This analogy persisted, being used by the Secretary and Chief Executive of the Institute of Chartered Secretaries and Administrators, Barry Barker, at the end of the 1970s when he stated that: 'The shareholder, that is the individual shareholder, has long since been disinterested in the company in which he has invested, provided that the share price is maintained or improved and dividends arrive regularly and are in sufficient amount. He has become a mere investor, who contemplates the share price list in the press as a racegoer does a race card, studying form and listening to or disregarding the tipsters' advice, based on anything from highly sophisticated analysis of macro- and micro-economic situations and company reports down to guesses' (Barker (1982) 86).

[35] The corresponding depictions of the Stock Exchange as a casino, by figures no less influential than Harold Wilson, supported this view of equity investing (see Kynaston (2001) 494). The Labour MP Maurice Edelman was also reported to oppose wider share ownership and 'protested against the coming of the "gamblers' State" with its pools, premium bonds, Stock Exchange speculations and take-over bids' (Davenport (1961a) 341). The connection between gambling and investing was commonplace, as was demonstrated in the Wider Share Ownership Council 1968 publication, in which one surveyed working man stated: 'It's not for the working man to buy shares, to gamble. For some rich people it's a living, isn't it?' And as similarly stated by a working woman: 'It would be a nice feeling to have a sense of ownership but it's a bit of a gamble isn't it, and I never had the chance' (Naylor (1968) 47 and 99). See Whiting (2004) 105.

[36] 'Meeting the Shareholders' (1964) 646.

[37] 'Silent Shareholders' (1963) 385.

[38] 'Meeting the Shareholders' (1964) 646; see also ch 2, section VI.A.i in this volume.

shareholders' interests were clearly at stake, as with nationalisations, directors struggled to increase shareholder attendance and engagement at general meetings.

Although these were dismal, if unsurprising, attendance levels by shareholders, the companies themselves were partly to blame, scheduling meetings for midday on weekdays or, when located outside of London, making them logistically difficult to attend.[39] This disregard for shareholder accessibility demonstrates a residual dismissiveness by company boards, even when they claimed to be seeking the support of their equity owners in the face of systemic threats. In 1976, *The Economist* substantiated the impression of a passive and uninformed shareholder base, observing that the only contact shareholders have with management is the annual AGM, when the shareholders exercise (or fail to exercise) the rights given to them in a company's articles of association and through the Companies Act, reporting that according to a survey of 48 major companies, the average AGM lasted 20 minutes and attendance rarely represented more than 1 per cent of the shareholder body.[40] In general, AGMs were not well attended, with only a small percentage of the eligible shareholders making an appearance and most not returning proxy cards to confer their vote to a representative, behaviour often attributed to the belief that dispersed shareholders will remain disengaged as long as they receive reasonable dividends.[41]

Similarly, in a 1973 paper, the Conservative Research Department presented its view on equity shareholders, which remained stubbornly consistent, that:

> Except in times of crisis, the annual general meeting in Britain is usually a formality. The majority of shareholders are apathetic and detached, with no sense of personal involvement in the company's operations ... Only a handful of individual shareholders are in a position to influence the appointment of company directors on their own.[42]

Not all observers, however, condemned shareholders for their lack of engagement, with some recognising the basis for their inaction, as expressed in a 1974 study of shareholder democracy undertaken by Mr Midgley of Brighton Polytechnic, reported in the *Financial Times*:

> The low level of shareholder participation ... may not indicate apathy but may suggest that private shareholders adopt pragmatic approaches to their role. It is probably true to say that they are realistic rather than irresponsible about formal company control procedures.[43]

From these accounts, directors' pleas for action in the face of state expropriations were made to small AGM audiences, although the events of the general meetings would have reached more people than just those in attendance as they

[39] 'Meeting the Shareholders' (1964) 646.
[40] 'Who Owns What?' (1976) 22.
[41] Jervis (1966) 34.
[42] Abbott (1973) 15.
[43] Blanden (1974) 7.

were also reported in detail by the financial press.[44] Whether shareholders not present at the AGMs received the messages intended for them and whether they took any action to try to influence political outcomes as a result is uncertain. Moreover, the press reports of AGM speeches reached a readership beyond a company's existing shareholders, including potential voters, other stakeholders and prospective investors, as well as the politicians who sought the support of the British public. As for the supporters of nationalisations and of the systemic transformation of British industry that elevated the interests of labour over those of equity owners, shareholder apathy and impotence aided their cause by undermining the justifications for shareholder primacy.[45]

In 1977, the Lord Bullock's *Report of the Committee of Inquiry on Industrial Democracy* based its recommendation that shareholder rights be reduced on the understanding that the shareholders' meeting is a 'reactive and passive body' that hardly ever makes changes to a company's constitution, and on the rare event that a resolution is proposed, it very rarely gets carried against the advice of the board.[46] The regular refrain claiming that shareholders were interested only in the affairs of the company when it affected profits and dividends remained constant to the end of the post-war period, and beyond, influencing proposals for shareholder and industrial democracy and perpetuating the impression, whether accurate or not, that shareholders are not engaged in the broader issues impacting how their companies are managed. This perception of shareholders as hapless fools endured past the post-war period and companies continued to act on the premise that investors can be easily fooled and their attention deflected away from core systemic issues, as is demonstrated with the various 'greenwashing', 'purpose washing' and 'impact washing' campaigns.[47]

E. The Uninformed Shareholder

The criticisms of shareholders were not limited to accusations of apathy and inaction, and the disparagements came not only from the anti-capitalist left but also from the directors and managers whose company's shares they owned.

[44] The financial newspapers were a key medium used by public companies to communicate with investors and the wider public, with detailed reporting of meetings appearing in the press. In a period of insufficient disclosure requirements, the financial press was often considered the only reliable, if limited, means for the small investor to obtain investing information and advice, as is discussed in Naylor (1960) 37. See also Lee and Tweedie (1977), a survey on private shareholders that shows that they were regular readers of the financial press, with the *Financial Times* being the most popular source; 86 per cent of respondents read one or more financial source, which is broken down into 39 per cent reading one source, 31 per cent two sources, 16 per cent three or more sources, and only 14 per cent no sources (at 21 and Appendix 6).

[45] Shenfield (1971) 12.

[46] 'Look Who the Owners are' (1977) 82; Lord Bullock *Report of the Committee of Inquiry on Industrial Democracy* (Cmnd 6706, 1977) 59, 81. See also ch 7 of this volume on the Bullock Report.

[47] There is an extensive body of research on the integrity of corporate reporting and representation; see, for example, Laufer (2003); Höchstädter and Scheck (2015); Schons and Steinmeier (2016).

In 1961, after a decade of Conservative governments, one reader of the *Financial Times* lamented that industrial leaders used the same language as the radical anti-capitalists to describe shareholders, which they treated with disdain, taking the position:

> [T]hat in general he [the shareholder] is stupid, motivated only by greed and fear, and by the desire of short-term gains, and that management is concerned with him only to obtain the loan of his money on the cheapest terms, to inform him only to the extent required to keep him sweet tempered, and above all to keep him from asking damn-fool questions.[48]

This perception highlights the tension between managers' low regard for shareholders and their need for them, both as equity providers and as supportive equity owners.

A further negative representation of shareholders was that they were potentially disruptive and value-destructive, building on the stereotype that pre-dates the post-war period; the grandstanding gadfly may no longer be a regular participant at AGMs, but his or her legacy at company meetings persisted in the post-war period, be it through targeted activist strategies or individual shareholders making vocal demands of the board.[49] Although the individual shareholder was often dismissed by directors as passive and ineffectual, every shareholder still possessed the power to be disruptive, even if it was exercised irregularly, as expressed in *The Economist* in 1959 during the high-profile takeover battle for British Aluminium, referencing mutterings from the Barclays Bank-United Dominions Trust deal:

> 'The shareholder may be supine, indifferent and even stupid in ninety-nine cases out of a hundred', but when provoked sufficiently, then in the hundredth case he will show his teeth and prove that he is not entirely powerless.[50]

In both these transactions, the directors and their City advisors were viewed as disregarding the interests of existing shareholders.[51]

[48] Mace (1961) 8.

[49] Despite the difficulty for small shareholders to exert their power, shareholder primacy was validated when battles reached the courts, as was seen in the early 1970s when the board of Lonrho, the multinational company, sought to fire its CEO, Mr Tiny Rowland, an infamous corporate raider, a decision that was contested and reached a High Court's decision. When the court did not support Rowland legal challenge of the board's decision, it was by a vote at an extraordinary general meeting (EGM) that Rowland received the support of the shareholders, against the wishes of the majority of the board, to keep him in his role. Rowland had the backing of around 25 million votes, and his opponents had only between 4 and 8 million, out of a total of 65 million shares, resulting in the individual shareholders getting their way, although 'the spectacle of shareholder democracy in action was not always pretty'. It should be noted that the company registry at the time of the EGM listed almost no institutional shareholders, whose decisions might have differed from those of small shareholders, but which had mostly deserted the company during the circus of the court battle ('For the Shareholders to Decide' (1973) 96; 'That Old Black Magic' (1973) 103).

[50] 'Shareholders and Directors' (1959) 612; Rubner (1966) 132.

[51] 'Shareholders and Directors' (1959) 612.

Frequently, equity owners were characterised as impotent in the face of increasingly sophisticated directors. As described in Labour's *Industry and Society*:

> [A]s companies grow larger and their affairs more complex, management becomes increasingly important, increasingly hierarchical, increasingly specialist and increasingly professional. More and more it assumes a life of its own. In the large companies, it is the managers who now undertake the functions once performed by capitalist owners.[52]

The neglect of the equity owner by management, and the portrayal of the shareholder as an ineffective participant tolerated for his or her cheap capital, benefited those pressing for structural reforms to the existing system; as described in the economist Alex Rubner's *The Ensnared Shareholder* in 1965:

> They [shareholders] are 'stupid', 'business-shy', 'ignorant'; when these fools attend AGMs this is a sure sign of their being busybodies and cranks. (Many directors hold this view, only they do not publish it.) Most observers seem of one mind, that shareholders are wholly impotent to influence corporate policy.[53]

The depiction of shareholders as uninformed, or badly informed, was bolstered by the reality that many small investors relied on the press rather than on financial advisors for advice, and there was a general lack of investment education, with few in the City willing to dedicate resources to meeting the needs of mass-market investing, which was seen as unprofitable and time-consuming.[54] Although the dismay at the lack of financial literacy is a chronic and persistent complaint, the democratisation of investing and the widespread involvement in share ownership (mostly indirectly) contributed to growing public awareness of the financial markets, no matter how inadequate. Despite having limited financial expertise, surveys in the 1960s show that approximately 40 per cent of individual investors took no advice at all when deciding on whether to accept or reject a takeover bid or other investing-related issues at investee companies; those who did take advice turned to brokers, the press and bank managers.[55]

In 1968, the British Market Research Bureau issued a report examining the influences on shareholders during the landmark General Electric Company – Associated Electrical Industries (GEC–AEI) bid intended to create a behemothic industrial company, which found that whereas the institutional investors made their decisions regarding the bid based on financial analysis, the behaviour of individual shareholders was more surprising; according to the survey, the small investor demographic was split roughly 50:50 between men and women, most of whom were long-term holders of over five years and were over 55 years of age, were relatively unsophisticated, did not recognise the individual players

[52] Labour Party (1957) 16.
[53] Rubner (1966) 132.
[54] 'Shareholders: Why So Few?' (1966) 52.
[55] Lex (1968) 1.

in the GEC–AEI bid and were unaware of the company's poor performance.[56] This lack of basic awareness by small shareholders was despite the high profile of the GEC–AEI merger, which was described as 'the first major post-war bid where the name of the personality – Arnold Weinstock – became bigger than the already well-known name of his company'.[57] These typical small investors were mostly ignorant of the most rudimentary details of the transaction involving the company in which they held shares, despite it being both publicly prominent and very contentious.

According to *The Attitudes of Private Shareholders to Mergers and Acquisitions* published in 1971, most individual shareholders were prepared to accept the recommendation of the board on a bid, but thought that, as a rule, it was a good idea to resist the first offer, and three-quarters of the shareholders surveyed wanted 'their company' to be approached by at least two bidders and also believed that if 'their company' was buying, then times were good; when it came to seeking advice, these shareholders turned equally to bank managers (1/3), stockbrokers (1/3) or no one (1/3), with the largest shareholders relying more on stockbrokers.[58] In addition, women shareholders were found to be slower to invest in the equity markets than men, with less than 50 per cent of women acquiring shares before the age of 35, compared to 75 per cent of men; women were more likely to ask for advice, generally from their bank managers, and were described as more 'emotionally involved' with their shares and the company in which they were held – for example, four times more women than men would not like to see redundancy occurring as a result of a merger.[59] According to this research, shareholders also expressed responsibility to other stakeholders, with a majority agreeing that a company should not raise prices sharply to deliver higher profits and that they had a greater duty to customers than to management; men were more inclined to stick by company management than women.[60]

Similarly, reporting on another survey conducted by the British Market Research Bureau for Thompson and Partners on the shipping company P&O's bid for Bovis in 1973, *The Economist* described how most individual shareholders did not know if the bid price was too high or too low, that they rarely consulted their stockbrokers (who were considered to be generally unhelpful) and that they did not remember the names of the players involved in the transaction; the determinants influencing these small shareholders were the long circulars sent by P&O (23 per cent), the press (17 per cent) and stockbrokers' advice (11 per cent).[61] In addition, 70 per cent of the individual shareholders who were asked claimed that advertising about the deal was not helpful in making

[56] Lex (1968) 1.

[57] Littlewood (1998) 156.

[58] Readhead (1971) 19; this might be a product of the level of attention larger shareholders would receive from their stockbrokers relative to those with smaller holdings and, possibly, less capital to invest.

[59] Readhead (1971) 19.

[60] Readhead (1971) 19.

[61] 'Ads & Takeovers' (1973) 105.

their decision.[62] Of those surveyed, 25 per cent had acquired the shares through inheritance and 51 per cent had owned them for over 10 years, suggesting that these individual shareholders were not active traders, but that they were 'sticky' investors who were loyal to the company (or too passive and/or uninformed to sell).[63] Other surveys of individual shareholders produced comparable results, with small shareholders often uninformed on the particulars of their investee companies, unable to understand the circulars when they arrived and, in many cases, having inherited the shares rather than choosing the investments themselves, further contributing to the passivity of their behaviour.[64]

The Private Shareholder and the Corporate Report, a survey published in 1977 on the use and understanding of company financial reports by individual shareholders, emphasised the challenges that small investors faced when presented with sophisticated financial information, showing, for example, that the chairman's report was the most widely read, with only 7 per cent of respondents not reading it (52 per cent 'read thoroughly' and 41 per cent 'read briefly for interest'), that the most important quantitative sections – the profit and loss account and the balance sheet – were 'read thoroughly' by 39 per cent and 29 per cent respectively, and that the auditor's report received the least amount of attention by shareholders of all the sections, with 48 per cent not reading it at all.[65] In addition, only 5 per cent of individual shareholders read the full report thoroughly, with the same amount reading none of it.[66] For the rationally apathetic shareholder, becoming informed was not worth the time or the resources, requiring a level of understanding and financial expertise beyond the reach of most individual investors.[67] Not surprisingly, 53 per cent of respondents thought that annual reports should be simplified to improve their use and understanding.[68] In the post-war decades, companies were increasing their disclosure, although aimed at meeting the expectations of the more sophisticated and increasingly influential institutional investors and financial analysts, and not at the particular needs of individual shareholders.[69]

II. TYPES OF SHAREHOLDERS

A. The Individual Shareholder

The changes in the shareholder body in the post-war period are fundamentally important to understanding the evolution of the financial markets during

[62] 'Ads & Takeovers' (1973) 105.
[63] 'Ads & Takeovers' (1973) 105.
[64] Lee and Tweedie (1977) 27ff; Bartlett and Chandler (1997) 247.
[65] Lee and Tweedie (1977) 54. This also gives explanations of the methodology, respondent details, full results and recommendations.
[66] Lee and Tweedie (1977) 62.
[67] Black (1990) 524.
[68] Lee and Tweedie (1977) 122.
[69] Lee and Tweedie (1977) 127.

this period and contextualising the developing relationships amongst different constituents and stakeholders.[70] The recalibration of the ownership of equity shares from individual small shareholders to institutional investors is a thematic arch that underpins the examination of the various movements of shareholder, corporate and industrial democracy in the post-war period. The shift by individual investors from direct to indirect shareholding accelerated after the Second World War, when small investors were net sellers of directly held equities in British companies and institutions became increasingly dominant, a trend that continued to define the shareholder body and was only partially addressed by the privatisation of nationalised industries after the Conservatives returned to power in 1979.[71] By the end of the post-war period, the individual direct shareholder was a minor player in the equity capital markets, overtaken by the institutions.[72]

i. By the Numbers

Research into the identity and behaviour of the small shareholder only began to appear in a methodical way in the late 1940s, prior to which fewer details are known about shareholders in UK listed companies.[73] The study of the equity ownership of industry conducted by Ellinger and Carter published in the *Financial Times* in 1949 was one of the first serious attempts to examine shareholder numbers and to probe the long-held assumptions about share ownership in Britain.[74] This research estimated that, at the time, there were only 1.25 million shareholders, representing just 2.6 per cent of the population.[75] As these numbers suggest, these shareholders were not representative of the British public and that the democratisation of the shareholder body was unrealised.[76] The dramatic shift in the post-war period of both the size of the British shareholder base and its composition demonstrates a systemic change in the financial markets that was often disambiguated from the political rhetoric and from the public understanding of who constituted an equity investor.

In the decades following the end of the Second World War, total shareholding by individuals, direct and indirect, was still far from what could be viewed as widespread equity ownership. In a 1958 study by George Copeman, co-founder of the Wider Share Ownership Council (WSOC), securities were examined as a group, and small shareholders were found to invest mostly in bonds, not equities, whose ownership remained more concentrated and with

[70] Cheffins (2008) 87.
[71] Grout (1987a) 60.
[72] Cheffins (2008) 344.
[73] 'An Association of Investors?' (1949c) 4. See also Rutterford and Sotiropoulos (2017) 520ff for a comparison of the UK with the US.
[74] 'An Association of Investors?' (1949c) 4.
[75] Rutterford and Sotiropoulos (2017) 521. A full breakdown of the research data by company can be found in 'An Association of Investors?' (1949c) 4.
[76] Rutterford and Sotiropoulos (2017) 521; 'An Association of Investors?' (1949c) 4.

increasing fragmentation of large shareholdings.[77] There were fewer British companies with owners who held concentrated stakes, and the pool of investors who were buying British equities was relatively small; Copeman estimated that only 100,000–150,000 individuals owned at least 50 per cent of quoted-company ordinary shares, concluding that fragmentation had not resulted in widespread dispersion of share ownership.[78] The contemporaneous studies of the shareholder body showed that the movements for shareholder democracy, including increased worker share ownership, were falling short of their goal of having many more small direct investors owning stakes in British companies, with little evidence of the 'democratisation of investments'.[79]

In a 1965–66 survey by the London Stock Exchange (LSE), it was estimated that there were 2.5 million share owners, which represented approximately 7 per cent of the UK population.[80] In 1966, *The Economist* described these 2.5 million individual investors as 'half-hearted capitalists', with even fewer (just 4 per cent) holding shares directly in industrial and commercial companies.[81] Although direct equity investing did not hold a dominant place in the pattern of British savings in 1966, many more small investors had savings in other types of investments, including government securities, investment trusts, pension funds (6.3 million members) and life insurance (22.7 million policyholders), all of which provided tax incentives to attract investors and through which individuals were the indirect beneficiaries of equity investments (at the time, life societies held a fifth to a third of their investments in equities and pension funds held even more).[82] As demonstrated by the disappointing results of the efforts for wider share ownership, investing behaviour was nudged by unfavourable tax treatments for direct shareholding and the availability of more tax-efficient institutional-investment options, gradually changing how individuals invested.[83] Whereas the institutions grew their assets under management with the burgeoning demand for indirect investing by a population increasingly able to save, the percentage of the British public with direct ownership of equity shares remained stable – in 1979 that level remained approximately the same as in 1966, with only about 4 per cent of the British adult population owning shares.[84]

Whereas individual direct investing might tell a humdrum tale, an analysis of the shareholder body as a whole depicts a more interesting story. Before the

[77] Copeman (1958) 34, 38. See section IV.C below on the WSOC.

[78] Copeman (1958) 39.

[79] Rutterford and Sotiropoulos (2017) 34.

[80] Naylor (1968) xvii. In comparison, 17% of the US adult population had direct investment in shares ('Shareholders: Why So Few?' (1966) 52).

[81] 'Shareholders: Why So Few?' (1966) 52.

[82] 'Shareholders: Why So Few?' (1966) 52.

[83] Munro (2012) 775; Kellett (1962) 32; P Myners, *Institutional Investment in the United Kingdom: A Review* (6 March 2001) 27.

[84] Fisher (1979) 31.

Second World War, over 80 per cent of UK public company shares were owned by individuals, decreasing to 66 per cent in 1957 (the first post-war year for which reliable detailed statistics are available), 54 per cent in 1963, then falling below 50 per cent to 47.4 per cent in 1969, 42 per cent in 1973 and 28.7 per cent in 1979.[85] Furthermore, individual shareholders owned, on average, much smaller stakes than those of the institutional shareholders, with very few individuals holding positions comparable to those of an institution.[86] Showing a similar trend, Lord Diamond's 1975 Royal Commission on Incomes and Wealth found that between 1963 and 1973, the proportion of equity shareholdings held by individuals (persons, executors and trustees resident in the UK) fell from 58.7 per cent to 42.0 per cent, which represented approximately two million individual shareholders, worth about £17 billion in December 1975.[87] According to the Commission's findings, when the equity shareholdings of the financial institutions were allocated to their respective beneficial shareholders, individuals owned 50 per cent of all ordinary shares.[88]

The direct ownership of shares by individual investors took a further blow with the financial crash of 1973–74, with share prices falling 25 per cent from the year before by the end of 1973 and by more than 50 per cent in 1974, making it the biggest financial collapse ever recorded in Britain (greater than 1929), understandably impacting how individuals felt about investing in the financial markets.[89] Statistics reported in 1976 showed a continuation of the decline in individual direct investing, with small investors as net sellers of ordinary shares and securities. As reported in the *Financial Times*, the Central Statistics Office released accounts for 1976 that showed small shareholders cut holdings in company securities by £1.2 billion, after a cut of £1.38 billion in 1975, which was offset in 1976 by the purchase of gilt-edged and other government securities to the amount of £1.69 billion, and investments in life insurance and pension funds rising by 28 per cent in 1976 to £5.54 billion.[90] Individuals in the post-war period were investing more, just not directly in equities.

[85] Littlewood (1998) 257; Cheffins (2008) 344. See Cheffins (2008) 355, fig VI for the market value of UK industrial shares, gilts and fixed interest investments from 1953 to 1962. For comparison, Moyle (1971) examines ordinary share ownership from 1957 to 1970 in companies quoted on the LSE using a sampling scheme. The results for registers holders on 1 July 1957, 31 December 1963 and 31 December 1969 are 61.8%, 51.0% and 44.7%, respectively (Moyle (1971) 7).

[86] Acton Society Trust (1959) 48 (£17 billion in 1975 is worth approximately £183 billion in 2023; see www.officialdata.org/UK-inflation).

[87] Lord Diamond, *Royal Commission on the Distribution of Income & Wealth. Report No 2: Income from Companies and its Distribution* (Cmnd 6172, 1975) s 64, Table 10; 'Two Diamonds' (1975) 12; 'Who Owns What?' (1976) 22. These individual shareholders are in addition to the indirect investors that make up the 13.5 million members of occupational pension schemes and 14 million savers through life insurance.

[88] 'Who Owns What?' (1976), 22; by this calculation, charities own 5.2%, and insurance companies and pension funds 35.6%.

[89] Gleeson (1981) 116.

[90] Riddell (1977) 11.

ii. The Identity of the Individual Shareholder

Within the context of wanting to apply the principles of democracy to company ownership, shareholders were increasingly the subject of closer investigation by those observing and reporting on the financial markets as well as by those engaged with the growing disciplines of management science.[91] Companies were also becoming more interested in understanding the make-up of their shareholder registries and in obtaining detailed demographic breakdowns of their investors, particularly when that information helped directors anticipate how shareholders might vote.[92] Prior to the 1950s, there was a general lack of research into the behaviour of small investors, as was lamented in the 1962 Hobart Paper *Ordinary Shares for Ordinary Savers*: 'We do not know much about them [ordinary shareholders] as individuals, and no-one in authority … has bothered to do any research.'[93]

Three years earlier, in 1959, the Acton Society Trust published a survey on the small investor, which profiled the demographic details of the average investor.[94] In keeping with the social science trends and increasing interest in the ordinary shareholder, the researchers created a composite of the target investor, seeking to better understand who this individual was and how he or she behaved. According to the survey:

> The typical small investor is a man who left school at sixteen, is now married, with one child who will soon be independent. His income is about £17 a week and if you want to hang a class label on him he is lower middle. Before buying shares he had a bank account … and a life insurance policy … If he does not own his house, he will within ten years … he took the plunge into the market without asking anyone's advice … His first investment after the war amounted to £75: he now has about £1,000 worth and he is thinking about staking £100 next year and perhaps the same sum the following year.[95]

The growing awareness of how little was known about the average small investor, and that previous assumptions might be inaccurate, drove more company boards to examine who owned the equity in their companies – for example, '[i]t is because of the widespread ignorance of what makes up a small shareholder, that Chesham Amalgamations has commissioned a study called *The Attitudes of Private Shareholders to Mergers and Acquisitions*'.[96] This survey confirmed some of the traditional views of small shareholders, such as that more than a third of the shareholders had never bought a share themselves and only half

[91] See, eg, Acton Society Trust (1959); Jervis (1966); Naylor (1968); Moyle (1971); Shenfield (1971).

[92] Readhead (1971) 19; Trafford (1974) 17.

[93] Kellett (1962) 9.

[94] Acton Society Trust (1959).

[95] Acton Society Trust (1959) 51. See also 'Profile of the Small Investor' (1959) 8; and 'Who is the Small Investor?' (1959) 6 (£17 in 1959 is worth approximately £506 in 2023 and £1,000 is worth approximately £29,769 in 2023; see www.officialdata.org/UK-inflation).

[96] Readhead (1971) 19. As reported by the *Financial Times*, this survey was conducted over eight weeks, during which 3,892 shareholders were contacted.

had ever sold one, and that they are essentially passive, although not as much as was assumed, particularly when it came to takeovers.[97] The survey showed that half of these shareholders owned shares in an average of three companies, 55 per cent owned shares worth £1,000 or less, 27 per cent owned shares valued between £1,000 and £10,000, and 25 per cent had received a bid for their shares, but only 3 per cent had acquired any as a result of a merger.[98] *The Economist*, reporting on a separate contemporaneous study, *The Pattern of Ordinary Share Ownership, 1957–1970*, which was published in 1971, noted that the typical private investor averaged six separate shareholdings, each worth approximately £1,320, which was not within the means of the ordinary working man or even much of the aspiring middle class, and this average investor 'hardly fits the picture of the "small shareholder" depicted by the protagonists of wider share ownership'.[99] The attempts to understand their shareholders also considered the differences between types of investors – for example, Fisons, the drug and fertiliser company, conducted multiple surveys that examined the discrepancies between what institutional investors and small shareholders thought was important, such as earnings-per-share growth, dividend increases, management capabilities and investment risk.[100]

B. Institutional Investors

The movement for shareholder democracy aimed at making the shareholder base more inclusive faced further complications with the accelerating growth of the institutional investors, which became an increasingly large percentage of total shareholders.[101] The impact of the ascendancy of the institutions was not immediately observed in the post-war period, as was described in a Labour Party pamphlet criticising the effectiveness of shareholders in 1957:

> [I]n the typical large firm, large shareholdings are, taken individually, too small and, taken collectively, too numerous for effective control to be exercised. It is also clear

[97] Readhead (1971) 19.

[98] Readhead (1971) 19.

[99] 'Who Owns What?' (1972) 73; Moyle (1971). Included in the data on shareholders are regional trends for individual investors. According to this study, Scottish and Welsh investors are more likely to invest in the largest companies than the English and the Northern Irish; for small investors, Scots have 90 per cent of their investments in the 300 largest companies and the Welsh have 88 per cent. Scots are also particularly patriotic with their investing, with private Scottish investors accounting for 28 per cent of all personal holdings in Scottish-registered companies compared to 8 per cent of personal holdings overall; the Welsh, for their part, are under-represented as equity investors and account for only 1.9 per cent of the value of personal shareholdings, even though they represent 4.9 per cent of the population.

[100] Trafford (1974) 17. In the 1975 survey conducted by the company, which was preceded by surveys in 1969 and 1972, it was discovered that the company's individual shareholders were ageing, with 52 per cent over the age of 65 (and 19 per cent over the age of 75) compared to 41 per cent in 1972 ('Zzzzz' (1976) 138).

[101] Cheffins (2008) 344.

> that so far, at any rate, the decline in large individual holdings has not been offset by a rise in large institutional investments.[102]

The equity capital markets were undergoing a systemic shift that resulted in the dominance of institutional investors by the end of the 1970s, a development that produced a more sophisticated and powerful shareholder base; the post-war history of the stock market demonstrated that the shareholder changed from 'an uninformed poor relation to a controlling power' and although the financial returns between 1964 and 1979 were unremarkable, the equity shareholder gained considerable influence and status.[103]

Alongside the gradual decline in direct individual investing, institutional investors replaced the small shareholder as the dominant holder of equities in the UK, a fundamental change in the ownership of British industry that went virtually unnoticed outside of the City.[104] The growth in institutional investing was the result of policies, like tax and dividend limitations, that penalised investment income and disadvantaged small individual investors, pushing investment capital towards products that were designed to circumvent these penalties.[105] In addition, as statutory restrictions on the types of securities that unit trusts and investment trusts could buy were lifted, their equity holdings increased, not least because in the inflationary post-war environment, equities offered attractive risk-return options, making institutional investors an increasingly important part of the equity shareholder body.[106] Institutions with growing pools of money needed

[102] Labour Party (1957) 20.

[103] Littlewood (1998) 276.

[104] Plender (1982) 14; Davies (2017) 40. A detailed analysis of the different types of institutional investors in the post-war period is beyond the scope of this study. A majority of institutional investors in the UK capital markets in the post-war period fall into one of four groups – insurance companies, pension funds, investment trusts and unit trusts – each of which developed differently and under conditions influenced by incentives such as tax treatment and regulations. Although these are the four major categories, they are not the only institutions that were invested in the equity markets: for example, merchant banks and non-depository financial institutions acted as external fund managers to some smaller institutions. Trusts, government agencies, charities, churches, livery companies, educational institutions, friendly societies and trade unions all invested in the capital markets to varying degrees, although the combined investments of all these other institutions was small. The 1975 Diamond Royal Commission on Incomes & Wealth gives the following breakdown of percentages owned of quoted ordinary shares as of 31 December 1973: banks and other financial institutions (3.3 per cent), non-financial companies (4.3 per cent), charities and non-profit-making bodies (4.4 per cent), and the public sector (2.5 per cent) (Lord Diamond, *Royal Commission on the Distribution of Income & Wealth. Report No 2: Income from Companies and its Distribution* (Cmnd 6172, 1975), s 64, Table 10). It should be noted that the 3.3 per cent for 'other financial institutions' includes investment trusts, grossly inflating this number, which would otherwise be very small, partly because most merchant banks refrained from investing directly in equity shares (Cheffins (2008) 88). The UK banks did not hold large amounts of equities, the result of regulations designed to limit their exposure, and the subsequent path dependency that remained even after obstacles to equity investing were relaxed (Black and Coffee (1994) 2004). Furthermore, private trusts, charities, small pensions and other small institutional investors were relatively inactive investors (Morgan and Thomas (1962) 182).

[105] Cheffins (2008) 341. For a comparative overview of UK institutional investors through to the mid-1990s, see Black and Coffee (1994) 2007ff.

[106] Kellett (1962) 25; Morgan and Thomas (1962) 180. See Stapledon (1996) 20–24 for a summary of ownership of UK equities. For a post-war contemporaneous description of the investment products,

to put capital to work and they were net buyers of equities, through initial and secondary offerings, as well as directly from the individual investors who were selling their holdings in the market.[107] Even when the institutions were still a minority of total equity shareholders, they were the majority of new investment capital coming into the equity markets, with the insurance and pension funds dominating.[108]

These new professional investors were the representatives of a much broader distribution of wealth as the individual saver, the 'ordinary' man or woman, chose to invest indirectly in equities through life insurance policies, pension plans and, increasingly, investment products like unit trusts.[109] Buying shares directly in companies was no longer viewed as the only or even the most attractive way to invest in the stock market, and institutions offering investment products competed for savings.[110] Furthermore, individuals who previously shied away from investing in the markets in favour of savings accounts were seeking better risk-adjusted returns and increasingly placed their savings in investment vehicles.[111] Governmental policies had structural consequences for the market, creating disincentives for small individual investors to own equities directly and increasing the appeal of indirect investing.

i. Dominance of the Pension Funds and Insurance Companies

During the 1950s and early 1960s, pension funds were the fastest growing of the institutional investors, with contributions outpacing economic growth as benefits expanded and companies invested in new pension schemes, often with funds withdrawn from insurance company plans.[112] In post-war Britain, the state left it to the individual and his or her employer to provide for its citizens in old age, leading to the growth in employee schemes.[113] 'The provision of pensions by employers is almost entirely a twentieth century and very largely a post-war development' and the increase in pension schemes based on life assurance policies, which were popular with universities, the self-employed and small businesses, contributed to the growth in insurance total funds, although larger companies usually preferred to administer their own pension funds.[114] In addition, both insurance companies and pension funds, many of which lacked in-house investing expertise, directed capital to investment trusts, accounting

see Acton Society Trust (1959) 92ff. These include unit trusts, which are open-ended trusts, and investment trusts, which are closed-ended and were not trusts, but limited liability companies that trade on the stock exchange.

[107] Cheffins (2008) 345.

[108] Morgan and Thomas (1962) 181.

[109] 'Equity Investment and its Responsibilities' (1964) 75. For a contemporaneous examination of unit trusts, see du Cann (1959). See also Whiting (2004) 102ff.

[110] Cheffins (2008) 344.

[111] Acton Society Trust (1959) 53, shows the sources of funds for buying shares.

[112] Littlewood (1998) 128, 256. These values also represented an increase in the number of unit trusts: 121 in 1965, 240 in 1970, 353 in 1975 and 493 in 1980.

[113] Davies (1991) 132.

[114] Morgan and Thomas (1962) 176.

for most of the trusts' new assets in the post-war period.[115] With the overall growth of indirect investing, the pool of capital increased, distributed amongst the different vehicles.

In 1953–55, insurance and pension funds held 16 per cent of UK stocks and shares and individuals held 62 per cent.[116] In 1957, the estimated percentage of ownership of UK equities by institutions was 18 per cent, rising to 25.6 per cent in 1963, 30.7 per cent in 1969, 38.3 per cent in 1973 and breaking through 50 per cent to 52.3 per cent in 1979.[117] The two largest groups of institutional investors, the insurance companies and the pension funds, saw their assets under management grow from £7 billion in 1957 to over £85 billion in 1981.[118] The relative positions and influence of individual small direct investors, on the one hand, and the professional managers who represented the collective beneficial interests of many individuals, on the other, were not balanced, with the latter far outweighing the former. This imbalance accelerated with the growing institutionalisation of equity investing in UK companies.

The increase in the size of the equity holdings of institutional investors meant that more shares were held directly in fewer hands, but that the beneficial ownership of the shares continued to expand and represent more and more British savers.[119] In 1971, the Department of Economic Affairs in Cambridge found that insurance companies, pension funds, investment trusts and unit trusts collectively owned 32 per cent of quoted securities in the UK, individual investors owned 44.7 per cent, with the remainder owned by other institutions like banks, charities and universities; for larger companies, individual investors owned an even smaller percentage – 41 per cent (valued at over £66 million).[120] In 1972, *The Economist* reported that of the £15 billion a year in equities traded in London, institutions accounted for approximately 40 per cent or about £6 billion, of which about £5 billion was in (what was then considered)

[115] Cheffins (2008) 345; Morgan and Thomas (1962) 178. The composition of the investment trusts' portfolios changed over time, increasing the percentage of ordinary shares; in 1948 ordinary shares made up 62% of trust investments, increasing to 89% in 1957 (Morgan and Thomas (1962) 178).

[116] Morgan and Thomas (1962) 180. The remainder were held by government agencies (3%) and 'other' (19%).

[117] Littlewood (1998) 257.

[118] Plender (1982) 14. By the second half of the 1970s, they absorbed up to four-fifths of all new government stock each year and by 1970, they owned more property than the approximately 90 listed property companies. Even unit trusts, the weakest of the institutional investors, had £400 million under management by 1964, £500 million in 1965, £1.32 billion in 1970, £2.55 billion in 1975 and £4.24 billion in 1980 (Littlewood (1998) 128).

[119] The growing financial institutions that were investing through the various vehicles on behalf of individuals were themselves important providers of income to their own equity shareholders; as explained in 1954 by J Blakey, FCA, President, Institute of Chartered Accountants in England and Wales: 'This is the day of the institutional investor – the banks, the insurance, investment and finance companies, which are themselves owned by a multitude of small holders, and pension fund trustees. Dividend income from industrial shares is the lifeblood on which millions depend for the security of their insurance policies and their pensions' ('Institute of Chartered Accountants' (1954) 2.).

[120] Spiegelberg (1973) 47.

large trades of over £50,000.[121] Lord Diamond's 1975 Royal Commission on Incomes & Wealth analysed the pattern of distribution of equity ownership and found that at 31 December 1973, institutional investors, which included insurance companies, pension funds, investment trust companies and unit trusts, held 38.2 per cent of quoted ordinary shares in UK companies, with 28.4 per cent owned by insurance companies and pension funds, representing 13.5 million beneficial investors who were members of occupational pension schemes and 14 million who were savers through life insurance.[122]

By 1975, with the market rebounding from recession, institutional investors owned almost half of the equity market, with the insurance companies as the dominant players and individual institutions like Prudential having material stakes across the market; for example, Prudential owned more than 1 per cent of three-quarters of the 40 largest British companies, indicating that the shareholder dispersion of the British capital markets was changing, with fewer but larger direct shareholders representing an increasing number of indirect beneficial holders.[123] Meanwhile, UK pension funds almost tripled their share of equities from 1957 to 1970, when they held over £3.4 billion and represented 9 per cent of shareholders.[124] In 1975, the estimated ownership of UK equities by insurance companies and pension funds was 15.9 per cent and 16.8 per cent, respectively, and unit trusts held approximately 4.1 per cent of UK equities, up from 2.9 per cent in 1969 and above the 3.6 per cent level of 1981.[125]

III. THE EVOLUTION OF THE FORMS OF SHAREHOLDING

A. Democratisation and Indirect Investing

The calls for increased participation in the equity markets were occurring at the same time as direct investment by small shareholders was shrinking and indirect investing was increasing, which seen through the lens of democratisation can be viewed as being less inclusive, as shareholder duties were transferred from the many to the few. This resulted in the accumulation of shareholder power in

[121] 'With a Quaint Device, the Banquet Vanishes' (1972) 102.

[122] Lord Diamond, *Royal Commission on the Distribution of Income & Wealth. Report No 2: Income from Companies and its Distribution* (Cmnd 6172, 1975), s 61 Table 8; 'Two Diamonds' (1975) 12; 'Who Owns What?' (1976) 22.

[123] Kynaston (2001) 419. By the 1970s, almost all large companies had widely distributed shareholder bases. The Diamond Commission found that amongst a sample of 30 of the largest British companies, there were only 19 holdings of 5 per cent or greater, and only five of these were owned by individuals or nominees; there were few large companies where one shareholder, or a small group of controlling shareholders, can outvote the rest ('Who Owns What?' (1976) 22).

[124] Moyle (1971) 18.

[125] Littlewood (1998) 442. Unit trusts suffered from the capital controls implemented during the Second World War that were not removed until 1958; when the controls were lifted, new trusts were issued, with assets under management growing from £60 million in 1957 to more than £200 million in 1960 (Gleeson (1981) 73).

the hands of a relatively small number of fund managers, as the percentage of the stock market owned directly by individual shareholders fell from 54 per cent in 1963 to 28 per cent in 1981; this decline in direct share ownership by individuals is offset by the growth of the institutional investors such as insurance companies, pension funds, unit trusts and investment trusts.[126] Despite their efforts, the forces pushing for a 'democratic control of industry by millions of individual shareholders' were facing a losing battle against the unrelenting momentum propelling indirect institutional investing.[127]

Although calls for shareholder democracy were politically popular as an alternative to socialist policies and systemic upheaval, and appealed to those seeking ways to address the inequalities in British society, the desired increase in direct ownership of public company shares by average citizens did not reflect post-war market trends.[128] The rhetoric and political clamouring for shareholder democracy and the broadening of share ownership was unsuccessful – that is, fewer individuals, of any group or class, were directly owning equity stakes in British companies and small shareholders were increasingly dispersed and without influence.[129] The incentives established by the existing system led to the decrease in direct ownership by individuals in favour of the investment vehicles offered by the professionally managed financial institutions, a trend that continues unabated.

B. The Investment Managers

The fund managers at the large institutions that controlled the growing pool of investment capital were a small cohort whose members would have been mostly known to one another and who were becoming part of the City elite as their influence increased.[130] As a result, this select group of investors, which was becoming even smaller as insurance companies, investment trusts and unit trusts merged and consolidated, had a growing influence on public companies through their expanding ownership stakes.[131] The shareholder body, whose members were not necessarily aligned in their incentives or investment goals, was often treated as a monolith, which did not take into account the potential conflicts of interests of institutional and individual shareholders, as well as amongst the different types of institutional investors.[132] As early as the 1950s, there were concerns over

[126] Grout (1987a) 60.

[127] Evershed (1968) 6. See Black (1990) 574 for a comparable US phenomenon: 'the model of public companies as owned by thousands of anonymous shareholders simply isn't true. There are a limited number of shareholders, and they know each other'.

[128] Rutterford and Sotiropoulos (2017) 34.

[129] Davies (2015) 355.

[130] Kynaston (2001) 218.

[131] Spiegelberg (1973) 48.

[132] Black (1990) 595.

'the potential abuse of power arising from the concentration of personal savings into the hands of a small number of institutional investors'.[133]

The individual fund managers had the potential to be very powerful and were responsible for making investment decisions and deciding whether to take activist positions, although how that power was exercised, and the governance surrounding decisions, varied from institution to institution. In his 1973 study of the City, the journalist Richard Spiegelberg observed these differences in institutional behaviour, which ranged 'from virtual autocracy at one end to reasonably democratic processes at the other. The big insurance companies still tend to stick rigidly to the committee system of investment management'.[134] The dangers of the concentration of power in the hands of the institutions were identified earlier by the social policy researcher and professor Richard Titmuss, who warned in a 1960 Fabian Tract, *The Irresponsible Society*, that the institutions had:

> [A] power, a potential power, to affect many important aspects of our economic life and our social value in the 1960s. It is a power concentrated in relatively few hands, working at the apex of a handful of giant bureaucracies, technically supported by a group of professional experts, and accountable, in practice, to virtually no-one.[135]

Within the self-regulating and insular culture of the City, with its seeming untouchability within the British system, '[t]here was also, as a further source of non-accountability, the huge shift of investment power to the big institutions'.[136] As expressed in the *Financial Times* in 1977:

> The private investor is fading away, while the institutions, they suspect, are dominated by financial technicians whose interests are almost entirely short-term. This may be widely unfair, but it is part of a set of attitudes which, unless actively and convincingly countered, threatens the shareholder-based system with extinction.[137]

Contemporary post-war commentators, including *The Economist*, raised concerns about the dominance of the institutional investors, framed explicitly in terms of evaluating the shareholder base as being more (or less) democratic; by increasing the share of equities held by institutions, the control of companies was increasingly in the hands of fewer people, that is, professional investment managers.[138] Spiegelberg quotes the economist Alex Rubner:

> When politicians suggest that corporate democracy has been advanced because tens of millions of people have become indirect investors through these institutional

[133] Titmuss (1960) 17. The Fabian Tract was a revised and expanded version of a lecture given in 1959. See also Chiplin, Coyne and Sirc (1977) 27.

[134] Spiegelberg (1973) 56.

[135] Titmuss (1960) 17; Plender (1982) 19.

[136] Kynaston (2001) 427; Spiegelberg (1973) 245.

[137] Owen (1977) 2.

[138] 'Small Mercies' (1974) 80; Littlewood (1998) 276. In most instances, the small shareholder lacks power against the institutions, especially when the institutions join together to act as a group. There were, however, examples of the small shareholder having the better position, usually delineated in a

> channels, this is little short of claptrap; the institutional managers are autocrats in their fields and subject to little democratic control.[139]

A small group of professional managers were increasingly responsible for investing on behalf of individual beneficiaries, resulting in shareholder power becoming concentrated and under the control of institutions.[140]

This changing ownership distribution resulted in differing incentives amongst shareholders as the managers of investment funds did not share the same downside risk as the underlying investors who owned the equity shares, although they did enjoy the upside of any increase in share prices.[141] Furthermore, fund managers made decisions about an investee company that could reflect other considerations beyond the individual company, such as the fund, the industry or the economy.[142] Institutional investors were encouraged to engage more actively with the governance of investee companies based on the idea that they will act in the interests of all shareholders and other stakeholders, an assumption that ignores the potential conflicts of interests and is based on a simplified notion, and lagging understanding, of the shareholder body.[143] Despite the post-war push for shareholder democracy, shareholder power was being consolidated amongst a small number of institutional equity owners with the power to influence management decisions, leaving fewer individuals, and genuine outsiders, in positions to monitor and influence company boards.

Direct individual share ownership was no longer able to meet the ballooning capital demands of post-war British industry, although the small investor was still needed as a funding source. Increasingly, however, the capital of the small shareholders was found in investment vehicles managed by the institutions:

> It is equally apparent that the modernisation and expansion of British industry can hardly be financed without the assistance of comparatively small investors. The wealthy 'capitalist' is nowadays somewhat of a historical figure, if indeed he ever existed at all in the sense of the bogey man conjured up for us by our Socialist governesses.[144]

Although not the direct shareholder democracy that was envisioned at the beginning of the post-war period, by the end of the post-war consensus more individuals had exposure to the UK equity capital markets, albeit through the (perceived) safety and under the professional guidance of the institutional

company's articles of association. In the examples of Lloyds Bank, for example, small shareholders owned 30 per cent of the equity in 1979, but they also had overwhelming voting control because the articles restricted each shareholder's voting rights to a maximum of 500 shares, irrespective of how many shares were held, which was a legacy tool from the nineteenth century used to block unwanted takeovers. The institutional investors were understandably unhappy and demanded a rule change from management, which the small shareholders were unlikely to fight, but for which they sought compensation ('Sorry, We Slept' (1979) 122; Black and Coffee (1994) 2034).

139 Spiegelberg (1973) 55.

140 Plender (1982) 16; Grout (1987a) 62.

141 Jung and Dobbin (2012) 54.

142 Davies (1991) 136.

143 Hill (2015) 65.

144 Naylor (1968) xiv.

investors who were the caretakers of individual savers and were becoming increasingly powerful members of the City establishment. The growth of the institutions represented a systemic change in the shareholder body that financed British industry, which was achieved without disrupting the dominant place of the financial firms within that system; the City's hold on power confirms its durability in face of tremendous challenges.[145]

C. Active Shareholders and Shareholder Activism

With the exponential growth of the equity stakes held by the institutions, the ability for the individual shareholder to hold a position large enough to influence management, even when the will was there, decreased, and the onus for shareholder activism shifted to the institutions.[146] The institutional investors, in turn, were increasingly the subject of criticism for passivity and for shirking their responsibilities as overseers of the corporate governance of the companies in which they invest.[147] The characterisation of the apathetic shareholder was directed at both individual and institutional shareholders, with *The Economist* describing the ineffective shareholding middle class as the 'booboisie' who, alongside the passive institutional investors, fail to stand up to the 'boardoisie'.[148]

In the immediate post-war environment, equity owners were admonished to wake up, become engaged and support industry in resisting the forces undermining the British capitalist system, as was expressed by Sir Alexander Roger, chairman of British Insulated Callender, in 1947:

> It is up to investors ... to join with directors, and all ranks in expressing an active and vocal and, if necessary, an organised interest in the impact of political and economic developments on the success or otherwise of the business in which they are concerned. Investors should cease to be the sleeping partners in industry: silence is taken as to give consent.[149]

There was growing acknowledgement that the professional investment managers of the institutional funds should take action, whether alone or as a group, to compel underachieving boards to improve their performance, including more effectively balancing the interests of the shareholders with other stakeholders, including the workforce and national interests.[150] On shareholders in the 1960s, Anthony Sampson wrote:

> The shareholders, the theoretical owners of industry, are still a pathetically ineffective army; directors can bamboozle them with phoney accounts, and write each other fat

[145] Cheffins (2008) 350.
[146] Maltby and Wilkinson (1997) 48.
[147] Nolan (2006) 93.
[148] 'Booboisie and Boardoisie' (1966) 53.
[149] Lex (1947) 1.
[150] Spiegelberg (1973) 50.

> service contracts to make sure they are not sacked. But some investors are beginning to stir; major holders like insurance companies and pension funds are intervening in management.[151]

The possibility of the institutions taking an active and productive role guiding management towards more accountability and improved decision-making existed alongside the frustration with shareholder passivity, apathy and reticence.

i. The Reluctant Institutional Activist

As companies became more complex and their management teams more professional, the individual shareholder, already facing structural and behavioural impediments to active involvement, was even less able to influence the companies in which he or she was invested.[152] Even the institutional shareholders, managed by investment professionals, were considered to have limited relevant industry expertise with which to support directors in managing investee companies, making their active involvement in operational decisions unlikely.[153] Activism by institutional investors was often not welcomed by directors and their financial advisors, who questioned the credentials of fund managers to get involved in operational and managerial issues, and accused them of arrogance in thinking that they had anything more than capital to contribute to British industry.[154] Furthermore, financial institutions, already sensitive to the threats of nationalisations and state intervention, feared a political backlash against them if they intervened in the management of companies, drawing attention to their influence.[155] The demands of increased shareholder involvement and stewardship were not enthusiastically embraced by the institutions or by the companies in which they owned equity stakes.

This reluctant activism aligned with the attitude by many institutional investors that resisted the call for increased involvement and preferred the traditional response of selling out of positions when they were dissatisfied with management, an approach based on the premise that they had neither the time nor the knowledge to get involved in the operational details of industrial companies.[156] The individuals responsible for investing the funds under management were not themselves proven industrial managers with a proscribed set of qualifications. In other words, the insurance companies were dominated by actuaries and the pension funds and other investment vehicles were run by finance professionals, yet they were being asked to influence decisions that impacted not only shareholder interests but also the health and wellbeing of companies, their employees

[151] Sampson (1971) 657.
[152] Maltby and Wilkinson (1997) 48.
[153] Barker (1982) 87.
[154] Plender (1982) 74.
[155] Black and Coffee (1994) 2067. See also ch 2, section VIII.A in this volume.
[156] Spiegelberg (1973) 49; Singer and Ron (2018) 423.

and other stakeholders.[157] Proficiency in financial management did not (and does not) necessarily convert to industrial expertise, creating tensions between the institutional investors seeking returns for their beneficiaries and other stakeholders expecting more active involvement by equity owners whose position of primacy was accompanied by rights and responsibilities, and who were seen to have 'a non-delegable duty to engage with the companies in which they invest'.[158]

Post-war institutional investors were not necessarily well-coordinated, strategic market participants and they faced regular criticisms of their actions, or lack of actions. Even with the institutions overtaking individuals in the ownership of quoted ordinary shares, in most cases they were not viewed as helping to improve the accountability of management:

> It certainly seems true that they have not been adequate substitutes for private investors, perhaps because they themselves are primarily managerially controlled enterprises and traditionally have been rather reluctant to interfere with the management of companies in which they own sizeable slices of the share capital.[159]

Sleepy insurance companies and conservative investment vehicles did not naturally seek the responsibilities that came with their growing importance, often resisting calls to engage more actively, although some, like Prudential, did start to take increasingly active positions to engage with management of investee companies considered to be flagging.[160] As reported in *The Times*, at the 1956 EGM of Birmingham Small Arms Co, in response to the reports of the misuse of company funds by the ousted chairman and managing director, the representative of Prudential stated to a hostile room that:

> It is our clear policy in the Prudential not to interfere in the management of industrial companies in which we invest ... In this case where there were no other large individual shareholders whom we might consult we came to the conclusion we had a duty to all the shareholders as well as to ourselves, to take some action.[161]

Thus, a traditional insurance company embraced a more public activist stance towards its shareholder responsibilities.

Before the widespread dispersion of share ownership that occurred in the post-war era, investors who owned the largest equity stakes in companies were regularly actively involved in management decisions, often for companies to which they had strong personal, family or community links, but the decline of these types of shareholders created a governance vacuum.[162] Institutional investors were reluctant to fill this gap, despite pressure from other stakeholders,

[157] Plender (1982) 32.
[158] Hill (2015) 66.
[159] Chiplin, Coyne and Sirc (1977) 27.
[160] Spiegelberg (1973) 49.
[161] Kynaston (2001) 218.
[162] On the decline in family ownership, the impact of institutional investors and the market for corporate control, see Franks, Mayer and Rossi (2004).

including law-makers and policy-makers.[163] Unlike the controlling or major shareholders of the past, the institutional investors did not have the same incentives or resources to be actively involved in every investee company, resulting in the burden of governance sitting uneasily on their shoulders.[164] Although there was, and continues to be, appeasing rhetoric by the institutions that suggests that they are taking more responsibility, the voting patterns of these shareholders change very slowly – much slower than their public relations announcements suggest.[165]

ii. 'Behind Closed Doors' Activism

The option of selling out of positions when management fails or underperforms was increasingly difficult for some investors with sizeable holdings in those companies, leading the institutional shareholders to pursue activist solutions and to put pressure on boards, often from behind the scenes. Institutional investors interacted with directors and management more regularly, subjecting them to detailed assessments of their financial and business performance, which, it was claimed, resulted in a virtuous circle of improved management, better results and elevated share prices.[166] Even when there was no clear evidence of activism, there was often speculation about the pressures being exerted on management privately, particularly when an investor had a position that was too large to liquidate, requiring operational improvements to unlock what was perceived as trapped value.[167] Furthermore, the motivation for discretion was high as public knowledge of institutional intervention or activism impacted share prices. As Spiegelberg reported in 1973: '"We prefer backdoor moral suasion", said one pension fund manager. "It is better than shouting from the rooftops."'[168] Often, it was only when these behind-the-scenes discussions failed that the activism became public, putting pressure on directors, particularly those of underperforming companies.[169]

A delicate balance was needed, however, as institutional shareholders tried to protect, and enhance, their investment positions. The large institutions sought to keep their active involvement confidential in order to avoid driving down a company's share price, and the removal of management would reveal their activism, resulting in a fall in share prices that they were working to prevent.[170]

[163] Cheffins (2008) 373. For a study on the challenges to activism faced by institutional investors, see Ivanova (2017) 181ff.

[164] Admati and Pfleiderer (2009) 2645.

[165] Rissman and Kearney (2019) 10193; Soohun and Yoon (2020) 24; Lund (2020) 11. On activism and cooperation amongst institutional investors, see MacNeil (2010) 431ff.

[166] Littlewood (1998) 276.

[167] Spiegelberg (1973) 51; Davies (1991) 129; Ireland (1999) 51.

[168] Spiegelberg (1973) 52. This approach continued beyond the post-war period; see Black and Coffee (1994) 2002.

[169] MacNeil (2010) 426.

[170] Littlewood (1998) 276; Spiegelberg (1973) 51.

The institutions that were taking active positions to improve the performance of companies were seeking to 'make shareholder democracy work', as described by one interventionist and advisor.[171] These institutions were increasingly pushing companies, and the markets in which they traded, to increase efficiency and competitiveness, arguably benefiting not only themselves and their beneficiaries but also the whole economy.[172] The claims that the institutions did not have the expertise to intervene in investee company decisions became less relevant when performance was improved, as did the assumptions that the lack of public activism meant that nothing was being done to protect shareholder interests.

iii. The Emboldened Institutions

With increased activism in the post-war era, no matter how reluctant, the institutions came under growing scrutiny when dealing with investee companies. In 1978, *The Economist* questioned whether the institutions, once shy of throwing their weight around, were now emboldened, taking no notice of who gets hurt, particularly the small shareholder; critical of institutional behaviour, it concluded that this was not necessarily the case, although not because of any consideration for the individual shareholders, but because it was increasingly clear that there was little consistency as to which battles institutional shareholders chose to fight.[173] Institutional shareholders were selective in deciding when to take action, and those choices could seem more arbitrary than systematic, leaving the individual small shareholders exposed. It took the development of a more methodical approach to activism before the institutions, some of which would eventually have specific mandates for shareholder activism, developed and applied organised and disciplined methods to their interventions.[174]

The traditional institutional shareholders of the post-war period were in some ways similar to the 'reluctant activists', or 'reluctavists', of today – that is, taking positions based on long-term hold strategies but opportunistically, and often tentatively, behaving as activists when the situation required it and where the expected returns justified the investment of resources, when they were available.[175] Unlike the rationally apathetic dispersed individual shareholders, the institutional investors were 'rationally reticent' – that is, responding to proposals on governance issues, but unlikely to take the initiate themselves.[176] Meanwhile, the post-war small shareholders were becoming more marginalised and at the mercy of the decisions of their fellow equity owners, the institutions;

[171] Spiegelberg (1973) 50. With the increase in activism by the traditional institutional investors, there was also a burgeoning of advisory services to help investors engage with boards.

[172] Littlewood (1998) 276.

[173] 'Divided We Stand' (1978) 125.

[174] Cheffins (2008)382.

[175] Davies (1991) 140; Benoit (2016) C.1.

[176] Gilson and Gordon (2013) 867. See also Bowley and Hill (2022) for a current examination of 'rational reticence' in the context of investor behaviour and ESG.

the 'free rider' was not necessarily in agreement with the direction of travel.[177] Despite the ascent of the more sophisticated institutional investors and the relative weakening of the direct individual small shareholder, the expectations of increased governance and oversight did not result in systemic changes to the relationship between directors and equity owners.

As the shareholder body evolved and its interplay with investee companies changed, there was a growing tension between the idea of the shareholder as a passive supporter of the board and that of the shareholder as an active owner of a company in which he or she was invested. On the one hand, there was a chorus of complaints about the lack of shareholder activity, except when it involved dividend distributions or when the company had crossed a red line of distress; on the other hand, there were criticisms of shareholders that were actively involved with investee companies and were seen to be prioritising their own interests. The institutions, whether individually or as a group, seemed:

> [T]o be in a 'no-win' situation. If they fail to act – or cannot publicise actions they have taken – they are criticised for their sluggishness. If they act – and are seen to act – they are open to charges of using power without accountability.[178]

iv. The 1973–74 Crash: An Activism Inflection Point

At the end of 1974, with the markets in steep decline and the City in distress, one of Prudential's investment managers, as described by the historian David Kynaston:

> Apparently on his own initiative, without any push from the Bank of England … decided it was time that the investment institutions stopped sitting on piles of cash and instead put some money into the equity market with a view to encouraging a recovery in prices.[179]

Three other insurance companies, Legal & General, Commercial Union and Sun Alliance, joined Prudential in investing £20 million in the equity markets, although this was not enough to stop the decline.[180] The Bank of England, having to draw on its own reserves, turned to the insurance companies to help prop up a number of major financial institutions on the verge of collapse; although some agreed to help address the crisis, others, like Edinburgh-based Standard Life, did not.[181] The insurance companies were accountable to their

[177] See Armour, Deakin and Konzelmann (2003) 17 on how increased institutional ownership impacts the 'free-rider' problem.

[178] Palmer (1982) 108; Spiegelberg (1973) 49. In 1973, the Bank of England created the Institutional Shareholders' Committee that represented all financial institutions, except commercial banks, but it never realised its potential for activism and was dormant by the end of the 1970s, although it was revived in the 1980s (Black and Coffee (1994) 2019).

[179] Kynaston (2001) 514.

[180] Kynaston (2001) 514 (£20 million in 1974 is worth approximately £267 million in 2023; see www.officialdata.org/UK-inflation).

[181] Kynaston (2001) 515.

policyholders and the pension funds for whom they invested, and whereas some invested a portion of their cash in equities, acting as a backstop to collapsing financial institutions in a crashing market was a step too far for many. There was also speculation about insurance companies working behind the scenes, and at the end of 1974 there were unconfirmed reports that they were supporting the market to avoid a depression era-type collapse.[182]

Although the institutions were instrumental in avoiding a depression during the 1973–74 stock market crash, the change in the make-up of the shareholder body in the post-war period also contributed to the dramatic capital markets reaction to the economic stresses that precluded it; even if the reasons for the crash were justified, the extent of the fall in share prices was disproportionate to the problems driving the correction.[183] A consequence of individuals being deterred from investing directly in equities by a variety of contributing factors, including rising trading costs and unfavourable tax treatments, resulted in capital markets that were increasingly dominated by institutions; meanwhile, these institutions executed larger trades with higher risks to the market-makers, leading them to become less willing to take contrarian positions, thereby potentially amplifying market trends, both positive and negative.[184] The dominance of the institutions was not only making the equity markets less representative, but was also having structural impacts on how shares were traded, how markets moved and how much volatility was introduced.[185] The stock market crash of 1973–74 was a demonstration of the influence of these factors.

IV. THE DEVELOPMENT OF SHAREHOLDER DEMOCRACY

A. The Shareholder and the Post-war Democratisation Movement

The movement for shareholder democracy developed alongside the more general post-war calls for democratisation, which were part of the political, economic and social shifts that were transforming Britain and were addressing the lack of equality and inclusion in the established capitalist order.[186] The post-war recalibration of the state's relationships and engagement with its citizens impacted industry and influenced how the equity shareholder, as well

[182] 'Steady as She Sinks' (1976) 47. A comparison can be made to the behaviour of financial institutions and institutional investors during the 2007–08 global financial crisis.

[183] Gleeson (1981) 117.

[184] Gleeson (1981) 117.

[185] A recent example of the consequences of material changes in the types of equity shareholders on the capital markets and how these impact individual small investors is high-frequency trading (HFT). In December 2020, HFT represented approximately 50 per cent of trading volume in US equity markets and between 24 per cent and 43 per cent in European equity markets (Breckenfelder (2020)). For an overview of HFT, see Sánchez Serrano (2020); and see Golumbia (2013) on HFT and democratisation.

[186] Garrard (2001) 280; Moss et al (2016) 443.

as other stakeholders, were perceived and treated, which continued to evolve within an ever-changing political environment. Following the Second World War, the political muscle of the common citizen strengthened and demands for broader applications of the principles of democracy, participation and inclusion increased on different political, economic and social fronts.[187] When it came to investing their capital, just as in the political sphere where the ordinary voter was no longer prepared to defer to what was traditionally considered the ruling class, the ordinary shareholder was increasingly unwilling to accept unquestioningly the decisions of company directors, regardless of how those choices impacted his or her interests as a shareholder.[188]

The concepts of 'shareholder democracy' and 'corporate democracy' were appearing regularly in the discussions on shareholder engagement and corporate behaviour, with calls on equity owners to shrug off their historical complacency and exercise their rights, as well as on companies to empower their shareholders to increase participation and to vote on meaningful issues.[189] In the post-war era, the relationship between shareholders and directors was increasingly seen through the lens of democracy, creating parallels to that between legislators and voters, as well as positive references for democratic participation and action, an approach that continues to be revisited, including following the global financial crisis of 2007–08.[190] Within the context of needing to reach their audience effectively, like the efforts to fight against nationalisations and the Labour Party's socialist policies, the language of democracy was a powerful tool that could be used by chairmen and other leaders of industry and commerce to communicate with investors, with the markets more broadly, and with policy-makers and law-makers.[191]

Shareholders were not only equity-owning stakeholders in companies but were also participants in the broader political and social events that were shaping post-war Britain. The political engagement with and treatment of shareholders, and how they, in turn, reacted to political pressures and decisions, influenced how law-makers and policy-makers addressed shareholder interests when drafting policy, proposing legislation and reforming (or not reforming) company law.[192] Against this backdrop, shareholder democracy was promoted as a means by which to address the shortfalls of corporate governance, countered by critics who turned to industrial and stakeholder democracy as the legitimate avenues for reform.[193] What is notable, however, is that none of these proposed avenues for change resulted in material transformations in core law, despite the efforts, and accompanying clamour and bluster, made by those seeking to disrupt the gravitational pull of an entrenched system.

[187] Moss et al (2016) 443, 448.
[188] Moss et al (2016) 443; Clarke (1977) 353.
[189] Singer and Ron (2018) 441.
[190] Singer and Ron (2018) 422.
[191] 'Meeting the Shareholders' (1964) 646.
[192] Black and Coffee (1994) 2005; Singer and Ron (2018) 425.
[193] Singer and Ron (2018) 425.

i. The Cohen Committee

The post-war movement for shareholder democracy developed in an environment of increased consideration to the individual, be it the rights and interests of voters or shareholders. The Committee on Company Law Amendment (known as the Cohen Committee), which was tasked in 1943 by the wartime coalition government with making recommendations on amendments to the 1929 Companies Act, reported in June 1945, addressing the need for more explicit protections for investors, shareholders and the public.[194] The Committee:

> [S]ought to find means of making it easier for shareholders to exercise a more effective general control over the management of their companies. The result, we believe, to strengthen the already high credit and reputation of British companies. We must emphasise, however, that this objective will be attained more by the selection by the shareholders of the right governing body of each company than by the provisions of any statute.[195]

The Cohen Report preceded the reforms of the 1947 and 1948 Companies Acts, which introduced some shareholder-friendly changes – for example, voting by proxy, the ability for shareholders to force an EGM with 10 per cent of the voting equity, and making it easier to remove directors.[196] The Committee's recommendations provide a window into the thinking of law-makers at the end of the Second World War, which recognised the need for shareholder protections while acknowledging their limited power and that 'the divorce between financial interest and power of management is a fact'.[197]

Whereas the Cohen Committee recommended reforms to the Companies Act, these were not enough to address the systemic weaknesses faced by the increasingly dispersed shareholder body, as explained by the legal scholar Sir Otto Kahn-Freund in his 1946 review of the Committee's report: 'Control over the management cannot be exercised by shareholders through the mechanism of a "shareholders' democracy", and analogies taken from constitutional law of a Parliamentary Democracy are singularly inept.'[198] Despite Kahn-Freund's rejection of the use of political democracy as a model for the ownership of companies, it was a useful rhetorical tool for those promoting the expansion of shareholding based on the illusion of control, not unlike that which existed for individual voters. The *Financial Times*, in the 'Secretaries' Column', addressed with scepticism the Cohen Committee's claim that, in accordance with legislative intent, the shareholders can exercise control over the board, countering that: 'In practice, directors too often control the company and tend

[194] Mr Justice Cohen, *Report of the Committee on Company Law Amendment* (Cmnd 6659, 1945); Clift, Gamble and Harris (2000) 61; Kynaston (1999) 505. See also Kahn-Freund (1946).

[195] Mr Justice Cohen, *Report of the Committee on Company Law Amendment* (Cmnd 6659, 1945), para 5.

[196] Franks, Mayer and Rossi (2009) 4017.

[197] Kahn-Freund (1946) 245.

[198] Kahn-Freund (1946) 246.

to become dictators.'[199] The Cohen Committee Report also emphasised the reticence of law-makers to use statutes to strengthen shareholder rights, especially the post-war Labour politicians who resisted accepting capitalist principles and adhered to the socialist notion that company directors are the adversaries of labour, thereby leaving the responsibility for governing in the hands of each company through their articles of association and the selection of directors.[200] Whereas some statutory reforms increasing investor protections were made in the 1948 Companies Act, the Labour government did not prioritise legislative changes to company law, and an opportunity for greater advancements in addressing shareholder rights and interests was missed.[201]

B. Calls to Increase Individual Savings

In the post-war era, alongside the democratisation movements, efforts were made to encourage British citizens to save more and to increase the number of individual investors in public companies, expanding the equity shareholder base and promoting shareholder democracy.[202] As the country recovered from the Second World War and the peacetime economy stabilised, the British population, traditionally amongst the 'world's least enthusiastic savers', was increasingly in a position to save and/or invest, even if individually on a very small scale, through life insurance policies, pension funds and other types of savings vehicles.[203] In post-war Britain, personal savings as a proportion of net personal incomes increased from 0.9 per cent in 1950 to 4.9 per cent in 1955, 6.0 per cent in 1959, and 8.3 per cent in 1960.[204] In 1956, the *Financial Times* reported that Sir John Braithwaite, chairman of the LSE, addressing the Institute of Bankers, pushed for at least five million individual stockholders:

> It seems to me very desirable, from every point of view, that there should be a great increase in the number of individual men and women who own stocks and shares; and this is becoming possible because of the very considerable redistribution of wealth that has taken place in recent years. If only some of the hundreds of millions of pounds that are poured down the drain each year in betting on horses, dogs and football could be attracted into investment in British Industry what a fine start could be made.[205]

The Labour Party, normally at odds with the interests of the City and preferring policies of state intervention, gave support to working-class share ownership as a substitute for gambling, which would benefit both the investor

[199] Head (1945) 3.
[200] Clift, Gamble and Harris (2000) 53.
[201] Franks, Mayer and Rossi (2009) 4017; Clift, Gamble and Harris (2000) 65.
[202] Jackson (2005) 430.
[203] Plender (1982) 35; Gleeson (1981) 76, 96.
[204] Kellett (1962) 15.
[205] 'S.E. Chairman's Call for 5m Shareholders' (1956) 9.

and the nation.[206] The post-war attitudes that encouraged investment by average men and women nurtured the expansion of equity share ownership, albeit mostly indirect, that became an integral part of the British economy and of modern financial markets.

The increase in share ownership was viewed as a means by which to include workers in the capitalist system and its benefits. As advocated by the Rt Hon Sir Toby Low, a Conservative Party politician, in his work *Everyman a Capitalist*:

> The wider spreading of an interest in the shares of industry will, I think, bring to an end the idea that industry's ownership is an oligarchy, will lead to a better and wider understanding of the working of the free enterprise system, and will more closely and more practically mark the identity of interest between capital and labour ... it would be a natural and logical development of the free democratic capitalist society as it has grown up here.[207]

Share ownership was seen by some, especially on the political right, as the favoured means by which to increase the involvement of workers and the working classes in industry beyond just as providers of labour. As the Rt Hon Sir Toby Low urged, 'every man should have the opportunity of being a capitalist in the stricter or narrower sense of the word: that he should be able to own shares in industry and should not be discouraged from so doing'.[208]

The movement to increase share ownership amongst workers and the working class was promoted by advocates with diverse political agendas, with the political left looking to address the perceived inequities of the British capitalist system and the political right, motivated by different goals, seeking for ways to fortify and preserve that system.[209] With the post-war push for citizens to boost long-term savings, the British working class was targeted by policymakers for increased involvement in the financial markets and, more specifically, the equity markets.[210] Since the 1950s, the Conservative Party saw share ownership, and worker participation in industrial ownership, as a part of a broader programme to expand the property-owning democracy, demonstrating how the Party increasingly saw the ownership of capital assets as a fundamental aspect of a transformational effort to address and reshape popular perceptions of, and attitudes towards, capitalism.[211]

British industrial leaders recognised that shareholder democracy was a way to expand the sources of capital available to British companies seeking to finance growth and to meet the demands of the changing post-war economy, while also addressing the social and political calls for more inclusion. In 1960,

[206] Whiting (2004) 101.
[207] Lord Hailsham of St Marylebone (1958) 26.
[208] Lord Hailsham of St Marylebone (1958) 25.
[209] Clarke (1977) 351.
[210] See, for example, the work of the WSOC, which claimed to have supporters from across political parties (see Naylor (1968)). See also Davies (1994) 258 on post-war long-term savings and the growth of institutional investing in equities.
[211] Edwards (2016) 108; Francis (2012) 280.

Reginald Maudling, President of the Board of Trade, explained: 'It must be an unhealthy situation if too high a proportion of equity investment in this country comes from too few sources. The greater the spread of share ownership that can be achieved, the better the state of industry and the health of the community as a whole.'[212] Conservative politicians led efforts to promote savings and share ownership, and whereas the Labour Party was seeking to dismantle private ownership, the Conservatives were acting to protect and extend property-owning democracy.[213] In addition to its stated broader social goals of increased inclusion and wealth accumulation, the democratisation of the shareholder base was also part of the efforts to make British industry's need for capital more acceptable to those opposing a capitalist system that they viewed as an inequitable, unfair and unrepresentative.

C. Property-Owning Democracy

The ownership of equity shares, which made up a meaningful portion of private wealth in the UK in the decades following the Second World War, was at the centre of the ideological debate on the relationship between capital and labour, and although the British public invested in different types of assets, '[a]ttention [was] focused on one type only, industrial ordinary shares, and the profits and dividends associated with them'.[214] Against this backdrop, the WSOC was founded in 1958 by a collection of politicians and men from the City to 'spread the enlightenment about the process of Savings and Investment' based on the belief that wider share ownership would create 'a nation of well-informed capitalists, enfranchised in the economic life of the country' and that 'the widening of direct share ownership was not an end, but a means to an 'enlightened' capitalist society'.[215] This 'enlightened capitalist society' would provide the financing that industry needed to grow and would strengthen the status quo by encouraging more of the British public to be invested in its success. Democratisation and wider share ownership were promoted by both the political right and the political left as a means of addressing inequality, although they differed in their approaches.[216] Equity shares were a symbol of wealth inequality for those seeking to reform, or even reject, the existing system, making the

[212] 'Britain Needs Wider Share Ownership' (1960) 12.
[213] Labour Party (1956) 28; Labour Party (1957) 41; Francis (2012) 280; Grout (1987a) 59.
[214] Copeman (1958) 32.
[215] Edwards (2016) 103, 105, 108; Whiting (2004) 97ff. The politicians involved were mostly Conservatives, with some Liberals, although the Council struggled to retain Labour representatives (Edwards (2016) 105). Emphasising the importance of being viewed as non-partisan, the WSOC prefaced its findings with the statement that 'leading members of all three political parties are to be found amongst the supporters of the Wider Share Ownership movement' (Naylor (1968) xiv).
[216] Whiting (2004) 99.

movement to expand shareholding contentious as '[s]ome labour supporters are bound to oppose wider shareholding on the grounds that it implies acceptance of the private enterprise system; others are likely to be sceptical of the advantages claimed for it'.[217] In 1961, *The Spectator*, when reporting on the efforts of the WSOC to gain the same opportunities for the small investor as the wealthy to invest his or her savings in the stock market, identified this convergence of goals, observing that: 'This group [WSOC] is as dissatisfied as the Socialists with the present unequal distribution of wealth and is trying hard to work out a philosophy which will appeal to all the workers by hand and brain.'[218]

The Conservative Party, committed to broadening participation in the capitalist system, promised in its 1964 general election manifesto that:

> To secure a still higher volume of savings, a Conservative Government will introduce new incentives. In particular we aim to devise a contractual savings scheme, giving attractive benefits to those who undertake to save regularly over a period of years. We shall also encourage the successful efforts which are being taken to widen the field of share ownership.[219]

Share ownership was identified as a foundational aspect of property-owning democracy and, as the Conservative MP Maurice Macmillan stated in his 1967 introduction to the WSOC's *Sharing the Profits*, 'as the housing shortage diminishes, the desirability of owning other forms of property will become the more obvious … The ownership of equity shares in industry is perhaps the most important of such other forms'.[220]

Despite its initial optimism in promoting shareholder democracy and the importance of share ownership, the WSOC struggled to progress its cause and was unable to get the tax incentives and legislative advances needed in the 1960s and early 1970s to boost direct ownership by individuals on a meaningful scale.[221] When Margaret Thatcher became leader of the Conservative Party in 1975, the principles of popular capitalism and property-owning democracy were bolstered, which brought optimism to the WSOC, as did the Conservatives' plans to privatise nationalised industries; ultimately, however, Thatcherism prioritised the interests of the financial institutions and favoured the City above individual investors.[222] The growing dominance of institutional investors was thereby assured, scuttling the hopes for widespread direct shareholder democracy and increasingly pushing the small individual shareholder into the role

[217] Acton Society Trust (1959) 6.
[218] Davenport (1961a) 341.
[219] Conservative Party (1964); Dale (2000a) 153. The savings ratio rose from 8.9 per cent to 15.4 per cent between 1970 and 1975, although most of this new capital was not being invested directly in equity shares, particularly not after the crash of 1973–74, but in indirect investment vehicles, in fixed income and in gold (Gleeson (1981) 119).
[220] Naylor (1968) xv.
[221] Edwards (2016) 109.
[222] Edwards (2016) 109.

of indirect investor, profoundly impacting the development of the shareholder body.[223]

D. The City and Shareholder Democracy

Within a post-war environment of reconstruction and societal transformation, representation and public perception were integral to the tension between the powers of reformation and those of preservation, and the institutions of the establishment (and especially the City) were sensitive to their vulnerabilities in the face of political pressure from those representing a large section of the population that were mostly ignorant of the ways of the financial markets, even if they were also increasingly invested in it (albeit mostly indirectly).[224] The City, steeped in its traditions and instinct for aloofness, and under increasing scrutiny, was reluctant to adapt to the changing post-war political mood and to espouse the movements for more democratic and inclusive capitalism, and showed little interest in embracing shareholder democracy and wider direct individual share ownership, which was not viewed at the time as being economically attractive.[225]

In the changing mood of the post-war era, the City, and the LSE more specifically, attempted to address the growing criticisms of the existing system by making small gestures in support of the popular capitalism embracing wider share ownership, although no meaningful steps were taken to realise this goal.[226] Appearing to address popular demands for change was an important part of protecting the City's privileged position and required a communications strategy that created a veneer of progress without disrupting the foundations underneath. Furthermore, the City's resistance to shareholder democracy is not surprising considering that the individual investor was often characterised as unknowledgeable, ineffective and unengaged or, alternatively, as a parasitic interloping speculator threatening the establishment with greed and ruthlessness.[227] In the post-war decades, the City establishment focused its efforts on protecting its entrenched position and power from the perceived threat of those advocating for democratisation, and it would take the Big Bang reforms of the Thatcher era to impose changes in attitudes and behaviours on these reluctant incumbents.

[223] Cheffins (2008) 344.

[224] Kellett (1962) 20.

[225] Edwards (2016) 108.

[226] Kynaston (2001) 161. The City's attitude to the post-war demands for increased shareholder democracy was similar to more recent calls for stakeholder capitalism that, despite the rhetoric, have resulted in minimal statutory changes to the core pillars of UK corporate governance – ie, the Companies Act, the Takeover Code and the corporate governance codes (Armour, Deakin and Konzelmann (2003) 550).

[227] See Kynaston (2001) 63 for an example of the City's attitude towards 'outsiders' (ie, speculators and financiers) taking stakes in public companies.

4

Corporate Purpose and the Shareholder

IN THE POST-WAR era, political, economic and social forces created an environment of recalibration, and questions on how the company was understood, how its directors behaved and to whom it was accountable were no exception. Following the disruptions of war, the victory of the Labour Party in 1945, and the subsequent post-war nationalisation and reconstruction policies, there were opportunities for change as the accepted norms of industry and financial markets were challenged by an evolving shareholder body. During this transformational period, the understanding of the purpose of the company, as well as the interests of shareholders and other stakeholders, developed, reflecting the political and social tensions of the period and the changing demands of the markets.[1]

I. SHAREHOLDER PRIMACY AND SHAREHOLDER DEMOCRACY

The principle of shareholder primacy that is fundamental to UK company law is based on the assumptions that the company is managed for the ultimate benefit of the shareholders, that the shareholders are paramount amongst stakeholders, and that the shareholders are the only stakeholder to which, by law or by social norm, directors had to account.[2] The legal understanding of directors' powers were developed in the nineteenth century, with the Joint Stock Companies Act of 1844 delegating these powers to the shareholder contract, which then empowered directors, who then formed the board of directors (this is in contrast to the US, where directors' power comes from the state).[3] The question of in whose interest companies are managed, to which the traditional response of common law has been the shareholder body, has been central to interpreting the legal duties of directors.[4] The understanding of directors' duties, and whether (or not) shareholder primacy should be the accepted meaning of acting in the interests of the company, is core to understanding the obligations to shareholders and the treatment of their interests.

[1] Konzelmann, Chic and Fovargue-Davies (2020) 15.
[2] Hansmann and Kraakman (2001) 441; Sneirson (2020) 76; Millon (2013) 1013. See also Moore (2018) 145ff on the legal basis of shareholder primacy in UK company law.
[3] Kershaw (2018b) 288.
[4] Cabrelli (2008) 9.

Adolf A Berle asserted in 1931 that:

> [A]ll powers granted to a corporation or to the management of a corporation, or to any group within the corporation, whether derived from statute of charter or both, are necessarily and at all times exercisable only for the ratable benefit of all the shareholders as their interest appears.[5]

The ongoing debates on the role and obligations of the company that were central to the interpretations of UK company law were also occurring in the US, influencing how these concepts were considered in both countries.[6] Whereas the shareholder primacy debate had characteristics that were specific for each jurisdiction, the US and UK positions informed and influenced each other, and took into consideration the arguments made by scholars and commentators on both sides of the Atlantic.

The shareholder primacy principle maintains that the shareholder, unlike other stakeholders, does not have conflicting priorities and therefore can focus fully on the company's financial results and profitability without the distractions and interference that the other stakeholders' interests might create for management.[7] Furthermore, it was argued that if directors focus on one goal (that is, profitability), they would be more efficient, and that requiring them to consider the interests of other stakeholders on a par with those of shareholders would hamper corporate results.[8] This singular focus on profits as an argument supporting shareholder primacy, although straightforward, was also used by those opposing the principle as proof of harmful shareholder greed, of short-termism and of equity owners enriching themselves at the expense of other stakeholders and of the company itself.[9]

The post-war questioning of the assumptions underlying shareholder primacy occurred at a time when vocal elements in society, emboldened by Labour governments and the empowerment of left-wing political movements, were challenging the existing social order, including how financial markets and industry functioned, and the nature of the relationships amongst its various actors.[10] The principles of democracy, whereby 'every person ought to have some degree of influence over every decision made by a group of which he or she is a member and which will have an effect on his or her life', were being applied to companies and the interests of its diverse stakeholders, pushing back against the assumptions upholding the existing system.[11] Although shareholder primacy was often presented as uncomplicated and fundamental, and has become a

[5] Berle (1931) 1049. See also Berle and Means (1967). On Berle, see Stewart (2011).

[6] Konzelmann, Chic and Fovargue-Davies (2020) 11. See also Williams (2018) 664ff. For a detailed comparison of UK and US corporate fiduciary law, see Kershaw (2018b).

[7] Knight (1982) 8.

[8] Keay (2007) 583; Keay (2010) 382ff; Moore (2013) 77.

[9] Hansmann and Kraakman (2001) 444.

[10] Fox (1985) 362.

[11] Caste (1994) 168.

foundational element of UK company law, 'there is no universal basis for arguing that shareholder value is the objective which is best suited to the governance of the modern company'.[12]

II. ENLIGHTENED SHAREHOLDER VALUE

Despite the legal basis for shareholder primacy and its position in UK company law, there was an intensifying push to require directors to consider the rights of other stakeholders, such as employees and customers, in addition to those of the shareholders.[13] From the outset, the theory of shareholder primacy faced opposition, with Marrick Dodd arguing in 1932, the same year that Berle and Gardiner Means publish their foundational work *The Modern Corporation and Private Property*, that he:

> [B]elieves that it is undesirable, even with the laudable purpose of giving stockholders much-needed protection against self-seeking managers, to give increased emphasis at the present time to the view that business corporations exist for the sole purpose of making profits for their stockholders. He [Dodd] believes that public opinion, which ultimately makes law, has made and is today making substantial strides in the direction of the view of the business corporation as an economic institution which has a social service as well as a profit-making function.[14]

Already in the 1930s, deliberations on corporate accountability and purpose challenged the legal and social bases for shareholder primacy.[15] As the shareholder base evolved and became increasingly institutionalised in the post-war era, investor behaviour changed, and the understanding of what was in the shareholders' best interests along with it, with broader implications for how company boards interacted with their equity owners, as well as with other stakeholders. The small individual shareholder was becoming less central to how directors thought about equity ownership, with boards focusing more on the increasingly influential financial institutions when seeking shareholder approval.[16] The growing dominance of the institutions helped to strengthen the arguments in favour of shareholder primacy, countering the claim that shareholders had lost their power in relation to investee companies and facilitating the transition to the governance approaches of the 1980s.[17]

Under pressure from stakeholder advocates, company boards sought to demonstrate that profit maximisation served broader interests than just those of shareholders and to emphasise the links amongst all its stakeholders as they

[12] Gamble and Kelly (2001) 110.
[13] Smith (1998) 280.
[14] Dodd (1932) 1147; Berle and Means (1967); Black and Coffee (1994) 2034.
[15] Konzelmann, Chic and Fovargue-Davies (2020) 11ff; Armour (2020) 333.
[16] Moyle (1971) 7.
[17] Davies (1991) 137.

determined what was in the best interests of the company.[18] As explained by GL Wates, the Chairman of Johnson & Phillips, in 1956:

> No industry could exist without the shareholder and his capital. The shareholder is not a villain ... [the shareholder] is an essential partner in the enterprise, as is the second partner, the worker ... and the third partner, the customer.[19]

This sentiment reflects the idea that company directors had a duty to act in the best interests of the company, which could be interpreted as supporting the principles of enlightened shareholder value (ESV) – that is, taking into consideration the interests of different stakeholders to create value for shareholders in the long run.[20] Accordingly, directors needed to balance satisfying their responsibilities to shareholders, and appealing to future shareholders, with acknowledging the interests of other stakeholders; quite simply, a company cannot be successful without pleasing its customers, satisfying its suppliers, servicing its creditors and contributing to its community.[21] The law required that directors act in the interests of the company, which was reflected in the acceptance of the principle of shareholder primacy, but the reality for those running and managing companies was more complicated, with managers and directors needing to combine their legal obligations with good business decisions, as well as responding to what was expected from them by society.[22]

As attitudes towards corporate responsibilities evolved, company boards faced growing pressure from different constituents, including employees, executives and the government, to act in ways that were not always in the clear interests of the ordinary shareholders.[23] Moreover, many directors accepted stakeholder demands as legitimate, particularly as different stakeholder groups increasingly began to overlap; the shareholder might have other identities – for example, as an employee, a customer, a supplier or a local resident – but it was only as the owner of equity that he or she had a legal right to a vote on the management decisions of the company.[24] Expectations of what constituted good corporate behaviour were not static, leading to the recognition that, despite the legal

[18] Keay (2007) 581.

[19] 'Johnson & Phillips, Limited (Cable Makers, Electrical & General Engineers & Contractors)' (1956) 4.

[20] Armour, Deakin and Konzelmann (2003) 7; Keay (2007) 578.

[21] Bebchuk and Tallarita (2020a) 15. Although the focus is often on the more sympathetic constituents (eg, workers, the environment or the community), non-shareholder stakeholders also include creditors and lenders, who are often perceived by the public with the same suspicion and distrust as financiers and investors, despite their critical roles in the economy. Company directors, however, were acutely aware of the importance of creditors as stakeholders, as was expressed in 1970 by the chairman of Lines Bros, the toy manufacturer facing serious financial challenges, who explicitly stated that he felt he was responsible not only to shareholders but also to the banks that supported the company, the loan stockholders, the staff all over the world and the customers (Lines (1970) 96). (Note: In 1971, not long after these remarks were made, Lines Bros collapsed.)

[22] Smith (1998) 280.

[23] 'Shareholders and Directors' (1959) 612.

[24] Keay (2007) 578.

duties to shareholders, there were obligations that went beyond simply what was required by law, as well as a willingness by directors to defend this approach. In 1960, for example, the chairman of Rugby Portland Cement spoke on the responsibilities of the public company, referring to the '[d]uty to our shareholders to whom we have a definite obligation; a duty to all our employees, for profits are the bulwark behind all our wages and salaries and our continuity of employment; and a duty to the nation'.[25]

At the time that this proclamation was made, and without any changes in core company law, shareholders were seen as being just one party (albeit the paramount one) amongst a consortium of different interests, and that the leaders of industry and commerce were aware of this shift in perception and the need to be responsive to it.[26] Similar sentiments continued to be communicated by company boards and although there were still no changes in the law by the 1970s, the adherence to the principle of shareholder primacy was not without dissent, as exemplified when the directors of British Leyland stated in 1975 – the year that the distressed company was nationalised – that the company had a 'much wider responsibility than merely serving the interests of the shareholders'.[27]

The concepts underpinning the movements for stakeholder capitalism and stakeholderism are identifiable in these post-war discussions, as are the roots of the debates on the effectiveness of shareholder primacy as a corporate model and whether legal reform was needed to elevate stakeholder interests.[28] Within this context, there were, and continue to be, demands that the interests of other stakeholders (and not just shareholders) be considered by company directors when making decisions.[29] Labour's post-war policies challenged the existing system based on shareholder primacy, advocating for increased state control and demonstrating a willingness to forfeit shareholder interests, as expressed in the Party's 1956 policy paper on social justice, *Towards Equality*:

> The managers and owners of private industry should be trustees responsible to the nation: in more than one sense, all business is the nation's business. But the mechanisms of control which are supposed to operate in the private sector are clearly inadequate. Control by shareholders over company affairs is virtually non-existent and, even if such control was possible, it would certainly not be in the public interest to revive it.[30]

Labour's suggested solution to the questions of industry's responsibility to stakeholders and to the shortcomings of the existing system that prioritised shareholders, as presented the following year in *Industry and Society*, was to review the Companies Act with the intention of introducing more accountability

[25] Reddish (1960) 470.
[26] 'Reforming Company Law' (1960); Cheffins (2008) 341; Freeman and Liedtka (1997) 287.
[27] 'Shareholders on the Rack' (1975) 38.
[28] On the current debate, see, for example, Bebchuk and Tallarita (2020a); Mayer (2020). For an analysis of the historical debate, see Avi-Yonah (2005).
[29] Cheffins (2008) 341. See Freeman (1994) on stakeholder theory.
[30] Labour Party (1956) 16.

that would require boards to manage in a way that 'coincides with the interests of the community'.[31]

At the time that this was proposed, there was no statutory requirement for directors to consider stakeholders other than shareholders when making management decisions in the best interests of the company, even under the pretence that a more inclusive approach to stakeholder considerations was for the good of the shareholders – that is, ESV.[32] The narrative of the post-war period illuminates the tensions between those who supported statutory reforms to elevate stakeholder interests, even when they conflict with shareholder interests, and those who advocated for the preservation of shareholder primacy and relied on legal and regulatory solutions other than company law to protect stakeholders (employment law, contract law, insolvency law, environmental regulations, etc).[33]

III. CONFLICTING INTERESTS AND THE CALL FOR REFORM

Within the framework of the debate on shareholder primacy, the fundamental questions were asked, and continue to be asked, as to whether there should be a formalisation of a company's expanded responsibilities beyond those to shareholders, and whether changes in British company law and/or policy were required.[34] In her research on company boards published in 1971, Barbara Shenfield considered these issues, with her findings showing that there were explicit acknowledgements by company directors that they needed to manage their companies in socially responsible ways, particularly when it served the company in the long term.[35] Shenfield, in discussing the responsibilities of directors when there are conflicts of interest amongst stakeholders, observed that:

> In cases where boards believe long-term conflicts do exist, and where they wish to resolve them in favour of interest other than the shareholders, the question arises as to whether there needs to be some reformulation of company law to remove doubts as to the legality of their actions.[36]

The calls for legal reforms were directed at the need to bridge the gap between what was happening in practice and the Companies Act, as well as to provide a statutory framework for directors to address the interests of their various

[31] Labour Party (1957) 49. For additional recommendations that continue to be recycled (eg, requiring a 'code of conduct' for companies), see Labour Party (1957) 53; Kelf-Cohen (1958) 273.

[32] Armour, Deakin and Konzelmann (2003) 537.

[33] Armour, Deakin and Konzelmann (2003) 541. For a short overview of stakeholderism, see Bebchuk and Tallarita (2020a) 10). See also Williams (2018) 667ff, on stakeholder theory; and Moore (2013) 63ff on the private nature of Anglo-American corporate law.

[34] Ireland (1996) 300.

[35] Shenfield (1971) 162; Blanden (1971) 19.

[36] Shenfield (1971) 162. The question of whether existing company law can accommodate stakeholder interests alongside those of shareholder remains at the centre of the discussions on corporate purpose and stakeholder capitalism, which are revisited and rediscovered by new generations of market participants (Kershaw and Schuster (2019)).

stakeholders and not just shareholders.[37] Shenfield's analysis of company boards considers these governance questions, amongst others:

> The internal government of companies, the ways in which the interests of other groups such as employees, customers and creditors as well as those of shareholders are balanced, and the relation of companies with the communities in which they operate, are all said to be in need of review and clarification, and the debate centres upon the ways in which companies can be made to recognize and serve certain social responsibilities without impairing their efficiency.[38]

Alongside the constancy and unchanging nature of core company law exists the consistency and familiarity of the narrative considering the need for reform.

Creating laws to regulate the treatment of diverse stakeholders was not a straightforward task as there was no consensus on which of the various interests should be included, how they should be prioritised, how they should be managed and against which benchmarks they needed to be judged; trying to create a law or code to address these issues was challenging.[39] Although there were calls to find an alternative to shareholder primacy, particularly when shareholders were characterised as greedy, apathetic, and both unsuitable and unable to direct management in making decisions for the efficient and productive running of British companies, these were not being met easily.[40] Throughout the post-war period, and against the backdrop of societal changes that profoundly impacted the development of British industry, issues of stakeholder interests and shareholder primacy were discussed in business, legal and political circles, yet neither the Companies Act 1948 nor the Companies Act 1967 reflected suggested reforms.[41] Despite the widely acknowledged need for company law reform that would address the changing nature of UK companies, including the disconnect between ownership and the control, relevant statutory changes were not introduced and no alternative to shareholders was found to fill the (often nominal) role of monitoring boards and enforcing accountability, with UK company law preserving the rights and interests of equity owners.[42] As a result, the gap between the law and practice continued to widen, in full view of the financial markets and all its stakeholders, and although the shareholders' primacy was preserved, the challenges faced by chairmen and directors were evident as

[37] Although shareholder primacy was safeguarded by company law, stakeholders could use other legal means to assert their claims – labour law, contract law, employment law, insolvency law, tax, environmental regulations, etc (Armour, Deakin and Konzelmann (2003) 541).

[38] Shenfield (1971) 14.

[39] Shenfield (1971) 149.

[40] Sampson (1971) 657. See ch 3, section I in this volume.

[41] Durham (1982) 568. Section 172(1) of the Companies Act 2006 makes considering employees a duty of company directors, although these interests remain subordinate and related to shareholder interests (Licht (2019) 9; Moore (2018) 145). For a discussion of the law that preceded s 172 (ie, s 46 of the Companies Act 1980, followed by s 309 of the Companies Act 1985), see Moore (2018) 151ff. See also ch 8, sections III and IV of this volume.

[42] Shenfield (1971) 11.

'any company that ignored the claims of employees, creditors, or consumers, will soon find itself in deep political water'.[43]

IV. THE UK COURTS

The UK courts, hesitant to interfere in the internal management of companies, took a non-interventionist approach to interpreting shareholder primacy – that is, that directors do not have to manage exclusively for short-term results and to maximise profits, allowing boards to apply commercial judgement to their decisions. UK case law suggests that whereas directors adhere to the principle of shareholder primacy when managing companies, they have wide discretion in what factors contribute to their assessment of what constitutes the best interests of the company.[44] Directors were accepted as the authorised voice of the shareholder body, which typically followed the recommendations of the board, and it was only when a majority of shareholders agree that there has been wrongdoing that they can exercise their power and vote to remove directors, with shareholder litigation being a much less likely outcome.[45] Although the UK system provided some flexibility and protection for directors exercising their judgement, this should not be confused with an acceptance of stakeholder interests to be on a par with those of shareholders or that directors can make business decisions that are harmful to shareholder interests in the short or long term.[46] Ultimately, shareholder primacy was preserved and the interests of other stakeholders were considered through that lens, with stakeholders other than shareholders having little or no influence on the decision-making process of directors.[47]

In the 1962 case *Parke v Daily News Ltd*,[48] the shareholders in the *Daily News* took the company and the directors to court for making a decision that they deemed to be beyond the company's powers – that is, to pay employees compensation for lost pension rights that resulted from a merger between newspapers.[49] A director of the *Daily News* in charge of labour relations told staff that the company had no legal obligation to pay compensation, but proposed it nonetheless; the court ruled that this decision by directors, no matter how well meaning in its intention, was not conducive to the interests of the company and found in

[43] 'Look Who the Owners are' (1977) 82.

[44] Keay (2007) 581; Keay (2010) 388; Moore (2018) 147, 152. See also Moore (2013) 144ff on the internal management doctrine; Mukwiri (2013) on questioning the shareholder primacy assumption in English law; and Davies (2015) 366 on common law and the pro-shareholder position.

[45] Moore (2013) 147; Davies (2015) 366; Cheffins and Black (2006) 1399ff. For a detailed discussion of derivative actions, including the statutory reforms introduced with the Companies Act 2006, see Kershaw (2012) 601ff. For a comparison of UK and US derivative actions, see Scarlett (2011).

[46] Kershaw and Schuster (2019) 11.

[47] Keay (2007) 605.

[48] *Parke v Daily News* [1962] Ch 927.

[49] 'Daily News Shareholder Wins £1.12m Action' (1962) 19; Moore (2018) 154.

favour of the shareholder who opposed it.[50] This example demonstrates how, despite directors' willingness to take a more stakeholder-friendly approach in their management decisions, shareholders could take action to protect the interests of the company, that is, to act to benefit the shareholders as a general body, successfully contesting this example of directors' prioritising other stakeholder interests.[51]

That this decision was based on an interpretation of what was in the best interests of the company, which was not clearly defined, emphasises the ambiguities in how the duties of directors were understood and how directors could be held legally accountable to shareholders.[52] As described by Barry Barker, Secretary and Chief Executive of the Institute of Chartered Secretaries and Administrators in a series of papers delivered in 1978/79:

> Traditionally they [the directors] had felt that they held the company in trust for the shareholders; but now they find themselves assailed by demands for accountability to employees, to creditors, to government policies over wage rates and prices, to the conservationists and environmentalists generally … Yet our systems of law and practice are still such that these boards of directors, though many sections of society yap at their gates, are self-perpetuating oligarchies accountable to no one, provided that they don't put their hands in the till.[53]

Relying on the courts to protect shareholder primacy was challenging in the post-war period; without more clarity on what constitutes the interests of the company, it was difficult to assess the behaviour of directors, contributing to the perception of a lack of accountability by company boards and to limited shareholder litigation.[54]

V. PRESSURES ON THE PRINCIPLE OF SHAREHOLDER PRIMACY

The strain on the principle of shareholder primacy was felt when boards used company profits for the benefit of stakeholders other than shareholders, without shareholder consent or guidance for such actions in the company's constitutional documents, raising questions as to whether companies that invested in worker recreational facilities, gave donations to charities or kept prices lower than those supported by the market, to give some examples, were going against

[50] 'Daily News Shareholder Wins £1.12m Action' (1962) 19.

[51] Moore (2018) 154; Keay (2006) 340; Attenborough (2009) 343. Section 74 of the Companies Act 1980 introduced changes to reverse the decision of *Parke v Daily News* [1962] Ch 927, allowing the company to make payments to employees in connection with the cessation or transfer of its business even when it is not to the benefit of the company (Arden and Eccles (1980) 4, 123). See also ch 8, section III.B of this volume.

[52] Keay (2006) 341; Moore (2018) 156; Bavoso (2014) 216.

[53] Barker (1982) 87.

[54] Keay (2010) 385; Moore (2018) 156. The limited amount of shareholder litigation in the UK was another contributing factor to director behaviour (Tomasic and Akinbami (2011) 237).

company law by not maximising the distribution of net profits to shareholders.[55] Shareholder primacy was not just being questioned by other stakeholders, however, but by shareholders who saw their interests as being broader than just short-term profits, as was expressed by TJ Palmer, the General Manager of Legal & General, at a seminar held at the London Graduate School of Business Studies in 1973:

> Shareholders are not a separate community from the general population and are the same people who are showing increasing concern for human rights and the environment. It seems to me therefore that directors who act upon the assumption that shareholders are prepared to support new forms of social responsibility by companies are not failing in their statutory obligation to promote the interests of shareholders.[56]

Those calling for the increased protection of stakeholder interests, which included workers and consumers, and for companies to be accountable to the community and to the nation were pushing against the prioritisation of shareholders over all the other stakeholder groups that contributed to a company's activities.[57]

In the post-war era, there was a growing movement advocating for companies to have greater and more general obligations that were not necessarily at the expense of shareholder interests, but which used a wider lens through which these interests were seen.[58] Confronting economic challenges and industrial unrest, British industry faced public scrutiny and calls for increased oversight as it struggled against the challenges of nationalisations, restructurings, and other industrial and corporate actions that threatened the established corporate order:

> Since their success or otherwise in output and exports is seen to be directly related to the balance of payments and other national economic problems, this gives support to the idea that companies must be subjected to such control as will make their profit-seeking congruent with the Government's overall economic strategy, and thus responsive to the needs of the community as a whole.[59]

That companies needed to consider the interests of stakeholders other than equity shareholders was a widely mooted concept in the post-war decades, although there remained a chasm between declarations for purpose and actions that would result in company law reforms, a discrepancy that persists with the movements for stakeholderism and enlightened shareholderism.[60]

The assumption that shareholders were focused exclusively on profits was countered by certain investors as they sought to communicate a more

[55] 'Shorter Note' (1965) 1029.

[56] Palmer (1982) 106.

[57] See Keay (2007) 586; and Kiarie (2006) 332 on the communitarian view of the company and of directors' duties to stakeholders.

[58] Keay (2010) 376.

[59] Shenfield (1971) 13.

[60] See Bebchuk and Tallarita (2020a).

enlightened position; TJ Palmer, of Legal & General, made the following observations in 1973:

> Quite apart from the views of society at large there is no evidence today that either the stock market or our shareholders expect us to be 'profit maximisers' to the exclusion of all else. In the first place there has been a radical change in the climate of thinking on these matters over the post-war period and particularly in the last few years and the belief that companies have a duty to act as responsible members of society is not confined to social theorists or crusading newspapers.[61]

This statement by a senior manager at a leading institution is indicative of how these issues were being considered by the financial community – that is, the acceptance that the company did not exist exclusively for its equity owners, but also had responsibilities to other stakeholders whose interests were distinct from (although not necessarily in conflict with) those of its shareholders, as well as the importance of communicating this position.[62]

In this climate of shifting expectations of the social responsibilities and accountability of companies, the CBI, as the organisation representing the interests of UK businesses, established a committee under Lord Watkinson, which reported its findings in 1973.[63] As reported in the *Financial Times*, the CBI committee concluded that 'directors have responsibilities not only to their shareholders but to employees and society at large', and called for a code of corporate behaviour, findings that were accepted as reflecting the views of the majority of the British public on corporate responsibility.[64] Taking a similar stance a few years later in *The Responsibilities of the British Public Company*, the CBI declared that:

> Companies must in our view recognise that they have functions, duties and moral obligations that go beyond the immediate pursuit of profit and the requirement of the law … The company must pay proper regards to a variety of interest other than those of shareholders, both inside and outside the company itself.[65]

The CBI also urged the government to consider establishing a non-binding advisory Code of Corporate Conduct 'to guide boards of directors in making decisions with a social or ethical content; to provide them with a body of doctrine and to help raise the general standard of corporate behaviour'.[66] The movements for stakeholderism and corporate social responsibility were not transitory trends, but consistent and constant components of the ongoing discussion on corporate governance.

[61] Palmer (1982) 104.

[62] See Keay (2007) 605 on the UK's enlightened 'third way' that combines shareholder and stakeholder interests.

[63] Confederation of British Industry (1973a); Confederation of British Industry (1973b); Cheffins (2015) 400; 'Shareholder Pressure' (1973) 18.

[64] 'Shareholder Pressure' (1973) 18; Confederation of British Industry (1973a) 4.

[65] Confederation of British Industry (1973b) 4; Davies and Lord Wedderburn of Charlton (1977) 201.

[66] Confederation of British Industry (1973b) 3. See ch 8, section VIII.C of this volume on later developments on a code of corporate governance.

There was increasing public pressure for legal reforms that would provide directors with a statutory framework that reflected these evolving views, rather than a system that relied on shareholders to direct boards, as well as one that required public accountability from companies.[67] The CBI demonstrated an awareness of the dangers of appearing unresponsive and was encouraged to lead its members to compromise; whereas business organisations recognised the need to adopt a narrative of change, albeit one that serves to protect the status quo, it was by no means certain that their affiliates and members would follow their lead.[68] The CBI's willingness to consider stakeholder interests can be understood as an enlightened approach to corporate responsibilities or, alternatively, as an attempt to project an image of progress that camouflaged a commitment to preserving the existing shareholder primacy system.[69] The cyclicality of these narratives, during which very little changes in the underlying core laws, suggests the latter explanation may be more credible than the former, as is likely the case in subsequent iterations of stakeholderism.

A. Distillers Thalidomide

Equity shareholders remained focused on returns and distributions, but there was an awareness of wider concerns, as well as of the impact on the share prices and profitability of public companies that did not acknowledge the interests of other stakeholders.[70] In extreme examples of greed or negligence, particularly when they received public attention, these concerns were magnified; the Distillers Thalidomide episode, in which Distillers, the drinks and pharmaceuticals company that was the distributor of the drug that resulted in severe birth defects when taken by pregnant women and that reached a settlement with victims in 1968, but, under unrelenting pressure, agreed to further compensation agreements in the 1970s, was identified by the *Financial Times* as one of the first cases 'where institutional investors seemed – whatever their real motives – to put pressure on a major company to recognise social obligations which go beyond those demanded by company law'.[71] In 1973, *The Economist*, commenting on the responsibilities of the company and its shareholders in addressing the ongoing Thalidomide situation and the possible responses, observed that:

> Its directors have conducted themselves in a way that indicates that they consider their primary duty is to their shareholder … There is no apparent moral responsibility on the shoulders of the Distillers' directors. The moral responsibility on the

[67] 'Shareholder Pressure' (1973) 18.
[68] Fox (2017) 211 (originally published in 1977).
[69] Davies and Lord Wedderburn of Charlton (1977) 201.
[70] Armour, Deakin and Konzelmann (2003) 546.
[71] 'Shareholder Pressure' (1973) 18; Vernon, Middleton and Harper (1973) 4.

company is the one that its shareholders are prepared to accept on the company's behalf.[72]

This description of the situation shows both an adherence to the principle of shareholder primacy and a clear demonstration of how profit maximisation might not always be the priority of shareholders (although acknowledging that reputational damage impacts share prices).

Acting in a socially responsible way was in the company's long-term interest as the public relations fallout, fed by relentless media coverage demanding a more comprehensive response, had profound impacts on the company's returns, leading its leadership to 'not let the company's interests suffer from falling into public disrepute' and to make decisions that would allow for public, and investor, forgiveness.[73] This example raises the question of whether changes in company law would have led to a different outcome; in her research, Shenfield concludes that where there is a need to balance the interests of various constituents, of which equity shareholders are one, it is not clear that legal restructuring or policy interventions were effective, other than to provide clarity as to the discretion that boards can take to act in socially responsible ways that do not appear immediately profitable for the shareholders.[74] In the Distillers' example, and in keeping with company law, it was the shareholders and not the directors who took the initiative to act in the interest of the other stakeholders – that is, its customers.

VI. CORPORATE COMMUNICATION

In an environment that was putting increasing pressure on the existing system of shareholder primacy and calling for the elevation of stakeholder interests, companies were looking for ways to communicate change that would be publicly recognised and rewarded, without sacrificing the interests of their equity owners.[75] Increasingly, company boards sought to communicate to investors and the market, as well as to other stakeholders – for example, trade unions, law-makers, policy-makers and the general public – a corporate image of social responsibility and willing engagement with the community, using the rhetoric of inclusion.[76] Company boards were making public pronouncements supporting stakeholder interests without any changes to their legal obligations, but as a reaction to shifts in public and political perceptions and expectations. As with nationalisations, boards were reaching out to their shareholders, although not necessarily as a reaction to a looming crisis like state expropriations.[77]

[72] 'The Thalidomide Issue' (1973) 9.
[73] 'The Thalidomide Issue' (1973) 9; Sunday Times of London Insight Team (1979).
[74] Shenfield (1971) 162.
[75] Bebchuk and Tallarita (2020a) 18.
[76] Fairfax (2006) 697.
[77] See ch 2 of this volume on nationalisations.

Corporate statements referencing the protection of stakeholder interests became increasingly common in the annual statements by company chairmen, often without acknowledging any legal constraints.[78] As expressed by John BH Jackson, Director of Philips Industries Ltd, at the end of the 1970s:

> The real situation emerges when one examines the way in which directors say they carry out their duty of acting in the best interests of their company. Many of them talk about 'balancing interests which normally coincide but occasionally conflict'. Few of them if any, talk, as the Courts would wish them to, about admitting the interests of others only insofar as they coincide with the interests of shareholders. Most of them insist on the importance of the future in the context of both shareholders' and employees' interests.[79]

Laporte, the British chemicals firm, was an example of a company taking a proactive approach in seeking to communicate its commitment to other stakeholders as well as shareholders, taking out advertisements that proclaimed that it is 'a free-enterprise British public company working on behalf of its customers, employees, shareholders and country'.[80] Increasingly, directors explicitly and publicly communicated that they understood that a company cannot, and should not, ignore its customers, suppliers, workers, community and other stakeholders to focus solely on its shareholders, and that they were addressing stakeholder interests when making their strategic and operational decisions.[81] Company boards were projecting that they were sensitive to all stakeholder groups, including shareholders, and sought ways to demonstrate how they included all their interests in their decision-making.[82] Directors were responding to the shifts in the political atmosphere and were widening their approach to address stakeholder interests, acknowledging that they had a responsibility to consider a range of constituents to ensure the success of their business and that the laws upholding shareholder primacy did not preclude them from acting accordingly or, at least, adjusting their public statements to communicate that they were taking a more inclusive approach.[83]

The change in how companies were communicating also extended to shareholder engagement. In the late 1970s, Shell, the oil and gas company, started holding less formal public meetings at which shareholders and other constituents could meet with management, creating an opportunity for the company to boost its engagement with investors; these informal gatherings were part of a wider initiative to communicate more with shareholders, the general public, employees and other groups, including financial analysts.[84] This type of

[78] 'Conscience Calls' (1975) 70.
[79] Jackson (1982) 18.
[80] 'Laporte' (1974) 48.
[81] Davies and Lord Wedderburn of Charlton (1977) 201; see also Armour, Deakin and Konzelmann (2003) 537 on 'enlightened shareholder value'.
[82] Cheffins (2008) 341.
[83] Elliott (1984) 102.
[84] Leslie (1977) 21. Financial analysts are included in this list of constituents, reflecting their growing importance.

increased engagement was a way to improve investor and stakeholder relations, with the hope that these efforts would have a positive impact on a company's share price, contributing to shareholder value. It was not only individual companies promoting the image of a more inclusive approach to how they were being managed; the CBI sought to help its members adapt to changing attitudes, calling on boards to interact more with their shareholders in general, and with the institutional investors in particular, as well as advocating for non-executive directors to play important interfacing and facilitating roles between boards and their shareholders.[85]

Corporate communications increasingly reflected the mood of the nation, although whether this genuinely represented changes in the attitudes of directors, or whether it was no more than calculated attempts to deflect criticism with well-drafted proclamations of corporate purpose, is less clear. The inclusion of stakeholder interests in company communications reflects evolving societal expectations, regardless of legal stasis, and that directors chose to express concern for stakeholder interest in their public communications suggests possible dissatisfaction with the existing shareholder primacy norm.[86] By adopting approaches that included the more visible aspects of inclusion, British industry was using corporate communications to direct the narrative, adapting to meet the mood of the times and taking steps to protect itself.[87]

VII. THE 1970S AND THE FRIEDMAN DOCTRINE

In 1970, in the last decade of the post-war-consensus era, there was an ongoing, high-profile debate amongst academics and members of the business community on the responsibilities of the company, to which the economist Milton Friedman contributed his infamous 1970 *New York Times* article 'A Friedman Doctrine – The Social Responsibility of Business is to Increase its Profits'.[88] The orthodox adherence to shareholder primacy is often attributed to the wholesale embracing of what has become known as the 'Friedman Doctrine', even though the primacy of shareholders was already well established in mainstream thinking and legal discourse about corporate behaviour and responsibilities.[89] Friedman's promotion of shareholder primacy became the guiding force for many corporate leaders and their advisors, as well as being endorsed by the law and economics movement, with the shareholder-wealth-maximisation approach

[85] Colchester (1978) 34. The development of the role of the non-executive director is an important aspect of corporate governance, but is beyond the scope of this work. See Moore (2013).

[86] Fairfax (2006) 699.

[87] Fairfax (2006) 705.

[88] Williams (2018) 665.

[89] Friedman (1970) SM17; Cheffins (2020) 5. For a history, beginning in the 1970s, of the use of the term 'shareholder primacy' and a contrast between 'radical shareholder primacy' and 'traditional shareholder primacy', see Millon (2013). See also Gindis (2020) on the influential Jensen and Meckling publication on the definition of the firm (Jensen and Meckling (1976)) and Davis (2021) on shareholder primacy and the democratisation of corporate purpose.

influencing directors in the US and the UK.[90] This interpretation of directors' responsibilities was based on the debates of the preceding decades, the nuances of which often fell by the wayside as advocates of what became understood as the Friedman Doctrine used shareholder primacy to justify prioritising profits above any other corporate consideration.[91] Shareholder primacy came to dominate corporate thinking, bleeding into short-termism and an orthodox definition of shareholder interests that has become closely identified with the subsequent Thatcher and Reagan era.[92]

Milton Friedman's arguments are often construed to be anti-stakeholder, a misreading that gained popularity amongst both the supporters and the critics of unfettered laissez-faire capitalism, even though Friedman's position did not oppose board decisions that were positive for stakeholder interests and also created shareholder value.[93] In his *New York Times* article, Friedman addressed the contemporaneous debate on the 'doctrine of social responsibilities' for business asserting that:

> In a free-enterprise, private-property system, a corporate executive is an employee of the owners of the business. He has direct responsibility to his employers. That responsibility is to conduct the business in accordance with their desires, which generally will be to make as much money as possible while conforming to the basic rules of society, both those embodied in law and those embodied in ethical custom.[94]

Notably, Friedman placed the goal of profit maximisation within society's legal and ethical boundaries. His explanation of shareholder primacy remains at the centre of the debate on corporate purpose and social responsibility that has been ongoing for decades, despite its occasional repackaging with a veneer of originality for new audiences.[95]

In his earlier work, *Capitalism and Freedom*, Friedman argued that the board is the agent of the shareholders and it is not the role of the company director or corporate manager to deploy resources to social or other causes beyond the creation of long-term shareholder value; company directors and managers are not qualified to allocate these resources effectively outside the core competencies of the business.[96] Nonetheless, even the most traditional interpretations of

[90] Keay (2010) 373; Bruner (2013) 61.
[91] Deakin (2005) 13.
[92] Konzelmann, Chic and Fovargue-Davies (2020) 17.
[93] Bebchuk and Tallarita (2020a) 16; Friedman (1970) SM17.
[94] Friedman (1970) SM17. The article references *Capitalism and Freedom*, where Friedman wrote: 'The view has been gaining widespread acceptance that corporate officials and labor leaders have a "social responsibility" that goes beyond serving the interests of their stockholders or their members. This view shows a fundamental misconception of the character and nature of a free economy. In such an economy, there is one and only one social responsibility of business – to use its resources and engage in activities designed to increase its profits so long as it stays within the rules of the game, which it to say, engages in open and free competition, without deception or fraud.' Friedman (1962) 133.
[95] Williams (2018) 664ff.
[96] Friedman (1962) 133–34.

shareholder primacy allow managers to consider other stakeholders: a company without workers or suppliers cannot produce goods, without customers it cannot sell its products to generate revenue, and without engaging with regulators and governments it cannot function.[97] Companies need stakeholders beyond just shareholders, regardless of legal primacy, and although often distilled to a simplistic binary relationship of shareholders against other stakeholders, this is not how companies operate; the focus on creating profits for shareholder does not extinguish the requirement to consider the interests of other stakeholders, without which there would be no profit to distribute to equity shareholders. Outside of the theoretical realm, profit maximisation cannot drive all management decisions, as argued by Paul Davies in 1978:

> Neither shareholder control (whether by institutional or private shareholders), the forces of market competition, the market in corporate control via takeovers, nor the threat of liquidation seem for various reasons to be sufficient to impose upon corporate managements the discipline of profit maximization. There is consequently vested in such managements, in fact if not in law, an element of discretion – the degree of which varies from case to case – in the setting of corporate goals.[98]

The accepted interpretation of directors' responsibilities, according to both legal and societal expectations, was under scrutiny and corporate leaders struggled with harmonising the demands of different stakeholders, including shareholders.[99]

When Friedman was writing in 1970, shareholder primacy was not understood as a doctrine that espoused focusing exclusively on shareholder interests at the expense of every other constituent, but rather that by serving the interests of the equity shareholders, stakeholders are better off.[100] It was in the 1980s, the 'greed is good' decade of the corporate raider, Margaret Thatcher and Ronald Reagan, that the identification of shareholder primacy with singularly focused short-term profits, as it was often presented and understood, flourished.[101] The concept of 'shareholder value' was often confused with the imperative to maximise company profit, leading to a distortion of how shareholder primacy was (and is) understood and presented.[102] Corporate leadership increasingly focused on delivering short-term results to their burgeoning institutional shareholders based on the premise that this was the legal mandate of shareholder primacy, whereas it was market forces and social norms that were the primary drivers of shareholder expectations and managerial decisions.[103]

[97] Chen and Hanson (2004); Wells (2002); Roe (2001); Jensen (2001).
[98] Davies (1978) 264.
[99] Cheffins (2020) 5; Roe (2021) 7.
[100] Chen and Hanson (2004) 43.
[101] Cheffins (2020) 5; Sneirson (2020) 83; Langevoort (2020) 379. See Stone, O (Director) *Wall Street* (American Entertainment Partners; Amercent Films, 1987).
[102] Keay (2012) 26.
[103] Millon (2013) 1040. Short-termism was also driven by reporting requirements and the market's focus on share-based performance metrics and equity-linked compensation. On short-term managerial focus, see Bhagat and Hubbard (2020) 7.

Milton Friedman, although very much an economist of the US, was also interested in economic developments of the UK and from the late 1960s his influence on the UK policy debate, and in particular on inflation control and monetary policy, was profound.[104] Friedman gave lectures at UK institutions and was interviewed by the UK media; his positions were widely cited (and refuted) in the UK, and his views on shareholder primacy would have been noted by participants in the debate on both sides of the Atlantic. With the election of Thatcher in 1979, Friedman became an even more influential figure in the economic discourse about the future of the UK.[105] The subsequent influence of the Friedman Doctrine on managerial decision-making in the US, the UK and elsewhere reflected the changing business and economic environments, including the loss of the nuances of Friedman's original arguments in the rush to justify the focus on short-term profits.[106]

The shareholder primacy norm at the core of UK company law has resisted reform and its statutory status was strengthened by section 172 of the Companies Act 2006, although this was presented as merely codifying an existing legal position.[107] Despite the historical success at withstanding legal reform, and based on the precedents of prior cycles, it is not certain that the British public will continue to accept the principle of shareholder primacy or whether the peripheral regulatory and legal adaptations that have been implemented will be enough to repulse demands for fundamental systemic legal changes.[108] By the end of the post-war era, and with the economy entering a new phase with Thatcherism, the momentum behind the calls for company law reform slowed; whereas the debate on shareholder primacy persisted, it took a global financial crisis decades later to refocus attention on the arguments that had driven the demands for legal change that culminated in the unsuccessful attempts at company law reform in the 1970s.[109]

VIII. MISSED OPPORTUNITIES: THE 1973 COMPANIES BILL

The 1973 Companies Bill, introduced by Edward Heath's Conservative government, sought to increase the protection of shareholders (and creditors) from insider trading and nominee share warehousing.[110] The Bill also aimed to make the duties and powers of directors more explicit and introduced the idea that directors, still guided by the principle of shareholder primacy, could take the interests of other stakeholders – that is, employees – into account, with

[104] Nelson (2009) 466.
[105] Nelson (2009) 495.
[106] Owen (2021) 11.
[107] Companies Act 2006, s 172; Moore (2018) 150. See ch 8, section IX.A of this volume on s 172.
[108] Moore (2018) 165.
[109] Gamble and Kelly (2001) 112.
[110] 'Recent Developments' (1974) 542.

The Economist proclaiming that the Bill 'makes it old-fashioned, almost illegal, to say: "my only duties are to my shareholders"'.[111] The Bill, in permitting the consideration of employee interests, reflected existing business practices, but it did not seek to introduce a statutory requirement and was viewed as weak and ineffective. The Bill was seen as an obvious and hollow public relations exercise that provided no real protections for employees – for example, in the case of an unwanted takeover – and undermined any attempt to address shareholder primacy and to elevate stakeholder (that is, employee) interests.[112] That this Bill that proclaimed to advance employee interests was introduced by the Conservatives reflected the prominence of the movements for industrial democracy and an indication of the widespread acceptance by British industry for directors to consider a stakeholder other than shareholders.[113] Although presented with the expectation of being introduced into law, the 1973 Companies Bill lapsed with the change of government in 1974, scuttling the proposed legal reforms.[114]

The acknowledgement of the need to consider the interests of stakeholders, and employees in particular, was not extinguished with the failure of the 1973 Companies Bill and the ousting of the Conservatives from government.[115] In June 1974 the Labour Party, which returned to government in February 1974 with a minority, published a Green Paper on the reform of company law that sought to increase the government's oversight of the City, including supporting the interests of non-shareholder stakeholders, on the basis that shareholders, in whose name companies were nominally run, had failed to exercise their control.[116] The Labour victory, followed by their majority win in the October 1974 election, occurred alongside the 1973–74 market crash, which in June 1974 saw the FT Index and All Share Index down more than 50 per cent from their peaks, inflation at a post-war high of 16.5 per cent, and financial hardships for many British companies and their investors.[117] The Green Paper, delivered in the midst of the financial crisis, rejected the existing approach of

[111] 'Shades of the Prison House' (1973) 87; Companies Bill 1973–74, c 53; *Company Law Reform* (Cmnd 5391, 1973) para 59. The Bill also recommended more disclosure requirements, which its critics claimed 'enlarges the gap between this fiction and fact by giving the non-existent rational shareholder even more power that he will fail to use than he has now' ('Shades of the Prison House' (1973) 87). Unlike today's listed company reports that are heavily regulated and conform to specific standards, directors in the post-war era not only had a lot more freedom in what information they shared with, or withheld from, the public, including their own shareholders, but were accustomed to limiting disclosure and typically resisted adding to the information that they were required to produce; Cheffins (2015) 401.

[112] Mackenzie (1982) 688.

[113] UK Parliament (1973) 20. See chs 5 and 6 of this volume on industrial democracy.

[114] It was also on 1 January 1973 that the UK joined the European Economic Community, which had consequences for the trajectory of the development of UK company law and corporate governance. See ch 6, section IV.C of this volume.

[115] Kynaston (2001) 478.

[116] 'Very Interesting' (1974) 96; Kynaston (2001) 478.

[117] Littlewood (1998) 208.

self-regulation and called for a commission, like the American Securities and Exchange Commission (SEC), staffed by 'City men', to oversee the securities markets and other areas of the financial markets, which would adopt a more interventionist and legislative approach than that taken by the existing collection of voluntary bodies (eg, the Takeover Panel, the Department of Trade and the Bank of England).[118]

The calls for a formalised watchdog to protect the interests of shareholders and to oversee mergers and acquisitions were resisted by the City, which continued to rely on self-regulatory instruments and processes.[119] Alongside this opposition, there were also a few voices within the City that were critical of the effectiveness of British self-regulations – for example, the stockbroker Victor Sandelson criticised the Takeover Panel for failing to stay in control of events and called for the creation of something like the SEC to regulate the financial markets, which could no longer depend on the discipline imposed by an English gentleman's needs to preserve his reputations.[120] Further progress was made with the Companies Bill 1978, introduced by James Callaghan's Labour government, which addressed the interests of employees, although not as a statutory obligation, 'requiring directors to have regard, in the performance of their functions, to matters which include the interests of the company's employees generally, as well as the interests of its members', which was then reflected in the Companies Act 1980.[121] Despite calls for statutory reform, the proposals to consider employee interests as expressed in the failed Companies Bill 1973 and in the later Companies Bill 1978 did not introduce changes to core law – it was never the law that employee or other stakeholder interests could not be considered, but only that they could not be in conflict with the interests of the company.[122] Even if the Companies Bill 1973 had become law, it would not have had a meaningful impact on the legal duties of directors in relation to the primacy of shareholder interests, although it would have explicitly identified the legal requirement to consider employee interests alongside them.

[118] 'Very Interesting' (1974) 96. See 'Reforming Company Law' (1960) 144 on earlier considerations of an UK SEC-type body.

[119] Kynaston (2001) 556.

[120] Kynaston (2001) 467. The Green Paper also called for the nationalisation of the nation's banks and insurance companies, which would bring these powerful financial institutions under the control of the state (Kynaston (2001) 478; see ch 2, section VIII.A of this volume on the nationalisations of insurance companies and financial institutions). In addition, the Green Paper called for a two-tier board system, but did not go so far as supporting the idea of the worker shareholder as an essential means of distributing corporate power (see ch 5 of this volume on worker shareholders).

[121] Companies Act 1980, s 46; Knight (1982) 13; Durham (1982) 568; Prentice (1981).

[122] Birds (1980) 72.

5

Industrial Democracy and the Worker Shareholder

I. POST-WAR RECONSTRUCTION AND THE MOVEMENT FOR INDUSTRIAL DEMOCRACY

THE POLITICAL ENVIRONMENT of the post-war consensus, and its evolution under different governments and prime ministers, with changing economic conditions and shifting societal expectations and norms, was the backdrop to the rise of a new stage in the movement for industrial democracy.[1] Britain was undergoing major changes in its institutions and policies, both domestic and international, and while the general public faced the hardships of post-war austerity, controls and rationing, 'Labour Britain was a laboratory of social engineering and reconstruction'.[2] Industrial democracy was part of the late nineteenth- and twentieth-century movements for the empowerment of labour and the enfranchisement of the working classes, which increased in intensity with the profound societal changes following the end of the Second World War.[3] After the political, economic and social dislocations of two world wars, as well as the upheavals of the Russian Revolution and the spread of socialist and communist regimes in different parts of the world, the calls for increased workers' rights within Britain were growing in intensity as they were taken up by mainstream political parties to become part of the national political debate.[4] The broader post-war political narrative was infused with ways of expanding democratic ideals and inclusiveness, which were applied to how various constituents, including workers, were perceived and what inadequacies of

[1] On the background for post-war industrial democracy, see Clegg (1960) 3ff; see also Coates and Topham (1975a); Coates and Topham (1975b); Coates and Topham (1975c). For a nineteenth-century study of industrial democracy, see Webb and Webb (1897).

[2] Morgan (1992) 30.

[3] See Clegg (1951) 1ff for a history of the development of industrial democracy. See also Blumberg (1971) 141ff for a discussion on Clegg, 'one of Britain's leading industrial relations experts', and his role in the evolving definition of industrial democracy as a reflection of a changing understanding of political democracy.

[4] For a contemporaneous understanding of how scholars at the height of the Cold War viewed the topic of worker shareholders, including the ideological struggle between Russia and the West, see Copeman (1958) 10ff. See also Lord Hailsham of St Marylebone (1958) for an example of how the Soviet threat to capitalism was portrayed; and see Copeman (1958) on the Russian system and the struggle between capital and labour.

representation needed to be addressed, although, as observed by the journalist John Elliott in his work on trade union power and industrial democracy, until the mid-1970s:

> [F]ew companies gave much thought to a wider positive role for unions or their members, although some did gradually realise the need to try to communicate more with their employees about company affairs, while others had been driven by the conflict traditions of their factories to consider whether there were better methods of running their labour relations.[5]

Within this context and as part of the various political attempts to address the challenges of the era, which included nationalisations and shareholder democracy, there were mounting demands for increasing participation by workers in the ownership and management of British industry through the various forms of industrial democracy.[6]

As the post-war political landscape shifted to make room for the support of the socioeconomic platforms of the political left that were manifested in the 1945 Labour electoral victory, there were growing demands for greater representation by and more equitable treatment of the British working class, of which share ownership, including increasing the number of worker shareholders, was one aspect.[7] Industrial democracy was an important expression of workers' demands for participation, and alongside the growing influence of organised labour, there was a push to see workers improve their position within industry and become equity owners.[8] For some supporters of the movements to democratise British industry, it was the worker's right to be an equity owner in the company for which he or she laboured, to profit from his or her work as an owner and not just a labourer, and to have the right to be heard and the authority, as a shareholder, to instruct.[9]

In an environment that was encouraging shareholder democracy more broadly, workers were seen as desirable group to target for increasing participation, meeting the goals of both widening the shareholder base and including workers in the ownership of industry.[10] The post-war calls from certain corners for the working man (and, by extension, the working woman) to have not only full legal rights but also a political voice as an equal participant in the democratic process were extended to industry and the financial markets, including seeing share ownership as a means to achieve industrial democracy.[11] The encouragement of share ownership by workers, like the WSOC policies that endorsed an

[5] Elliott (1984) 111.
[6] Gumbrell-McCormick and Hyman (2019) 92.
[7] Copeman (1958) 3.
[8] Goss (1973) 5.
[9] Copeman (1975) 41.
[10] Naylor (1968) xvii; Copeman (1958) 28.
[11] Edwards (2016) 107; in contrast to the WSOC, the TUC discredited the concept of employee ownership schemes (Trades Union Congress (1973) 35; see also section IV.B of this chapter).

increase in employee shareholding as part of its more general goal for wider share ownership, was based on the belief that it would benefit the country as a whole.[12]

A. Industrial Democracy within Democratic Frameworks

The zeitgeist following the Second World War that was reflected in the creation of the post-war settlement was one of growing inclusiveness, with elements of the financial and industrial communities, some of whom were working with the new Labour government on its economic plan, recognising the need to heed the calls for increased inclusion and democratisation that were emanating from across the political spectrum.[13] Industrial democracy was a reflection of the movements for political democratisation demanding representation, as expressed in the 1974 Fabian Tract, *Working Power: Policies for Industrial Democracy*, authored by Giles Radice:

> Democracy is infectious. This is one of the main strengths of the industrial democrat's case. For, in a society in which democratic rights are increasingly recognised, it becomes more and more difficult to maintain that industry should be excluded. Why should industry remain one of the major areas to which democratic principles do not apply?[14]

Industrial democracy as a movement went beyond the questions of ownership that were central to shareholder democracy, addressing key elements of post-war industrial relations.[15] The British labour movements used the language and ideas of democracy as part of their platform seeking to improve the conditions and increase the rights of workers as part of the programme for post-war reconstruction:

> The claim to share in the control of industry rests primarily on the simple democratic right of workpeople to have a voice in the determination of their industrial destinies. It is supported by the knowledge that it is only by recognition of this claim that the potentialities, experience and good sense of the workers can be drawn upon and the full productive powers of industry be effectively realised.[16]

The analogy of democracy, taken from the political sphere, was applied to industry, notwithstanding the fundamental differences between citizens and workers, and their relationships to the state and to work, respectively.[17]

[12] Naylor (1968) xviii. See ch 3, section IV.C of this volume on the WSOC and shareholder democracy.
[13] Eatwell (1979) 68.
[14] Radice (1974) 6.
[15] Copeman (1958) 24.
[16] Trades Union Congress (1944) 7.
[17] Clegg (1951) 23; Clegg (1960) 81ff.

To advance its agenda, the industrial democracy movement needed a usable policy framework that was based on more than just the conceptual recognition of workers' interests and rights, although there were differing views on what that framework should be; as explained by Hugh Clegg, one of the most important post-war British authorities on industrial relations, just as the existence of enforceable rules keeps political democracy functioning, so 'a system of industrial democracy must provide mechanisms for protecting the rights and safeguarding the interests of industrial workers. Otherwise it does not deserve to be called democratic'.[18] The parallels between industrial democracy and political democracy were not, however, without its critics, a position expressed by Tom Clarke, a researcher of industrial sociology, in his 1977 essay 'Industrial Democracy: The Institutionalized Suppression of Industrial Conflict?':

> A primary weakness of the contemporary case for industrial democracy is the presupposition that democracy has been attained in the political system with the existence of parliamentary representation, the principles of which may be usefully emulated to provide for the democratic control of industry. Yet, when examined critically, the achievements of parliamentary democracy have been modest to say the least.[19]

For some, at least, political democracy was a weak model to emulate. For its advocates, however, democracy was a means by which to include disparate groups within an established system, countering the efforts of those wanting systemic upheaval:

> All the claims of all the pressure groups cannot be met. But so much of what they seek can be given them, together with such good reasons for refusing the rest, as to make them think that they are being treated fairly, and that their bargaining is giving them as much as they could reasonably expect. The consequence of this system is that most groups in society are integrated of their own free will into the political system. They choose to seek their political aims within the existing system, and thus to add to its stability.[20]

For the supporters of industrial democracy, the conflict between labour and capital was at the core of post-war British democracy, as was expressed in 1968 in the Institute for Workers' Control's pamphlet *The Labour Party's Plans for Industrial Democracy*:

> If the battle for workers' control does not form up at the very centre of the unions' strategy during that collision it will be a bleak day for labour, and, almost certainly, a bleak day for democracy. The present lethargic drift of the British economy will not continue indefinitely. Either Labour will conscript capital, and in the process of a democratic upsurge, unleash the vast creative initiative of the British working people to re-organise the whole structure on a human basis, or, failing that, capital will decide that political democracy itself is the impediment to the rationalisation of its

[18] Clegg (1960) 82.
[19] Clarke (1977) 352.
[20] Clegg (1960) 20.

> whole rickety edifice. Parliament is not eternal. Our strong man is lurking, somewhere, waiting for Mr Wilson and Mr Heath to conclude their pantomime. If he is to be held off and defeated, we must quickly awaken to the fact that democracy is a permanent self-deepening process, and that unless it is able to expand, it will die.[21]

For the Labour Party and the political left, industrial democracy and the empowerment of workers were at the core of the struggle with the stagnating established system for the future of democratic Britain.[22]

II. MOTIVATIONS FOR SUPPORT OF INDUSTRIAL DEMOCRACY

There were many catalysts for those promoting the principles of industrial democracy, from seeking to increase worker participation in the owning and managing of industry to improving working conditions and creating incentives for workers and their organised representatives to align their interests with those of directors and existing shareholders.[23] Worker share ownership was seen as a means by which workers could contribute not just their labour but also their capital – both directly and, to a greater and growing degree, indirectly – to the companies for which they worked, helping to entwine their incentives with those of the company and creating additional financial ties.[24] 'Industrial democracy' could be difficult to define, often reflecting the underlying ideological assumptions of its user, the term 'used to define both revolutionary, socialist aspiration for workers' control, and a limited reform which offers consultation, whilst preserving management's right to make the final decision'.[25] The proponents of industrial democracy as a means of reforming British society were suspicious of attempts by the establishment to co-opt the movement as a means of defanging it:

> The confusion inherent in the concept of workers' participation is not always intentional. True, some people consciously seek to cripple the workers' control movement which has arisen. But for others, the anxiety natural to reformers, to avoid any fundamentalism which might intensify the difficulties involved in securing change. However, it cannot be too strongly urged that, in its usual meaning, participation has the closest and ugliest relationship with a whole train of mean and sleazy predecessors in the sequence of devices for 'heading off' a growing working class demand for control.[26]

Industrial democracy was a broad movement that called for workers to have a more active role in the decisions made at the companies where they worked and to benefit more from the product, and profits, of their labour beyond just

[21] Coates and Topham (1968b) 7.
[22] Foote (1986) 231.
[23] Heller (1979) 3.
[24] Goss (1973) 19.
[25] Fatchett (1977) 2.
[26] Coates and Topham (1968a) 228.

their wages; the definition of 'industrial democracy' is neither singular nor categorical, encompassing numerous approaches and schools of thought, which underwent conceptual evolutions.[27]

Industrial democracy is about worker representation and participation, creating opportunities for employees to have real influence on company management and the decisions of both private and public firms and across industries. As explained by Clegg:

> As soon as we reject any simple and unique definition of industrial democracy we can see that a number of combinations of its elements – trade union opposition and willing participation of workers with management in a common enterprise – is possible, and that there may be ample room for argument about which combination is the most democratic … In fact, there exist many combinations of the elements of industrial democracy in different establishments and in different industries, and different combinations may seem to give equally satisfactory and unsatisfactory results.[28]

Industrial democracy was part of a dynamic post-war political and social landscape, and its various manifestations were influenced by the ability of competing constituents to gain, or retain, control in a modernising Britain.[29]

A. Worker Share Ownership and Societal Inequalities

Increasing share ownership amongst workers as a means by which to address societal inequalities was a concept that was promoted by advocates from the political left and right, with the former looking to reform the existing capitalist system and the latter seeking ways to fortify and preserve it.[30] Whereas Labour were committed to their policies of nationalisations and bringing private industry under state control, the Conservatives encouraged equity investing, with

[27] Clegg (1951) 1. Clegg (1960) 3 writes that the term can 'cover any theory or scheme so long as it is based on a genuine concern for the rights of workers in industry, particularly their right to a share in the control of industrial decisions'.

[28] Clegg (1951) 36.

[29] Poole (1986) 13; Elliott (1984) 99. The legacy of the post-war period endures in the Labour Party platform, which preserves the ideals of industrial democracy and the criticisms of the inequity of shareholder primacy; as recently as the 2019 general election, the Labour Party ran on a platform that advocated seizing 10 per cent of shares in large UK companies and placing them in Inclusive Ownership Funds (IOF) that would hold these shares on behalf of workers, be managed by workers and pay dividends to workers (Labour Party (2019) 60). The *Financial Times*, in an analysis done with the law firm Clifford Chance, estimated that this would result in a transfer of value worth £300 billion in 7,000 companies (Pickard (2019) 1). The 2017 Labour manifesto promised to broaden ownership in the UK economy, stating that 'Britain is a long-established democracy. But the distribution of ownership of the country's economy means that decisions about our economy are often made by a narrow elite. More democratic ownership structures would help our economy deliver for the many and lead to a fairer distribution of wealth' (Labour Party (2017) 19). In 2019, Labour also promised to change the laws that protect shareholder primacy: 'We will amend the Companies Act, requiring companies to prioritise long-term growth while strengthening protections for stakeholders, including small suppliers and pension funds' (Labour Party (2019) 63).

[30] Clarke (1977) 351.

wider share ownership, including worker participation in industrial ownership, as a part of a broader programme to expand property-owning democracy and to change popular attitudes to capitalism through the ownership of capital assets.[31] As part of the post-war reconstruction efforts, there was a push for all citizens (including workers) to increase long-term savings, and the British working class was targeted by policy-makers to become more invested in the financial markets, and specifically the equity markets.[32]

By the mid-1950s and 1960s, employee shareholder schemes were promoted as effective ways to encourage savings and investment, as well as a means to improve industrial relations and address inequalities.[33] A driving force behind the push to increase worker share ownership by promoters like George Copeman was the belief that it would help blur the established class distinctions between owner and labourer by advancing the goal of wealth redistribution: 'Closing the gap between capital and labour is largely a matter of giving employees similar incentives and facilities for capital ownership to those now possessed by business owners.'[34] Industrial democracy sought to break down the traditional bifurcation between capital and labour, with its supporters, who came from across the political spectrum, advocating for different ways in which this might be achieved, including making workers shareholders in the companies where they worked.[35]

For those advocating in favour of industrial democracy, the structural and systemic changes needed to empower workers were manifold. As explained in the 1958 pamphlet 'The Insiders', published by the *Universities and Left Review*:

> To democratize power in industry means, in fact, to give as much power, as great a degree of play for responsibility to the individual worker as is possible to do. Unless this is done, the worker remains the mere functionary of his machine. To achieve this today it is clear that we must look, not for a single form of control, but to several different but complementary forms of participation.[36]

In a post-war environment that saw the political left advocate for the widespread expropriation of companies that transferred ownership from private hands to the state, worker control through shareholding was another potential avenue for systemic change.[37] This is especially relevant in light of Labour's failure to

[31] Edwards (2016) 108; Francis (2012) 280.

[32] See, for example, the work of the WSOC (see Naylor (1968)). See Labour Party (1956) 29 on Labour's encouragement of personal savings. See Davies (1994) 258 on post-war long-term savings and the growth of institutional investing in equities. See also ch 3, section IV.B of this volume.

[33] Naylor (1968) 55.

[34] Copeman (1958) 7.

[35] The focus of this research is the two parties, Labour and Conservative, that alternated in government during the post-war period. The Acton Society Trust survey summarises the position of the third major party, the Liberal Party, in favour of worker shareholding and co-partnership as a means 'to increase the status and sense of personal significance and responsibility of all and everyone in industry; and to spread more widely the wealth and power that industry creates' (Acton Society Trust (1959) 5).

[36] Coates and Topham (1975c) 87.

[37] Kelf-Cohen (1958) 269.

leverage its widespread nationalisation programme to put companies under workers' control, missing an opportunity to implement industrial democracy policies that could have created worker shareholders on a transformational scale.[38]

In a period that was seeing an expansion of industrial democracy measures, this reflected an increase in the adoption by companies of various schemes for employee profit-sharing, which Elliott observed might suggest a change in corporate behaviour, as 'in a more liberal and ideological vein, a few companies may be deciding that it is illogical of them to perpetuate the class divisions of company ownership when they are allowing employees increasing democracy in management affairs'.[39] In what was considered a radical step at the time, some companies had progressive and generous programmes that gave employees at almost every level the ability to invest in their employer companies.[40] With increased share ownership, there was hope that there would be a ripple effect in terms of greater awareness of how industry works, although it remained an open question as to whether employees understood what it meant to own shares or whether they saw schemes as just another handout.[41]

The support for industrial democracy as a means by which to bring capital and labour closer together, once considered a socialist policy, was increasingly mainstream, with growing recognition by experts in the field of industrial relations, like Clegg, that industrial democracy could exist within both capitalism and socialism.[42] From the perspective of the capitalists, expanding the number of worker shareholders was not a means by which to redistribute exiting wealth and/or to change the structure of society, which were the intentions of the labour movement and the political left, but was instead a way to involve workers in the fortunes of the company for which they worked by sharing in the new wealth that was created through their efforts.[43] There was growing management support for 'giv[ing] their workers a slice of the company's growth, at the same time hoping to encourage a greater identification with its objectives'.[44] This alignment of interests sought to transform workers from resisting the existing system to becoming willing participants in it.[45] Employee shareholder schemes and vehicles for collective savings were particularly appealing to the Conservatives, whereas Labour, partly due to the influence of the trade unions, remained more committed to representation and consultation as a way to expand industrial democracy.[46]

The idea of workers being invested through equity share ownership in the companies where they worked, in particular, and the success of the capitalist

[38] See ch 2, section III.C of this volume on the missed opportunity for workers' control of nationalised industries. See also Eatwell (1979) 162; Kynaston (2007) 140.
[39] Elliott (1984) 187.
[40] 'Privileged Shareholders' (1957) 1183.
[41] Fisher (1979) 31.
[42] Blumberg (1971) 141.
[43] Elliott (1984) 187.
[44] Blanden (1973) 17.
[45] Whiting (2004) 114.
[46] Plender (1982) 30; Elliott (1984) 65.

system, more generally, was presented as a stabilising and moderating approach in uncertain and factitious times.[47] Like the movement for shareholder democracy, industrial democracy was a means of assimilating a potentially hostile constituency into the existing system and introducing workers to more of the benefits of the British capitalism.[48] The various manifestations of post-war industrial democracy nurtured the connection between capital and labour, which was strengthened further through the normalisation of the idea of workers owning shares, albeit usually indirectly and almost always passively.[49] The relationship between these two groups was being reframed, acknowledging that 'although workers and capitalists may differ over the respective shares of wages and profits, as joint producers they have a *common* interest in maximising the surplus of revenue over costs of production'.[50]

B. Bridging the Gap between Capital and Labour

The movement for industrial democracy was not without its ideological complexities for the political left and the unionists, with the acceptance of the concept of the worker shareholder changing the framing of the struggle of labour against capital, as well as how to address the interests of the non-worker shareholders, in particular those who were characterised as profiteers who buy, own and sell shares to generate investment income; to the representatives of labour, equity shareholders, whose ranks the worker shareholder was joining, had always been a separate, elitist and often oppositional stakeholder with prioritised legal rights within a system that disadvantaged labour.[51] To become willing participants in a system that encouraged workers to become equity owners required an ideological pivot that could be viewed as bolstering the capitalist system that they had hitherto tried to reform or even dismantle.[52] Nonetheless, worker shareholding was an important component in the broader movement for industrial democracy, and the promotion of share ownership by workers gradually altered the narrative on shareholders.[53] For the groups on the political left that were ideologically hostile to the British capitalist system generally and the investor class specifically, there was a move away from seeing all shareholders antagonistically as the opportunistic 'other' towards acknowledging the benefits of equity ownership for their own constituents, the workers.[54] With the inclusion of workers as part of the shareholder base, the incentives of

[47] Lord Hailsham of St Marylebone (1958) 26.
[48] See ch 3, section IV.C of this volume.
[49] Copeman (1975) 127.
[50] Chiplin, Coyne and Sirc (1977) 98.
[51] Clarke (1977) 361; Elliott (1984) 66; see also ch 3, section I.A of this volume.
[52] Clarke (1977) 360.
[53] Copeman (1975) 26ff.
[54] Elliott (1984) 188.

these stakeholder groups became increasingly aligned, protecting the legal position of existing shareholders, including from the threats of nationalisation.[55]

Although on one level a shareholder primacy-based system was challenged by the demands of industrial democracy, on another it gained greater support as the shareholder body expanded to include previously hostile groups; the prioritisation of shareholder interests was an easier target when the shareholder body did not include workers and working-class savers on a meaningful scale.[56] Within the political context of the post-war period, the increased convergence of the worker and the equity owner/capital provider made a shareholder-centric approach to company law and corporate governance easier for opponents of the existing system to accept, contributing to a process of deradicalisation.[57] Once the cause for worker shareholding was adopted more broadly, the portrayal of the shareholder was ready for recalibration, although a complete repositioning was never fully realised, and despite the increase in worker share ownership, a lingering hostility persisted against the providers of capital by organised labour, its supporters and other critics of the capitalist system.[58] The opinion that share ownership was an effective levelling tool was not universally accepted, however, with some parties questioning the efficacy of increasing the number of worker shareholders to address societal challenges, recognising that 'the view one takes on the merits of wider shareholding will depend upon one's political viewpoint'.[59] Nonetheless, in the post-war period, the support for industrial democracy was expanding beyond its traditional base on the left, a trajectory of transitioning to the mainstream that is similar to other movements seeking to reform the existing industrial and financial systems – for example, ESV, stakeholder capitalism and corporate purpose.

III. BRITISH INDUSTRY AND A CHANGING WORKFORCE

A. Post-war Changes in Behaviour and Expectations

Although the most vocal advocates of industrial democracy came from the political left, there were those on the right of the political spectrum whose views on managerial prerogatives were evolving to address the changes of the post-war era.[60] The Conservative Research Department, describing the shifts in the dynamic between employers and employees, attributed the changes in the general workforce to '[t]he inevitable effect of extended full-time education coupled with high economic security', and to directors and managers becoming

[55] Naylor (1968) xiii.
[56] Davies (2017) 40.
[57] See Davies (2019) 86ff on Labour and ownership.
[58] Elliott (1984) 184.
[59] Acton Society Trust (1959) 5.
[60] See Abbott (1973).

more professional, leading to a recalibration in how these various parties interacted with one another, as well as the expectations and behaviours of each, with:

> [T]he average employee much less willing to accept traditional authority at his workplace. Today, most employees at all levels want to know not just what they have to do, but why; and they want some say in how it is done. This is participation in its simplest form – but it represents a change in the doctrine of management to which there is a substantial degree of resistance. Indeed, many managements, and some employers' associations, are still fighting to retain rights and privileges which have no place in a progressive industrial society.[61]

The managerial class might not have been enthusiastic about the evolution of the workforce upon which it depended, but there was a growing awareness of a need to address the demands of increasingly self-confident workers, and industrial democracy provided possible solutions.[62]

Alongside the changing profile of workers, the managers running British companies were becoming increasingly professional and independent.[63] Although industrial democracy was a movement that was identified with advancing the interests of the working class, there was an acknowledgement that it could also benefit different levels of the industrial hierarchy. Even if the manager's motivations for improving industrial conditions and relations were distinct from those of the employees:

> Whatever his purpose, whether it be to make a profit, to make a success of his undertaking, to leave a stable concern to his children, or to get through life as easily as possible, his interest is in getting his whole staff to work together as well as possible.[64]

Within the burgeoning debate on the effectiveness of industrial democracy to improve performance and efficiencies, the value of aligning the incentives of labour with the existing system by making workers shareholders in industrial companies was increasingly accepted by some of the established participants, as described by the Rt Hon The Viscount Chandos, chairman of Associated Electrical Industries Ltd (AEI):

> It is hardly an exaggeration to say that he (the worker) invests his life in an industry or a company or a process inside the company and I, like everyone else who I think has pondered on these subjects, would like to see him a part proprietor of the business.[65]

[61] Abbott (1973) 4; Labour Party (1957) 16; Coates and Topham (1977) 26.
[62] Davies (1978) 260.
[63] Maltby and Wilkinson (1997) 48.
[64] Clegg (1951) 30.
[65] See Copeman (1958) 184–85 for a selection of quotations by corporate leaders supporting employee shareholding. In 1974, the *Financial Times* reported favourably on one (atypical) example of industrial democracy: GR Speaker, the industrial company, then 54 per cent owned by the Belgian company Eternit, with the remaining 46 per cent of shares held by past and present employees who inherited them from the company's eponymous founder (and wife) and his partner and were sole owners until selling a controlling share to Eternit in 1971. In addition to the original bequests, employees were allowed to buy shares after one year of service and were awarded shares after seven years; bonus issues were made and dividends paid. Although fewer than half of the 260 employees

As the relationship between management and labour evolved, workers took on increased responsibilities and were acknowledged as being more than just disinterested labourers, strengthening the arguments supporting industrial democracy and for increasing worker shareholding, and as Copeman argued:

> [M]any of these employees are now doing some of the work of initiative and leadership formerly done by business owners. So there is a case, in equity, for extending to employees a concession which will encourage them to acquire and hold shares.[66]

Supporting these developments in the perception of workers' abilities, advocates for industrial democracy argued that employees had unique operational insights that contributed to improving the performance that benefited all shareholders, that workers had direct experience, often more than the directors, who were regularly from outside the industry, and that workers were even in a position to judge the competency of management.[67] Worker shareholders were presented as having the ability to exercise the oversight that is associated with share ownership, as well as to participate effectively in other forms of industrial democracy, such as board representation.[68] The competency of management was being challenged and workers were looked upon as a possible solution, as the Labour politician Derek Fatchett remarked in a paper on industrial democracy:

> There is no doubt that from the mid-1960s onwards, there has been a tremendous revival of interest in industrial democracy. This has not been associated with a demand for any one particular form of industrial democracy, but can be more adequately characterised by a general unease and criticism of the existing management of industry.[69]

From the opposition benches, Harold Wilson argued in 1973 that the growing abilities of workers supported the promotion of industrial democracy:

> The average worker today is more sensitive, better educated, more aware of his own talents, as well as his potential power, and much more confident than his father a generation ago. This also makes him more conscious of the frustrations that exist in

in 1974 owned shares, the largest holdings were not limited to management. The managing director claims that: 'The fact that he is working for the people [he] employ[s] has … helped efficiency and staff retention.' This example of industrial democracy was presented with the glow of idealistic aspirations, demonstrating a capitalist system that includes benevolent owners and worthy labourers ('Speaker's Worker Shareholders' (1974) 20).

[66] Copeman (1958) 7.

[67] Goss (1973) 9. On the need to better leverage the expertise of the workforce to manage companies, Harold Wilson proclaimed that: 'There is little doubt that we are at the beginning of a social revolution in this sphere and over the next 10 years it's bound to develop widely. One of the main reasons is that it is becoming increasingly difficult for management in the old sense to run modern industrial complexes without taking their work-force much more into their confidence and giving workers much greater scope to use their ingenuity, initiative and creative talents at the point of work' (Wilson (1973) 7).

[68] In the immediate post-war years, the trade unionists still accepted the superior capacity of management (Middlemas (1979) 393). See ch 6 of this volume on worker directors.

[69] Fatchett (1977) 9.

> modern industry – management incompetence and inefficiency, mass production-line boredom, and often the inadequacy of trade union representation.[70]

In the post-war period, the movements for worker shareholding were part of broader political and social aspirations for a more inclusive, and more democratic, form of ownership of British companies, itself a reflection of a more representative Britain.[71] The democratisation of British industry was twofold, both broadening and diversifying the shareholder base by increasing the number of small investors across socioeconomic background and, more specifically, by including more workers, who despite their progress from their pre-war position, remained heavily under-represented as a group within the shareholder body.[72]

Further strengthening the arguments supporting the increase in worker shareholding was the complaint that the traditional individual owner of equity shares was not, in most cases, an active participant in investee companies, as one letter writer to the *Financial Times* expressed:

> If three out of four shareholders treat the annual report as rubbish there is little argument left for the responsibility of shareholders to counter the Left-wing view that the work force should have at least as much control of industry as the shareholders – after all the work force wants more information about their companies, they are pressing for more responsibility, and their livelihoods depend on their employing companies.[73]

Those who supported industrial democracy, generally, and share ownership by workers, more specifically, attributed to workers a desire to be informed on company affairs and a natural activism, assuming that they had built-in motivations for involvement and engagement that other small dispersed shareholders, whose interests rested primarily in dividend payments and capital appreciation, lacked.[74] This theory supporting worker shareholding, as presented by the *Financial Times* letter writer above, suggests that workers have more incentives to be active shareholders than the existing (mostly apathetic) individual shareholders, assuming a deliberate strategy and clarity of purpose by these worker shareholders, as well as an absence of the (rational) apathy that is attributed to

[70] Wilson (1973) 7.

[71] Elliott (1984) 187.

[72] See Acton Society Trust (1959) 2, stating that: 'Our interest has been the socio-political implications of encouraging a large number of people, including wage-earning classes, to own ordinary shares (principally in British industry).'

[73] Harman (1974) 2. See ch 3, section I.D of this volume on the apathetic individual investor.

[74] See Copeman (1958) 188 for the 1957 memorandum of Courtaulds Ltd on the reasons given for sharing information with employees, including: '1. Employees tend more and more to look at industrial matters with a questioning mind, a state of affairs which has been aided and accelerated by the rise in educational level, by the impact of the popular press, the cinema, radio, television, by political propaganda and highly organised trade unionism. It is therefore highly desirable to place before them factual information about the structure of industry and the economics involved; if this is not done they will possibly acquire a number of misconceptions which will cause suspicions to arise and will mar good relations. 2. It helps employees to understand the system under which they work, 3. It is a means of identifying the interest of employees with that of the Company.' See also ch 6, section III.E of this volume on workers' rights to information.

other equity investors, even when workers' stakes are as small, if not smaller, than that of the typical individual shareholder.[75] This argument rests on the unproven assumption that whereas the ordinary equity shareholder had only a financial interest in an investee company, the worker was a long-term investor with more at stake and would therefore be motivated to take an active interest in how the company for which he or she worked, and in which he or she owned shares, was managed.[76]

i. Misalignment of Interests

The champions of industrial democracy as a means of empowering the working class accepted labour becoming, at least partly, the provider of capital, blurring the identity of the honourable worker with the oft-derided shareholder.[77] Conversely, with the spread of industrial democracy and worker shareholding, company directors saw labour potentially having an additional avenue for influence on managerial decisions through their rights as worker shareholders (or indirectly through pension funds).[78] The introduction of worker shareholders added potential conflicts of interest amongst shareholder groups; in addition to equity owners, worker shareholders were also employees, expanding the shareholder base to include participants from outside the typical demographic, and making the dynamics of share ownership potentially more complex as the opportunities for misaligned and differing incentives amongst the different shareholder groups increased.[79] In the case of the worker shareholder, his or her interests as an equity shareholder may only partially overlap with those as an employee, yet increasingly these may be the same individual. In theory, if worker shareholders coordinated their activities under the guidance of trade unions or other political groups, they could influence corporate behaviour in ways not necessarily aligned with the interests of the other non-worker shareholders at investee companies.[80] Even when workers acquired shares, however, there was no rush to influence the decisions of company boards through their new identities as equity owners; like other shareholders, the share-owning workers faced many of the same incentives for rational apathy.[81]

[75] Davies (1994) 268. See also ch 3, section I.D of this volume on shareholder apathy.

[76] The argument that worker shareholders have more than short-term financial incentives is also made for the institutional investors who are investing the capital of employees and pensioners: 'The institutions invest, typically, not the funds of speculators or the incomes of rentiers, but the earnings of workers, albeit better-off workers, who aim to save against loss of income in old age' (Davies (1994) 268).

[77] Elliott (1984) 187. On the post-war perceptions of shareholders, see ch 3, section I of this volume.

[78] Wheeler (2008) 176; Poole (1986) 63.

[79] See Wheeler (2008) 172ff on the aggregation of the power of worker-owners' capital through worker shareholder associations.

[80] Fairfax (2019) 1312.

[81] See Clarke (1977) 353 on rational apathy: 'the "apathy" ascribed to the majority of people is often only a realistic assessment on their part of their relative powerlessness, even if an attempt were

When the worker becomes the shareholder, just as when he or she becomes a company director, the tensions increase. Distinctions between groups are muddied, and the battling forces of democratisation (that is, shareholder democracy and industrial democracy) and how they are used by those seeking to bolster their own interests can become entangled and confused.[82] Whereas shareholder democracy, achieved through the growth of the shareholder base, was a means by which to protect and preserve shareholder interests, industrial democracy sought to strengthen the rights of workers, sometimes at the expense of current shareholders.[83] This friction magnified any existing conflicts amongst stakeholders when they also became shareholders – for example, worker shareholders, whose interests as workers and as shareholders could be misaligned.[84] For example, managers of the occupational pension funds had fiduciary duties to their members – that is, the workers who were indirect owners of the equity – that were not necessarily aligned with the best interests of the same individuals in his or her role as employee, who was also a pension plan participant.[85]

The principles of shareholder democracy, which advocated for more rights for shareholders, rubbed up against those of industrial democracy, which sought through various means to see workers increase their power and influence within the companies where they worked, often pushing the shareholder and the labourer into opposing corners, even when the very idea of the worker shareholder, which was also being promoted, grafted these stakeholders together.[86] The desire to see a more diverse and inclusive shareholder base is common to both shareholder democracy and industrial democracy, but the small individual shareholder and the worker were not one and the same, although they could be, and there were efforts from policy-makers, regulators and legislators to see an increase of the latter amongst the former.[87] Meanwhile, despite these efforts to bolster the influence of workers and their representatives, it was the institutional investors, and not small investors of any type, that were gaining the most

made by them to influence decisions within the system'. See also ch 3, section I.D of this volume on shareholder apathy.

[82] See Kahn-Freund (1977) 77 on conflicts of interest. See also ch 6, section II of this volume.

[83] Proposals for worker representation on boards impacted shareholders' statutory rights; for example, see KW Wedderburn (1977) para 1.13, in reference to the Bullock Committee proposals.

[84] Abbott (1973) 14.

[85] Plender (1982) 30. Examples include any form of long- and short-term board decisions that involve allocations of profits for reinvestment, pay adjustments and/or dividends.

[86] Although their incentives could be misaligned, labour and equity owners could also work together towards a common goal. This was seen in the case of Distillers addressing the Thalidomide settlement for victims, when shareholders were supported by the industrial pressure applied by the TUC to force the board to act in the interest of the company and negotiate a settlement with victims that would mitigate the adverse publicity and harm. Shareholders and stakeholders, in this case workers as represented by their union, found their interests aligned and acted in concert against the decisions of company directors. See David (1972) 15; McLachlan (1972) 24; and ch 4, section V.A of this volume.

[87] Copeman (1958) 5.

ground and increasing their share of the ownership of, and influence in, British companies.[88]

The unrelenting rise in the power of the financial institutions in the post-war era was met with resistance and stimulated (unsuccessful) efforts to mitigate this trend, contributing to the support of the movement for industrial democracy that encouraged direct worker participation in the markets.[89] It was clear that the existing pool of small shareholders was not large enough to create a buffer against the institutions, and that worker share ownership was one way to 'stem the tide of institutional dominance over the stock market', as was proposed by one reader in a letter to the *Financial Times*, also adding that these shares must be earned by workers and not simply given to them, a familiar theme of those suspicious of the working class.[90] Expanding share ownership to include more workers was seen as a way to counterbalance the growing influence of institutional investors, although the tide would not be turned in this critical post-war period that saw the shareholder body shift irrevocably, introducing the advent of the dominance of institutional investors in their many forms, a trend that accelerated in the 1960s and 1970s, when the direct ownership of listed UK equities by individuals declined from 54.0 per cent in 1963 to 28.2 per cent in 1981.[91]

B. Worker Shareholding as a Solution to Industrial Unrest

The cross-party settlement reached at the end of the Second World War gradually eroded and by the 1960s the post-war consensus was weakening, and political cooperation fading, as the stability of the mixed economy was under pressure, leading to more industrial and political unrest as British voters sought change after more than a decade of Conservative governments that began in 1951.[92] Industrial democracy was part of the Labour Party's political programme throughout the 1950s and into the 1960s, with the National Plan promising British voters reforms that would stimulate productivity and increase worker involvement and representation.[93] Both major parties sought ways to address the industrial relations challenges and unrest that were major issues for

[88] See ch 3, section II.B of this volume.

[89] See Acton Society Trust (1959) 14 on the difficulties faced by small investors wanting to invest directly in equities and the incentives to use vehicles like Unit Trusts. See also Aldington (1959) 9ff on considerations for creating a share-owning democracy based on small savers and wage earners, highlighting the disadvantages faced by individuals investing in equities, and the admission that the diversification needed to mitigate risk is difficult when the amounts are small, necessitating the use of institutional investment vehicles.

[90] Grey (1978) 19.

[91] Davies (2015) 358. See also ch 3, section II.B in this volume.

[92] Middlemas (1979) 429.

[93] Labour Party (1966); Dale (2000b) 133.

voters, adopting increasingly divergent approaches that contributed to weakening the post-war agreement.[94] During the post-war period, which experienced escalating industrial strife, to have more working-class people (and especially labourers) directly holding shares in British companies was seen by many as necessary social progress and was encouraged by supporters of a mixed economy and a planned society; it was also seen as a means by which to draw into the established ownership system an increasingly disruptive class of citizens and at a relatively low cost.[95] For the supporters of worker shareholding, equity ownership was a way to make workers understand through direct experience that settling labour disputes sensibly and increasing industrial productivity were to their, and the country's, advantage.[96]

Worker shareholding was promoted as a way to address the industrial unrest that was disrupting British industry, although this view was not shared by all employers, and there was considerable scepticism from industrial leaders and industrial relations experts as to whether worker shareholding schemes contributed to the improvement of employer–employee relationships.[97] Although some industrialists were not convinced of the merits of worker shareholders as contributors to improved industrial relations, others embraced it. The Bow Group reported in 1973 that:

> The question of industrial ownership must be seen as a long term issue, but a vitally important one. Pride in ownership is a beneficial instinct, and one that must be developed in every individual for the benefit of both himself and of society as a whole … The merit of such profit sharing or share ownership schemes is that more individuals have an opportunity for deeper involvement in their company's future, and in the future of industry as a whole. If, over a period of years, this can be fostered, it would be of immense value to society as a whole.[98]

Beyond the ideological assertions, calls for increased industrial democracy had a pragmatic appeal for those seeking to address the industrial strife that was disrupting British industry and impacting national productivity. As set forth by Clarke:

> The general aim of management is to restrict conflict by containing it within joint regulatory institutions which blur the divergent interests of management and workers,

[94] Middlemas (1991) 448.

[95] This idea mimics that of a Marxist view of political democracy, which asserts that: '"Other things being equal, a democratic state form is cheaper to operate than a despotism; as long as it is possible, it is a bargain for a ruling class interested in keeping down overhead costs." The willing compliance gained by the appearance of democratic rule obviates the necessity for the constant deployment of the expensive apparatus of political coercion' (Clarke (1977) 353; see also Draper (1974) 119). See also Copeman (1958) 27 on using wider shareholding to close the gap between the conflicting forces of capital and labour.

[96] Naylor (1968) xiv.

[97] Elliott (1984) 187.

[98] Goss (1973) 19.

> erode the basis of independent worker organizations, and thereby inhibit the capacity of workers to take defensive action.[99]

Since the Second World War, productivity and efficiency were used as arguments in favour of industrial democracy and by the 1960s, it was increasingly accepted that: 'Industrial democracy is required to yield increases in "output per man-hour", to resolve "inter-group tensions", and to give "worker satisfaction" and good "communications".'[100]

The call to make owners from workers did not always stem from an idealistic drive to empower labour and bring capital to heel, with some supporters of industrial democracy seeking to use it to preserve the existing relationship between capital and labour.[101] For many Conservatives and those on the political right, industrial democracy, and share ownership specifically, were seen as a way to include workers more directly in the fate of the companies for which they worked, possibly helping to solve some of the pressing problems created by deepening industrial unrest. As one reader of the *Financial Times* wrote in 1970 in relation to the business and industrial challenges at the automotive company British Leyland Corp, 'all workers must become shareholders so that they suffer or benefit from their own actions'.[102] In a time of industrial instability, expanding the equity ownership base of British industry was considered stabilising, with the Conservatives advocating for wider share ownership, be it through direct investing or indirectly through pension funds, investment/unit trusts or other vehicles.[103]

The ideological motivations of different groups contributed to the general increase in attention to the idea of expanding share ownership by individuals, and specifically workers:

> When left-wing supporters are prepared to consider worker shareholding they tend to do so for different reasons from those influencing right-wing supporters. The latter tend to favour workers' shareholding in the expectation that it will make workers more responsible, whereas the former think of workers having a right to share in the prosperity of the capitalist class. Of course, many people may hold a combination of these two attitudes, but in their pure form they represent two markedly different reasons for favouring wider shareholding.[104]

In the decades following the post-war period, wider share ownership was eventually realised through indirect investing in institutional vehicles, although the relationships amongst companies, equity shareholders and other stakeholders stayed mostly constant, with the familiar commentary from both supporters and critics of the existing capitalist system remaining stubbornly persistent.

[99] Clarke (1977) 356.

[100] Clegg (1960) 84. Similar arguments were made in support of nationalisations; see ch 2, section III.A of this volume.

[101] Elliott (1984) 185.

[102] Edwards (1970) 2.

[103] Goss (1973) 19.

[104] Acton Society Trust (1959) 7.

C. The City and the Worker Shareholder

Although there was a growing acceptance by the City for the idea of worker share ownership, most workers remained removed from, and suspicious of, financial institutions, which did not actively pursue the business of small individual shareholders.[105] Even those workers who might have showed an interest in investing in the companies where they were employed were unlikely to engage with the City brokers, as was explained in the 1962 Hobart paper, *Ordinary Shares for Ordinary Savers*:

> A man on a welding job may know a lot about the product he handles and may follow their fortunes through the newspapers' financial columns. But he may dislike the idea of parting with his money to some distant City man whom he never sees and can 'know' only over the telephone.[106]

Furthermore, the brokers were not equipped to deal with an influx of small investors, even if they had been open to the concept of serving worker shareholders, which most were not.[107] There may have been increasing awareness by certain elements in the City of the principles of worker shareholding, but resistance remained as the movement for direct wider share ownership failed to gain broad support.[108] Ultimately, it took the growth of pension funds and other investment vehicles to give average workers broader exposure to investing in securities in general and the equity markets in particular.[109]

Even when the City endorsed worker share ownership, the response was often one of distrust, and any such concession from the financial community was interpreted as a manifestation of capitalists co-opting the principles of industrial democracy, as illustrated by Tony Benn, Secretary of State for Industry, when describing a dinner party in 1974 with men from the City (and their wives) following the February general election:

> They were talking about workers' participation and involvement and getting workers to buy shares, and all that Tory crap. The guys were mainly hereditary bankers who sent their kids away to public school and they had no fight, never been through the fire; whereas up-and-coming trade union leaders and stewards are very formidable, and in the end they will win.[110]

Benn exemplifies the scepticism expressed by leftist critics of the establishment of any attempts by the City to implicate workers in the reinforcement of the existing capitalist system. His erroneous prediction about the victory of the

[105] Whiting (2004) 102; Rutterford and Sotiropoulos (2017) 38. See also ch 3, section II.A of this volume on small shareholders.

[106] Kellett (1962) 21.

[107] Aldington (1959) 13.

[108] Edwards (2016) 112.

[109] Whiting (2004) 96; Edwards (2016) 104.

[110] Kynaston (2001) 496; Benn (1989) 145. See also Jackson (2005) 432 on equity investment being used to make workers 'Tory-minded'.

trade unions over the privileged bankers of the City was a reflection of the political mood in 1974, a sentiment that had eroded by the end of the decade.[111]

Despite initial reluctance, by the end of the 1970s, worker shareholding was generally accepted by the City and its industrialist clients, and was seen by most as a way to expand capitalist values to workers and not as a threat to the existing system and the principles of shareholder primacy.[112] In 1979, Nicholas Goodison, chairman of the LSE, declared himself to be a supporter of 'people's capitalism' and that he was 'hopeful that the widening of the circle of share ownership to a greater number of employees could do much to counter the "anti-business ethos" that he feels has surrounded UK industry since the last century'.[113] The impression in the City that there was an anti-business ethos amongst workers would change with the new decade and the Conservative government, although the support of the concept of worker shareholders persisted.[114] Margaret Thatcher, then leader of the Conservative Party and an ally of the City, was on record as a supporter of worker shareholders, stating in the House of Commons that: 'It is our wish that people who work in industry, whether public or private, should make more strides in being real capital owners themselves.'[115]

IV. IMPEDIMENTS TO WIDESPREAD WORKER SHAREHOLDING

A. The Labour Party's Ambiguous Position on Worker Shareholding

The Labour Party identified share ownership as a contributor to inequality, although it did not necessarily embrace the idea of expanding share ownership amongst workers as a way to address it, stating in its 1957 policy statement *Industry and Society*:

> It is sometimes urged by those who are increasingly conscious of the facts of ownership that industrial property ownership should be 'democratised' – principally through profit-sharing schemes under which employees can acquire shares in the companies for which they work. Certainly, in recent years there has been much talk and even some action to this end. But although profit-sharing schemes may serve certain purposes – e.g. promoting good industrial relationships and providing work incentives – and although they may in fact increase the number of shareholders their effect on the distribution of shareholding is negligible.[116]

Labour presented the following analysis:

> If the distribution of share ownership in the UK is similar to that in the USA, then something like 50 per cent to 60 per cent of total capital gains will accrue to the

[111] Middlemas (1991) 334.
[112] Elliott (1984) 186.
[113] Fisher (1979) 31.
[114] Edwards (2016) 100.
[115] Fisher (1979) 31.
[116] Labour Party (1957) 32.

> wealthiest 5 per cent of shareholders. Since shareholders themselves account for no more than 6 per cent of the adult population, roughly 0.3 per cent of the population will enjoy at least 50 per cent of the capital gains.[117]

This was an amount that was estimated by the Minority Report of the Royal Commission on Taxation of Income and Profits at approximately £650 million a year.[118] Although increasing the share ownership by workers appeared to be an effective way to address inequalities, it would need to occur at outstanding rates to have impact, whereas the nationalisation of whole industries, for example, had immediate and profound effects on British industry and society.[119]

Worker shareholding was not a core element to Labour's programme for industrial democracy, which focused on board representation and participation in the management of companies, as explained in the 1967 working party report *Industrial Democracy*:

> [W]e are not enthusiastic about schemes for co-ownership or co-partnership in individual firms and plants. We are not against the idea of workers owning shares in the firms in which they work, but can see no future for any scheme of industrial democracy that does not start from the worker *as a worker*, within a framework of a representation that extends upwards from the workplace.[120]

This approach points to the need for a form of representation that provides real control and input into managerial decision-making and addresses the potential misalignment of interests between workers and shareholders, with the ultimate priority being the needs of labour as above those of any shareholder, including a worker shareholder.[121] It also suggests Labour's discomfort with the inherently capitalist nature of share ownership that, instead of reforming a system that has taken advantage of labour, absorbs the worker into the management-controlled status quo.[122]

Labour's *Industrial Democracy* explains the Party's position:

> [W]e have been witnessing a considerable concentration of economic power within the private sector of our economy, and unless the new pattern of wider social accountability, and tripartite (community, industrialists, trade unions) participation in decision making, can offer a significant re-distribution of economic power, there is a further danger to our democracy from concentrated and non-responsible economic power.[123]

[117] Labour Party (1957) 34.

[118] Labour Party (1957) 34 (£650 million in 1957 is worth approximately £20 billion in 2023; see www.officialdata.org/UK-inflation).

[119] Clift, Gamble and Harris (2000) 71. Under Thatcher, share ownership schemes were part of a wide-ranging programme to extend the private property ownership (Francis (2012) 275), which also corresponded with a deterioration of worker rights and protections and increased inequalities (Gatti and Ondersma (2020) 47; Gatti and Ondersma (2021) 12).

[120] Labour Party (1967) 33.

[121] Clift, Gamble and Harris (2000) 71.

[122] Gumbrell-McCormick and Hyman (2019) 93; Ramsay (1977) 485; Whiting (2004) 100; Poole (1982) 193.

[123] Labour Party (1967) 13.

Equity ownership remained a symbol of wealth inequality and a central focus of Labour's policies to elevate the interests of workers; the 'new pattern of wider social accountability' described in 1967 still resonates, underlining the constancy of both the rhetoric and the stubbornness of the entrenched system.[124] Although Labour's policy paper advanced the argument that share ownership by workers is not an effective method to redistribute wealth, the problems inherent in the exclusivity of the distribution of wealth from equity shareholding in private companies remained part of their programme for increasing equality and a foundational issue to be addressed with their policies for industrial democracy.[125]

B. Trade Union Resistance to Worker Share Ownership

The trade unions resisted the idea of workers owning shares, which they viewed suspiciously as potentially drawing workers away from the interests of the unions and towards the side of capital, exemplified by Clegg's description of profit-sharing schemes in the 1951 Fabian Society study *Industrial Democracy and Nationalization*, as 'anti-trade union devices of industrial paternalism'.[126] The trade union's antagonism to worker shareholding as a means of industrial democracy resulted in employee ownerships schemes not usually being found in the more unionised companies as employers tried to avoid clashing with the unions on this issue.[127] Although the workers themselves were not typically against ownership schemes, the unionists opposing extending share ownership saw it was a way for capitalists to embroil workers in the existing system and to undermine the power of the unions as their rightful representatives.[128]

Despite the wariness about share ownership, it was noted in an Acton Society Trust survey for the WSOC from 1964/1965, which questioned 536 male factory workers at six major British manufacturing companies, that trade union members were slightly more likely to support share ownership than non-members (46 per cent versus 45 per cent), whereas trade union officials were 53 per cent in favour, although the survey authors explained that this different in attitudes between officials and regular union members may be partly attributed to the former being more articulate than the latter (that is, that they are better able to express their views) rather than an indication of real ideological differences.[129] In answering the same survey question, trade union officials were also more likely to express a view against shareholding (28 per cent) as compared to regular members (3 per cent) and non-members (15 per cent), and were less likely to answer 'don't know' (17 per cent), as compared to regular members (30 per cent) and non-members (45 per cent), suggesting, perhaps unsurprisingly, that the

[124] Labour Party (1967) 13.
[125] Labour Party (1957) 34; Whiting (2004) 100.
[126] Clegg (1951) 8; Ackers (2007) 86.
[127] Elliott (1984) 187.
[128] Francis (2012) 291; Gumbrell-McCormick and Hyman (2019) 93.
[129] Naylor (1968) 51.

union officials had more developed views on share ownership.[130] Although in most cases, trade unions in the 1960s were dismissive of employee shareholder schemes, the positive attitudes to share ownership as expressed by individual union officials surveyed may foreshadow the unions' eventual shift in position towards an approach to industrial democracy that was more integrated into the existing system, although with the emphasis more on worker directors and less on worker shareholders.[131]

The TUC policy statement from 1974 addressed the topic of shareholding, in which it acknowledged shareholders' ultimate right as the owners of capital to withdraw that capital, and elucidated its objections to company-based schemes of co-ownership and profit-sharing on the following grounds: (i) such schemes do not provide any real control over managerial decisions; (ii) there is no advantage to workpeople tying up their savings in the firm that employs them since this doubles the insecurity; and (iii) they do little or nothing to reduce the degree of inequality of wealth and they do not include industry's public sector.[132] Furthermore, the trade unions were protective of their position as the sole agents of workers, requiring that boards deal only with them as the representatives of labour, which could be threatened by worker share ownership.[133] By the mid-1970s, the historical resistance of trade unions to worker shareholding was softening, particularly in relation to collective funds rather than individual ownership, and by ensuring that any worker share ownership schemes were under union control.[134] With the change in approach, the question posed by the WSOC persisted, 'whether or not industrial democracy provides a potential for unions to switch from their present negative and reactive role to one of positive and constructive responsibility in which they put aside some of their traditional tactics'.[135]

V. WORKERS' ATTITUDES TO SAVINGS AND EQUITY OWNERSHIP

There were gradual changes in post-war working-class attitudes to savings and the accumulation of capital, as described in the sociologist and economist Ferdynand Zweig's 1961 study of British workers' developing opinions:

> The traditionally-minded workman was known for his contempt for money, which went very well with his contempt for the moneyed class. This contempt is largely disappearing. The worker to-day doesn't want to waste his money. His pattern of

[130] Naylor (1968) 51.

[131] Naylor (1968) 107; Elliott (1984) 66. In 1974 the TUC declared that: 'Company-based schemes of co-ownership and profit-sharing are discredited' (Trades Union Congress (1974) 26). See also Elliott (1984) 66, 184; and ch 6 of this volume on worker directors.

[132] Trades Union Congress (1974) 36.

[133] Poole (1982) 187. See also ch 6, section I.E of this volume on the attempts by trade unions to control worker representation on boards.

[134] Elliott (1984) 188.

[135] Naylor (1968) 51, 75.

> consumption turns to more durable good; he spends his money more wisely and more economically ... in this way a large section of the working-class population becomes a property-owning class. For the time being it is mostly property for the worker's own consumption – a house, a car, TV, a washing machine, refrigerator, post-office savings, savings bonds, insurance rights – but the overspill to capital assets is already on its way. I came across workers with considerable nest-eggs up to £3,000, well invested. In this way a new type of a bourgeois worker appears on the stage.[136]

Property-owning democracy was spreading and the saving patterns of workers were changing, although not yet including material investments in equity shares, whether directly or indirectly.[137]

Despite the support for worker shareholding and the perceived shifts in attitudes towards saving, the workers themselves did not embrace direct share ownership in the way hoped for by those who saw worker shareholders as a positive for British industry, as well as by worker representatives and advocates.[138] In the 1964/1965 Acton Society survey for the WSOC, 40 per cent of workers did not think that the working class should become shareholders, 42 per cent felt that the working class would not buy shares themselves (58 per cent gave the reason as having no surplus money), 65 per cent thought worker shareholding would have no effect on industrial relations, although only 17 per cent of respondents thought share ownership would have no effect on the company, while a full 85 per cent of those surveyed did not know any shareholders.[139] Even the few workers surveyed who owned shares did not necessarily support the idea of working-class share ownership, most providing the reason that the working man's savings should not be exposed to the risks of investing.[140]

For politicians and other advocates on both the right and left, the principles of industrial democracy were based on ideological positions, whereas for most of the workers there seemed to be little dogma involved in their decisions to own, or not to own, shares; most of the workers surveyed had never even thought of investing in equity shares.[141] The Acton Society survey also asked workers about their political affiliations, with support for share ownership differing depending on how they identified politically. The party breakdown of workers in favour of shareholding was: 61 per cent Conservative, 43 per cent Labour, 43 per cent Liberal and 35 per cent with no party preference; the percentage of workers against shareholding was: 20 per cent Conservative, 17 per cent Labour, 21 per cent Liberal and 17 per cent with no preference.[142] Interestingly, more Conservatives and Liberals opposed share ownership than Labour supporters,

[136] Zweig (1961) 206.
[137] Davies (2019) 95; Whiting (2004) 105.
[138] Copeman; Rumble (1972) 33; Naylor (1968) Pt One.
[139] Naylor (1968) Pt One. See also section IV.B above on trade union member responses to the survey.
[140] Naylor (1968) 48; Whiting (2004) 106.
[141] Naylor (1968) xvii.
[142] Naylor (1968) 52.

for which there are a multitude of explanations, ranging from ideological influences to whether there was a basic understanding of the concept of equity ownership. As one Liberal supporter surveyed commented: 'Encouraging everybody to be a "little capitalist" is rather alarming.'[143]

There were no suggestions offered by the survey participants to help increase worker share ownership, the majority believing that 'they did not see any possibility of working-class people ever being interested in shares'.[144] Writing in 1972 about the Acton Society survey, George Copeman commented that:

> My clear impression from these studies has been that the average employee in Britain was not interested in share ownership. He was not against it or for it, he just had more urgent things to do with his money. But the studies also showed that further up the ladder of industrial responsibility, there was much greater interest in share ownership.[145]

Whereas workers might not be embracing share ownership in a way hoped for by the backers of industrial democracy, employees who were higher up the hierarchy – that is, supervisors, managers and executives – were taking advantage of the growing opportunities to buy equities.[146] Accordingly, the more general movement for shareholder democracy – that is, broadening the shareholder base to include more skilled employees and managers – was more successful than the more targeted industrial democracy efforts focused on equity ownership by manual and clerical workers.[147] It is only after the end of the post-war era, with the opportunities created by the widespread share offerings of the Thatcher-era privatisations, that there was a widening of working-class interest in share ownership.[148]

A. Workers as a Subset of Ordinary Shareholders

Copeman's 1958 research provides statistics that show the low number of individuals in Britain who owned shares, and how few within that group were workers, reporting that:

> There are no direct figures of the number of ordinary shareholders, but only 5 ½ % of all income units, or 1 ¼ million out of a total of 22 million, own negotiable securities of any kind (National Survey of Personal Incomes and Savings, 1952). This includes those who own bonds issued by governments, municipalities and public boards, as well as those owning company shares.[149]

143 Naylor (1968) 52.
144 Naylor (1968) 48; Whiting (2004) 105.
145 Copeman and Rumble (1972) 33; Whiting (2004) 105.
146 Copeman and Rumble (1972) 38.
147 Copeman and Rumble (1972) 38.
148 Rutterford and Sotiropoulos (2017) 34; Francis (2012) 290. See also Grout (1987a) 63 on the high level of participation by employees in the privatisation share offerings.
149 Copeman (1958) 33.

Copeman's research also gives a breakdown of these security holders, of whom approximately half own less than £500 worth, only 1 per cent are unskilled manual workers and 7 per cent skilled manual workers; furthermore, he stipulates that it is rare for small securities holders to own company shares, concluding that 'the number of actual shareholders may be considerably less than 1¼ million'.[150] This research did not support the popular preconception, encouraged by the political left, that equity shareholders were rich capitalists; a breakdown of security holders shows 42 per cent have incomes under £400 per annum, 25 per cent with incomes between £400 and £999, 22 per cent between £1,000 and £1,999, and only 11 per cent with incomes above £2,000, although even amongst the lowest band there would be very few unskilled and skilled manual workers.[151]

Whether or not a worker believed that he or she should own shares was not, however, the same question as whether he or she could participate in equity ownership, and in post-war Britain, even when employees did buy shares, most could only afford to invest small amounts of capital in the companies where they worked, which would not lead to the accumulation of stakes large enough to give them any real influence on management decisions.[152] Compared to the positions held by the growing institutional investors, that of the typical individual small shareholder was negligible; this, of course, accepts the premise that any dispersed shareholders, whether small individuals or institutions, could influence managerial decisions.[153] Much like in the political realm, where the everyman or everywoman feels that his or her one vote is inconsequential and his or her ability to effect change is non-existent in the face of greater political forces, so the worker shareholder, like other small shareholders, felt without influence or control amongst many fragmented owners.[154]

As outlined by Copeman when contrasting the worker shareholders with business owners:

> [T]he employee who is allowed, in companies such as ICI, to participate in the future prosperity of the business through an issue of shares, does not expect to control the business. He is only one of a large number of employees who receive shares, and each of their holdings is small. None can give himself security in his position of employment by controlling the majority of shares.[155]

[150] Copeman (1958) 33 (£500 in 1958 is worth approximately £14,946 in 2023; see www.officialdata.org/UK-inflation). In 1958, the UK population was approximately 51.7 million (see www.ons.gov.uk/peoplepopulationandcommunity/populationandmigration/populationestimates/adhocs/004356ukpopulationestimates1851to2014).

[151] Copeman (1958) 34. See also ch 3, section I.B of this volume.

[152] Naylor (1968) 10ff. A detailed breakdown of savings is given for the workers surveyed, with only 23 per cent saying that they were 'saving for security or retirement' and that this group had the highest amount of savings; in total, 10 per cent of those surveyed were both long-term savers and had over £500 saved (Naylor (1968) 77). Shares (3 per cent) and government bonds (3 per cent) were the least popular forms of savings amongst those surveyed (Naylor (1968) 3).

[153] Elliott (1984) 184.

[154] Copeman (1958) 29.

[155] Copeman (1958) 84. Elliott (1984) 185 gives the example of how ICI's scheme operates, which was the best known of the existing schemes. Copeman and Rumble (1972) 32 also discuss the ICI

A much larger stake than those typically held by a worker shareholder was needed to have the influential and powers of ownership; the expectation that the typical worker shareholder would feel that his or her interests were aligned with management, which in turn might improve labour relations and/or the conditions of the workers, a main argument in favour of industrial democracy, was improbable.[156] It did, however, make a compelling story for those looking for project inclusivity and reflect modernising values on the British capitalist system.[157] Even with millions of workers owning shares in companies indirectly through their pension schemes, these represented tiny individual holdings and 'little more than an impersonal claim on the revenues generated by industry and commerce, and it entails few responsibilities or obligations – and virtually no power'.[158] Furthermore, the institutions investing on behalf of the worker beneficiaries were only partially representative, as insurance funds, pension funds and other indirect investment vehicles might correspond to a certain concept of employee interests, which was by its nature incomplete and not fully representative, as well as not being transparent.[159]

The belief that workers would materially increase their income through equity investments was, in most cases, exaggerated, although there were industrial democracy advocates who pointed sophistically to individual, unrepresentative, examples where a low-wage worker had, over time, through thrift and self-denial, accumulated a meaningful portfolio of investments.[160] The calls for workers to become shareholders encouraged a small number of blue-collar employees with savings to take small direct equity stakes in the companies for which they worked, blurring the class lines between labourer and capital provider, a phenomenon that accelerated with indirect investing by the British workforce through different investment vehicles.[161] Despite the exceptions, however, large numbers of workers directly buying shares in the companies for which they worked did not materialise and there was a general lack of enthusiasm for share ownership by the working men and women at whom industrial democracy was aimed.[162]

Although the various investment plans and schemes designed to increase worker participation in direct share ownership received considerable attention, they failed to gain traction, and because of a:

> [F]undamental lack of desire on the part of most employees to become shareholders, the pioneers of employee shareholding schemes have generally gone to great lengths to provide a special incentive for employee saving and investment – an incentive that is not normally given to outside investors in company shares.[163]

scheme, which 'decided that their employees would be shareholders in their own right, with no strings attached. This was a milestone of progress'.

[156] Regan (1962a) 6.
[157] Edwards (2016) 107.
[158] Plender (1982) 198.
[159] Davies (1994) 268.
[160] Regan (1962b) 8.
[161] Zweig (1961) 206; Naylor (1968); Plender (1982) 31.
[162] Whiting (2004) 109.
[163] Copeman (1958) 172; see also Whiting (2004) 102ff.

Even with these plans that offered preferential treatment and attractive incentives, widespread enrolment did not occur, and even when workers did participate, this did not normally lead to any further direct equity ownership. The Acton Society Trust survey from 1964/1965 concluded that although there was a relatively positive response to profit-sharing schemes in the companies that it studied, there was no clear evidence that employees becoming worker shareholders through schemes were more disposed to buy shares outside the schemes.[164] Employee ownership programmes were not the industrial democracy gateway to broader shareholding amongst workers and the ambitions of the post-war supporters of industrial democracy for workers shareholders were only realised, to a degree, through the increased participation in pension funds and other investment vehicles, even if not in the way imagined and certainly without the desired governance oversight that a critical mass of property-owning individual shareholders, including workers, was expected to contribute.[165]

VI. WORKER UPTAKE

The policy debates on the initiatives for industrial democracy examined the pros and cons of workers holding shares in their employer companies without necessarily considering whether workers were able, or willing, to divert wages to equity investments, as observed by the economist Derek Matthews in his study of profit-sharing:

> [M]ost workers were not sufficiently well off to afford to save, especially in the form of shares. Indeed, holding savings in the shares of one company, particularly one's employer, is simply an unwise speculation. Therefore, for good reason, given the choice, workers would take a cash bonus, but given shares these would be sold immediately. If this was forbidden the shares were looked upon as 'dead money'.[166]

Although it is unlikely that the pros and cons of diversification were the main drivers of workers' decisions on whether to invest in their company's shares, the need for cash to meet daily needs was undoubtedly a salient consideration. Some schemes directly acknowledged the preference, often based on short-term needs, of many workers for cash distributions over company shares; for the average post-war British worker, the need for cash came before an interest in equity and the accompanying ownership rights.[167] Although there was an ideological

[164] Naylor (1968) 73. In addition to the survey of male workers, a sample of women (both married and unmarried) was also interviewed for the survey (Naylor (1968) 92ff).

[165] Edwards (2016) 104.

[166] Matthews (1989) 461.

[167] Copeman (1958) 85. Copeman discusses the disadvantages of cash-based profit-sharing schemes, ie, that they do not adequately address the problem of fair distribution because much of the real profits do not appear in the profit and loss account, but are spent on growing the business, and asset growth is not all captured in the balance sheet, meaning that profits for cash distribution do not represent growth in the way that the distribution of company shares does (at 90).

appeal of turning workers into shareholders, in most cases, workers benefited more from an increase in wages than from any rise in dividend payments or capital appreciation earned through shares from an employee-ownership scheme.[168] For workers, most of whom had limited engagement with the financial markets, the reasons to take advantage of share-owning schemes were too remote and/or abstract to inspire broad participation.[169] There appeared to be a disconnect between the policy-makers and the working-class constituents who they claimed to serve: does the average labourer concern himself or herself with the tax implications of equity investing when he or she is preoccupied with meeting his or her daily sustenance needs?

The economic situation of most workers meant that they were unable to become investors outside of company shareholder schemes, and those who did save typically invested not in equities, but in National Savings (National Savings Certificates, Post Office and Trustee Bank Accounts, Premium Bonds and Defence Bonds) and building societies, in gilt-edged securities and in contractual savings such as mortgages, life insurance and pension policies.[170] The structural impediments to individual investing were high hurdles to widespread worker shareholding outside of schemes, as expressed in 1959 in the Conservative Political Centre pamphlet *Everyman a Capitalist*:

> [I]t is not the role of Government to single out industrial shares and urge people to invest in equities: rather it is their duty to secure conditions in which total savings through whatever medium match the requirements of our economy and to ensure that facilities exist whereby people of all income groups and of all occupations may invest their savings as they choose … It therefore seems to us that the Government can fairly be asked to remove the disadvantages in the way of investment in industry by the small saver, disadvantages suffered in comparison to other means of saving which are open to him.[171]

Despite the motivations of the politicians seeking to broaden and democratise the shareholder base to include the working classes, it was often not in the financial best interests of these workers to use whatever disposable income that they might have to invest in company shares, unless it was on favourable terms.[172]

At the time of the Acton Society survey in the 1960s, there were still major obstacles to having grassroots support for this aspect of industrial democracy, and whereas share ownership was promoted by politicians and policy-makers from all parties, it was removed from the daily existence of factory workers and

[168] 'Vote for Reform' (1966) 1170. According to the Conservative Trade Unionist pamphlet *Participation: A New Way Ahead*: 'Analysis has shown that if no profits were distributed to shareholders, and dividends given instead to employees, the average pay increase would be 6%. Of course, the result of such an action is that investors would withdraw and capital would dry up' (Conservative Trade Unionists (1970) 13).

[169] Naylor (1968) 44.

[170] Copeman (1958) 41; Matthews (1989) 461.

[171] Aldington (1959) 10.

[172] Naylor (1968) xx.

was not embraced broadly by the workers themselves. As described in the 1967 joint comments by the Right Honourable Lord Shawcross and the MP Maurice Macmillan of the WSOC, 'there is no antagonism to equity investment as such amongst the workers in industry: it is simply that they do not appreciate the practical possibility of it for themselves'.[173] Most workers felt detached from management and had no real attachment to the companies for which they worked, although some saw share ownership as a possible means to improve this situation, as expressed in a letter to the editor of the *Financial Times* written in 1962:

> Speaking as an ordinary working man, I cannot help feeling that when one reads the daily newspapers about the profits that are being made by big combines in various industries and institutions, one is left with the feeling that one should be receiving a much larger share of those profits in one's wage packet for the effort one puts into production to justify those profits. Putting it mildly, he feels he is not getting a fair crack of the whip. Speaking as an individual, a remedy could be in the form of the average worker taking a much larger part in in share ownership alongside the big insurance companies and city institutions, letting him feel that his savings count for something.[174]

Ultimately, however, despite attempts by those encouraging industrial democracy as a means by which to alter the composition of the shareholder body, both to align worker incentives with those of industry and to increase worker participation in company profits, a systemic shift resulting in worker shareholders becoming direct owners of British industry on a meaningful scale did not happen, keeping most workers in the role of stakeholders, without ownership rights, whose interests, under existing company law, remained subordinate to those of the equity shareholders.[175]

As argued in the 1977 Hobart Paper *Can Workers Manage?*:

> It is sometimes suggested that weakness of labour management could be resolved by making workers owners of the capital. This solution might deal with the problem of responsibility, but it would hardly alter the low propensity to save. Concentration of ownership in a much smaller number of hands would follow in due course, as careful owners become separated from careless owners.[176]

The worker shareholder remained relatively rare, and its promise as a tool for reform unfulfilled. The support for wider share ownership by workers was often by organisations, like the WSOC, whose interests were aligned with the existing system, preserving the status quo under the cover of the rhetoric of change.[177]

[173] Naylor (1968) xiv; Whiting (2004) 105.

[174] Regan (1962a) 6.

[175] Acton Society Trust (1959) 6. There were various policies to encourage wider share ownership, although most were not specifically targeted at workers, and individual direct shareholding continues to decline as a percentage of the overall shareholder body. It would take until the denationalisations of the 1980s to see a reverse in this trend and an increase in direct small shareholders; see Grout (1987a) 59.

[176] Chiplin, Coyne and Sirc (1977) 80.

[177] Francis (2012) 280.

Meanwhile, existing shareholders benefited from the change in the political narrative that led to the impression of a more representative shareholder base, even though a new age of empowered and informed workers directly owning shares did not occur, but was replaced instead by the continued growth of institutional investing and the spread of indirect share ownership.[178]

A. British Workers and the Risks of Investing

The unknown risks and/or benefits of share ownership that lay sometime in the future were not relevant for most workers with little or no savings and who relied on their wages to meet immediate and short-term needs, for which they often still fell short.[179] The post-war individual investors of modest means often avoided equities, and as a Bow Group report from 1973 argued, typical workers 'will not consider buying investments whose value fluctuates on the market until they have a greater buffer of liquid savings than a majority of employees can hope to achieve', and if this fundamental barrier to turning workers into equity shareholders on a broad scale was to be addressed, legislative action was needed.[180] Not only were workers mostly unable to invest directly in equities, the participation schemes designed to encourage share ownership were considered by some critics as still being too risky for the average worker, who could suffer considerable losses in the event of his or her company failing.[181] Labour's *Industry and Society* argued against workers having 'skin in the game' through equity investments in the companies where they worked, presenting the downside of worker share ownership:

> The shares of any one firm are subject to short-term fluctuations in value … [T]o a worker who as few other resources and who may need to sell his shares at short notice, fluctuations and the risk of loss are crucial. Moreover, there is a definite danger to the employee-shareholder that a fall in the value of his capital will coincide with a reduction in his earnings or even a loss of employment.[182]

Worker shareholder schemes went against the risk-mitigating investment strategy of diversification, with workers having their wages and their savings tied to the same company and, as a result, exposed to the same concentrated risks:

> [T]here are disadvantages which can be serious – especially where employees in a failing company find their savings depreciating in value about as fast as if they had been left in fixed-interest stocks over the past decade. It can be even worse where a man's whole savings are locked up in such a company.[183]

[178] Davies (2019) 82; Edwards (2016) 101.
[179] Whiting (2004) 106.
[180] Goss (1973) 19.
[181] Moore (2013) 77.
[182] Labour Party (1957) 33.
[183] Kellett (1962) 26; Grout (1987a) 64; Grout (1987b) 16.

Unlike with unit trusts, which supported diversification, worker shareholder schemes concentrated workers' interests in their employer companies.[184] The arguments that worker share ownership was too risky, however, were refuted by the companies that supported the plans, which asserted that profit-sharing schemes were incentives that provided workers with *extra* cash and did not put their core earnings at risk.[185]

The limited financial literacy of most British workers would have further increased their vulnerability to the risks of the equity markets.[186] The promoters of wider share ownership amongst workers needed to contend with the widespread belief that working-class men and women were 'not capable of understanding the mechanics of investment on the Stock Exchange as it operates today'.[187] In addition to the financial and knowledge barriers that kept British workers from investing in shares, there was the overhang of a class system that reinforced the idea that investing was not for the working class, a view often expressed by the workers themselves, which could be addressed through '[t]he spread of information, the removal of class prejudice and the provision of practical assistance to make investment easy to understand and to undertake – these are the essential starting points for wider share ownership'.[188] This was noted by the Conservative Political Centre in its pamphlet advocating for increased equity investing by 'wage earners and other small investors', exemplified by an individual who can:

> [P]articularly ill afford to lose any part of his savings. We have therefore attached considerable importance to minimising the risk of loss. The small investor must be enabled to enjoy the advantages of skilled advice and spread the risk which are open to the large investor, and which he considers essential.[189]

The encouragement of workers to invest in equities was not limited to shareholder schemes and direct ownership, and was also directed at unit trusts and other vehicles, which were less risky than the direct investments that exposed them to the profits and losses of the companies where they worked.[190]

B. Investment Incentives

In an attempt to address the reluctance of workers to participate in equity ownership, many of the employee shareholder plans in Britain were designed

[184] Whiting (2004) 107.
[185] Elliott (1984) 184.
[186] See ch 3, section II.A of this volume on individual shareholders (not limited to worker shareholders).
[187] Acton Society Trust (1959) 84.
[188] Naylor (1968) xix.
[189] Aldington (1959) 12.
[190] Beck (1962) 12.

as profit-sharing and co-partnering schemes, often alongside share-purchase schemes, using different models to try to entice workers into becoming shareholders or, at the very least, to increase their knowledge and understanding of investing with the goal of future equity ownership.[191] Different scheme structures were proposed, including those that protected against any losses to worker shareholders, but without the support of the government and targeted legislation, share ownership as a means for expanding industrial democracy (and corporate democracy) would not be widely adopted by the British workforce.[192] Employee schemes faced the headwinds of unfavourable legislation that pushed investment capital towards indirect investment through the vehicles offered by the financial firms. This dynamic of frustration is described by the historian Amy Edwards:

> [T]he [Wider Share Ownership] Council spent much of the 1960s and early 1970s in the 'doldrums'. It struggled to make any concrete progress in advancing greater tax concessions for investment practices or employee share schemes. If anything, moves towards wider share ownership suffered legislative set-backs, including the extension of capital gains tax to employee share option schemes by Heath's Conservative Government.[193]

Suspicion of the motives of company management that introduced worker shareholder schemes, although not necessarily unjustified, was a further impediment to their success and widespread adoption, as was explained by GP Waddington, Director of G Waddington & Son Ltd, in 1957:

> The greatest difficulty – and sometimes this seems an insuperable one – lies in the prejudice of employee to employer, the suspicion ingrained in man to master which has endured over the centuries, and which can never be wholly dissipated. The result of this is an almost heart-breaking difficulty in 'getting over' to the employee the fact that C-Partnership and employee shareholding exist for his benefit. His instinctive reaction is – 'What's the boss getting out of this?'; the necessarily somewhat complex explanations of the schemes, either verbally or by written notices – even at Meetings where questions are invited, and answered carefully in simple language – often leave this question unanswered in the minds of some workers.[194]

In the 1964/1965 Acton Society Trust survey, employees at one of the six companies being studied ('Riverside') responded to a question on what they thought was the aim of having an employee shareholder scheme, with 31 per cent answering that they believed it was used as an incentive to keep labour, 25 per cent to get workers to take greater interest in their work, 22 per cent for tax avoidance or to keep money in the company, 15 per cent for political motives and 7 per cent

[191] Naylor (1968) xix; for detailed results on employee shareholder schemes for the companies interviewed for the survey, see 53ff.
[192] Copeman and Rumble (1972); Edwards (2016) 109. See also ch 3, section IV.C of this volume.
[193] Edwards (2016) 109; Acton Society Trust (1959) 8. See also Copeman (1975) 140ff on unfavourable tax treatment.
[194] Copeman (1958) 199.

because the company was progressive.[195] In addition, the surveyed workers had divergent views on whether share ownership impacted industrial relations, with some stating that whether or not they owned shares had no bearing on how their supervisors and managers treated them, whereas others saw the schemes as primarily politically motivated – that is, as a way for company management to appear to address the concerns of labour and to avoid nationalisations rather than genuine efforts to elevate workers.[196] The views expressed by these surveyed British workers do not unambiguously reflect the theories supporting worker share ownership as a means to influence industrial relations or to better align the interest of labour and capital, demonstrating a rupture between the perceptions of policy-makers and law-makers, and of the reality of the working-class population whose interests they claimed to represent.[197] The willingness of boards to offer shareholder schemes was in itself grounds for suspicion by those opposed to the capitalist state; company directors, for their part, were generally not opposed to these schemes, viewing them as a way by which to align the incentives of the workforce with those of their companies.

Ultimately, however, if governments wanted to encourage greater direct equity investments in British industry by its workers, good intentions and suggestive nudges were not enough, and laws and regulations were needed; like the tax relief and incentive schemes aimed at top executives that were addressed in the 1971 budget and the Finance Act of 1972, worker shareholder schemes also needed to be legislated if they were to become effective policy and not just rhetorical expressions of the principles of industrial democracy.[198] Unlike the senior executives, directors and founders of publicly listed companies, who regularly invested in the shares of the companies for which they worked and for whom there existed incentives to do so, the typical post-war labourer would not have expected to invest in his or her company and would have given the idea little (or no) thought were he or she not prompted by targeted schemes and by the efforts of activists working for the cause of industrial democracy.[199]

Profit-sharing schemes and share-ownership plans gradually became part of worker expectations from their employers, although, unlike for senior management and in highly competitive and skilled industries, in most cases these benefits were not meaningful sources of wealth or influence for the typical worker.[200]

[195] Naylor (1968) 60.

[196] Naylor (1968) 60, 65, 108.

[197] Whiting (2004) 98.

[198] Sampson (1971) 596; Copeman (1975) 171.

[199] For a more detailed contemporaneous analysis of incentive schemes for executives conducted in the early 1970s, see Copeman and Rumble (1972). In the UK in 1977, it was reported that there were 1,000 share-ownership programmes for top executives, whereas there were barely 100 schemes for workers, most of which only involved around 10 per cent of employees (Elliott (1984) 185).

[200] For a description of the different types of employee shareholding schemes, in this case divided into nine types, see Copeman (1958) 95ff. See also Acton Society Trust (1959) 55ff for a summary and survey of five shareholding schemes; and Copeman and Rumble (1972) for a discussion of more than 150 American and British schemes and programmes.

Workers, the vast majority of whom had no experience as investors, needed to be given strong government-backed incentives to take up the equity options being offered to them as part of the wider efforts to increase saving rates whilst also expanding the shareholder base – for example, with the introduction of preferential tax treatments.[201] It was only in 1978 that Labour's Finance Act passed, creating financial incentives for companies to introduce profit-sharing schemes with tax advantages for participating employees.[202]

C. Indirect Worker Share Ownership

The post-war transformation of the shareholder base resulted in individual shareholders, of which worker shareholders were included, indisputably losing ground to the financial institutions and their expanding influence on the equity markets. The schemes designed to increase worker share ownership did not succeed in countering this trend; instead, individual investors became the indirect beneficial owners of company shares through the investment products managed by the professional managers of financial institutions.[203] Share ownership schemes were starting to become a normal benefit of employment, but it was through life insurance policies and other investment vehicles that billions of pounds worth of investment capital came under the control of institutions – that is, the insurance companies, pension funds, investment trusts and unit trusts.[204] The profit-sharing schemes and attempts at creating more inclusivity by turning workers into direct owners of shares never reached the scale needed to provide workers with real influence, whereas the growth of indirect ownership created increasingly powerful institutions that could, when the will existed, influence management decisions, although not necessarily always in alignment with how the individual beneficial owners would act if they had a direct say.[205]

The post-war financial institutions, meanwhile, were not seeking hands-on control of British industries; they were deliberately slow in increasing their exposure to equities, reluctant to take more than 1–2 per cent in a single company, as well as limiting themselves to holding stakes that were small enough to be liquid, thereby shying away from coming close to anything like financial control.[206] The institutions that managed the investments of British workers did not seek to become vehicles for promoting the ideals of industrial democracy, sticking to their duties as (mostly passive) stewards of the invested capital.[207]

201 Blanden (1973) 17.
202 Finance Act 1978, c 42, pt III, ch III. See also Grout (1987a) 62 for the mechanics of the Act's treatment of profit-sharing schemes.
203 Plender (1982) 13ff; Edwards (2016) 109. See also ch 3, section II.B of this volume on institutional investors.
204 Plender (1982) 14.
205 Davies (1994) 267.
206 Copeman (1958) 43.
207 See ch 3, section III.C of this volume on shareholder activism.

Indirect ownership of shares might have turned workers into equity holders, but it did not give them access to the decision-making powers of investee companies, or, as was observed by Copeman in 1958, 'the indirect share ownership that institutions give to their policy holders is too remote to have much effect in closing the psychological gap between capital and labour'.[208] For the proponents of equity shareholding as a means of increasing industrial democracy – that is, of workers having a say in the companies for which they work – one of the disadvantages of indirect investing through investment vehicles 'is that those who invest in industry in this way will not themselves have a vote in any industrial firm, or receive directly from the companies in which they are interested a balance sheet or report'.[209] For those who viewed wider share ownership as a means of engaging individuals in the capitalist system, the institutionalisation of shareholding decoupled the individual from the market, keeping the British public 'ignorant of the benefits of a free economy, and was thus left vulnerable to the false promise of socialism'.[210] Furthermore, as the benefits of worker shareholding, both direct and indirect, were questioned, workers were accessing another avenue of influence – that is, board representation. The 1977 Hobart Paper *Can Workers Manage?*, which was responding to the Bullock Committee, argues that, whereas it was acknowledged that dispersed small shareholders had very limited influence on company decisions, the involvement of trade unions as worker representatives meant that '[w]orkers' direct democracy, the possibility that they themselves could take all decisions, is on the contrary frequently promised as a feature of so-called "industrial democracy" and a remedy for "alienation"', which occurs when workers elect organisers to act on their behalf.[211]

[208] Copeman (1958) 43.
[209] Aldington (1959) 20.
[210] Davies (2019) 100.
[211] Chiplin, Coyne and Sirc (1977) 73. See also ch 6 of this volume on worker directors; and ch 7 on the Bullock Committee.

6

Industrial Democracy and the Worker Director

ALONGSIDE THE POST-WAR movement for worker shareholders, the democratisation of industry was also pursued through the representation of workers on company boards. Whereas Chapter 5 considered the worker as shareholder, this chapter examines how the movement for industrial democracy put pressure on the rights of existing shareholders through the demands for worker representation. Building on the understanding of industrial democracy as it addressed the worker shareholder, the other side of the shareholder coin is considered – that is, how equity shareholder rights and interests could be restricted or diminished through industrial democracy. The post-war movements for industrial democracy sought not only to turn workers into shareholders but also to introduce legal requirements for designated board seats for workers or their union representatives. Worker representation became a core demand of industrial democracy and remains part of the Labour Party platform that advocates for:

> [O]ne-third of boards to be reserved for elected worker-directors and give them more control over executive pay – because when those who depend on a company have a say in running it, that company generally does better and lasts longer.[1]

Whereas creating shareholders from workers was an exercise in expanding the shareholder base, the demands for worker representation on boards were encroachments on the rights of existing equity shareholders, whose interests could be in conflict with workers, and an attempt to rebalance the interest of key stakeholders.[2] By the end of the post-war period, the calls for British workers to have a direct say in managerial decisions became the primary manifestation of industrial democracy, evolving from below-board consultations with workers and collective bargaining to proposed legislative changes that gave employees a seat at the (board) table.[3] Although initially the pressure for representation was not necessarily aimed at the board level, which was a potentially divisive approach to worker participation, it became the main focus as the struggle amongst the various constituents crystallised in the mid-1970s.[4]

[1] Labour Party (2019) 64.
[2] Daniel and McIntosh (1972) 139.
[3] Elliott (1984) 139ff.
[4] Lewis and Clark (1977) 324.

The relationship between labour and capital and the stakeholder–shareholder dynamic are central to understanding the development of industrial democracy, which came to focus on the issues of worker representation, joint consultations, collective bargaining and the means by which labour can be a managerial partner, with workers exercising real influence on the decisions at the companies for which they toiled.[5] Industrial democracy evolved from a pre-war socialist theory based on the exploitation of workers by the capitalist system to a post-war movement dominated by the trade unions, as the representatives of labour, functioning within the same system that they had opposed.[6] As explained in the 1978 *A Guide to the White Paper on Industrial Democracy*:

> Industrial democracy means that employees should have an opportunity to take part in the development of corporate strategy, contribute to decisions before they are taken and share responsibility for their implementation. While employees, employers and government work together at national level to formulate social and economic policies there is a gap in the development of the employee role at company level in spite of the fact that many board decisions have major implications for employees' long-term interests.[7]

In keeping with this understanding of the movement, in the post-war period industrial democracy came to be identified with worker representation on company boards, which addressed how the interests of different stakeholder were prioritised under the law, questioning the principle of shareholder primacy and the status quo that it supports.[8] The extensive post-war scholarship on industrial democracy is dominated by the study of representation, including how its development was influenced by the trade unions, which had their own agenda and motives, not the least of which was to increase their power and influence as the agents of labour within the established system.[9]

The concept of the worker director raised several questions: with the inclusion of worker directors on company boards, were directors still expected to represent all shareholders without prioritising a subset of constituents? Were worker directors expected to put the interests of workers above the interests of all shareholders and other stakeholders? If the worker directors are representatives

[5] See Webb and Webb (1897) ch IV, 'Trade Unionism and Democracy', 806ff; see also Clegg (1960).

[6] For a history of industrial democracy and its ideological developments, see Clegg (1951); Clegg (1960); Ackers (2007) 86.

[7] Ream (1978) 2. It should be noted that the term 'industrial democracy' was seen by some on the left as an instrument used by the establishment to undermine the principles it represents: 'The very term is shrouded in such confusion, and used so indiscriminately, that it may itself become a weapon against socialist advance' (Coates and Topham (1968a) 228).

[8] Worker representation on boards exists in other jurisdictions, of which the two-tier Germany structure is the most often referenced example. For a contemporaneous discussion on German and European industrial relations as they relate to British considerations of industrial democracy, see Abbott (1973) 5ff; Horner (1974) 187ff.

[9] Clements (1977) 317. There is an extensive bibliography that addresses the issues of worker representation in the board room, including: Clegg (1951); Coates (1968); Coates and Topham (1975a); Brannen et al (1976); and Batstone, Ferner and Terry (1983).

of union members only, should they be prioritising union interests over those of all workers, as well as above those of other shareholders and stakeholders? How does existing law accommodate for the concept of the worker shareholder as envisioned by supporters of industrial democracy? If worker directors were not expected to prioritise the interests of the employees, do they lose their value as an instrument of industrial democracy as they are absorbed into the traditional board processes and methods of decision-making? Does the very existence of worker directors and their participation within the established corporate structure potentially undermine other ways by which workers and unions exercise their power (for example, collective bargaining) and did it weaken workers' negotiating positions against management, with which worker directors are now affiliated as members of the board?[10]

I. THE TRADE UNIONS AND WORKER REPRESENTATION

A. Worker Participation and Nationalisations

Worker representation was a priority for the trade unions and labour movements since before the Second World War, initially focusing on nationalised industries and attempting to influence legislation for the public ownership of companies, with the TUC arguing in 1945 that it is 'essential that their organisation shall make proper provision for the representation and participation of workpeople, and to this end statutory provision be made for the interests of workpeople to be represented on the Governing Board'.[11] These aspirations for the role of workers within newly organised nationalised industries seemed possible with the election of the Labour government in 1945, and the TUC pushed industrial democracy as integral to the nationalisation policies, beneficial not only for workers but also for another key stakeholder, the public:

> [I]t should be realised that the extension of public control over the national economy is by no means inconsistent and may in fact be equivalent with the extension of participation by workpeople and the public as a whole in the determination of their economic destinies.[12]

In pursuing the goals of industrial democracy, the merging of the interests of the workers with that of the general public was a way to broaden the audience sympathetic to the empowerment not only of workers but also of anyone excluded from the control of British industry, including the community and consumers.[13]

[10] Daniel and McIntosh (1972) 140.
[11] Trades Union Congress (1944) 10. See also ch 2 of this volume on nationalisations.
[12] Trades Union Congress (1944) 18.
[13] Radice (1974) 15.

The TUC in 1945 did not, however, limit its demands for worker rights and representation to nationalised industries, but extended them to private companies, in which it acknowledged the role of the owners of industry, but sought the inclusion of workers in managerial decisions:

> Private undertakings must necessarily operate by reference to the interests of their owners. It is essential, however, that the operations of private industry as a whole should be subject to a control representative of the public interest; and in the framing of that control not only has the viewpoint of the workpeople a special right to consideration, but such a control can be made fully effective only if it makes proper provision for participation by organisations representative of the workers in industry in its operation.[14]

The TUC called for the recognition of the rights of workers alongside the rights of shareholders and for an increased role of labour in management decision-making, emphasising the interests of workers amongst all other stakeholders, as its approach to industrial democracy evolved over the post-war decades.[15] The trade unions played a central role in advocating for the rights of workers, for an increased role in industrial decisions, and as beneficiaries of corporate profits, fortifying their position to make demands with the ability to disrupt access to labour and to disturb industrial production.[16] The public interest was the flag with which the movements for workers' rights and industrial democracy draped themselves, with the TUC taking a measured approach to the need for a radical extension of industrial democracy by working within the established system and integrating labour within the existing managerial power structure, as opposed to calling for the end of capitalism and the dissolution of property rights.[17]

B. The Labour Party and the Trade Unions

The political parties both on the right and on the left adapted their platforms to address the post-war demands of industrial democracy and the building pressures of industrial relations, but it was the Labour Party that embraced the movement and made it an explicit part of its political platform, as expressed in the 'Industrial Democracy' section of its 1950 manifesto:

> We have begun to build up a flourishing partnership between Government, management and workers. More has to be done, both in public and private enterprise. Too many managements still pay lip-service to join consultation and then do little to make it effective. They should consult with workers' representatives before decisions affecting them are taken, and not after; they should make available to these representatives

[14] Trades Union Congress (1944) 19.

[15] Lewis and Clark (1977) 334 ff.

[16] Crosland (1959) 11.

[17] Lord Bullock, *Report of the Committee of Inquiry on Industrial Democracy* (Cmnd 6706, 1977) v; Clift, Gamble and Harris (2000) 62; Fox (2017) 208.

> the accounts and records on which managerial decisions are based. Upon the trade unions lies the responsibility for further equipping and training members for service and the country.[18]

Although at the time of the 1950 manifesto the Labour Party was still years away from including the demand for board representation in its programme, there was already debate on how companies were implementing worker consultation, with calls by the unions, politicians and law-makers for more to be done.[19]

The demand for worker participation in management was an established tenet of industrial democracy and was promoted as a core demand in the nineteenth century and in the decades just before and immediately after the First World War, whereas, as the Labour politician and socialist intellectual CAR Crosland observed in 1959: 'To-day one hardly hears a whisper of these matters at Labour Party or Trade Union conferences.'[20] The drumbeat for this manifestation of industrial democracy – that is, worker representation – grew louder in the later decades of the post-war consensus, a consequence of the social progress made by workers during the war and because the demands for increased consultations and expanded collective bargaining contributed to the changing attitudes by most of the union leadership that culminated in the 1970s.[21] This shift of emphasis to the demand for worker directors corresponded with the waning of public support for nationalisations and was aligned with the second Labour government of Harold Wilson, whose party was committed to working with the trade unions through the policies of the Social Contract and was willing to deploy political capital to promote systemic changes.[22] Socialists had long been asserting that workers had the right to a say in the running of industry, just as the working class had a right to be heard within a political democracy, as explained by Crosland:

> [B]ut only through workers' control could he [the British worker] achieve effective industrial power, and raise his status above that of a 'commodity, bought and sold like any other article of commerce'. It was assumed that the coveted power could be achieved only by direct workers' management, or at least participation in management.[23]

[18] Labour Party (1950) 4; Dale (2000b) 65. Although the two main political parties that formed governments in the post-war years from 1945 to 1979 are the focus of this research, the Liberal Party was also part of the political debate. The Liberals viewed both management and organised labour as impeding the industrial growth that Britain needed, stating in their 1959 manifesto that: 'Britain's production and productivity lag. It must expand so that jobs are waiting for them – Restrictive practices both by management and labour must go. The causes of crippling industrial disputes must be eliminated. It can be done if rank and file trade unionists are ready to fight for more industrial democracy' (Liberal Party (1959); see also Dale (2000c) 100). The Liberals also supported a constitutional model of the company that included company law reform to put employees on par with shareholders (Clift, Gamble and Harris (2000) 74, fn 97).

[19] Clift, Gamble and Harris (2000) 67.

[20] Crosland (1959) 10.

[21] Elliott (1984) 65.

[22] Dorey (1995) 129. See also section II.D below on the Social Contract.

[23] Crosland (1959) 10.

The promotion of the different aspects of industrial democracy evolved over time, with the trade unions initially reluctant to embrace worker representation and consultations that they saw as undermining their position as the opposition to management, particularly when it included all workers and not just union members. In reference to works councils, which were joint committees of workers and managers from within a factory:

> The trade unions were usually suspicious, for they were bodies outside industry and here were representative organizations of the worker within industry over which they had little control, and because employers often encouraged works councils as an alternative to trade unions.[24]

The support for worker directors is an example of how the trade unions, led by the TUC, consolidated their power by transitioning from opposing the existing system from the outside to preserving it as cooperating participants within it.[25]

C. Industrial Change and the Expansion of Union Membership

In the post-war period, union membership underwent transformation and expansion, impacting the development of its industrial democracy policies and positions.[26] The change in union membership reflected the developments in British industry, with the decline in manufacturing and the growth in non-manual labour, as well as the diversification of the workforce, which influenced what type of workers were represented by organised labour.[27] For example, for the 1955 general election campaign, the Labour Party made promises to change company law, accompanied by a declaration to improve working conditions 'in shops and offices', suggesting a broadening of the traditional classification of workers to beyond the factory floor.[28] The development of the industrial democracy movement coincided with a shift in the rhetoric used by unionists to identify 'the worker', which was reflected in the changing demographics of trade union membership.[29]

In laying out its political platform, the Labour Party did not limit its support of industrial democracy to manual labourers, who were still its base and the main constituents of the highly influential trade unions, but also included the growing pool of office and technical workers, signalling an evolution in the attitudes towards, and a recognition of, different types of workers.[30] This change reflected the increased unionisation of white-collar workers, a group that in the

[24] Clegg (1951) 7.
[25] Trades Union Congress (1974); Fox (2017) 197.
[26] Davies (2019) 87; Melling (2003) 249; Pollard (1992) 282; Fox (2017) 211.
[27] Melling (2003) 249.
[28] Labour Party (1955); Dale (2000b) 86.
[29] Melling (2003) 246.
[30] Pollard (1992) 281.

past would not have identified with the masses of blue-collar workers or their representatives, but that was now capitalising on the growing power and influence of organised labour.[31] For the groups of workers who were between the labourers and directors – for example, middle management and other white-collar employees – which were historically left out of the industrial relations negotiations, there was a clear motive to become unionised and to profit from the benefits of industrial democracy.[32]

The inclusion of more workers of different types under the umbrella of the TUC, which saw an increase in office and other non-manual members from the late 1940s, contributed both to the change in the federation's membership and to the evolution of its policies on industrial democracy, with organisations that had historically remained separate from other trade unions joining the TUC and becoming a meaningful minority. These groups were not a moderating influence on the TUC, as they included postal workers, civil servants, teachers and healthcare workers, who had all recently taken industrial action (that is, gone on strike) to advance their interests.[33] Between 1948 and 1960, union membership increased: manual unions +0.6 per cent and white-collar unions +33.6 per cent, with the density of union membership in local government rising by 16 per cent to 84 per cent and in national government up 19 per cent to 83 per cent.[34] The increase of managers, who were often overlooked in industrial relations, joining unions created additional complexity to the questions of representations as more layers of the workforce became unionised; as observed in the Fabian Tract *Working Power*, 'managers, who are now joining trade unions in increasing numbers, must be able to play their part through their own trade union machinery'.[35]

The growth in union membership was boosted not only by the increase in white-collar workers but also by more women members, mostly in the public sector.[36] These demographic changes had implications on how the unions interacted with the industrial establishment, with the TUC's increasing willingness to work within the system occurring as growing numbers of managers and white-collar employees were becoming aware of the power of unionisation, swelling the unions' membership and altering its collective expectations.[37] The unions themselves were being democratised as they came to represent a more diverse collection of workers, a phenomenon that was not unlike the changes in the shareholder base that was expanding beyond its pre-war demographic.[38] In both

[31] Melling (2003) 249.
[32] Fox (1985) 397; Fox (2017) 211.
[33] Pollard (1992) 282.
[34] Pollard (1992) 282.
[35] Radice (1974) 14.
[36] Edgerton (2018) 370; Runciman (1966) 132.
[37] Runciman (1966) 133.
[38] See the Rt Hon Lord Donovan, *Report of the Royal Commission on Trade Unions and Employers' Associations 1965–1968* (Cmnd 3623, 1968) for details on the trade unions. See also Webb and Webb (1897) on the early focus and study of industrial democracy, which examines trade

cases, popular perceptions did not necessarily reflect the increasingly complicated composition of these groups, which were traditionally seen as having very little overlap.[39]

D. The Perceived Managerial Capabilities of Workers

In 1945, in support of its programme for industrial democracy and the advancement of workers, the TUC argued that the worker could be as competent as the managerial class at directing the companies for which they work:

> There is to-day a conviction that given equal opportunity workpeople who have gained their experience in the day-to-day work and in the Trade Union organisation of industry are as capable of undertaking administrative responsibility as those who have been assisted in its attainment by the possession of certain advantages.[40]

Despite this endorsement of the capabilities of workers and the support for consultation and representation, there remained an acknowledgement of the limitations to the wholesale takeover of companies by workers, no matter how ideologically desirable, because of what was seen as an inability of workers to manage companies effectively, as the majority of trade union leaders accepted the greater expertise of management.[41] In addition to demanding inclusion, the unions also recognised the need to train workers to be equipped to be successful representatives, often leveraging skills gained through below-board participation, and addressing the concerns as to their managerial capabilities and skills.[42] For workers to become equal partners in management, sitting as directors alongside the representatives of equity shareholders, they needed not only to demonstrate that they had the necessary skills but also to challenge the entrenched perceptions of their abilities, including with their own union leaders, and to address the negative bias against them that stubbornly persisted throughout the post-war period.[43] Based on similar stereotypes and prejudices, just as the worker was deemed by some as unable to make investment decisions as a shareholder, he or she was also considered unqualified to manage companies effectively.[44]

unions and the democratic nature of these institutions of 'manual working wage-earners, associated according to occupations' (at vi).

[39] Rt Hon Lord Donovan, *Report of the Royal Commission on Trade Unions and Employers' Associations 1965–1968* (Cmnd 3623, 1968) from para 111 onwards; Melling (2003) 248; Jobson (2013) 125; Davies (1978) 253.

[40] Trades Union Congress (1944) 20.

[41] Middlemas (1979) 393.

[42] Davies and Lord Wedderburn of Charlton (1977) 209.

[43] Shackleton (1977) 232; Middlemas (1979) 393.

[44] See ch 5 of this volume on the perceptions of the worker shareholder.

The industrial relations scholar Harvie Ramsay observed that, despite a narrative by management supporting the principle of worker participation, this commitment:

> [I]s readily subordinated where conflict would be too risky, often with the excuse that workers are not educated or responsible enough to become involved in these areas [economic or financial matters] yet. Nearly any business text on the topic will confirm this stereotype almost to the letter; the style and expression are remarkably monotonic. The vague platitudes of this view have also informed the manifestos of all three main political parties in the elections of the 1970s. Yet management continue to shy away from specific legislative requirements or proposed structure of participation, with weak arguments which ill disguise the felt need to keep control over the whole process and to excise participation if it does not meet their needs.[45]

In an environment that was full of promises but lacked actionable reforms, a large majority of workers supported board representation; yet, as determined by a 1969 Gallup poll, 48 per cent thought it would not affect them whatsoever.[46] British industrial and political leadership made encouraging gestures, but resisted legislative changes, using the appearance of compromise to deflect from the lack of reforms and the preservation of the status quo, an act of public theatre that did not convince many workers.[47]

E. Trade Unions as Gatekeeper

As the movement for industrial democracy gained pace, the TUC, as the largest federation of trade unions in the UK, positioned itself as the gatekeeper to British workers, of which many, but not all, were union members.[48] Even before its endorsement of worker representation and the specific demand that the trade unions control that process, the TUC sought to capture control of the advancements in the processes of industrial democracy.[49] Dating back to the immediate post-war period, the TUC advocated for public sector control of industry and trade, with their support of policies, ranging from the complete nationalisation of industries to various other partial measures, including the creation of Industrial Boards:

> Such Industrial Boards would need to be representative of all sections of the industry and should be composed of representatives of workpeople and employers in the

[45] Ramsay (1977) 495.
[46] Daniel and McIntosh (1972) 146.
[47] Fox (1985) 400.
[48] Clift, Gamble and Harris (2000) 68; Poole (1982) 196.
[49] Trades Union Congress (1944) 15; Rt Hon Lord Donovan, *Report of the Royal Commission on Trade Unions and Employers' Associations 1965–1968* (Cmnd 3623, 1968) paras 723–27.

> industry in equal proportion … Representation of the workpeople on the Boards would necessarily have to be organised by the trade unions.[50]

The trade unions increased their influence alongside the growing industrial unrest in Britain, positioning themselves as the sole legitimate representatives of workers and taking control of the process through which companies were expected to interface with labour, a move that the Labour Party, which relied on the unions for support, was prepared to accept; at the party conference in 1968, Labour gave its endorsement of a single channel of communication between workers' representatives and management through the development of existing union machinery.[51] By the time of the Bullock Report of the mid-1970s, the concept of single-channel engagement through the TUC was well established.[52] Once directors acknowledged that engaging with workers was desirable and in the best interests of their companies, they accepted the trade unions as the natural and most effective medium with which to interact with their workforce.[53]

The goal of advancing the interests of the worker as the primary stakeholder, and of placing workers' rights (at least) on a par with shareholders through statutory changes, became a *cri de guerre* of the trade union leadership, which sought to make itself essential to any agreement for worker representation, including by excluding workers who were not union members.[54] In making itself the gatekeeper to worker representation, the TUC narrowed the inclusiveness of its version of industrial democracy, leaving non-unionised workers outside and unrepresented, excluding a portion of the workforce on whose behalf the industrial democracy movement was supposedly working.[55] The requirement by the TUC that workers must have union membership to access the right to representation undermined the claim for an expansion of democracy in industry, demonstrating how popular terminology, in this case the broadly defined 'industrial democracy', was used to advance a position, and to gain popular public support, even when its original meaning and intentions were modified to suit a specific purpose.[56]

Although the study of industrial democracy and worker representation emphasised the trade unions, and much of the debate on and promotion of the movement was advanced by the unionists, a distinction should be made between the trade unions and the individual labourers that were their constituents,

[50] Trades Union Congress (1944) 15.

[51] Clift, Gamble and Harris (2000) 68.

[52] See ch 7, section II.A of this volume; Lord Bullock, *Report of the Committee of Inquiry on Industrial Democracy* (Cmnd 6706, 1977) from ch 10, para 6 onwards.

[53] Daniel and McIntosh (1972) 111.

[54] Poole (1986) 128.

[55] Davies (1978) 253.

[56] Elliott (1984) 130; Clift, Gamble and Harris (2000) 69. The single-channel model of industrial democracy advanced by the TUC excluded not only non-unionised workers but also senior managers below the board level, who were also employees but not union members, and any overseas workers employed by British companies (City Company Law Committee and Great Britain Committee of Inquiry on Industrial Democracy (1977) 18).

especially as not all British workers were union members.[57] For those that opposed them, the unions' ability to dictate the narrative on the rights of all workers was problematic; the Conservative Trade Unionists, for example, made this point in a 1970 pamphlet on participation, stating that: 'We must break the attempted myth that unionised labour is the sole representation of workers – what about the 13 million non-unionised not to speak of doctors, dentists, farmers and the self-employed.'[58] Despite the trade unions' success at claiming to be the sole representative of workers, which was facilitated by their close relationship and policy alignment with the Labour Party, which was augmented further when Labour were in government, as well as the trade unions' usefulness as a convenient counter-party and antagonist to the opponents of industrial democracy and organised labour, the rhetoric of the unionists did not reflect the will of all workers.[59]

II. CAPITAL AND LABOUR: CONFLICT OR CONVERGENCE?

A. Promoting Industrial Democracy from Outside the System

The trade unions did not initially offer their support for the mechanisms of industrial democracy that brought them, and the workers who they represented, inside the system, be it through the representation on the boards of private companies or through worker share ownership, as they believed that these would compromise their freedom and implicate them in a fundamental part of the capitalist structure designed to take advantage and suppress the rights of labour.[60] The establishment's growing acceptance of industrial democracy fuelled the suspicion that it was a way to undermine protections for workers and a tool for deflecting criticism and demands for genuine reform. In his 1977 essay on industrial democracy, Clarke describes how:

> [T]he industrial-democracy lobby wish to extend the methods of elitist representative democracy into the workplace which will involve undermining the existing participatory democracy entailed in unilateral shopfloor controls. 'Industrial democracy' is not a development of popular power but an attempt to forestall it.[61]

As one major trade union leader explained:

> [T]here is a fundamental and, in finality, irreconcilable conflict between Capital and Labour … 'Workers' participation' is, in my view, the greatest bulwark for preserving

[57] In the late 1970s, union membership at large British companies was approximately 70% (Davies (1978) 253).

[58] Conservative Trade Unionists (1970) 13.

[59] Clift, Gamble and Harris (2000) 74; Williamson (2016) 138.

[60] Furlong (1977) 99; Clegg (1960) 24ff.

[61] Clarke (1977) 357.

> a free enterprise society. It does not seek to change, it seeks to perpetuate. It seeks to create the idea that there isn't a fundamental difference between us.[62]

Those who believed that the way to advance the interests of workers was to dissemble the existing system feared that the trade unionists would be corrupted by workers within it, leading them to abandon their position as the opposition to capitalism, and 'the danger that trade union representatives may become involved in responsibility for rationalisation decisions which will undermine security of employment and bargaining power'.[63] As Clegg argues:

> [W]orkers' participation in management was not only irrelevant to the question of industrial democracy but could actually be harmful to workers' interests and to the extension of 'democratic' social relationships in industry, principally because of the problems of role conflict experienced by workers on decision-making bodies, but second because of the inherent danger that they might acquire managerial definitions of the proper functions of the enterprise.[64]

The trajectory of the post-war progression of the movement for industrial democracy began from the outside and moved inside, going from opposing the system to working within it.[65] Just as the working class fought to improve its position within the broader political context, workers also challenged the industrial system, although it was initially argued that they must do so by remaining outsiders. As expressed by Clegg: 'Organized opposition is a prerequisite of democracy, at least on a large scale. Only as long as the trade unions act as an opposition to management will they serve the interests of industrial democracy.'[66] Writing almost a decade later in his 1960 book, *A New Approach to Industrial Democracy*, Clegg laid out the three principles of industrial relations: (i) trade unions must be independent of both the state and management; (ii) only the unions can represent the industrial interests of workers; and (iii) ownership of industry is irrelevant to good industrial relations.[67] Accordingly, trade unions must remain outside the system to represent workers' interests, rejecting worker shareholders and worker directors as a means of addressing industrial unrest.[68]

The worry that the trade unions would be absorbed and subsequently weakened (at least to a degree) into the existing system was prevalent within the Labour Party, as explained in the 1967 working party report on industrial democracy:

> Historically, workers and their trade unions have been suspicious of any proposals for their partnership in a system of unbridled capitalism. This suspicion arose not only

[62] Clarke (1977) 356.
[63] Coates and Topham (1968a) 239; Clegg (1951) 131; Blumberg (1971) 142ff.
[64] Ackers (2007) 95; Poole (1986) 132.
[65] Clegg (1951) 141.
[66] Clegg (1951) 141. For a more detailed review of Clegg's legacy and work, see Ackers (2007).
[67] Clegg (1960) 21.
[68] Clegg (1960) 24.

> because of the feeling that such proposals might seek to by-pass or to emasculate the independent trade unionism they had built. It arose also from hostility towards the aggressive profit maximisation that the system pursued, and its likely concomitants of consumer exploitation and ruthless disregard of the social costs involved.[69]

The ideological commitment to being the opposition conflicted with the idea of workers' representation on company boards and, as expounded by the historian Geoffrey Foote in his work on the political thought of the Labour Party,

> The demand for industrial democracy seems to have wavered as the efficacy of workshop bargaining has declined, and the problems of mass unemployment have overridden many other industrial issues ... Most crucially, in its emphasis on a change in the relationship between labour and capital so that the former was given more power, it failed to pose the abolition of the system of wage-labour.[70]

The acceptance of board representation as a means of improving the conditions of workers was controversial within the Labour Party as it blurred the line between workers and management, although increasingly the unions acknowledged the benefits of using the existing industrial system as a way to promote changes alongside, and not in competition with, other methods of industrial democracy like collective bargaining.[71] The insertion of trade unionists into the managerial mechanisms of the corporation was opposed by those who saw it as a means by which the government undermined the power of organised labour, interpreting the establishment's willingness to work with the unions as 'a smokescreen of rhetoric about industrial democracy, in which attempts to embroil trade unions in responsibility for hostile acts against their members will be coupled with marginal concessions to particular representatives of the workpeople'.[72] In the case of worker representation, as well as other forms of industrial democracy, tension existed between the demands for workers to have a say in management and how this inclusion then makes them part of that system, deconstructing the clear distinctions between labour and capital on which traditional trade union and socialist ideologies are based.[73]

B. The Trade Unions' Pivot to Embrace Worker Directors

Consistent with the arguments supporting nationalisations and worker shareholding, worker representation was also promoted as a means by which to improve the conditions of workers and address inequities, which both confirmed the framework of the company board and sought to alter its composition.[74]

[69] Labour Party (1967) 24.
[70] Foote (1986) 333.
[71] Clift, Gamble and Harris (2000) 66.
[72] Coates and Topham (1968a) 239.
[73] Clarke (1977) 357.
[74] Fox (2017) 196.

The TUC's 1974 statement of policy in support of worker board representation was a watershed event in the development of organised labour's approach to industrial democracy, in which it accepted the existing system as the platform from which to advance its goals.[75] Employee and shop-floor consultations were the traditional methods for amplifying workers' voices and the pivot to espousing worker directors as the preferred organ for change occurred amid political and economic volatility and increasing industrial unrest as the post-war consensus unravelled.[76] The endorsement of worker representation on boards went against the traditional position of the trade unions that there was a fundamental conflict of interests between capital and labour, with the TUC claiming that having worker directors was an extension of, and not in conflict with, existing practices, expanding into areas that were outside the scope of collective bargaining and addressing the lack of legal requirements for consultations:

> There is, legally speaking, no responsibility on the part of the board to its employees collectively, or to negotiate or consult with their representatives. Collective bargaining of course provides a de facto control and involvement in management decisions but has no legal foundation in company law.[77]

The TUC's change in position was not viewed by all parties as purely about the advancement of industrial democracy, with some critics perceiving it as a way for the unions to increase and consolidate their power.[78] In his work advocating for industrial democracy, George Copeman identified this contest for power, explaining: 'The struggle is at the top level, between the organised forces of capital and labour. The dignity and even the careers of powerful leaders on both sides are at stake.'[79] The trade unions, and their role in British industry, were evolving and by the end of the post-war period were well integrated into the established order and sought to take control of it, a development noted by John Elliott:

> By the time Labour had been returned to power in 1974 the TUC was determined to change the existing system, which had little if anything to do with employee participation and which had often meant that right-wing and elderly trade union leaders, who were regarded as 'safe bets' by the Civil Service, industrialists and ministers, did well and boosted their income before and after retirement to the tune of thousands of pounds a year.[80]

Partnering with industry and government, the trade unions had advanced the cause of labour while ensuring that their own agenda was served and their power preserved, or enhanced, by advocating for changes for the workers that they

[75] Trades Union Congress (1974) 37; Ogden (1982) 550.
[76] Williamson (2016) 121.
[77] Trades Union Congress (1974) 12; Lewis and Clark (1977) 328.
[78] Cottrell (1978) 58.
[79] Copeman (1958) 2.
[80] Elliott (1984) 210.

represented, albeit in ways that kept the union leadership firmly in control.[81] As described in 1978 by Sir Allan Cottrell, former Conservative government Chief Scientific Advisor:

> Shop-floor worker participation is one thing, but what is now in some quarters is called 'industrial democracy' is quite another. The name of the game here is 'power' and the prize is control of the 'commanding heights of the economy'.[82]

By examining the TUC and the adjustment of its position on worker representation, the tensions between the power gained from working within the system and the clarity of purpose afforded to the opposition working from without are made clear.[83] Ultimately, the ideals that underpinned the movement for industrial democracy frayed under the pressure of political compromise, which left statutory requirement for worker directors an unrealised goal.[84] That industrial democracy, in general, and worker participation, in particular, had returned as a political priority in the rhetoric of the major parties and as a core part of political discussions was a sign of progress, although an increase in political noise does not necessarily translate into action or meaningful reform.[85]

Although the trade unions agreed that unionised workers needed more influence and control over management decisions, they disagreed as to how this was best achieved, with not all unions supporting the TUC's new approach.[86] According to those who opposed worker representation, anything that weakened the trade unions, which included being absorbed into the structure of management, was harmful to the interests of workers, and it was on this basis that the TUC's unionist critics opposed it, with dissenting unions attempting to resist what they saw as the TUC's assimilation into the establishment.[87] The TUC responded to these unionist challenges by pushing critics to the margins, creating rifts and fissures amongst the trade unionists, which might have contributed to the success of the union busting of the following decade.[88]

C. Moderate Labour under Fire

Just as the TUC was criticised for its stance on worker representation, the political left harshly criticised the Labour government that was elected in 1964 on a platform committed to industrial democracy, which was described in a 1968 Institute for Workers' Control pamphlet, *The Labour Party's Plans for Industrial*

[81] Clements (1977) 325.
[82] Cottrell (1978) 58.
[83] Fox (2017) 197.
[84] Clift, Gamble and Harris (2000) 81.
[85] Clift, Gamble and Harris (2000) 65.
[86] Lewis and Clark (1977) 324.
[87] Clift, Gamble and Harris (2000) 66; Williamson (2016) 132.
[88] Williamson (2016) 132.

Democracy, as being the product of 'paralysing pseudo-politics ... based on a virtual conspiracy to avoid all the major issues of power, and fudge all the basic conflicts, which beset modern society'.[89] The movement for industrial democracy gained momentum during Labour's time in government and became a central policy issue, although this did not result in any major reforms to core company law.[90] Furthermore, Labour's position was criticised for its naiveté in relation to the role of the state and its organs:

> For a century and more, the State has been anything but neutral in the tug-of-war between capital and labour. It has intervened in every major upsurge of industrial unrest, in the face of every significant push towards industrial democracy, to head off and hold back the forces which might limit or control the powers of capital.[91]

The post-war Labour Party, which now had the exacting experience of governing, was seen to be fortifying the very system against which many of its supporters struggled, resulting in the dilution of the principles at the foundations of industrial democracy that sought to oppose rather than prop up the establishment.[92] For some, industrial democracy was a movement aimed at disrupting the existing system, whereas for others, industrial democracy was not about disassembling the system, but about buttressing it, finding ways to increase the power of the state in the affairs of private industry, or even as a means of absorbing the trade unions into the establishment.[93]

In the second half of the 1970s, the weakening Labour Party and a shift in electoral support resulted in a disconnect between the expectations for change and the ability to enact it.[94] The replacement of Harold Wilson by James Callaghan in 1976 was a reflection of the further deradicalisation of the Labour Party, pushing the more orthodox defenders of labour in the struggle against capital towards the political margins, all while the British voting public turned increasingly to the right.[95] By the end of the 1970s and into the following decade under the new Conservative government, the changing political winds impacted the nature of the debate on industrial democracy and the campaign for worker directors, as well as the general public's attitude towards, and tolerance for, industrial unrest and the associated societal and economic disruptions.[96]

[89] Coates and Topham (1968b) 2.
[90] Clift, Gamble and Harris (2000) 70.
[91] Coates and Topham (1968b) 2.
[92] Clift, Gamble and Harris (2000) 68.
[93] Manne (2007) A.23.
[94] Clift, Gamble and Harris (2000) 81.
[95] Morgan (2010) 123. Wilson and Callaghan clashed over the misguided 1969 Labour White Paper *In Place of Strife*, which was opposed by the trade unions and eventually withdrawn, a saga that is beyond the scope of this study, but offers insights into the ideological camps within the post-war Labour Party, the changes of leadership, and Labour's relationship with the trade unions (see Morgan (2010) 133).
[96] Pollak (2013) 106; see also Hanson and Rathkey (1984) 154ff.

D. The Social Contract

Labour's October 1974 manifesto delineated the party's recalibrated relationship with organised labour, stating that: 'At the heart of this manifesto and our programme to save the nation lies the Social Contract between the Labour Government and the trade unions, an idea derided by our enemies, but certain to become widely accepted by those who genuinely believe in government by consent.'[97] Unsurprisingly, the correlation between the power of the trade unions and the impact and intensity of the demands for worker representation was particularly notable when Labour was in power, fortified by the Social Contract that re-established that partnership.[98] The Social Contract affirmed the cooperation between Labour and the TUC, whose relationship had undergone considerable stress in the preceding years, putting industrial democracy firmly at the forefront of their combined political agenda.[99] Five years earlier, the 1969 publication of Labour's White Paper, *In Place of Strife*, was a divisive, ineffective and ill-advised attempt to weaken the trade unions that badly damaged their long-standing alliance; with the Social Contract, a restored TUC reclaimed its position as an insider, from where it promoted the merits of worker representation.[100] As explained in the 1974 Fabian Tract *Working Power: Policies for Industrial Democracy*:

> 'Industrial democracy' is now on the political agenda for the first time since the 1930s. The TUC is debating a major report on industrial democracy at its 1974 conference. The minority Labour Government has promised legislation soon. All three major political parties will be putting to the electorate proposals to increase 'participation'. Journalists, management consultants, enlightened managements spend much time discussing the issue. Even the CBI has agreed that some changes are needed.[101]

The return of Labour to government in 1974, and Wilson's encouragement of the industrial democracy project, gave organised labour confidence that the momentum would lead to the statutory changes that they endorsed and that the UK's adoption of industrial democracy policies was imminent and inevitable.[102] There was an atmosphere of empowerment on the left, prompting the trade unions to act more boldly, although paradoxically this occurred just as the lawmakers and politicians who were their partners and natural supporters – that is, Labour – were losing the ability, and in some cases the will, to deliver on their promises.[103] The trade unionists' confidence was overblown and legislation was not forthcoming as the calls for statutory changes echoed back unanswered

[97] Labour Party (1974b); Dale (2000b) 198.
[98] Middlemas (1990) 234ff, 370.
[99] Lewis and Clark (1977) 324.
[100] *In Place of Strife: A Policy for Industrial Relations* (Cmnd 3888, 1969). On this, see Dorey (2019); Middlemas (1990) 234ff, 370.
[101] Radice (1974) 1.
[102] Moore (2018) 157.
[103] Morgan (1992) 414.

both by the sitting Labour government and by the Conservative government that followed.[104] The assumption that this impetus for reform, backed by many different constituents, could not be halted or diverted was brash and serves as a warning to promoters of movements for systemic legal reform, including for corporate purpose, stakeholder capitalism and the various forms of ESG.

E. An Evolving Narrative

By the 1970s, many company directors were showing sensitivity to the public mood and the political atmosphere of increased awareness of the principles of industrial democracy, and were more likely to indicate that they did not necessarily interpret their obligations, and make their decisions, based on a strict shareholder primacy interpretation of the law.[105] The shift in the rhetoric did not change the underlying principle in UK company law that directors' duties were to act in the best interests of the company – that is, the interests of the shareholders – and were not accountable to other stakeholders. Nonetheless, there were also those in the business community who joined the appeals for a more equitable system and recognised the unequal treatment of workers' interests, as Stephen Abbott, writing for the Conservative Research Department, explained:

> Under present company law, directors are individually and collectively responsible to the shareholders in administering the company. They have no general duty to consider the interests of employees – except in so far as a failure to do so might harm the company and be damaging to shareholders' interests. I believe this approach to be inequitable and divorced from present-day reality. It lends support to the 'them and us' posture which is the source of so much suspicion, resentment, and conflict.[106]

Although this language suggests a sympathetic attitude towards stakeholder interests, the concern is not necessarily for the welfare of the workers or for the democratisation of industry, but for the impact of this position on industrial relations and resulting disruptions (which would also affect shareholder value).

Meanwhile, within this evolving political atmosphere, some company boards took a more inclusive approach to dealing with stakeholders, including engaging more with the trade unions, and sought ways to address the concerns of workers while preserving their own position, particularly as the labour disputes of the post-war era became increasingly enflamed and disruptive. In the post-war period the position of workers and the working class was advanced in various ways, with the response of management not necessarily to encourage participation in the decision-making of industry, but to develop more paternalistic

[104] Davies (1978) 247; Williamson (2016) 132; Clift, Gamble and Harris (2000) 79.

[105] Moore (2018) 157. For the contemporary debate on shareholder primacy and stakeholder interests, see, for example, Armour, Deakin and Konzelmann (2003); Fairfax (2006).

[106] Abbott (1973) 9.

human resource and personnel policies to try to improve working conditions.[107] Management began to address the interests of workers and not just those of their equity shareholders in a more organised and public way, and there was a growing acknowledgement of needing both to work with the trade unions and to appear to be more accountable to society at large.[108]

It was increasingly accepted by industrial leaders that it was in the interests of company directors to try to cooperate with the trade unionists, seeking to compromise on certain issues and to build better relationships with the workforce, while incorporating the (potentially disruptive) workers as participants into the existing system. Derek Fatchett identified the issues, stating that:

> If one can be bold and state the managerial problem of the 70's [*sic*] in one sentence, it is that management needs to acquire the means to reintegrate the worker, so that there is a more general sharing of the company's objectives. For many managers (and indeed some politicians) it is a stick job; the fear of the lengthy dole queues should be sufficient to re-establish industrial discipline. But there are other managers who recognise that an occasional carrot is necessary, and that industrial democracy, based upon job enrichment and enlargement could provide a necessary stimulant to efficiency, without fostering demands for workers' control over strategic decisions.[109]

As long as the trade unions had the power to disrupt the sources of labour needed to power British industry (a tendency that intensified in the 1970s), most company directors, fearing industrial action, preferred to engage with the trade unionists and to support elements of industrial democracy, like below board-level worker consultations or schemes to increase worker shareholding, in an attempt to avoid others, like the more threatening demands for board representation.[110]

III. INDUSTRIAL DEMOCRACY AND LEGISLATIVE CHANGE

The post-war era witnessed intensifying opposition to the legal principle of shareholder primacy, with trade unions demanding parity with shareholders on company boards, insisting on being given top-level representation – and possibly even control – and not just influence.[111] Nationalisations were the initial post-war threat to equity shareholders, and with the waning of that movement, the calls for there to be statutory requirement for worker directors on company boards put shareholders' ownership rights at the centre of the debate on worker

[107] Poole (1986) 44.
[108] 'RTZ' (1974) 42.
[109] Fatchett (1977) 10. That industrial democracy increases efficiency is often cited as an argument in its favour, although it was not universally accepted: 'Clegg questions the claim that "Industrial democracy is good for business" ... For him, there is "no logical connection between democracy and efficiency" and probably not much evidence either, while the case for industrial democracy rests on political principles alone' (Ackers (2007) 91). See also Clegg (1960) 84; Martin (2003).
[110] Middlemas (1979) 453; Elliott (1984) 117.
[111] Elliott (1984) 134.

representation at all companies, both private and public.[112] Although the industrial democracy movement appeared to be gaining momentum amongst a wider audience, a hurdle in its development and adoption was the need for legislative reform to compel comprehensive changes in corporate behaviour.[113] Whereas the discretionary implementation of policies for increased worker participation was becoming more broadly accepted, the demands to formalise these requirements through law were considered a more radical, and more problematic, stance to endorse.[114] In its political manifesto of 1955, the Labour Party adopted a policy that went further than just ideological commitments to industrial democracy, making reforms a statutory priority: 'We will encourage schemes of industrial democracy and introduce long overdue legislation to improve working conditions in shops and offices.'[115] This political expression of support by Labour for legally enforced industrial democracy was about working conditions, which included issues such as wages, injury and redundancy compensation, and human resource departments, campaigns that were typically spearheaded by the trade unions, but, significantly, it did not call for worker representation that would put employees on the board.[116]

Undoubtedly there are those, including some trade unionists and socialist ideologues, who believed that the movements to democratise industry could lead to systemic changes, yet, despite loud and forceful arguments in favour of reforms, the legal status quo remained intact. The 'stickiness' of a system based on shareholder primacy persisted, alongside the clamouring for stakeholder representation and industrial democracy, with the core legal framework remaining static.[117] Furthermore, the fact that the support for the democratisation of industry was coming from different quarters suggests that the very concept was malleable to the specific needs of separate interest groups, a development on which Clarke commented:

> It is exceedingly rare that a concept gains such widespread support from so many diverse organizations as 'industrial democracy' has recently acquired. Political, business and trade union leaders (many of whom are not otherwise distinguished in their commitment to democratic principles and practice) have queued to assert allegiance to the promise of this reform.[118]

This could be interpreted as the widespread endorsement of systemic reform that benefits many constituents or, alternatively, as a banner under which many players could march to appear supportive of a popular movement, but that does not result in substantive changes.

[112] Elliott (1984) 101.
[113] Clift, Gamble and Harris (2000) 73.
[114] Kahn-Freund (1977) 72; Williamson (2016) 129.
[115] Labour Party (1955); Dale (2000b) 86.
[116] Middlemas (1979) 397.
[117] Davis (2021) 906; Clift, Gamble and Harris (2000) 73.
[118] Clarke (1977) 351.

Industrial democracy, including worker representation, was positioned as bringing necessary challenges to a system that kept labour outside of the management suite, but these demands for change remained contained within the existing framework.[119] Even if the Companies Act were reformed to require companies to have worker directors, this change in core law would still preserve the structure of the corporation even if the make-up of the board were altered.[120] Post-war nationalisations programmes called for the disassembling of large portions of private industry that was meant to bring transformative change to the British economy, which is in contrast to the statutory inclusion of worker directors on boards, which bolstered the preservation of private industry and the existing role of the equity shareholder, albeit with more limited powers.[121] Whereas the former sought to disrupt the status quo, the latter was simply tinkering with the levers that did not require systemic change. Through this lens, the demand for worker directors was seen by those who opposed the established system to be a subversive force that strengthened the capitalism that they were targeting for dismantling, refuting the claim that industrial democracy was a way to strengthen labour from within by eroding the power of capital.[122]

A. Compromise and Discretionary Requirements

With the increased interest in industrial democracy in the mid-1960s, there was a shift in the position of the trade unions on how they envisioned its implementation, with many unionists seeking to cooperate with companies to find discretionary solutions, not yet demanding statutory change, a compromise position on which Kahn-Freund remarked: 'Even in 1966 the TUC advocated legislation "of a discretionary character" designed to enable companies by agreement with the unions experimentally to adopt a participation scheme, and compulsory legislation was rejected.'[123] Although the TUC was advocating for some legislative changes, these were not compulsory and were within a framework that preserved management's control, while increasing its own power as its partner, and it was not until their policy shift in the 1970s that a general scheme of participation was endorsed.[124] For much of the post-war era, the trade union leadership was, for the most part, aligned with employers in their opposition to the statutory requirement for worker directors in British companies.[125]

In a period when industrial strife was intensifying in Britain, industrial democracy was seen by those on both the political right and left as a means by

[119] Fox (2017) 201.
[120] Williamson (2016) 130; Clift, Gamble and Harris (2000) 81.
[121] Barry (1965) 372; Elliott (1984) 260.
[122] Cressey and MacInnes (1980) 6.
[123] Kahn-Freund (1977) 72.
[124] Kahn-Freund (1977) 72; Clarke (1977) 357.
[125] Kahn-Freund (1977) 71.

which to address the grievances of the workforce and engage with their union representatives.[126] The questions of how to address the issues of industrial democracy included whether they should be solved with statutory solutions, and the Conservative Party, whilst in opposition, pledged in its 1966 manifesto to pass a new Industrial Relations Act and to establish a (not legally enforceable) Code of Industrial Relations Practice, which the Labour Party and trade unions strenuously opposed, and that were part of the programme on which the Conservatives returned to power under Edward Heath in the 1970 general election.[127] The Conservatives' approach to addressing Britain's industrial relations challenges did not include the use of legislation to promote industrial democracy. The Conservative Trade Unionists expounded upon this position, citing the need for customised solutions that could not be achieved through statutory requirements:

> [B]ecause participation is linked so closely with the place of work, there can be no rigid rules or legislation on the application of participation to each enterprise. Instead, participation must be geared to the needs of the individual workplace and employer. The participation must be flexible, free to evolve and able to adjust appropriately to changing circumstances. Participation is a living thing, compounded as it is of the individual talents of the workplace – it must not be strangled by the shackles of unduly detailed legislation.[128]

The support for voluntary changes and the need to preserve management's right to decide was positioned as defending British industry against the heavy-handed promoters of oppressive legislation; in their fight to fend off calls for legal reform, the proponents of the existing system portrayed mandatory statutory requirements as the enemy of industry and the tool of the anti-capitalists seeking to repress productivity and growth.[129]

B. Industrial Relations Legislation

Heath's Conservative government introduced the 1971 Industrial Relations Act and the non-binding Code of Industrial Relations Practice of 1972 that interpreted the Act's guiding principles.[130] The Industrial Relations Act, the first comprehensive legislation addressing industrial relations in the UK, focused on the responsibilities of management to employees and their union representatives,

[126] Goss (1973) 3.
[127] Abbott (1973) 13; Conservative Party (1966); Dale (2000a) 167. The Act was subsequently passed by Parliament in 1971 (and repealed in 1974). Abbott comments that: 'It is ironic that the active implementation of this Code [the Industrial Relations Code of Practice] – the provisions of which are the immense benefit to trade unions and employees alike – has been retarded because of the "non-cooperation policy" of the TUC' (Abbott (1973) 20).
[128] Conservative Trade Unionists (1970) 5.
[129] Williamson (2016) 127; Conservative Trade Unionists (1970) 5, 13.
[130] Gould (1972) 1442.

although neither the statutory rights of stakeholders nor the legal underpinning of shareholder primacy were changed.[131] In contrast to the calls for increasing the representation of workers on boards, or even for the requirement for directors to consider workers' interests as was proposed in the failed 1973 Companies Bill, the Act diluted the rights of the trade unions, which, by weakening this key stakeholder, served to strengthen shareholders.[132] The Act, which established limitations on 'unfair' practices of both employers and employees, and which used legal restrictions, including limiting the unions' use of economic sanctions in industrial disputes, was pointedly ineffective at realising the goal of having more control over workers.[133] Unsurprisingly, the Act was opposed by the Labour Party, the political left and the trade unions, which saw their rights eroded, resulting in strikes, boycotts and further disruptions in industrial relations.[134] The trade unions took the decision not to cooperate with the Act, which was 'presented as unnecessary, harmful and counterproductive, accusations that could only be rebuffed in the absence of industrial unrest'.[135]

In defence of the heavily criticised Act, Conservative proponents argued that this legislative progress 'represents a change in the doctrine of management; a recognition by Parliament that employees have become increasingly integrated in the enterprise for which they work'.[136] Even the supporters of the Act, however, recognised that it did not fully address the issues at the core of the industrial democracy movement, acknowledging that:

> Yet, to date, company law still fails to accept the reality that they [workers] are at least as much a part of the company as the shareholders. If there is to be more co-operation and less conflict in British industry and commerce one of the first essentials is that Boards of Directors should be regarded as trustees of shareholders and employees alike.[137]

The flawed Act's failure was not unexpected as both its underlying premise and its enforceability were questionable, and its demise served as a warning to later governments attempting to construct new legal frameworks for labour relations, and then trying to enforce them despite opposition from all sides.[138]

True to their electoral promises and to the terms of the Social Contract, Labour repealed the Industrial Relations Act in 1974 when they returned to power, although by then the legislation had already been defanged by the judiciary.[139] Labour promised in their February 1974 election campaign not only

[131] Robertson and Sams (1972) 48; Gould (1972) 1443.
[132] See ch 4, s 4.8 on the 1973 Companies Bill.
[133] Davies (1978) 247; Gould (1972) 1443. See also Rideout (1971).
[134] Robertson and Sams (1972) 52.
[135] Warner (2019) 549.
[136] Abbott (1973) 13.
[137] Abbott (1973) 13.
[138] Robertson and Sams (1972) 52.
[139] Abbott (1973) 4; Dorey (1995) 103; Dorey (2019) 202.

to repeal the 1971 Act but also to replace it with an Employment Protection Act and an Industrial Democracy Act, thereby creating legislation to 'increase control of industry by the people'.[140] Following the February election that gave neither party a majority, the subsequent resignation of Heath and the inability of Wilson to form a majority coalition, a second general election in 1974 was called.[141] With the results of a hung Parliament in February, the Conservatives, citing national unity as their reason but also perhaps recognising the direction of the political currents that were keeping them from power, changed course and pledged in their October election campaign not to re-introduce the Industrial Relations Act.[142]

For the October election campaign, the Labour Party went further than the commitments it made in February, promising to back up its industrial democracy policies with statutory changes and declaring that it:

> [W]ill introduce new legislation to help forward our plans for a radical extension of industrial democracy in both private and public sectors. This will involve major changes in company law and in the statutes that govern the nationalised industries and the public services.[143]

How much these industrial relations positions contributed to the election results is difficult to measure, but it was Labour that the electorate returned to government.

C. Labour's Redoubled Commitment to Industrial Democracy

Labour's victory with a three-seat majority in October 1974 transferred power back to a party that was cooperating closely with, and was heavily influenced by, the trade unions, giving them a mandate to introduce policies that would increase workers' rights, including making changes to company law to enact legal requirements for British companies to take employee interests into consideration.[144] The building-up of industrial tensions and the increasing power of the trade unions were central to these political developments, and the Labour Party became bolder in its commitment to addressing industrial relations, appearing intent on introducing statutory reforms that would result in structural changes to the relationship between the owners of industry and labour.[145] When addressing the questions of ownership and the control of British industry, the Labour

[140] Labour Party (1974a); Dale (2000b) 189; Fatchett (1977) 23; Lewis and Clark (1977) 325.

[141] Edgerton (2018) 363.

[142] Conservative Unionist Party (1974b); Dale (2000a) 230. The February 1974 Conservative Party manifesto remained committed to the essential structure of the Industrial Relations Act, albeit one that it would amend following consultations and with the benefit of experience; see Conservative Unionist Party (1974a); Dale (2000a) 210.

[143] Labour Party (1974b) 13; Dale (2000b) 203.

[144] Radice (1974) 4.

[145] Clift, Gamble and Harris (2000) 65.

Party and those on the left of the political spectrum, including the unionists, pushed for the formalisation of increased inclusion through the mechanisms of industrial democracy, with the aim of achieving statutory support for these policies that would result in changes in UK company law.[146] In the mid-1970s, the promise of industrial democracy legal reform burnt bright, although the fulfilment of the commitments made in opposition proved challenging once faced with the realities of governing.

The Labour Party's return to power in 1974 occurred in a political environment that corresponded with the accelerating accumulation of power by organised labour, and that year the TUC adopted its important policy statement on industrial democracy, laying out its detailed position, expectations and demands, which included proposed legislation.[147] The repeal of the Industrial Relations Act by the Labour government was supported by organised labour, and the TUC's expectation was that new legislation, in the form of an Employment Protection Act and an Industrial Democracy Act, would be introduced to strengthen the rights of workers and trade unions, and that there would be a reform of the Companies Act that reflected the advances of industrial democracy.[148] The TUC's proposed changes to the Companies Act were mostly concerned with board composition and responsibilities, including a two-tier board structure, and that there was the requirement that '[t]his change should be reflected by a statutory obligation of the companies to have regard to the interests of workpeople as well as shareholders'.[149]

Having legal requirements for worker representatives on company boards added complexity to the relationships amongst directors, shareholders and workers, and blurred the lines separating these different stakeholders.[150] In an attempt to adopt a more inclusive form of capitalism, one group of directors (that is, worker representatives) were given powers that could marginalise other groups in pursuit of outcomes that were not in the interests of all shareholders – for example, worker directors voting for wage increases instead of greater distributions of profits.[151] The TUC, in its 1974 endorsement of worker directors and of a two-tier board structure, explained in its policy statement that 'the system of two-tier boards is probably a desirable development in that the structure gives workers' representatives a degree of joint control over all major decisions of the company: closures redundancy, major technological

[146] Elliott (1984) 212.

[147] Trades Union Congress (1974).

[148] Trades Union Congress (1974) 44.

[149] Trades Union Congress (1974) 45.

[150] Kahn-Freund (1977) 76.

[151] Kahn-Freund (1977) 76. This concern was not limited to worker representatives, but applied to any shareholder group that could exercise effective control. This same argument is made for the benefits enjoyed by any shareholder groups with concentrated control, of which worker shareholders could be one (Armour (2020) 329; Shleifer and Vishny (1997) 747). See ch 5, section III.A.i of this volume on the misalignment of interests between worker shareholders and other shareholders.

changes, mergers, etc'.[152] The TUC's proposal for the requirement of this board structure explicitly demanded legislative changes that subjugated the shareholder to the worker directors:

> The supervisory board would be the supreme body of the company and while it would take into account the interests and views expressed at the AGMs of shareholders it would not be bound by them. The supervisory board would be responsible for determining company objectives, the policies necessary for their achievement, and for monitoring and reporting progress to workpeople as well as the shareholders and, through returns to the Registrar of Companies, to the wider public … The management board would be appointed by the supervisory board and would be responsible to it for the day-to-day running of the company, according to the objectives and policies laid down.[153]

Alongside these recommendations by the TUC, the new Labour government had plans to strengthen its position on industrial democracy through changes in law, taking steps to meet the objectives set out in its manifesto, including 'to provide the means by which company law can be revised in the light of the changing needs of shareholders, consumers, workers and the community as a whole'.[154] The proposed reforms would fundamentally alter the relationship amongst stakeholders and recalibrate a system based on shareholder primacy, goals that proved easier to promise than to implement when faced with the need to address the (often competing) interests of all constituents.[155] The ongoing calls for stakeholder capitalism, including (but not limited to) worker representation, continued to face challenges – that is, that the rhetoric promising the reforms comes much easier than their enactment, especially when changes to core law are required.

The TUC, which had previously limited its support to the discretionary implementation of industrial democracy policies, encouraged by the new Labour government and its socialist mandate, expressed confidence that the government would support its demands for industrial democracy by introducing legislation, stating boldly that: 'Participation is about power. Industrial democracy will lead to a socialist society. It's our show that is on the road.'[156] Statutory worker representation became a central issue in the struggle amongst the various players wrestling for control of the policies that would direct the British economy and shape it for the future, with the questions of legislative solutions impacting both workers and shareholders in British industry.[157] This change in approach by the TUC to call for statutory requirements for worker representation on boards corresponded with a more general change in attitudes in Britain towards

[152] Trades Union Congress (1974) 38.
[153] Trades Union Congress (1974) 39.
[154] Labour Party National Executive Committee (1975) 5.
[155] Clift, Gamble and Harris (2000) 80.
[156] 'The TUC Goes for Parity' (1976) 79; see also Davies and Lord Wedderburn of Charlton (1977).
[157] Davies (1978) 247.

regulation, precipitated by the difficult economic conditions of the 1970s and the end of the post-war settlement – that is, that the self-regulation norm that protected the position of the entrenched elite was no longer acceptable.[158] Although the post-war governments intervened in major ways – for example, establishing the welfare state and the privatisation of certain industries – there were also significant areas of social and economic activity that were left mostly untouched by the state as Britain remained committed to preserving self-regulation as the predominant means of regulating its economy.[159]

D. Worker Directors and Shareholder Interests

The political left and the trade unions took positions that challenged shareholder primacy, supporting statutory requirements for worker directors that impacted the interests of existing shareholders, including their right to appoint and remove all directors, and the proposal to introduce directors who were not the representatives of shareholders was a fundamentally transformational reform.[160] The building pressure for increased industrial democracy targeted the shareholders who provided companies with risk capital, and the demands for worker representation was one step along the continuum of the ongoing ideological struggle in Britain between labour and capital. Anthony Touche, the retiring chairman of the Association of Investment Trust Companies, stated in 1973:

> Shareholders' interests must be remembered in the various proposals being put forward for business reform and increasing worker participation ... 'Much has been heard this year about the face of capitalism ... The healing of the warts on this face is necessary, and the criticism valuable only if it leads to a stronger and more healthy system. There is a danger, however, that this criticism may lead to a denigration of capitalism in general and of the role of the shareholder in particular.'[161]

For Touche, representing a segment of the increasingly dominant institutional investors, it was politically expedient to make statements about change and inclusion, but it was preserving the rights of shareholders and the capitalist system in which they function that were the primary concerns.[162]

Whereas the idea of the worker shareholder became more acceptable to, and even encouraged by, the politicians who sought to preserve the existing system,

[158] Yeung (2010) 74. For an overview of the development of the regulatory state in Britain, see Moran (2001). See also Fox (1985) 381 on the establishment's fear of encroachments on their freedom and independence.

[159] Moran (2001) 20; Fox (1985) 381.

[160] City Company Law Committee and Great Britain Committee of Inquiry on Industrial Democracy (1977) 10.

[161] Owen (1973) 28.

[162] See Chiplin, Coyne and Sirc (1977) 34 for a contemporaneous discussion on the economic implications of the change in property rights that results from an extension of industrial democracy.

the demands to have worker-appointed trade union representatives on boards were not widely endorsed, with the Conservatives taking the position that:

> The appointment of worker-directors is not the first or the most obvious way of achieving real participation involving the whole of the labour force. A Conservative Government will encourage the implementation of schemes which fully involve all employees in the operations of their companies. Schemes for financial participation will also be encouraged.[163]

For the established market players, a balance needed to be achieved between meeting the calls to address the inequities of capitalism that were being manifested in disruptive industrial unrest and ensuring that all participants have a stake in the existing, if evolving, system, thereby making it in their interests to preserve it.

E. Workers' Rights to Information

The right for workers, and not just shareholders, to access company information was another aspect of industrial democracy for which there were attempts at more rigorous legal obligations.[164] The employees' right to information, specifically on matters that directly affected them, was a concept advanced by the Conservative government that enacted the (ineffectual) Industrial Relations Act in 1971, acting on a 'new principle: ie, that employees should be entitled to information similar to that provided to shareholders'.[165] The failed 1971 Act was a legislative milestone for statutory disclosure obligations, creating a duty for companies to share information with the trade unions and, when the Labour government repealed the Act, new legislation was introduced to replace, and expand, these requirements.[166] In the 1970s there was a growing trend by company boards to create special reports for employees, which was not a legal requirement, although by the end of the decade there was a decrease in the number of companies starting to offer employee reporting. These special reports were widespread and, according to one 1979 survey cited in *Towards a New Industrial Democracy*, a study by the industrial sociologist Michael Pool, 42 per cent of the surveyed companies reported this practice, as did 80 per cent of those with over 1,000 employees.[167] Voluntary employee reports were promoted as a way to increase the level of engagement between directors and their employees, and were widely available despite professed concerns by critics

[163] Thomson (1977) 38; Labour Editor (1976) 3.
[164] Clift, Gamble and Harris (2000) 64.
[165] Abbott (1973) 14; Dorey (1995) 112. As part of the shareholder democracy movement, shareholders were also engaged in a struggle for increased disclosure, with access to company information being a lynchpin issue of corporate governance. See Kellett (1962) 47; Garrett (1956–57) 312.
[166] Poole (1986) 54.
[167] Poole (1986) 54.

that access to information would strengthen the trade unions in their opposition to management.[168]

The Labour Party's position on industrial democracy supported workers' rights to information and consultation: 'Workers should have the right to information on, for example, manpower and labour costs, ownership and control of the company, the projected work-load, pricing policies and development, production, and investment data.'[169] Likewise, the TUC objected to existing company law only requiring that information be disclosed to shareholders, seeing information not only as a right of workers but also as a necessity for effective negotiation and bargaining for their members.[170] For some advocates of industrial democracy, limitations on what information workers received were unacceptable and inconsistent with a broader definition of managerial accountability, with the case being made by the Institute for Workers' Control that:

> Information which is needed by workpeople for bargaining purposes is even more needed for planning purposes ... If disclosure is restricted to employees on the basis solely of their rights in employment, then it cannot possibly become the basis of the necessary information input for democratic regional planning.[171]

There was opposition from within industry to sharing information with employees, as there was for increasing disclosure to shareholders, although the CBI deviated from the views of some of its members by taking the more progressive position of not opposing the idea of sharing more company information or having below-board consultations with the aim of increasing worker participation, with Sir John Methven, the CBI's Director-General, stating that: 'We believe employees should have the rights to information, rights to be consulted about all decisions that affect them, where possible before they are taken, and rights to access the senior executives in the company.'[172] In 1973, the CBI declared that 'we support full disclosure of information to employees, subject to the important proviso that information of interest to shareholders must be given to them no later than it is given to the employees'.[173]

The willingness to share information with workers was a way for companies to show progress in support of industrial democracy and contributed to positive corporate public relations, regardless of whether or not employees (or their union representatives) made use of it, and this access to additional information was presented as a way for workers to increase their knowledge and their ability to contribute more to the managerial control that they were seeking.[174] The trade unions and management did not always agree on the

[168] Poole (1986) 53.
[169] Wilson (1973) 12.
[170] Trades Union Congress (1974) 12.
[171] Barratt Brown and Coates (1975) 12.
[172] Elliott (1978) 7.
[173] Confederation of British Industry (1973a) 18.
[174] Hanson and Rathkey (1984) 164.

quality and comprehensiveness of the information provided by companies, a matter that required legislative solutions if the standardisation of disclosure and its content were to be enforced.[175] Disclosure requirements and the control of information were central to the post-war industrial democracy considerations and the efforts to empower workers, and were important levers in the struggle for power amongst stakeholders.[176]

IV. THE UNREALISED POTENTIAL OF POST-WAR INDUSTRIAL DEMOCRACY

Industrial democracy has been part of the wider debate on the relationship between capital and labour since the nineteenth century, but it was in the 1970s, when the post-war agreement was drawing its final breaths, that it entered mainstream discourse and was viewed as a key issue by politicians and legislators, albeit one that failed to achieve systemic reforms.[177] In 1970, British voters removed Wilson's Labour Party from government in an election for which industrial democracy was an explicit part of Labour's platform, with the manifesto asserting that 'political democracy is of limited value unless it is underpinned by industrial democracy'.[178] With the Conservatives in power for the first four years of the decade, industrial democracy was not a policy priority for the government, although it remained part of the ongoing discussions on industrial relations and was central to the conflicts over the 1971 Industrial Relations Act.[179]

Although the Conservative Party did not make industrial democracy and employee participation an explicit part of its platform, these remained important issues for the legislators, politicians and policy-makers seeking to address the difficult economic conditions and crises of the 1970s, as well as the social and political challenges posed by the gradual dissolution of the post-war consensus as 'civil society willingly tolerated a resurgence of the central, metropolitan-oriented state as the only means of subordinating chaos'.[180] In the 1973 Bow Group report on employee participation in British companies, it framed the question of employee participation within the more fundamental issue of democratic enfranchisement, stating that:

> The question now is not who has a right to elect the Government, but who has a right to take part in those decisions in business and industry which immediately affect the lives of the employees or have far-reaching implications for society as a whole.[181]

[175] Poole (1986) 54.
[176] Confederation of British Industry (1977) 24; Fatchett (1977) 16.
[177] Williamson (2016) 138.
[178] Labour Party (1970); Dale (2000b) 174.
[179] For a contemporaneous overview and analysis of the Act, see Rideout (1971). It is notable that, unlike for the Labour Party, the term 'industrial democracy' does not appear in any of the Conservative Party election manifestos from 1945 to 1979.
[180] Middlemas (1991) 449.
[181] Goss (1973) 1.

Worker representation was a concept that fit comfortably into the broader societal discourse on democracy and embodied the changing attitudes of increased inclusion, but without disrupting the existing capitalist framework. As industrial unrest, mirroring the methods of political upheaval, threatened the status quo, industrial democracy and the rights of stakeholders in general and workers in particular were part of the larger historical struggle for political participation and democratisation.[182]

A. Political Polarisation

Calls for radical upheaval and systemic revolution were mostly pushed to the margins during the political cooperation of the post-war settlement; however, a relatively ambitious platform for reform, of which industrial democracy was a key tenet, was forming in the Labour Party in the period leading to their return to government in 1974, a time of industrial unrest and economic stress caused by the 1973–75 recession that ended the period of post-war economic growth and led to the end of the consensus that had defined British politics since the end of the Second World War.[183] British politics was reverting back to its equilibrium and, as described by the historian Keith Middlemas:

> The polarisation in the public debate which the appeals of a radical left and right began to induce weakened the liberal, pluralistic and elitist conventions which had facilitated intermediate levels of activity within the state for thirty-five years.[184]

Witnessing the building momentum and public support for the principles of industrial democracy, the trade unions, as the organised representatives of labour, positioned themselves to take the lead in these developments, placing themselves as the agents of the necessary changes to a system that until then had made only token gestures to industrial democracy through worker representation on the boards of nationalised companies.[185]

Industrial democracy remained a foundational element of the Labour Party's platform, with Wilson, whilst in opposition, declaring in a speech at a regional Labour Party conference in 1973 that:

> Unless radical changes are made in relations between management and shop-floor it will be become increasingly difficult for modern industry to function effectively. It is no longer a question of whether workers should play a greater part in their day-to-day factory life – but how this is to be done.[186]

In the same speech, Wilson also proclaimed that: 'The whole history of the Labour movement is based on our realisation that political democracy is an

[182] Poole (1982) 191.
[183] Morgan (1992) 356ff.
[184] Middlemas (1991) 178.
[185] Elliott (1984) 210.
[186] Wilson (1973) 11.

empty symbol without economic democracy, and that economic democracy is meaningless without industrial democracy.'[187]

B. British Industrial Democracy in the Face of Political and Economic Headwinds

Alongside the popular sentiments that led to the Labour electoral victories, the political tide was rising in support of non-shareholder stakeholders having more influence in the decision-making of British industry, which was a byproduct of a business environment that had changed dramatically since the end of the Second World War, including with economic ownership and control increasingly being exercised by company directors and senior management.[188] The political, economic and social conditions in the mid-1970s worked against the advancement of meaningful industrial democracy initiatives, and although Labour replaced the Conservatives in government in 1974, they struggled with parliamentary minorities and instability under both Wilson and Callaghan.[189] There was no general consensus on the needed reforms as economic hardships and industrial unrest undermined Labour's programme, and it was in this environment that the Bullock Committee, a new committee on industrial democracy, was established:

> [A]gainst the background of the British economy's persistent weakness, reflected in problems of management and industrial relations as well as the recurrent crises in the balance of payments and the currency. In the 1970s the situation further deteriorated with the onset of the worst recession in the capitalist world since the 1930s, and the marked relative decline of investment in British manufacturing industry.[190]

The stock market crash of 1974 and the inflationary economic conditions weakened the Labour government's position, and questions about the viability of a mixed economy and a planned society were raised as the post-war consensus was increasingly challenged by Britain's declining global trade position and growing industrial unrest.[191] The Labour government saw inflation peak at 25 per cent in 1975, the result of a number of economic events, including the negative effects of the 1973 oil crisis, the pressures of negotiated wage increases by the unions and rising food prices associated with the European Community policies, which created doubts about Labour's economic competence and ability, as well as their suitability to steward Britain to recovery.[192]

It was in this difficult economic environment that the trade unions intensified their demands for the formalisation of the mechanisms of industrial democracy,

[187] Wilson (1973) 4.
[188] Lewis and Clark (1977) 323.
[189] Dorey (1995) 126.
[190] Lewis and Clark (1977) 323. See ch 7 on the Bullock Committee.
[191] Dutton (1997) 105.
[192] Dorey (2019) 206; Morgan (1992) 376.

even as the governing Labour Party became less able to deliver meaningful systematic changes. Fatchett discussed these circumstances in his 1977 paper:

> Workers and their trade unions have been increasingly forced by events to recognise their own inability to influence the major strategic decisions of industry. The merger process of the last decade [from the mid-1960s onwards], and the subsequent centralisation of decision making, have resulted in a situation in which a company's economic decisions now process far ranging economic and social implications, but still without being subject to effective trade union control. As technology passes into an increasingly labour saving phase, and as the structural weaknesses of the British economy result in more redundancies and rationalisations, so an ever increasing number of trade unionists have sensed the need for joint regulation of industry's strategic decisions.[193]

In these difficult economic conditions at the end of the post-war consensus, support for industrial democracy weakened, with the British public, disillusioned with Labour and suffering the effects of the industrial unrest of the 'winter of discontent', choosing in 1979 the Conservatives' capitalist platform as the path to recovery.[194]

C. The European Economic Community

In addition to the mounting domestic economic challenges of the 1970s, the process of joining the European Economic Community (EEC) added another existential political event that challenged the Labour government. The legal implications of joining the EEC introduced a new aspect to the British debate on industrial democracy, and Wilson's initial intention to bring UK law into line with that of the EEC fanned domestic ambitions for employee parity and board representation similar to what was required in certain European jurisdictions.[195] The European examples of industrial democracy were examined in close detail as British industry considered its own future within an economic union that had alternative templates of industrial relations and corporate governance.[196] Britain's membership of the Common Market required it to engage with the European Commission's draft Fifth Directive on company law and the draft Statute for the European Company, both of which supported worker representation on company boards.[197]

[193] Fatchett (1977) 9.

[194] Elliott (1984) 294.

[195] Pollak (2013) 106.

[196] Brannen et al (1976) 210ff; Abbott (1973) 240ff; Conservative Trade Unionists (1970), 15ff; Williamson (2016) 123. See also Lord Bullock, *Report of the Committee of Inquiry on Industrial Democracy* (Cmnd 6706, 1977) ch 1, paras 6–8, ch 3, paras 13–14, ch 4, paras 10–12 and ch 6, paras 48–50 on Europe and the EEC.

[197] Lewis and Clark (1977), 323; Davies (2010) 292ff. The Fifth Directive (September 1972) was part of the Commission's proposal to harmonise company law amongst Member States; see Abbott (1973) 9. In Trades Union Congress (1974) 15–19, the TUC gives an overview of the implications for

The influence went both ways across the Channel and the UK's joining the EEC also affected the development of European industrial democracy, weakening support for a mandatory two-tier board system, as well as introducing strong opposition to the initiative to use the German model to harmonise the national company laws.[198] Adding to the economic and political uncertainty of the second half of the decade, and foreshadowing the more recent events in Britain, Wilson, who inherited the decision for Britain to join the EEC from his Conservative predecessor and was unhappy with the terms that were agreed, put the question of membership to the British public in a referendum in 1975, with 67.2 per cent voting to remain in the EEC.[199] Despite Wilson's objections to the terms on which Britain had joined the EEC, the supporters of the agreement argued that industrial relations would be enhanced by the influence of European attitudes, even though there were no provisions for the harmonisation of industrial relations policies amongst Member States.[200]

Pressure was being put on the government to review Britain's approach to industrial democracy and employee participation, including to consider statutory changes to provide for worker representatives on boards that are common in EEC member countries, although on different terms from those that were promoted by the TUC in Britain.[201] The TUC, committed to the idea of two-tier boards since its 1974 policy statement, demanded that worker representatives be tied to the unions, a principle that was not found in the European examples.[202] The TUC's requirement that the trade unions be the only vehicle through which workers would gain access to board representation was a uniquely British approach and contrasted with the more inclusive European methods that did not tether worker directors to union membership, a stipulation that potentially disenfranchised non-unionised employees.[203]

industrial democracy of Britain's entry into the EEC and its summary of the attitudes of European countries to worker participation, including the EEC proposals of a statute for the 'European Company', a new legal entity, and the Fifth Directive of Company Law, which proposed a similar structure that would balance the interests of the company, the shareholders and workers. On the CBI's objections, see Confederation of British Industry (1973a) 15.

[198] Horn (2012) 85.

[199] Dorey (1995) 133. The tides of political change were already being felt as the country voted 'yes' in the referendum and, in the same year, Margaret Thatcher, who supported remaining in the EEC, was elected leader of the Conservative Party, replacing Edward Heath, whose economic policies were supported neither by the City nor the Party's base.

[200] Clarke (1977) 357; Horner (1974) 187.

[201] Abbott (1973) 4. For a discussion on the differences between the TUC's recommendations (as presented in the Bullock Report) and the EEC's Fifth Directive, primarily the TUC's demand that worker representatives be tied to union membership whereas the EEC supported representation for all workers, as well as the UK's unitary board system as contrasted to the EEC's two-tier board system, see City Company Law Committee and Great Britain Committee of Inquiry on Industrial Democracy (1977) 7ff; Clift, Gamble and Harris (2000) 70.

[202] Middlemas (1991) 180; City Company Law Committee and Great Britain Committee of Inquiry on Industrial Democracy (1977) 8.

[203] See section I.E above on the TUC as gatekeeper.

Wilson's decision to hold a referendum was also driven by his desire to pacify the left of the Labour Party that opposed membership of the EEC on the grounds that it was a collective of capitalist states that supported free trade. As a socialist party, it was natural that there were objections as Britain joined an economic system that preserved the existing relationship between labour and capital, and joined a federation whose power relied on strengthening and expanding a joint market, which the Labour left saw as a 'capitalist club'.[204] In contrast, taking a position against the Labour Prime Minister and serving as a strong example of the gulf between the financial community and the government, the City was resoundingly in favour of membership, with a letter to members from the Stock Exchange Council stating that 'the withdrawal of the United Kingdom from the EEC would be disastrous both for the Nation and, in particular, the City', a position supported by the *Financial Times*, which maintained that voting against EEC membership was 'a gratuitous act of irresponsible folly'.[205]

Joining the EEC created a revised political landscape that accompanied Britain out of the mindset of post-war reconstruction and into a new era that included European membership and the economic policies of the Thatcher years. Britain's entering the EEC, like its recent exit from the European Union, was not without its complications, including questions of industrial democracy and worker representation, and how Britain's approach differed from those of its fellow members.[206] Britain curtailed the discussions and blocked attempts at European harmonisation of company law, although pressures from Europe to establish common accounting standards and other regulatory frameworks remained.[207] The Companies Act 1980 implemented the EU Second Directive, which dealt with share capital and company classifications, and the Companies Act 1981 implemented the Fourth Directive on company accounts.[208] European countries provided examples of alternative ways of addressing the demands of workers and unions, and the proposition of Britain conforming to the regulations of Europe was embraced by some and shunned by others. On the issues of industrial relations, the British legal, regulatory and corporate traditions were not easily aligned with those of Europe and, with some idealistic exceptions, UK law-makers were not looking to change.[209]

[204] Dorey (1995) 131.

[205] Kynaston (2001) 521. This divergence between the Labour socialists and the City on the subject of Britain's membership in the EEC is recognisable to current observers of the end of Britain's membership in the European Union and an example of the durability of these positions.

[206] Clift, Gamble and Harris (2000) 71; Horn (2012) 89.

[207] Gamble and Kelly (2000) 43.

[208] Farrar and Hannigan (1998) 23.

[209] Davies (2010) 292ff.

7

The Bullock Committee

A Paper-Tiger Attack on the System

I. ESTABLISHING THE COMMITTEE OF ENQUIRY

AMIDST THE POLITICAL volatility of the mid-1970s, the debate on industrial democracy was gaining momentum as the ideological camps became increasingly entrenched in their respective positions and the post-war consensus buckled under the weight of economic hardships and societal stress.[1] Harold Wilson's Labour government, eager to reach agreement amongst the various constituents on a statement of principles, was conspicuously slow in producing the anticipated White Paper on industrial democracy; the government did eventually establish a Committee of Enquiry in December 1975, led by Alan Bullock, but only after it was pressured by a Private Member's Bill introduced by the MP Giles Radice.[2] This Committee of Enquiry was expected to produce the promised White Paper, which, in turn, was regarded as a prelude to long-awaited industrial democracy legislation. At the time of its creation, the Bullock Committee held the promise of delivering the hoped for systemic changes based on legal reforms.[3]

Under the terms of the Social Contract, the establishment of the Committee of Enquiry into Industrial Democracy was a material step in fulfilling the Labour Party's commitment to the trade unions to introduce industrial democracy legislation.[4] The announcement to the House of Commons of the creation

[1] Williamson (2016) 125.

[2] Middlemas (1991) 180; Lewis and Clark (1977) 325; Williamson (2016) 126. A total of 250 MPs voted for the Bill, which was given a second reading and went to a Standing Committee for consideration. Its suspension by the government's announcement of the Committee was seen by some of its supporters as a means of evading the actions required by the Bill. See Clift, Gamble and Harris (2000) 76.

[3] Elliott (1978) 263.

[4] Fatchett (1977) 23. In addition to the Chairman, Lord Bullock, the members of the Committee were: Professor G Bain, Director of the SSRC Industrial Relations Research Unit, University of Warwick; Mr NP Biggs, Chairman of Williams & Glyn's Bank Ltd and former Chairman and Chief Executive of Esso Petroleum Co Ltd; Sir J Callard, Former Chairman of Imperial Chemical Industries Ltd and Chairman of British Home Stores Ltd; Mr B Heath, Chairman of Guest, Keen and Nettlefolds Ltd; Mr C Jenkins, General Secretary of the Association of Scientific, Technical and Managerial Staffs; Mr J Jones, General Secretary of the Transport and General Workers Union;

of a committee 'to advise on questions relating to representation at board level in the private sector' framed its mandate as:

> Accepting the need for a radical extension of industrial democracy in the control of companies by means of representation on boards of directors, and accepting the essential role of trade union organisations in this process, to consider how such an extension can best be achieved, taking into account in particular the proposals of the Trades Union Congress report on industrial democracy as well as experience in Britain, the EEC and other countries, having regard to the interests of the national economy, employees, investors and consumers, to analyse the implications of such representation for the efficient management of companies and for company law.[5]

As described at the time in the *Industrial Law Journal*:

> This was, thus, yet another recent public statement accepting that the need for an extension of industrial democracy is beyond argument and defining industrial democracy in terms of worker representation on the board. Much of the credit, or blame, for this situation can be attributed to the efforts in recent years to the TUC which has consistently promoted the idea, and whose recent report on the subject the committee is to take particularly into account.[6]

With the creation of the Bullock Committee, the focus of industrial democracy in Britain was now on worker representation on company boards, which was made a priority by the most powerful trade unionists and by the government to which they gave their support and with which they partnered.

The Bullock Committee was established to address British industry's complicated industrial relations, with the Wilson government committed to pursuing the type of societal planning and re-engineering that was successful during the Second World War and its immediate aftermath, although by the mid-1970s Britain was lagging its European neighbours and failing in its own economic goals.[7] Industrial democracy embodied the belief that the labourer had a right to participate in the decisions of, or even the ownership in, the company for which he or she worked, a concept that gained considerable political momentum as the conflict between workers and the owners of industry intensified in

Mr D Lea, Secretary, Economics Department, Trades Union Congress; Professor KW Wedderburn, Cassel Professor of Commercial Law in the University of London (London School of Economics); and Mr NS Wilson, Solicitor. See Lord Bullock, Report *of the Committee of Inquiry on Industrial Democracy* (Cmnd 6706, 1977) Preface, para 2. There was one additional member of the original Committee, Mr J Methven, who signed neither the Majority Report nor the Minority Report and resigned when he became Director-General of the CBI, 'but his total opposition to the majority report is well known' (Confederation of British Industry (1977) 5).

[5] Lord Bullock, *Report of the Committee of Inquiry on Industrial Democracy* (Cmnd 6706, 1977) Preface, para 1.

[6] 'Reports and Awards: Industrial Democracy' (1975) 250.

[7] Morgan (1992) 429.

the 1970s, and labour unrest and industrial relations became central issues for the government as it addressed Britain's economic problems and the breakdown of the post-war consensus.[8] The pressure for worker representation was building, culminating in the TUC, with its membership of approximately 11 million workers, endorsing the policy and with the government's creation of the Bullock Committee to study the issues with the goal of making legislative changes:

> [P]erhaps the most immediate factor leading to the Bullock Committee was a decisive shift in trade union and labour movement policy, occurring at a time when close co-operation between the TUC and the Labour Party facilitated the translation of union policy into government action.[9]

The TUC backed the Labour government's decision to establish the Bullock Committee, which faced resistance from industrial groups and from the CBI, as well as from some individual trade unions.[10]

The Fabian Group, presenting evidence to the Bullock Committee in 1976, summarised the concept of industrial democracy, explaining that:

> The democratic case within industry has the same moral basis as democratic arguments elsewhere – that every individual should have a say in those decisions which affect his life. And at a time when democratic values are widely recognised throughout society, it is difficult to deny their validity within the factory and office … The move away from a 'deferential' community towards a more 'assertive' one has had a major impact on industry.[11]

Workers were less deferential and more openly critical of management, the result being that 'formerly unquestioned "managerial prerogatives" have come under increasingly strong challenge, and management have had to develop consultative and "participative" styles of work'.[12] The premise that post-war social changes had created more engaged and active workers was advanced by those promoting the organisational and legislative changes supporting industrial democracy and the empowerment of labour that formed the basis of the Committee's investigation and its findings, with the Industrial Society's guide to the Bullock Report, which sought to explain the findings to a mass audience, concluding that: 'Employees are less prepared to accept without question unilateral decisions by management. Traditional management prerogatives have come under attack.'[13]

[8] Williamson (2016) 121.

[9] Lewis and Clark (1977) 324. For a concise overview of the development of the relationship between the Labour Party and the trade unions, as compared to the corresponding development in Germany, see Frege (2003) 249ff.

[10] Furlong (1977) 98; Radice and Lewis (1976) 2; Fatchett (1977) 23.

[11] Radice and Lewis (1976); Clarke (1977) 353.

[12] Coates and Topham (1977) 26.

[13] Henderson (1977) 3.

A. The Bullock Report's Challenging Inception

The Labour government, facing pressure on its ruling majority, needed to balance the demands for action from its allies on the left, namely organised labour and the TUC, with not alienating or antagonising industry and the CBI or the dissenting trade unionists, and, unconvincingly, presented the Bullock Committee as a broad consultative body.[14] The Committee's members were announced in December 1975, the result of a highly divisive and polarised process, beginning with the fact that the Chairman, Lord Bullock, as well as the rest of the Committee members were vetted by the TUC.[15] Unsurprisingly, the CBI objected strenuously to the very principles on which the Committee was founded.[16] The CBI gave evidence to the Committee in 1976 that supported the business representative members, who reacted to the partisan nature of the Committee's composition by becoming more entrenched in their position, leading to a split recommendation, with the Majority Report representing seven of the 10 members, accompanied by a note of dissent from one member, and the Minority Report representing the remaining three members.[17]

Although the Committee was established under the leadership of Prime Minister Wilson, the Bullock Report was published in January 1977 under a Labour government led by the Party's new leader, the former trade union official James Callaghan.[18] This change in party leadership corresponded to a gradual, and meaningful, shift in the government's approach to industrial democracy.[19] When the first draft of the Bullock Report was presented to Callaghan's Cabinet, it was viewed as being fundamentally important, as Tony Benn, then Secretary of State for Energy, described in December 1976: 'I thought this was possibly the biggest decision the Government had to take during its lifetime and it was comparable in importance to the extension and development of the franchise.'[20] By the time the final Report was published, however, Benn's initial enthusiasm appeared overstated; as the CBI observed, 'there have been voices raised in total support of the Bullock Report, but significantly, even three months after publication of the Report, these voices have not so far included Mr Callaghan and his senior cabinet colleagues'.[21] The lack of coherent support within the Labour Party and the labour movement, as well as criticisms of the dominant role of the TUC in the Report's recommendations, created an opportunity for the Report's critics within Callaghan's cabinet to sideline it.[22]

[14] Middlemas (1991) 180.
[15] Middlemas (1991) 180; Lewis and Clark (1977) 326.
[16] Confederation of British Industry (1977) 3.
[17] Middlemas (1991) 181; Confederation of British Industry (1977) 3.
[18] Fatchett (1977) 23.
[19] Clift, Gamble and Harris (2000) 76.
[20] Benn (1989) 690.
[21] Confederation of British Industry (1977) 13.
[22] Clift, Gamble and Harris (2000) 80.

II. THE TUC, THE MAJORITY REPORT AND THE MINORITY REPORT

In the post-war period, the influence of the trade unions grew and the workforce that they represented became more empowered, with the unions making demands from industry and government that might appear commonplace today, but were viewed as radical and disruptive when initially mooted.[23] With the Labour Party back in government in the mid-1970s, it seemed like there was sufficient momentum to bring about systemic industrial democracy reform. Despite the lack of unanimity amongst supporters of industrial democracy, the goals of worker representation and parity alongside equity investors were consistent with the political agenda of the Labour government and the Social Contract with the trade unions.[24] Labour worked closely with the TUC on its industrial democracy strategy and this cooperation with the unionists was politically beneficial, delivering potential political dividends for politicians that could tap into the influence of the union leaders and access their members, an important constituency.[25]

A. The TUC's Position

The TUC demands from the Bullock Committee were, essentially, for the restructuring of the joint stock company and included: (i) worker representation on the board be a legal right that a recognised and independent union could demand; (ii) the selection of board representatives through trade union machinery; (iii) half the seats on the board to be occupied by worker representatives; (iv) these provisions to apply to all companies and groups that employed 2,000 or more people; (v) the responsibilities of worker representatives to be analogous rather than identical to those of shareholder representatives and that their reporting back to their constituents be safeguarded; (vi) a change in company law so that companies would have a statutory obligation to take care of the interests of employees, as well as shareholders; and (vii) that reform be carried out through the existing unitary board system (a reversal after initially requiring a supervisory board structure).[26] When giving evidence to the Committee, the TUC

[23] See ch 6, section I of this volume on the trade unions and worker representation.

[24] Elliott (1984) 36.

[25] Radice (1974) 2.

[26] Coates and Topham (1977) 33–34; Lord Bullock, *Report of the Committee of Inquiry on Industrial Democracy* (Cmnd 6706, 1977) ch 4, para 2-9; see also 'The TUC Goes for Parity' (1976) 79. For summaries of the Bullock Report, see Kahn-Freund (1977); Henderson (1977); Fatchett (1977) 26ff. Kahn-Freund's analysis of the Bullock, Report was decidedly critical and he summarises his views with the following statement: 'Though it might be a little unusual, I should like to have the privilege of ending this paper with a personal observation. My scepticism towards employee representation in the corporate organs of business enterprise goes back to the time of the experiment made in this direction more than half a century ago in the Weimar Republic. I recognise that much water has flown under the bridges of the Thames and also of the Rhine since those days, and that

revised and eased its demands, with the Report clarifying its original position on the two-tier board, stating that:

> In their [the TUC's] supplementary and oral evidence however they modified their view on board structure, indicating that their basic objectives could also be achieved in the context of a reconstituted form of the unitary board which presently exists in the United Kingdom. The TUC view is that such a reconstituted policy board should be the supreme organ of the company, with the ultimate right to overrule the general meeting of shareholders on certain specific issues.[27]

Although cloaked in language that suggested that the TUC had not softened its position and including proposed limitations of the shareholders through the organ of the general meeting, this rhetorical deflection did not conceal the major concession of accepting the existent unitary board structure, which was what the Report recommended.[28]

In addition to the structural changes, the TUC recommended to the Bullock Committee mechanisms by which the board, which would include worker directors, could not be overruled by the shareholders, with the shareholders conceding power to the new board in the following areas: (i) changing the company constitution; (ii) winding up; (iii) changes in the capital structure; (iv) proposing dividends; and (v) selling significant parts of the business.[29] Under the proposed recommendations, shareholders would also cede to the board the power to: (i) allocate or dispose of resources (including planning, investment, research and development, and budgeting decisions); and (ii) the appointment, removal, control and remuneration of management.[30] Although the TUC sought to limit shareholder power, it acknowledged that worker directors would have the same legal responsibilities as shareholder representatives and that there would be a statutory definition of directors' duties that would apply to all categories of directors, which required them to vote in the company's best interests, no longer accepted as being solely the shareholders' interests, and not to vote as delegates of any specific group (for example, workers).[31]

both the proposals of the Bullock Report and the present law for the Federal Republic and other European countries are very different from the feeble and half-hearted German scheme between the Wars. Nor can I forget how difficult it is, at an advanced age to abandon firm views formed in the past, and perhaps under conditions that are no more. For all these and other reasons I was determined to read the Bullock Report with an open mind – I was doing my best to find the road to Damascus and to turn from a sceptic into a believer. It is my painful duty to confess that I did not succeed' (Kahn-Freund (1977) 83).

[27] Lord Bullock, *Report of the Committee of Inquiry on Industrial Democracy* (Cmnd 6706, 1977) ch 4, para 7.

[28] Davies (1978) 267.

[29] Trades Union Congress and Great Britain Committee of Inquiry on Industrial Democracy (1977) 12.

[30] Trades Union Congress and Great Britain Committee of Inquiry on Industrial Democracy (1977) 12.

[31] Trades Union Congress and Great Britain Committee of Inquiry on Industrial Democracy (1977) 14; 'Look Who the Owners are' (1977), 82.

This concession by the TUC on directors' duties was in agreement with the position taken by industry, as expressed by the CBI:

> We consider that it is the duty of each member of the board to pay full regard to all interests which should be considered. Thus, each member must at all times have in mind interests such as those of shareholders, of all employees, of customers, of creditors and of the public in the country or countries in which it is operating. No member of the board should be entitled to disregard any of these interests; from which it follows that no member should serve one interest only.[32]

Similarly, as expressed by the Conservative Research Department:

> Under our present system, directors are under obligation not to actively represent sectional interests. All are equally responsible for promoting the overall interests in the company. Here is the crux of the matter. *No director should be appointed primarily to 'represent' any special interests – including those of employees.* (Emphasis in original)[33]

The composition of the board, and the division between the representatives of labour and of capital, was a key issue for the Committee to consider. The TUC's recommendations to the Committee were for there to be a statutory requirement for worker representation on boards:

> [D]emanding that the way in which policy is formed in an enterprise be altered to reflect *equality* between labour and capital in the running of enterprise. They argue that this equality should be expressed by allotting 50 per cent of the places on a reconstituted policy board to representatives of employees and 50 per cent to representations of shareholders. (Emphasis in original)[34]

The demand for workers to be on equal legal footing with shareholders, and to be able to block their decisions and limit their power, exemplified the unionists' (misplaced) confidence in their position and ability to promote their industrial democracy platform, which, by the end of the decade, proved to be unwarranted.

B. The Majority Report

Whereas the TUC's original arguments in favour of the two-tier board were considered, and the continental examples were studied and appraised, ultimately the Majority Report opted for the unitary board structure that the TUC had also come to accept, with the Committee members concluding that

[32] Confederation of British Industry (1973a) 16.

[33] Abbott (1973) 16.

[34] Lord Bullock, *Report of the Committee of Inquiry on Industrial Democracy* (Cmnd 6706, 1977) ch 4, para 6.

the two-tier system contravened company law and practice, and was technically too complex.[35] As explained (or justified) by the TUC Guide to the Bullock Report:

> It was clear to the Bullock Committee that it would be impractical to introduce this [European] two-tiered system to the UK. It was clear that worker representatives on supervisory boards have had very little power. The committee concluded that representatives should therefore be on the existing company board.[36]

The Majority Report proposed a definition of board powers and that the shareholders' meeting would retain the right to approve the board's proposals in certain circumstances, referred to as the 'attributable functions of the board', including: (i) winding-up of the company; (ii) changes to the memorandum and articles of association; (iii) recommendations to shareholders on the payment of dividends; (iv) changes to the capital structure of the company; (v) disposal of a substantial part of the undertaking; (vi) the allocation or disposition of resources to the extent not covered in points (iii) and (v) above; and (vii) the appointment, removal, control and remuneration of management, whether members of the board or not, in their capacity as executives or employees.[37] The Majority Report took a more moderate approach than the TUC, putting these functions in the hands of the reconstituted board, whose proposals the shareholders had the power to approve or reject.[38]

i. The 2x+y Formula

The Bullock Majority recommended that the board be composed according to what is known as the '2x+y formula', which stipulated that for going-concern companies with 2,000 employees or more in the UK, employees should have the right by law to be represented on company boards through the mechanisms of the trade unions, with company directors coming from three groups: (i) shareholders; (ii) employee representatives; and (iii) independent/co-opted directors.[39] The first two groups would be of equal size ('x') and the third group ('y') would be smaller, with 2x being roughly the size of the existing board (for example, if the existing board had nine members, the reconstituted board would have 15 members, of which six would be shareholders, six would be employee representatives and three would

[35] Lewis and Clark (1977) 331; Henderson (1977) 9.

[36] Trades Union Congress and Great Britain Committee of Inquiry on Industrial Democracy (1977) 10.

[37] Lord Bullock, Report *of the Committee of Inquiry on Industrial Democracy* (Cmnd 6706, 1977) ch 8, para 18.

[38] Henderson (1977) 22; Lord Bullock, *Report of the Committee of Inquiry on Industrial Democracy* (Cmnd 6706, 1977) ch 8, para 16.

[39] Lord Bullock, *Report of the Committee of Inquiry on Industrial Democracy* (Cmnd 6706, 1977) ch 9, para 21.

be independent directors.[40] The Report concludes that this composition of shareholders, employee representatives and non-executive 'co-opted' directors:

> [W]ill produce a mixture conducive to the efficient operations of companies. While we accept that many companies are efficiently managed by their boards, we do not take a complacent view that there is no room for improvement in this respect in British industry and we are confident that the proposed new board structure will have a considerable contribution to make to greater efficiency.[41]

The supporters of this radical legal overhaul of the relationship amongst shareholders, directors, senior management, employees and unions argued that it would be conducive to growth and efficiency, provide legitimacy to managerial authority, help to reduce industrial unrest and promote capital investment, both domestic and foreign.[42] In what could be interpreted as an attempt to appear moderate and appeal to industry and capital providers, the Majority Report's explanation of its recommendations explicitly focuses on managerial efficiency and not on the socialist principles that underpinned its industrial democracy programme.[43]

ii. A Note of Dissent

The Bullock Committee member NS Wilson, a solicitor, who signed the Majority Report, also submitted a note of dissent in which he did not accept the proposed formula for director representation, which he deemed unnecessary and he said would result in the creation of larger boards, limiting the flexibility needed to ensure maximum efficiency, concluding that the 2x+y formula would lead to 'horse trading' and polarisation:[44]

> To summarise, therefore, I find it impossible to believe that the 2x+y formula is a meaningful advance on the outright parity representation system which (as the Economist Intelligence Unit remarked) 'makes no provision for resolving any particular difference between the two sides except by means of some haphazard form of arbitration or compromise'.[45]

[40] Lord Bullock, *Report of the Committee of Inquiry on Industrial Democracy* (Cmnd 6706, 1977) ch 9, paras 25–29. See ch 9 of the Bullock, Report for the full discussion on the reconstitution of the board.

[41] Lord Bullock, *Report of the Committee of Inquiry on Industrial Democracy* (Cmnd 6706, 1977) ch 9, para 21.

[42] Lewis and Clark (1977) 330; Lord Bullock, *Report of the Committee of Inquiry on Industrial Democracy* (Cmnd 6706, 1977) ch 6, para 28.

[43] Lord Bullock, *Report of the Committee of Inquiry on Industrial Democracy* (Cmnd 6706, 1977) ch 6, para 28; Ogden (1982) 551. The Majority concluded that: 'We believe therefore that our twin aims of effective employee participation and efficient management can best be met in this country by introducing employee representatives on to present company boards' (Lord Bullock, *Report of the Committee of Inquiry on Industrial Democracy* (Cmnd 6706, 1977) ch 8, para 15).

[44] Lord Bullock, *Report of the Committee of Inquiry on Industrial Democracy* (Cmnd 6706, 1977) Note of dissent by Mr NS Wilson, para 6.

[45] Lord Bullock, *Report of the Committee of Inquiry on Industrial Democracy* (Cmnd 6706, 1977) Note of dissent by Mr NS Wilson, para 7.

In his dissent, Wilson insisted that employees should having fewer seats than shareholders, putting it at odds with the fundamental position of the Bullock Majority, so 'that one has the impression that he only signed the report in order to avoid being lumped with the Minority'.[46]

C. The Position of the Minority Report

The Minority Report, which was delivered by the three industrialist members of the Committee, took issue with the very premise of the Bullock Committee's remit that:

> [R]equired it 'to consider *how* such an extension' (representation on Boards of Directors) 'can best be achieved'; it did not require the Committee to consider *whether* 'a radical extension of industrial democracy' should be achieved by the representation of employees on Boards of Directors. (Emphasis in original)[47]

The CBI and other representatives from industry and the City gave evidence to the Committee, expressing views that were:

> [S]trongly critical of employee representation on the board based on any form of compulsion. The essence of the CBI's evidence, echoed in a number of other submissions, was a plea for flexibility in developing alternative forms of participation and for building on what had already been developed, free of any statutory right or obligation for employees to be represented on boards of directors.[48]

The Minority Report strongly rejected the proposed 2x+y formula, seeing it as 'the thin edge of the wedge, the method of infiltration which could lead eventually to Trade Union/worker control of what are in effect the management boards of the Private Sector of industry'.[49] It also objected to the formula on the grounds that it 'would introduce conflict and collective bargaining to the boardroom, was too rigid and legalistic and was fundamentally an unacceptable restraint on management freedom and action, which was equated with efficiency'.[50]

The CBI asserted unequivocally that the Bullock proposals would 'fundamentally change private enterprise in a damaging way'.[51] Because of the nature of the question asked and the assumption that worker representation on boards was taken as a given, these Committee members declared that: 'The proposals in

[46] Shackleton (1977) 231.
[47] Lord Bullock, *Report of the Committee of Inquiry on Industrial Democracy* (Cmnd 6706, 1977) Minority Report, para 1.
[48] Lord Bullock, *Report of the Committee of Inquiry on Industrial Democracy* (Cmnd 6706, 1977) ch 4, para 13.
[49] Lord Bullock, *Report of the Committee of Inquiry on Industrial Democracy* (Cmnd 6706, 1977) Minority Report, para 34.
[50] Lewis and Clark (1977) 334.
[51] Lewis and Clark (1977) 329.

this Minority Report therefore represent, in our considered view, the best ways of fulfilling what we regard as a far from satisfactory or even wise remit.'[52] The Minority Report recommendations should not be taken as an endorsement of the premise of Bullock's Committee, but, rather, as their response to the specific question put to them. The Minority made it clear that, whereas they supported some aspects of industrial democracy, they were not in favour of worker directors and argued that '[c]ertainly it is unwise to impose "democracy" on those who are unwilling or unready to receive it'.[53]

An underlying assumption of the Minority Report, proposed by the representatives of industry and the de facto defenders of the existing system, was that the behaviour in British boardrooms was without reproach – that is, the manifestation of the theoretical ideal, described by the economist JR Shackleton in his assessment of the Bullock Report, that 'highly talented and disciplined professionals take correct decisions in a constructive atmosphere free from conflict and faction'.[54] This view was based on an idealised theory of director behaviour rather than reflecting the range of conduct by the boards of British companies and the varied abilities of their members. The Minority asserted that:

> [N]o one should be misled into believing that the comparative objectivity with which complex economic and human problems are brought into focus by the professional Boards of our large companies in the Private Sector could be maintained, let alone improved, by the injection into these Boards of representatives of powerful sectional interests, whether or not organised by the Trade Unions.[55]

In addition to this unwillingness to acknowledge the shortfalls and limitations of management, and consistent with established biases towards workers, the Minority also emphasised what they saw as the lack of ability and weakness of employees, presenting them as unable to participate in board-level decisions, and claiming that their exclusion from representation was in the best interests of the workers themselves because having them on boards would 'place employee elected representatives in the wholly invidious position of being obliged to sit in on discussions to which they might have nothing to contribute because they were not properly equipped to contribute to this particular type of deliberation'.[56] Echoing the long-standing criticisms of industrial democracy, the opposition to the Majority's proposals to increase workers' power considered them

[52] Lord Bullock, *Report of the Committee of Inquiry on Industrial Democracy* (Cmnd 6706, 1977) Minority Report, para 1.

[53] Lord Bullock, *Report of the Committee of Inquiry on Industrial Democracy* (Cmnd 6706, 1977) Minority Report, para 9; Shackleton (1977) 232.

[54] Shackleton (1977) 232.

[55] Lord Bullock, *Report of the Committee of Inquiry on Industrial Democracy* (Cmnd 6706, 1977) Minority Report, para 32.

[56] Lord Bullock, *Report of the Committee of Inquiry on Industrial Democracy* (Cmnd 6706, 1977) Minority Report, para 33; Shackleton (1977) 232. See ch 6, section I.D of this volume on worker capabilities.

ill-equipped to make managerial decisions, claiming that labour could not be trusted in this new role of constructive responsibility that required the unions to adapt from their usual negative role of confronting and criticising management from outside the board.[57] That the Minority did not entertain the prospect that worker representatives could improve the management of British industry, compounded by their blinkered certainty in the quality of directors, was the very attitude against which the proponents of industrial democracy were pushing, attempting to make the managerial elite more accountable to workers and other stakeholders.[58]

The City Company Law Committee, an initiative formed by the Governor of the Bank of England in 1974 that gave evidence to the Bullock Committee, expressed opposition to legislating the changes in board composition:

> The Majority Report (7,23) rightly notes that in most companies the board is the apex of the decision-making hierarchy and the focus of managerial authority. Any legislation, however much it may purport to advance the aims of industrial democracy, which impairs the single-minded and cohesive determination of this 'apex' to further the interests of the company as a whole cannot, in our view, possibly be in the interests of anyone – customers, shareholders or employees.[59]

In addition, the City Company Law Committee argued that the trade unions' demand for compulsory employee board members 'has little to do with the true objective of what has come to be called "industrial democracy"', which it saw as workers' involvement in their work within the company, which might take many forms within a broader interpretation of the movement.[60]

The Minority Report explained its objections, declaring:

> We are completely opposed to the introduction into existing Boards of representatives of special interests of any kind which might provoke confrontation or extend the scope of collective bargaining into top level management decision-making.[61]

Employee participation was seen by its detractors as being inherently conflicted, allowing workers to use an additional avenue to strengthen their collective bargaining position, and that the worker directors would not serve the general interests of the company, but would prioritise the sectional interests that they represent.[62] For the Report's critics, the Majority recommendations were giving

[57] Elliott (1984) 66.

[58] For a discussion on the perceived low quality of British managers in the post-war period, see Cheffins (2008) 338ff.

[59] City Company Law Committee and Great Britain Committee of Inquiry on Industrial Democracy (1977) 8.

[60] City Company Law Committee and Great Britain Committee of Inquiry on Industrial Democracy (1977) 3.

[61] Lord Bullock, *Report of the Committee of Inquiry on Industrial Democracy* (Cmnd 6706, 1977) Minority Report, para 32.

[62] Cottrell (1978) 59.

labour an additional front from which to wage a war of attrition against capital, and introduced the risk of worker representatives interfering with, and diminishing, the management of British industry.[63] Although the Report's proposals were viewed as a weak compromise that brought labour inside the existing system by entangling it in the mechanics of industrial management, the proposal to install worker representatives on company boards made some opponents fearful of the distortions that could be achieved from within.[64]

III. THE BULLOCK REPORT AND SHAREHOLDER PRIMACY

A. Legal Rights of Shareholders

The recommendations of the Bullock Report dealt directly with the questions of shareholder rights and interests, with the intention that statutory changes would follow.[65] In its 1974 policy statement on industrial democracy, the TUC, taking a firm position on worker representation as a means by which to limit shareholder powers, called for 'stringent limits on the collective ownership rights of shareholders', although the evidence that it submitted to the Bullock Commission was less overtly hostile.[66] Both the TUC's policy statement and its evidence to the Bullock Committee acknowledged the status quo of shareholder primacy and the entrenched position of equity owners, and when addressing the Committee, the TUC conceded that it 'recognised the ultimate power which ownership of capital confers on shareholders, ie the right of withdrawal of capital, can only be altered by changing the pattern of ownership itself by political means'.[67]

The TUC, in supporting statutory employee representation on boards, advocated for revisions in company law:

> Their view is that present company law reflects a conception of management's responsibilities to capital and labour that is outdated and inappropriate in the prevailing economic and social climate. The law defines 'interests of the company' as the interests of shareholders as a whole in the long term. The TUC Report argued, as indeed did many other submissions of evidence, that the law should be altered to reflect the essentially joint interest of labour and capital in the enterprise by placing statutory obligations on companies to have regard to the interests of employees as well as shareholders.[68]

[63] Lord Bullock, *Report of the Committee of Inquiry on Industrial Democracy* (Cmnd 6706, 1977) Minority Report, para 32.

[64] Clift, Gamble and Harris (2000) 78.

[65] Elliott (1978) 263.

[66] Trades Union Congress and Great Britain Committee of Inquiry on Industrial Democracy (1977) 10; Lewis and Clark (1977) 328.

[67] Lewis and Clark (1977) 328.

[68] Lord Bullock, *Report of the Committee of Inquiry on Industrial Democracy* (Cmnd 6706, 1977) ch 4, para 5.

Existing company law, which upheld the principle of shareholder primacy, did not reflect the growing separation between ownership and control, the de facto control by management and directors, and '[t]he problem is that employees scarcely feature in company law, and are often no more than a marginal constraint on the power of top management'.[69] The Majority Report required that the board of directors take into account the interests not only of shareholders but also of workers, a proposal that had a precedent in the doomed Conservatives' Companies Bill in 1973.[70] The Majority Report was seen to address this issue:

> '[T]he company' is to be defined as embracing the interests of both of these groups … this proposal to redefine the interests of the company is usually regarded as uncontroversial, on the grounds that it is merely bringing the law into line with 'reality'.[71]

The Bullock Report recommended systemic and legal changes that transferred certain powers to the board of directors, on which there was worker representation and to which responsibility for certain key decisions was given – that is, those that affect the interests of employees – and for which the board alone can convene a meeting, although with shareholders retaining the right to vote on whether to pass these resolutions or not.[72] The Majority Report stated that:

> We are proposing considerable changes in the legal rights of shareholders, though it will be argued below that in practice the changes may not be as great as they seem. They are necessary because, if our proposals are adopted, the new concept of partnership between capital and labour in the control of companies will supersede the idea that a company and its shareholders (ie its 'owners' or 'members') are one and the same thing … The power of individual shareholders to sell their shares remains, of course, unaffected and constitutes the normal recourse to shareholders who dislike the way a company is being run.[73]

The Bullock Report recommendations limited the power of shareholders in some areas; that is, with the introduction of worker directors, shareholders

[69] Lewis and Clark (1977) 330.

[70] With the defeat of the Conservatives in 1974, the Conservative Party's Companies Bill was shelved. The Bill also addressed other aspect of shareholder democracy, eg, non-voting shares and insider dealing (Companies Bill 1973–74). See Fleming (1976) 7; Lord Carr of Hadley (1982) 97. See also ch 4, section VIII of this volume.

[71] Davies and Lord Wedderburn of Charlton (1977) 198; Lewis and Clark (1977) 332. Lord Bullock, *Report of the Committee of Inquiry on Industrial Democracy* (Cmnd 6706, 1977) ch 8, para 29.

[72] Lord Bullock, *Report of the Committee of Inquiry on Industrial Democracy* (Cmnd 6706, 1977) ch 8, paras 27–28.

[73] Lord Bullock, *Report of the Committee of Inquiry on Industrial Democracy* (Cmnd 6706, 1977) ch 8, paras 26. See Chiplin, Coyne and Sirc (1977) 52 for a critique of this approach by the Report: 'This development would not only be to the detriment of shareholders, over whose loss no tears are shed in our day when the functions of ownership are misunderstood. It would also damage the general public (workers as consumers) in whose interest capital should not be frittered away but invested where it produces the most output.'

lost the right to appoint all directors, re-allocating power away from shareholders to workers and their unions.[74] The Report's proposal that for certain decisions the board should have legal responsibility without needing to consult shareholders, who retained the right to approve or reject resolutions, was also a constraint on shareholders, which shifted more influence to directors, including to the new worker directors, chosen through the trade union selection process and not by the shareholders.[75] By using law to prescribe the division of powers amongst shareholders, the board and managers, rather than having the shareholders and directors decide, and by limiting certain rights of shareholders in favour of the board, the Report's recommendations broke with the core principles of partnership and required fundamental changes in British company law. It was not, however, calling for basic changes in corporate behaviour, as:

> [T]he substantive content of the proposed attributed functions would merely ratify what is in practice the common position of dominance of the board and retain for the board certain basic decisions that management literature generally asserts to be decisions the board ought to take.[76]

The elevation of workers' interests to be on a par with shareholders was not restricted to representation, with the Bullock Majority proposing to give workers other rights consistent with those of equity owners – for example, requiring companies to circulate reports not just to shareholders but also to employees, addressing a long-held demand of the advocates of industrial democracy.[77] This proposal reflected the calls by the TUC for increased transparency, requiring reports both to shareholders and to employees.[78] Access to information and increased disclosure were core issues for industrial democracy and shareholder democracy, with the former seeking parity between workers and owners, and the latter seeking to address the agency problem faced by shareholders.[79] These employee-empowering proposals were presented to the Committee as ways by which to strengthen the position of workers and to reintroduce management's legitimacy, thereby improving the working relationship between labour and management.[80]

[74] Lord Bullock, *Report of the Committee of Inquiry on Industrial Democracy* (Cmnd 6706, 1977) ch 8, para 32; Lewis and Clark (1977) 332.

[75] Lord Bullock, *Report of the Committee of Inquiry on Industrial Democracy* (Cmnd 6706, 1977) ch 8, para 27; Davies (1978) 257.

[76] Davies (1978) 258.

[77] Lewis and Clark (1977) 333. See also ch 6, section III.E of this volume on workers' right to information.

[78] Trades Union Congress and Great Britain Committee of Inquiry on Industrial Democracy (1977) 15; 'Look Who the Owners are' (1977) 82.

[79] See ch 2, n 173 of this volume on shareholders and information.

[80] Coates and Topham (1977) 34.

B. In Defence of Shareholders

The Majority proposals were met with resistance from constituents determined to preserve the principle of shareholder primacy, with the City Company Law Committee stating that it was:

> [D]eeply concerned with the impact the proposals would have on the fundamental basis of the joint stock company system as it has developed in this country over a period of more than one hundred years – a system based on the concept that the ultimate authority and control over a company rests with those who provide the capital (ie, the shareholders) in general meeting … This is the framework upon which the development of the joint stock company has been based – and this is the framework which the Bullock proposals would seek to replace by a neo-syndicalist structure of joint regulation by shareholders and union-appointed employees.[81]

In addition, and in agreement with a similar position taken by the CBI, the Institute of Directors also opposed employee directors as a threat to 'the essential role of a board, whose members should be the best available, appointed for their fitness to play a part in a well-integrated team'.[82] These 'best available' directors, seen through the lens of the industry and in the words of the Minority, were 'consisting primarily of persons with appropriate specialist and/or professional experience and training to fit them to plan and control the company's operations as executive directors'.[83]

Some opponents to the Bullock proposals focused on the rights being taken away from shareholders, something that was seen as a threat to the basic principles of property-ownership rights.[84] The CBI refused to accept three main elements of the Bullock Report's recommendations: (i) legally required worker directors; (ii) parity; and (iii) the trade unions' exclusive right to the nominations of worker directors.[85] The CBI rejected the TUC's industrial democracy proposals as an 'unacceptable erosion of both managerial prerogative and private property rights'.[86]

The City Company Law Committee broadly supported the CBI in its position that industrial democracy should be approached by companies on an individual basis to reflect specific needs and corporate structures.[87] Richard Dixon, the CBI's special affairs director, was quoted in the *Financial Times*

[81] City Company Law Committee and Great Britain Committee of Inquiry on Industrial Democracy (1977) 4.

[82] Ream (1978) 19.

[83] Lord Bullock, *Report of the Committee of Inquiry on Industrial Democracy* (Cmnd 6706, 1977) Minority Report, para 31.

[84] Batstone, Ferner and Terry (1983) 4.

[85] Middlemas (1991) 181.

[86] Radice and Lewis (1976) 2.

[87] City Company Law Committee and Great Britain Committee of Inquiry on Industrial Democracy (1977) 4.

in 1978 as stating that: 'Maybe some people want to overturn this traditional ownership structure; but our members don't want to, and we believe that many other people in the country do not want to either.'[88] The CBI sought to protect the status quo, the established order that the TUC's recommendations would upend, that is, that of shareholder primacy, arguing to preserve the existing system in which 'directors cannot allow any other financial interest or responsibility in their capacity as directors, other than responsibility to shareholders', effectively ruling out worker representatives on company boards.[89]

The objectors to the recommendations to dismantle the system of shareholder primacy claimed that, if adopted, they would threaten companies' access to equity financing:

> By restricting the power of shareholders over 'their' firms, it can be argued that the Bullock reforms would destroy the traditional functions of shareholder power of any description. The economic case for shareholder power – and, indeed, part of the justification for shareholder income – lies in two features of classical capitalism: the risk-bearing function and the element of market discipline of a stock exchange provides.[90]

The CBI characterised the proposals to restrict shareholder powers and the recommendations of statutory changes as threats to the liquidity and vitality of the capital markets, as quoted in *The Times*: 'If Bullock prevails, shareholders will more than ever be reduced to a passive role. Their legally sanctioned influence will be limited to voting only with their feet. Undoubtedly this is what many will do.'[91] Normative financial theory asserts that taking the control over management away from shareholders, even if this control was not being used, would lead to the decrease in the flow of risk capital to companies and an increase of financing by means other than equity.[92]

C. Confirming the Status Quo

The expressions of fear of what was viewed as the government's assault on shareholder primacy was seen in some quarters as exaggerated and histrionic, believing that the Bullock recommendations amounted to nothing more than shareholders being 'required to cede control which they rarely exercise to people who already partly own the business anyway' through their pension funds or other worker-shareholder schemes.[93] A gradual re-alignment of interests was

[88] Elliott (1978) 7.
[89] Trades Union Congress (1974) 12; Elliott (1978) 244.
[90] Shackleton (1977) 230. See also City Company Law Committee (1975) 8 on concerns regarding the effects of worker representation on companies' ability to borrow and raise capital.
[91] Confederation of British Industry (1977) 11.
[92] Shackleton (1977) 231.
[93] 'Look Who the Owners are' (1977) 82.

occurring at the same time as the unions were fighting for worker representation whereby a growing number of workers were becoming shareholders themselves, a few directly but most indirectly, which might make them less inclined to disrupt the operations of the companies in which they own shares.[94] By the time of the Bullock Committee deliberations, the stereotypical labourer with no thought for tomorrow was disappearing, replaced by workers who were increasingly likely to have pensions and/or to have invested through savings vehicles like unit trusts.[95]

The Bullock Report claimed that: 'Essentially therefore our proposals will have the effect of bringing law into line with reality, rather than reducing any real power or valuable rights that shareholders possess.'[96] This argument accompanied claims that company directors dismissed shareholders' meetings as little more than a formality, a contributing argument to the Committee's conclusions, which was also presented by Professor Wedderburn, a member of the Bullock Committee and a signatory of the Majority Report, in a 1977 paper, stating that:

> The shareholders' meeting normally goes along with management, and management can normally muster enough proxies in real life not to be worried too much by the shareholders' meeting. Indeed we had directors who said to us on the Bullock Committee: 'The shareholders? They are the last people we think of!'[97]

Regardless of whether the recommendations were codifying the realities that already existed or were truly revolutionary, the Bullock Report proposals called for a material change in the existing system, including core legal reforms. Shackleton made the argument that the Bullock Report was only reflecting what was already occurring – that is, that:

> [T]he proposals are only logical developments of processes already under way. Unions are *already* extending collective bargaining, managers *already* recognise the need to consider the interests of their employees; shareholders are *already* losing their power to control management, and so on. (Emphasis in original)[98]

For some, however, the implications of the Bullock Report's recommendations were momentous, or as John Methven, a former member of the original Bullock Committee who resigned to become the CBI Director-General, contended: 'Majority Bullock, by removing the ultimate control of shareholders, would be an act of confiscation, and would fundamentally change the free enterprise system as we know it.'[99] On the one hand, the Bullock recommendations were viewed as radical reforms and an assault on British capitalism, whereas, on

[94] See Davies (2019) 96 on pensions and industrial democracy. See also ch 5 of this volume on the worker shareholder.

[95] Zweig (1961) 206.

[96] Lord Bullock, *Report of the Committee of Inquiry on Industrial Democracy* (Cmnd 6706, 1977) ch 8, para 29.

[97] KW Wedderburn (1977) para 1.10.

[98] Shackleton (1977) 230.

[99] Confederation of British Industry (1977) 7.

the other hand, they were seen as little more than a continuation, and formal acknowledgement, of a systemic evolution that was already underway.

For the recommendations of the Bullock Report to be implemented, including that worker directors be nominated exclusively by the unions and to have parity with shareholders' directors, industrial democracy legislation was needed.[100] Shareholder primacy was intact despite decades of repeated and concerted attempts by other stakeholders (most notably workers, trade unions and their supporters) to bring about statutory changes to the existing system; nonetheless, in the face of vocal criticisms of shareholders and urgent calls for companies to address their responsibilities to other stakeholders, the core law enshrining shareholder primacy remained unreformed.[101] The Bullock Report was intended as the precursor to new legislation and legal changes to the Companies Act, yet despite the attempts to recalibrate the interests of the various stakeholders, this episode in British industrial democracy did not result in statutory changes to the laws supporting shareholder primacy, but, on the contrary, was followed by a change in government and an era that witnessed the strengthening of the shareholder, the capitalist system and the structures that nourished them.[102]

D. The Interests of the Company

In its desire to promote industrial democracy, the potential conflicts amongst the interests of different stakeholders were minimised in the Bullock Report's assumptions regarding the company's interests, which did not address the fundamental ways in which shareholders and employees differ in terms of their relationships to the company and how their interests can diverge. As explained by Kahn-Freund:

> The so-called 'interest of the company' is always identical with the interest of its shareholders, not *the* interest, but *an* interest. But the employees concerned with the dispute about the introduction of labour-saving machinery [for example] have nothing to gain from this measure: the company's interest may be irreconcilably opposed to that of each member of that employee group … the company's interests may be opposed to those of workers in a sense in which they cannot be opposed to the shareholders, not, for that matter, those of the creditor. (Emphasis in original)[103]

Expressing its concern over the potential conflicts of interest, the City Company Law Committee argued:

> We believe that the effective conduct of a company's business requires a unity of purpose on boards, and an ability to act collectively on behalf of and in the interests

[100] Ream (1978) 19.
[101] Williamson (2016) 135.
[102] Elliott (1978) 310; Moran (2001) 26.
[103] Kahn-Freund (1977) 76.

> of the company. An employee director would on occasion be called on to take part in decisions which, though in the long-term interest of the company, might be unpopular with some of his fellow employees or contrary to the policy of his union … Even if the employee directors constituted only a minority of the board, to participate in such decisions might well give rise to a conflict between their duty to as directors and their loyalty to their fellow employees or trade union.[104]

From the company's perspective, employees were an outside force, whereas shareholders represent groups or individuals, even when they are in conflict, are a force inside the company.[105] Furthermore, by demanding board representation for workers and curtailing the existing power of equity shareholders, the interplay amongst stakeholders was complicated even more, as the same individual could be a worker, a worker shareholder, a worker director and a union official, each identity motivated by differing incentives that were not always aligned.[106]

The opponents to the Bullock Majority rejected the assertion that worker directors would not priorities the interests of their constituents above those of the company, arguing that by introducing worker representatives, the nature of how boards function would change, with these new directors, who were not elected by shareholders, representing the interests of a defined group of stakeholders, as opposed to the traditional role (supported by law) of all directors representing the interests of all shareholders, regardless of their identity.[107] In the unitary board system that was the status quo and was ultimately recommended by the Majority Report, the worker directors were described as representatives and not delegates, requiring these directors to execute a challenging balancing act, a claim that was questioned, and 'what must be emphasised here is that the entire concept of the worker representative who is not a delegate rests on a dubious foundation'.[108] To complicate things further, the worker directors were chosen through the machinery of the trade unions, adding another level of potentially conflicting priorities, as well as an undemocratic stratification amongst workers depending on which union they joined or if they were union member at all.[109]

The Report's attempts to redefine the interests of the company and to undermine the accepted primacy of shareholders were contested: 'The fact that the shareholders' powers are seldom exercised does not mean that they are not real.

[104] City Company Law Committee (1975) 4.

[105] Kahn-Freund (1977) 76. For a detailed discussion of Kahn-Freund's views on worker representatives on boards and the conflict between shareholders and employees, see Moore (2018) 158.

[106] See also ch 6, section III.C of this volume.

[107] This argument for excluding worker directors can be countered with examples of company directors who represent controlling or majority shareholders.

[108] Kahn-Freund (1977) 77; Lord Bullock, *Report of the Committee of Inquiry on Industrial Democracy* (Cmnd 6706, 1977) ch 5, para 16.

[109] Williamson (2016) 127; Lord Bullock, *Report of the Committee of Inquiry on Industrial Democracy* (Cmnd 6706, 1977) Minority Report, para 33.

They can be exercised and, even where they are not, their existence remains an important check on the board.'[110] For those looking to preserve the principle of shareholder primacy, the weakening of shareholder control of companies, the acceptance of increased management discretion in determining what is in the best interests of the company, and the introduction of statutory requirements for worker directors were not welcome developments for interest groups like the City Company Law Committee, which observed in *A Reply to Bullock* that:

> Today, there seems to be no mechanism which will guarantee continuous, profit-maximizing behaviour on the part of the controllers of large companies. Neither shareholder control (whether by institutional or private shareholders), the forces of market competition, the market in corporate control via takeovers, nor the threat of liquidation seem for various reasons to be sufficient to impose on corporate managements, in fact if not in law, an element of discretion – the degree of which varies from case to case – in the setting of corporate goals.[111]

For the defenders of the status quo, Bullock's proposed introduction of worker directors threatened the interests of the company by limiting the shareholders' right to determine how their companies are managed.[112]

IV. (RE)DEFINING DIRECTORS' DUTIES

The 1975 City Company Law Committee's First Report addressed the TUC's proposals and their impact on shareholders and lenders of capital, raising concerns that labour lawyers 'will have to turn their attention now to company law and to some of the fundamental questions these raised as to the nature and purposes of corporate enterprise'.[113] The redefinition of directors' duties through changes to company law was considered one of the least controversial aspects of the Bullock Report, with 'everyone' agreeing to this change, according to Committee member Bill Wedderburn, a labour law academic and politician.[114] The legal scholar Paul Davies addressed the recommendations of the Bullock Report in 1978, arguing that because of the legal requirement to act in the best interests of the company, interpreted as acting in the best interests of the shareholders (that is, the members), altering the legal duties of directors was a major theoretical change in how the concept of the company was understood; director duties might include the interests of the employees as they relate to shareholder interest, both short- and long-term, but in law it is the directors,

[110] City Company Law Committee and Great Britain Committee of Inquiry on Industrial Democracy (1977) 10.
[111] Davies (1978) 265. See similarly Davies and Lord Wedderburn of Charlton (1977) 201.
[112] Elliott (1978) 260.
[113] 'Reports and Awards: Industrial Democracy' (1975) 251; City Company Law Committee (1975) 8.
[114] KW Wedderburn (1977) para 1.10.

and not the courts, who decide on what is in the shareholders' best interests.[115] Seemingly without much consideration for the impact on shareholders, or the scope of the proposed change on core company law, the Bullock Majority, and their supporters, recommended the independent recognition of employee interests, thereby diluting the existing rights of shareholders, furthering the cause of industrial democracy and the empowerment of workers based on the assumption that these proposed statutory changes were little more than a formalisation of the existing situation.[116]

The Majority Report's recommendations required the consideration of both shareholder and employee interests, and although it referred to the interests of consumers, it did not include them, or any other additional stakeholders, in the reconstituted board.[117] The Report also left open to interpretation how the interests of workers and shareholders were to be considered:

> Once it is understood that this new definition operates so as to specify the interest which the directors are to take into account and not so as to stipulate in any particular situation the weight which a director must attach to either interest, then it can be argued that the definition creates for the employee (or the shareholder) director maximum freedom of action within the context of an enterprise whose existence is seen to depend upon the continued participation of both labour and capital.[118]

For the opponents of the Bullock Majority, this 'freedom' was interpreted as a lack of clear guidance, with the City Company Law Committee's *A Reply to Bullock* drawing attention to this issue: 'Insufficient attention has been given to the fact that, if the interests of employees and shareholders are in conflict and both must be considered, there is no touchstone for determining what the directors should do.'[119] The Report does not provide for legal guidance in the event of such a conflict, introducing significant ambiguity into the interpretations of directors' duties. Consistent with the campaigns for stakeholder capitalism and the various movements that seek to challenge the shareholder primacy system, the legal details appear to be secondary to the higher-level ideas and ideals that fuel the calls for reforms, and in the post-war era the interests of workers were at the apex of these concerns, with other stakeholders – including consumers, the community and the environment – receiving less attention.[120]

[115] Davies (1978) 258.

[116] Davies (1978) 258.

[117] Lord Bullock, *Report of the Committee of Inquiry on Industrial Democracy* (Cmnd 6706, 1977) ch 5, paras 42–47.

[118] Davies and Lord Wedderburn of Charlton (1977) 198.

[119] City Company Law Committee and Great Britain Committee of Inquiry on Industrial Democracy (1977) 13; Davies and Lord Wedderburn of Charlton (1977) 202.

[120] This evolution in stakeholder prioritisation is beyond the scope of this study, requiring, amongst many other things, a detailed analysis of the rise (and fall) of trade union power, as well as of the development of social and environmental activism, as understood against a backdrop of the changing investor base.

V. POLITICAL RESISTANCE TO THE TUC PROPOSALS AND THE BULLOCK REPORT

A. The Political Left

Consistent with the criticism of industrial democracy more generally, the opposition to Bullock came not only from the industrialists, the City, and the political and economic conservatives reacting to what they saw as an attack on the system that they supported (and that supported them), but also from elements of the political left that saw the Bullock Report as a device to ensnare labour in a trap laid by capital.[121] The TUC's positions on industrial democracy, which was heavily reflected in the proposals of the Bullock Majority, were opposed not only by business groups that were the trade unions' natural opposition, but also by the Communist Party, which saw them as promoting the assimilation of labour into the capitalist system, as well as from factions from within the Labour Party itself that rejected worker representation on boards and for whom 'tough collective bargaining represents the legitimate limit of trade union and worker aspirations'.[122] The *Morning Star*, the left-leaning British daily newspaper, succinctly summarised the views of this opposition to the Majority Report, which was that the proposals were 'a bid to involve the working class man in supporting the capitalist system'.[123]

Industrial democracy's aim to change the relationship between labour and capital by empowering workers was undermined by the Bullock recommendations, which preserved the existing wage-labour system, perpetuating capital's hegemony whereby the 'hostility to *capitalists* left the social power of *capital* intact' (emphasis in original).[124] From the perspective of their critics, the TUC and the Bullock Majority might have made some gains for workers, but these were within a system that safeguarded capital's power over labour, thereby fortifying a system that they were meant to be opposing. The Bullock Committee was accused of being complicit in bolstering the existing system, with opponents on the left arguing that the fundamental weakness of Bullock is that it gives legitimacy to the established system and the capitalist control of industry to the exclusion of labour; the Bullock Majority proposals were rejected by dissatisfied factions from within the industrial democracy movement that saw the recommended changes as superficial, impotent and a tool with which to bolster the status quo that they sought to abolish.[125]

That the Report was being criticised from industry groups and the political right did not disqualify the political left from offering its own condemnations

[121] See ch 6, section II of this volume.
[122] Radice and Lewis (1976) 2.
[123] Confederation of British Industry (1977) 6.
[124] Foote (1986) 333.
[125] Clarke (1977) 360.

of the proposals. Bert Ramelson, a Communist Party industrial organiser, was quoted by the CBI – with clear self-interest in publicising criticisms of the Report from the political left – as saying: 'Workers should not be stampeded into accepting the Bullock report merely because for their own reasons the CBI and other big business representatives are making a big hooha against it.'[126] The opposition from the capitalist did not preclude the opponents on the political left from rejecting what were considered unacceptable, and potentially dangerous, compromises.[127] The Bullock Report satisfied few on either side of the political spectrum and, in its final muted form, failed to bring about genuine systemic reform or lead to industrial democracy legislation. Whereas the political left accused the Bullock Majority of bolstering the existing system, in contrast, the CBI and many of its members were suspicious of the trade unionists' industrial democracy demands, being concerned that the TUC was infiltrated by the radical left whose goal was to undermine and deconstruct the capitalist system from within.[128]

B. Union Opposition and the TUC

The TUC's position on worker participation and its recommendations to the Bullock Committee also faced resistance from individual trade unions that did not embrace its vision for industrial democracy.[129] Three major unions – the Amalgamated Union of Engineering Workers (AUEW), the General and Municipal Workers' Union (GMWU) and the Electrical, Electronic, Telecommunications and Plumbing Union (EETPU) – submitted detailed policy statements as evidence to the Committee in opposition to the TUC's proposals.[130] The engineering section of the AUEW preferred that worker representation on boards be limited to the public sector and rejected the TUC's proposed model for representation as a 'rubber stamp' that would only give the illusion of power.[131] The EETPU, a strong critic of formalised industrial democracy, opposed worker directors, but agreed that more managerial accountability was needed.[132] Expressing a long-held argument against worker representation, the EETPU was also concerned about the conflict faced by worker directors facing 'irreconcilable split loyalties' of organised workers' interests and those of

[126] Confederation of British Industry (1977) 13.
[127] Williamson (2016) 130.
[128] Middlemas (1991) 179.
[129] Brannen et al (1976) 3; Fatchett (1977) 23; City Company Law Committee and Great Britain Committee of Inquiry on Industrial Democracy (1977) 5.
[130] Lewis and Clark (1977) 326. For a full list of those who submitted evidence to the Bullock Committee, see Lord Bullock, *Report of the Committee of Inquiry on Industrial Democracy* (Cmnd 6706, 1977) Annex A.
[131] Middlemas (1991) 180; Fatchett (1977) 24; Lewis and Clark (1977) 327.
[132] Fatchett (1977) 24.

the enterprise as a whole.[133] Some unions, like the Association of Professional, Executive, Clerical and Computer Staff (APEX), accepted some of the TUC's recommendations to the Bullock Committee, but pressed for additional amendments, whereas other large unions (for example, the GMWU) disagreed on the very principle of worker directors being the best way to achieve greater industrial democracy, with the General Secretary of the GMWU, David Basnett, quoted as saying explicitly that '[t]he Bullock recommendation do not meet our union's position on industrial democracy'.[134]

Contrary to the TUC's position, many of the unions did not want their representatives sitting on company boards where they would be held responsible for management decisions and some, like leaders from the Electrical Trades Union (ETU) and the Electrical Power Engineers Association (EPEA), dismissed the Report altogether, while others, like the National Union of Bank Employees (NUBE) and the Association of Scientific Technical and Managerial Staffs (ASTMS), only partially accepted its recommendations.[135] Eager to leverage the disunity amongst the unions, the CBI published in *In Place of Bullock* a broad selection of quotations by opposing unionists to bolster its campaign again the Bullock Report's findings, for example, quoting Alan Sapper, the General Secretary of the Association of Cinematograph, Television and Allied Technicians (ACTT), as saying that: 'I do not think there is a majority in the trade union movement to give credence to implementation of the Bullock recommendations.'[136] Although much of the criticism of the Report came from industry and finance, as the CBI made clear, it was by no means confined to those who were assumed to have a vested interest in preserving the status quo.[137]

C. Objections to the TUC 'Power Grab'

The opposition to the Bullock Majority was also a rejection of what was perceived by some parties as a power grab by the TUC, whose influence on the Labour government and growing power were viewed with suspicion and resentment.[138] The TUC's backing of the government's programme for industrial democracy was an opportunity for it to consolidate power through legislative changes that ensured the TUC's representatives positions on company boards. As expressed

[133] Lewis and Clark (1977) 327.

[134] Fatchett (1977) 24; Confederation of British Industry (1977) 13. For more on the response to Bullock, and the GMWU's position in particular, see B Wedderburn (1977).

[135] Middlemas (1991) 182.

[136] Confederation of British Industry (1977) 13.

[137] Confederation of British Industry (1977) 7. Alan Fox argues that the unions, like business and finance, were part of the establishment that sought to protect itself from interference (Fox (1985) 381).

[138] Elliott (1984) 249; Williamson (2016) 134; Confederation of British Industry (1977) 6.

by the TUC in its guide to the Bullock Report, which asserted its existing position as the gatekeeper to labour:

> The report comes out unequivocally in favour of establishing a right for workers to equal representation with shareholders on boards of their companies, and is quite categorical that, for this representation to be constructive and effective, it must be based on trade union machinery.[139]

The TUC, in its push for the recalibration of the relationship between workers and their companies and its demand for statutory changes in the composition of boards, inserted itself into an essential role, a position that caused concern for the representatives of industry that identified a threat to the existing balance of power and responsibilities: 'The TUC proposals were seen as involving an extension of union power to a point where the exercise of management function could be effectively thwarted on all major issues.'[140]

Opponents to the TUC requirement that employee representatives be decided exclusively through the machinery of the trade unions saw this as a way to bring the conflicts of collective bargaining into the boardroom and of splitting directors according to interest groups, which would result in a weakened board.[141] The Chairman of the LSE, Nicholas Goodison, was quoted as stating that: 'The Bullock proposals do not seem to me to be about industrial democracy or the hopes and fears of real people. They are about the future advancement of trade unions power.'[142] The Stock Exchange's reaction to the Bullock Committee's recommendations was to declare that it could accept workers on company boards – itself a remarkable concession reflecting the changing attitudes of the time – but only 'provided that the appointment of such worker directors is always subject to the overriding right of shareholders as owners of the company to remove any director at any time', thereby insisting on preserving the existing removal rights and protecting shareholder primacy.[143]

An examination of the demands made to the Bullock Committee reveals the ambition of the TUC, exemplified by its willingness to exclude any worker not prepared to come under the TUC trade unionists' banner, with the Bullock Majority proposing that employee board representation be based on trade union machinery, although deviating from the TUC's recommendations by leaving the structure of how that was to be determined open to include other trade unions

[139] Trades Union Congress and Great Britain Committee of Inquiry on Industrial Democracy (1977) 7. See also ch 6, section I.E of this volume on the TUC as gatekeeper.
[140] Lewis and Clark (1977) 329.
[141] Ogden (1982) 557.
[142] Confederation of British Industry (1977) 8.
[143] 'Look Who the Owners are' (1977) 82. Director removal rights were granted in s 29 of the Companies Act 1947.

recognised by a company.[144] The Minority Report directly addressed this jockeying for power by the trade unions, stating that:

> It is necessary to be clear at the outset about the aims of any proposed new legislation. The TUC policy statement makes clear its view that the purpose of industrial democracy is to extend power – 'control' is the word used by the TUC in the report to the 1974 Congress – of organised labour.[145]

The CBI took a similar stance as the Bullock Minority, stating that 'the majority Bullock report was not about employee participation but about trade union control of industry'.[146]

The Bullock Report's recommendation to give trade unions control over which worker directors would join company boards, including deciding on the method for selection, was met with protest and resistance, and was seen as handing to the unions power over companies and allowing them to 'simply write their own ticket'.[147] The TUC's insistence that board representation must be controlled by the unions called into question its claim to represent the interests of all labourers and undermined the democratic basis of its efforts to reform British industry. The Minority Report used the principles of democracy to counter this requirement by the trade unions:

> It is one of the strengths of political democracy in the free world that every citizen has equal political rights and that no one has to belong to a particular party or organisation in order to exercise those rights. No citizens have to demonstrate their belief in collective representation before they can vote for a representative in Parliament. It would be a mockery of democracy as we know it to limit the rights of employees in any system of industrial democracy to those who have opted for collective representation through a Trade Union.[148]

The City Company Law Committee also objected in similar terms: 'We cannot accept the argument that the unions, because of their political power and importance in the industrial system, must monopolise any system of employee representation.'[149] The CBI rejected the unionists' attempts to empower only employees who were members of trade unions, instead supporting alternative industrial democracy legislation that included all employees, whether they were union members or not.[150] The rejection of this TUC demand by various parties

[144] Lord Bullock, *Report of the Committee of Inquiry on Industrial Democracy* (Cmnd 6706, 1977) ch 4, para 2 and ch 10, paras 8–12.

[145] Lord Bullock, *Report of the Committee of Inquiry on Industrial Democracy* (Cmnd 6706, 1977) Minority Report, para 13.

[146] Confederation of British Industry (1977) 6.

[147] Cottrell (1978) 59.

[148] Lord Bullock, *Report of the Committee of Inquiry on Industrial Democracy* (Cmnd 6706, 1977) Minority Report, para 25.

[149] City Company Law Committee and Great Britain Committee of Inquiry on Industrial Democracy (1977) 8.

[150] Confederation of British Industry (1977) 6.

and stakeholders, including the Minority members, the CBI and certain trade unions, made it a main point of strife, which contributed to the Labour government's dithering in its response to the recommendations.[151] As for the workers themselves, their views seem not to have been solicited by the Committee other than indirectly through the trade union leadership. A poll conducted by *The Times* in January 1977 showed that there was widespread support by employees for worker representation, although only 10 per cent agreed that these directors must be chosen through trade union mechanisms: 'However, this is, sadly, of little relevance as the ultimate outcome of the Bullock Report will be decided at national level by negotiations between the TUC, the CBI and the government.'[152] Thus, the democratic element of industrial democracy was diluted as the interests of the very stakeholders that the Committee was tasked with addressing were weakened by political brokering.

The rejection of the TUC's demand to be the single channel for union-selected worker representation on boards meant that the Majority Report proposals provided an avenue for representation for non-unionised and non-TUC employees, suggesting limitations to the TUC's power as the Committee diluted its final recommendations and subsequent White Paper.[153] Whereas the Wilson government that established the Bullock Committee leant heavily on the TUC and was committed to the implementation of the Social Contract, the Bullock Report, which was released during the Callaghan government, backed away from the wholesale recommendation of the TUC's policies.[154] The enmeshing of industrial democracy so closely with the power of the TUC exposed its weaknesses when the trade unions' influence waned alongside the change in governments, which subsequently impacted the effectiveness of the movements for industrial democracy and worker representation.[155] Despite claims by leaders from all sides to be supporting the interests of British workers, clamouring for position and power became a dominant focus, to the detriment of the principles of industrial democracy.

VI. THE CITY AND INDUSTRY

The likelihood of success for the recommendations proposed by the Bullock Report depended, to a degree, on the extent to which it was believed that the interests of shareholders, management and employees could be aligned, which seemed unlikely in the combative industrial relations environment of the

[151] Middlemas (1991) 182.
[152] Shackleton (1977) 233.
[153] Lord Bullock, *Report of the Committee of Inquiry on Industrial Democracy* (Cmnd 6706, 1977) ch 10, paras 10–12; Ream (1978) 7.
[154] Clift, Gamble and Harris (2000) 80.
[155] Fox (1985) 408.

1970s.[156] Framing its industrial democracy recommendations in a way that would appeal to opponents from industry and finance, the Bullock Report argued that its proposals would lead to efficiencies, which would compensate shareholders for their loss of primacy, an assertion contested by its critics.[157] Opponents of the Report rejected its attempted interference in the existing laws and practices, with the City Company Law Committee declaring that:

> We do not believe that such a fundamental change in the underlying concept of company law should be entertained unless it is shown to have the overwhelming support and approval of all those most directly affected – management, employees, and the investing public, both private and institutional. The public response to the Majority proposals indicates only too clearly that the necessary support and approval do not exist. Not only have the proposals received a hostile reception from representative bodies of management and investing institutions but also from leading trade union leaders.[158]

The Bullock proposals relied on the acceptance of their viability within the existing system and, in particular, whether it was believed that the worker representatives on company boards would support dividend payments and other measures that kept companies attractive to investors, thereby allowing them to continue to raise the equity capital needed to grow. If worker representatives voted only in what appeared to be the interests of the workers, public companies could alienate equity investors, a genuine concern in light of the prevalent attitudes of trade unions towards dividends and other shareholder benefits.[159] It should be noted, however, that although the alarm was raised about the threat to equity financing, at the time of the Bullock Report, British industry was not heavily reliant on equity raises, diminishing the importance of shareholders, and these circumstances were used by the critics of shareholder primacy to justify curtailing the rights of equity owners relative to other stakeholders, and especially workers.[160] To the presumed relief of industrialists and the City, the Bullock Report's proposed mechanisms for the joint representation on boards of both capital and labour were still at least within the existing governance framework and continued to use the comfortable language of capitalism, with the Report stating that:

> There must in the future be a new legitimacy for the exercise of the management function within a policy framework agreed jointly by the representatives of capital

[156] Batstone, Ferner and Terry (1983) 3ff.

[157] Lord Bullock, Report *of the Committee of Inquiry on Industrial Democracy* (Cmnd 6706, 1977) ch 5, paras 26–32; Lewis and Clark (1977) 338; City Company Law Committee and Great Britain Committee of Inquiry on Industrial Democracy (1977) 20.

[158] City Company Law Committee and Great Britain Committee of Inquiry on Industrial Democracy (1977) 5.

[159] City Company Law Committee and Great Britain Committee of Inquiry on Industrial Democracy (1977) 20.

[160] Lord Bullock, *Report of the Committee of Inquiry on Industrial Democracy* (Cmnd 6706, 1977) ch 2, Table 3 for a breakdown of the sources of financing of large quoted companies in manufacturing, distribution and other services from 1950 to 1975.

> and labour. We believe that this new legitimacy is essential for the long-term efficiency and profitability of the private sector and for the ultimate success of the economy itself.[161]

A. The Feared Economic Consequences of the Bullock Recommendations

Together with the dissatisfaction expressed about the Bullock recommendations, there were also fears of their impact on the struggling British economy, on industry and on the financial system if they were adopted and implemented.[162] As described by a reader of the *Financial Times* in 1977, expressing a lack of confidence in the Report's recommendations and their negative impact on the economy:

> Implementation of Bullock would not only damage direct and indirect shareholders, including pension funds. Side effects would include the break-up of successful management teams and a cessation of new equity (risk) investment in sizeable British companies. Also an unwillingness by successful groups to expand staff levels in the UK around the Bullock cut-off levels … Of course, Bullock will mean less foreign interference in our economy since the hated multinationals will gradually go away taking their technology and employment with them.[163]

The anxiety generated by the Report, even in its diluted and compromised form, was felt at British companies and amongst financial institutions, including the pension funds and other investment vehicles that represented the workers who were their beneficiaries and in whose interests the Bullock Committee claimed to be acting.[164]

The City was amongst the constituents raising the alarm at the consequences of the Bullock proposals, claiming that any legislative changes would harm confidence in the British financial system, with widespread negative effects.[165] The City Company Law Committee warned in its 1975 report on employee participation that parity of worker representation on boards, realised through union mechanisms, would be a disincentive to the capital markets and would hurt efficiency, productivity and profitability.[166] The opposition to the Majority proposals was widespread, with the City Company Law Committee declaring that:

> [W]e are strengthened in our belief that the *compulsory* introduction of employee board representation could damage rather than improve the efficiency and profitability

[161] Lord Bullock, *Report of the Committee of Inquiry on Industrial Democracy* (Cmnd 6706, 1977) ch 9, para 10.
[162] City Company Law Committee and Great Britain Committee of Inquiry on Industrial Democracy (1977) 5.
[163] Taylor (1977) 15.
[164] Confederation of British Industry (1977) 6ff.
[165] Fatchett (1977) 25.
[166] Lewis and Clark (1977) 329.

> of the private sector in the long term, while causing short term disruption to the management of every major company in the UK. (Emphasis in original)[167]

The Bullock Committee heard evidence from witnesses from the City who were concerned that '[c]onfidence might be damaged by the investors' perception of what might happen as a result of board level representation – the possibility of interference with the efficiency of management, leading to a reduction in the profitability of companies'.[168] Employer representatives gave evidence to the Committee against the recommendations and the attempt to implement a standardised system:

> Most employer and independent evidence similarly stressed the need for flexibility … [A]nother theme running through the employer evidence was the need to build up participation from the bottom rather than impose it from the top if commitment from employees is to be achieved … There were many other criticisms of the TUC's proposals on the grounds of democracy and accountability, but perhaps most of all there was criticism of the impact on efficiency.[169]

The Report explained that:

> A major source of concern, it was felt, would be that the objectives of employee representatives would be different from those of shareholder representatives. In consequence, lenders of capital would tighten their controls over existing loans and would be wary of lending money afresh to companies with employee representatives on their boards, and investors would look elsewhere for safe investment.[170]

The Majority proceeded to dismiss these considerations, claiming that 'fears about the detrimental effects for investors are thought to be misplaced' and that worker representation on boards would only strengthen private industry.[171]

B. Industry's Reaction to Worker Participation and Statutory Changes

The unsurprising response by industry was to reject the Bullock recommendations: 'In contrast to the trade unions, most evidence from individual firms, and managers and employer associations, was at the best, unsympathetic to the notion of extending industrial democracy and, at worst, openly hostile.'[172]

[167] City Company Law Committee and Great Britain Committee of Inquiry on Industrial Democracy (1977) 2.
[168] Lord Bullock, *Report of the Committee of Inquiry on Industrial Democracy* (Cmnd 6706, 1977) ch 6, para 35.
[169] Thomson (1977) 38.
[170] Lord Bullock, *Report of the Committee of Inquiry on Industrial Democracy* (Cmnd 6706, 1977) ch 6, para 35.
[171] Lord Bullock, *Report of the Committee of Inquiry on Industrial Democracy* (Cmnd 6706, 1977) ch 6, para 36.
[172] Fatchett (1977) 25.

The CBI, as the representative of British industry, rejected the proposal to give statutory rights to employees to vote for their own directors on the basis that it was only the shareholders who had the right to appoint a company's directors, although it did concede the need for greater participation by employees in the companies for which they worked, although below the level of the board.[173] This view was consistent with that taken by the Minority Report, which was presented 'in the confidence that our views will have the support of large sections of the industrial community', emphasising the importance of effective participation below the board level and broader representation by employees at all levels.[174] The CBI concluded that the Majority Report 'with its mechanistic obsession with Board level composition, was therefore a major disappointment'.[175] The CBI also expressed its support for the existing unitary board system and asserted that:

> [E]mployers were, on the whole, very much on the defensive in their approach to the extension of industrial democracy, torn between outright opposition to the implications of trade union proposals and the need to make the best of what they gradually realised was inevitable in some form.[176]

In comparison to the supporters of Bullock's industrial democracy proposals, the opposition from industry was not particularly effective in communicating clearly its ideological objections to the Majority Report in a way that gained wider public support. Davies argues that:

> This lack of a theoretical perspective has probably done more to hinder management opposition to the proposals than union promotion of them. The TUC effectively seized the initiative in its proposals of 1973 based on the need to make large companies more responsive to the needs of society in general and of the employees in particular, whist opposition by employers has tended to throw doubt either on the bona fides of those supporting such proposals or on the practicality of their schemes. Objections on the grounds of practicality are, of course, very important, but they do not directly address themselves to the question of the underlying rationale of private enterprise, implicitly raised by the report.[177]

The arguments based on why the proposals were flawed or why those championing them lacked credibility could not garner the same general approval as the substantive claims by the pro-Bullock advocates that the system itself needed to be reformed for the benefit of society as a whole.

Although there was clear opposition by industry representatives to the Bullock recommendations, some individual managers and company directors were seen to be more open to the principles of industrial democracy, as

[173] Furlong (1977) 101.
[174] Lord Bullock, *Report of the Committee of Inquiry on Industrial Democracy* (Cmnd 6706, 1977) Minority Report, para 4; Confederation of British Industry (1977) 5.
[175] Confederation of British Industry (1977) 4.
[176] Lewis and Clark (1977) 330.
[177] Davies (1978) 264.

explained by Tony Benn in response to Callaghan's concerns about alienating industry: 'We must also be careful not to be too much affected by the CBI view because working management was quite different, it was quite sympathetic, and managers were joining the trade unions in large numbers now.'[178] The attitudes of the management at individual British companies were, perhaps, more nuanced than those of the CBI, although they also almost universally rejected the Report's recommendations.[179] Sir Robert Fairbairn, the Chairman of Clydesdale Bank, expressed the mood amongst corporate leaders at the time of the Bullock Committee when addressing his company's AGM, warning about the dual threats of nationalisations and of the impact of the Bullock Report's recommendations.[180] As had become the accepted and expected of the speeches made by corporate leaders at the time, and which is reminiscent of corporate scripts that paid tribute to the stakeholder interests, he first acknowledged the value to the employer, the employed, the country and management, including employees in the discussions on the running and growth of the business, then, in reference to the specifics of the Bullock recommendations, explained that 'to suggest that the representation of shareholders and employees should be on an equal basis with a smaller number of outside Directors is surely going much too far'.[181] Whereas there was general agreement that directors should consider the needs of stakeholders other than shareholders, this did not extend to accepting the statutory requirement for worker directors.[182] Furthermore, in the daily running of their enterprises, company boards needed to address the interests of a variety of stakeholders in addition to employees and shareholders – for example, consumers, creditors, suppliers and the community – although the Bullock recommendations rejected the idea that the newly reconstituted boards should represent consumers or any other additional stakeholder representatives of the 'public interests'.[183]

By the time the Bullock Report was presented in 1977, industrial democracy was a mainstream policy issue, no longer the domain of radical socialists seeking to deconstruct the existing system, although it was still viewed with hostility by many in the establishment and, as was succinctly observed by Derek Fatchett: 'At the door of industrial democracy in general, and Bullock in particular, will be laid the responsibility for the further decline of British capitalism.'[184] The CBI described the broad-based reactions to the Bullock proposals: 'Many of these themes [criticisms of the Majority Report] were echoed in the editorials and letter columns of the national press, on television, radio and political

[178] Benn (1989) 690. See also ch 6, section I.C of this volume on the evolving trade union membership.
[179] Elliott (1984) 244.
[180] 'Report & Accounts' (1977) 130.
[181] 'Report & Accounts' (1977) 130.
[182] Davies (1978) 263.
[183] Kahn-Freund (1977) 79.
[184] Fatchett (1977) 31.

platforms in the weeks following publication.'[185] The mainstream media was also accused by the political left of being complicit in the struggle to preserve the existing system:

> Thus the capitalist press responded to the Bullock proposals with uniform hostility, and frequently misinformed, well orchestrated hysteria: of course, in damning the Bullock majority report, press commentators were keen to proclaim their democratic zeal, but then went on to suggest alternative schemes of the most paternalistic and disingenuous nature.[186]

In condemnation of the Majority Report and the TUC's motives, the CBI reported that: '*The Times* leader coined a new word "syndiarchy" [*sic*] for the extension of trade union power which the newspaper believed was at the root of the Bullock recommendation.'[187] *The Times* devoted 500 column inches to the Bullock Report the day after it was published, most of it critical and expressing fear of the 'syndicarchy'; similarly, the *Daily Mirror* was critical of the Majority Report and objected to 'shop steward power'.[188]

C. The 1978 White Paper

The Bullock Report was followed by the 1978 White Paper on industrial democracy legislation, a draft of which went before the Cabinet committee in the summer of 1977. Notably, the White Paper did not include a demand to codify the Report's recommendations and was the apex of this post-war industrial democracy exercise, as the Bullock recommendations never become law.[189] The Callaghan government, which did not have the same commitment to the project as when the Committee was established by Wilson, consulted widely amongst the various constituents. The White Paper did not result in a proposal to impose a proscribed pattern for employee participation, but proffered that the recommendations be adopted voluntarily, with statutory fallback rights for employees and trade unions only in circumstances when voluntary arrangements could not be made.[190] The White Paper was met with disappointment from all sides, from the supporters of Bullock for not going nearly far enough and from its opponents for going too far, although the latter group were relieved at how diluted the White Paper was compared to the Majority Report, which was already a diminished version of the TUC's initial demands.[191]

[185] Confederation of British Industry (1977) 7.
[186] Clarke (1977) 366.
[187] Confederation of British Industry (1977) 6. The correct term is 'syndicarchy'.
[188] Shackleton (1977) 232.
[189] 'Bullock is Dead. Long Live Workers' Participation' (1977) 125.
[190] Clift, Gamble and Harris (2000) 80; Ream (1978) 3.
[191] Williamson (2016) 136.

In the end, no changes were made to the Companies Act and there was growing ambiguity in the Labour government's attitude towards the responsibilities of directors and shareholder primacy.[192] The optimism that industrial democracy legislation would be introduced did not convert into a unified approach to the issue of worker representation, resulting in many iterations of the Report as industry representatives and the unions struggled against each other in trying to influence the government's policy decisions.[193] Despite the focus on worker directors by the Bullock Committee and the ongoing debate amongst supporters and critics, both the TUC and the CBI were reported to have objected to the Report's final proposals, and there was a view that 'Bullock's call for worker-directors was generally derided as utopian'.[194]

The lack of statutory requirements for worker directors was indicative of the TUC's loss of political influence, whereas the emphasis on voluntary agreements that were based on the specific needs of individual companies reflected the position supported by the CBI.[195] The CBI and the Institute of Directors, as well as other industrial supporters and members of the Conservative Party, may have viewed industrial democracy as inevitable, and may have even accepted certain aspects of it as potentially beneficial to businesses, but they took positions against the statutory enforcement of the White Paper recommendations.[196] Margaret Thatcher's Conservatives were not against the principles underpinning industrial democracy, that is, to give labour more of a say in industry, even if it rejected the Labour government's proposals.[197] In the context of the industrial relations challenges of the 1970s and with their eye on regaining power, the Conservatives declared that: 'The right of participation for the individual at work is as basic a tenet of Conservative philosophy as the right of the individual to participate in a political democracy.'[198] How that participation was to be realised, however, deviated from the recommendations of the Bullock Report and the resulting White Paper, and did not include mandatory worker directors and the dilution of shareholder primacy.[199]

D. The Post Office Experiment

Although the leaders of industry were mostly opposed to the recommendations of the Report, the calls for worker representation were taken seriously and in 1978–79 the Post Office, a public corporation, underwent an experiment

[192] Clift, Gamble and Harris (2000) 80.
[193] Clift, Gamble and Harris (2000) 80.
[194] Morgan (1992) 430.
[195] Confederation of British Industry (1977) 4.
[196] Ream (1978) 18.
[197] Elliott (1984) 223; Fisher (1979) 31.
[198] Ream (1978) 20.
[199] Elliott (1984) 223.

in industrial democracy by introducing a comprehensive co-determination structure that included union participation on its board, reflecting the proposals of the Bullock Committee and the 2x+y formula for board composition.[200] This experiment, which was the result of the Post Office Act 1977, was not an exact mirror of the Bullock recommendations; the board of the Post Office was increased, for a two-year period and as part of an agreement between management and the unions, to include seven management representatives, seven union representatives, five 'independent' directors (of which two were explicitly to represent consumers), all five of which were to be chosen by management and the unions together from a list supplied by the Minister, and an independent chairman appointed by the Minister.[201] This scheme for employee representation on boards did not change the power given to the Minister by the Post Office Act 1969 to appoint all members of the board, which meant that if employee representatives sought to influence management decision, they needed to act at the level of the Minister.[202]

The example of the Post Office involved union-nominated worker representatives taking positions on the pre-existing management board and did not include any changes of ownership, with there being no increased share ownership by workers.[203] The Post Office experiment was structured so that, in theory, the well-supported union representatives were able to challenge management:

> Nevertheless, in practice this influence was counterbalanced by the strategies of management and the divisions amongst the worker directors themselves. In particular, management curtailed the influence of the worker directors by holding informal meetings, keeping issues away from the board, inhibiting the floating of ideas and challenging the contributions of the unions nominees.[204]

The Post Office experiment in worker representation on boards demonstrates that, even in relatively conducive conditions, worker directors needed the willing cooperation and 'buy in' from the other directors to succeed and that mere structural changes are not enough, with incumbents capable of undermining reforms by acting outside the new framework.[205] Furthermore, the timing of the experiment at the Post Office almost certainly assured its failure, undertaken by a weakened minority Labour government that, in its attempt to stay in power, adopted an increasingly commercial approach to the public sector. Unsurprisingly, under the newly elected Conservative government that followed, the Post Office experiment in industrial democracy, and the question of its continuation, came under review.[206] The Post Office management was against

[200] Batstone, Ferner and Terry (1983) 1ff; Poole (1986) 164.
[201] Davies (1978) 248.
[202] Davies (1978) 249.
[203] Batstone, Ferner and Terry (1983) 2.
[204] Poole (1986) 165.
[205] Elliott (1984) 300.
[206] Batstone, Ferner and Terry (1983) 41, 152.

continuing with union representation on its board, and even though it was a public corporation, the Conservative government let the scheme lapse, a position that was consistent with its evolving economic policies of shrinking the public sector and weakening the trade unions.[207] The unions wanted to continue with the experiment, but, in the words of a union official: 'There is no possibility of experiments in industrial democracy under the Tories. It is a socialist concept and needs a government sympathetic to that. To expect Tories to embrace such philosophies is totally naïve.'[208] The Labour Party, meanwhile, was now in opposition and had more pressing political priorities in its struggle to rebuild the support that had led to its victories earlier in the 1970s.

VII. THE END OF THE POST-WAR CONSENSUS AND THE DIMINISHING OF INDUSTRIAL DEMOCRACY

A. A Weakened Labour Government

The blueprint and development of industrial democracy in post-war Britain were the result of ongoing negotiations and recalibrations by the interested parties, a movement that culminated with the Labour government's Bullock Report in 1977, and then wilted under the leadership of James Callaghan, who took a cautious approach to industrial relations reforms and did not pursue the implementation of the Report's recommendations.[209] With the CBI and British industry loudly opposing the Report and unwilling to negotiate with the TUC on fundamental aspects, members of Callaghan's cabinet began to indicate, at least privately, that they would not support the Bullock Report's recommendations.[210] The Labour Party's political failure to retain power in 1979 ensured that the Report's proposals would not be implemented and would be banished to the archives of history; the movement for industrial democracy was subsequently thrown off its trajectory with the crumbling of the post-war consensus and the rise of union-busting Thatcherism in 1980s Britain.[211]

Socioeconomic shifts and British society's growing focus on wealth and individual financial betterment did not bode well for the success of the Labour Party and its socialist ideology, creating divisions within the movement as it sought to retain power.[212] The British public, which had grown weary of the industrial unrest and the overly confident unions, turned away from the principles of industrial democracy, at least for the time being, resulting in a political backlash

[207] Batstone, Ferner and Terry (1983) 152–59.
[208] Batstone, Ferner and Terry (1983) 157.
[209] Morgan (2010) 141; Johnston (2020) 206.
[210] Middlemas (1991) 182.
[211] Pollak (2013) 106.
[212] Eatwell (1979) 154.

against the left. Furthermore, the dependence on collective bargaining and the absence of legally required participation structures for workers meant that there was a weak network of regulation that was easily overturned, which is what occurred in 1979 as the post-war consensus was replaced by a different political, economic and social reality.[213] Ultimately, the efforts for worker representation on company boards and for statutory requirements supporting worker shareholders and other aspects of industrial democracy were undermined by the changing political backdrop before which they played out, with Labour losing its majority in 1977 followed by a Conservative Party victory under Thatcher in 1979.[214] With the weakening of Labour and its return to the opposition benches, the trade unions lost their ally in government and their ability to influence industrial democracy policy was weakened.[215] The election of Thatcher saw a change in the British government's approach to dealing with industrial unrest, and whereas throughout the post-war consensus both Labour and Conservative governments tried unsuccessfully to use the law to control the trade unions and their power base, Thatcher proceeded to subdue and reform British industrial relations without even consulting the unions.[216]

B. Core Company Law Remains Unchanged

Despite the great effort expended in its creation and the potential it promised for an overhaul of the established system, the Bullock Report, and the subsequent White Paper, did not result in company law reform or the formalisation of industrial democracy, with the exception of introducing the requirement (generally considered unenforceable) that directors take into consideration the interests of employees and not just those of shareholders.[217] Even at the time that the Bullock Report was delivered, it was not viewed as a model for change that could lead to worker control and an actual expansion of industrial democracy, with its contribution assessed in the *Modern Law Review* in 1977:

> What the report does achieve is to initiate discussion on the nature of collective bargaining and trade unionism, the function of management, the role of the shareholders and the out-datedness of British company law, and more generally the relation between politics, the law, economic management and industrial relations.[218]

The discussion on the various elements of industrial democracy is ongoing, coming in and out of fashion depending on the political, economic and social

[213] Ackers (2007) 95.
[214] Pollak (2013) 106.
[215] Elliott (1984) 293.
[216] Kavanagh (1992) 188.
[217] Williamson (2016) 136. On this change to directors' duties, see ch 8, sections III and IV of this volume.
[218] Lewis and Clark (1977) 333, 338.

cycles, with the same (or similar) arguments made in the name of reform, whereas the underlying core law remains mostly static.[219]

Ultimately, despite the noise suggesting and simulating change, the result is a societal consensus that preserves the existing system that is based on corporate power, as explained by the sociologist of industrial relations Alan Fox:

> Moreover, in an important sense, corporations *are* the system – which means that all governments that wish, as all British governments do, to preserve the system must in the last resort help the corporations themselves. A further consequence of corporatism on the modern scale is that, given its massive all-pervasiveness, the individual is too easily conditioned and resigned to seeing it as inevitable and beyond the reach of major change except by an upheaval that is itself too daunting to contemplate. (Emphasis in original)[220]

The power of the status quo, and of inertia, as well as the perception that implementing systemic change is a complex challenge keeps the laws governing companies unchanged, even when the rhetoric of industrial leaders and law-makers suggests advancements in corporate behaviour and evolution in stakeholder relationships.[221]

During the post-war period, the basic questions that fuelled the industrial democracy movement reflected the evolving understanding of the company and company law. As observed by Davies in 1978: 'in a more fundamental way the report challenges the whole basis of our present company law, by posing the question: what is the company and for whom is it to be run?'[222] The debate on industrial democracy was ongoing and intense, fuelling the industrial relations conflicts and drawing in the disparate constituents, each jostling to promote their position and to protect (and expand) their power. The 1977 Preface to *The Shop Steward's Guide to the Bullock Report* declared that:

> No question is more important today than that of industrial democracy. More and more people are keenly discussing the issue, which quite recently was of concern only to the smallest minority. In the next year or so, it is perfectly possible that general elections will be fought in order to decide upon proposals for the democratisation of work.[223]

This prediction was realised with the Labour Party's loss and the Conservative government's pivot away from the industrial democracy initiatives that had produced the Bullock Committee and Report. Although the British economy continued to evolve, the underlying system on which it is built has been left largely undisturbed by the challenges from the industrial democracy movement

[219] Pollak (2013) 105ff.
[220] Fox (2017) 213.
[221] Clift, Gamble and Harris (2000) 52.
[222] Davies (1978) 263.
[223] Coates and Topham (1977) prefatory note.

that produced the Bullock Report, from the growing dominance of institutional investors at the expense on small individual direct shareholders, and from the increased focus on corporate responsibilities to all stakeholders and to society.[224] With the election of Thatcher and the Conservatives in 1979, governmental interference in restructuring the laws governing how, and for whom, companies were run was not on the agenda, with the focus shifting to promoting free market conditions, increased competition and economic growth.

C. Abandoning Bullock

The Bullock Report of 1977 represents both the promise and the failure of the post-war movement for industrial democracy, and the general election that returned the Conservatives to power in 1979 saw this opportunity dissipate and a new era of free-market capitalism begin.[225] The industrial strikes during the 'winter of discontent' of 1978–79 made the Labour government's position virtually indefensible to an exhausted public, demoralised by a sense of national decline, which turned against the trade unions and the Labour Party.[226] Labour's manifesto for the 1979 general election demonstrates how it eased away from its earlier push for industrial democracy legislative changes, although the Party was still committed to the expansion of industrial democracy principles and to establishing a committee to 'stimulate and monitor schemes of industrial democracy in the private sector and the nationalised industries'; these were vague promises that lacked any new initiatives, possibly an acknowledgement that the moment for radical action had passed, at least for the time being.[227] The failure of the recommendations of the Bullock Report did not put an end to the industrial democracy debate, and although the demands for the recognition of stakeholder interests have not progressed in a linear way, these issues remained central to the discourse on corporate behaviour and governance, and regularly returned to be focal points of the discussions on equality, fairness and societal norms that recur with the turns of the political and economic cycles.[228] Politicians and activists who seek structural reforms of the existing capitalist system through the various movements for increased corporate accountability and responsibility would do well to examine the historical circumstances within which the Bullock Committee was created, its recommendations delivered, and then abandoned.[229]

[224] Gamble and Kelly (2001) 112.
[225] Elliott (1984) 310.
[226] Dorey (2019) 208; Morgan (1992) 430.
[227] Labour Party (1979); Dale (2000b) 230.
[228] Coulter (2020) 4.
[229] See Pollak (2013) for a contemporary study by a Labour politician on the lessons that can be learnt from the Bullock Report affair.

The decades that make up the period of the post-war consensus demonstrate how company directors and corporate leaders can adapt effectively to echo the language of their critics and engage in a narrative that suggests change, whilst continuing to manage their companies within the existing system and for the paramount benefit of their equity shareholders. Using the right messages to divert criticism and to create the appearance of responsiveness allows companies to appeal to the broader public, and with the passage of time and shifting political winds, today's priorities become secondary to the more pressing demands of tomorrow – for example, industrial democracy movements were eclipsed by the glittering promises of 1980s free-market capitalism. Even when there appeared to be concessions by industry in favour of the principles of industrial democracy, these were often rejected as genuine reforms, being seen instead as attempts by the establishment to bring labour inside the tent of the existing capitalist system by integrating them into the mechanisms that perpetuate it.[230] Ultimately, the Bullock Report, and the TUC's overestimation of its position at the time when the Committee issued its recommendations, undermined the industrial democracy project that was rejected by the new Conservative government and the electorate that brought it to power.[231]

In April 1977, Bullock Committee member Wedderburn, optimistic that the Report would herald systemic change to company law, stated:

> I believe that if we are bold enough to confront the question of our own preconceptions, or our company law and of our labour relations, of the true issues of democracy in industry and society now, then the concluding works of the Report are true. Our descendants may indeed not only be grateful to us but probably will wonder what all the fuss was about in 1977.[232]

It was only a couple of years later that Wedderburn's predictions looked brash, with core company law remaining intact despite the growing public commitments to the principles of industrial democracy. The change in political fortunes in the late 1970s meant that the advocates of industrial democracy faced strengthening headwinds, while the principle of shareholder primacy was reinforced and remained entrenched as an accepted foundational legal norm spurred on by the changing corporate landscape of the 1980s.[233] The embrace of free-market capitalism in the Thatcher era saw the privatisations of state-owned companies, the result of which was that there were hundreds of thousands of trade unionists amongst the swelling number of first-time shareholders.[234] Thus, the unionists saw a convergence of their interests with those of existing shareholders as they joined them in being capital providers to British industry.

[230] Clarke (1977) 363.
[231] Middlemas (1991) 183.
[232] Wedderburn, KW (1977) para 1.19.
[233] Cheffins (2020) 36.
[234] Morgan (1992) 469; Grout (1987a) 63.

Alongside this expansion of the shareholder body, the 1980s saw an increase in shareholder protections with the Companies Act 1981 and the Financial Services Act 1986.[235]

D. A Cautionary Tale

By the time Labour was voted out of power in 1979, it was divided and politically weakened, and the defeated party watched as the recommendations of the Bullock Report were sidelined in favour of the more aggressive capitalism of the Thatcher era that severely weakened the trade unions.[236] The Labour Party's post-war programmes and political manifestos no longer met the needs of the British electorate, leading to a marked shift away from its traditional positions on labour relations and industrial democracy, as well as the eventual abandonment by New Labour of its programmes for industrial partnerships and stakeholder capitalism that were associated with the industrial unrest of the 1970s.[237] Even before Thatcher's union-busting policies and privatisations, and alongside the bruising economic policies following the financial crisis of 1976, it was the Bullock Committee's failure to realise any material reforms, and the Labour government's squandering of the opportunity to make structural changes to the economy that would benefit workers, that marked the watershed for this transition in the modern British political economy.[238] The Bullock Report can be pegged as the key turning point in post-war industrial democracy, after which the movement lost momentum (at least until the cycle was repeated with new iterations of movements campaigning for stakeholder interests). The advocates of stakeholder capitalism, ESG, corporate purpose and other initiatives calling for systemic reform should consider that, whereas the current support for change may seem unassailable, entrenched systems are built to protect themselves and their position with effectiveness and resilience.[239]

The Bullock Report can be seen as an example of how political intention and administrative theatre create the semblance of evolution without resulting in real systemic changes. For all the Committee's promise and effort, as well as the shift in public opinion to accept the principles of industrial democracy, the Bullock Report recommendations did not result in legislation that adapted company law to reflect the empowerment of workers and the limiting of shareholder rights,

[235] Cheffins (2008) 358.
[236] Dorey (2019) 210; Clift, Gamble and Harris (2000) 81. For a study of employee views of post-Bullock industrial democracy, see Hanson and Rathkey (1984).
[237] See ch 8, section VI.A of this volume on New Labour and the Stakeholder Society.
[238] Pollak (2013) 106.
[239] See Fox (1985).

with company law remaining unchanged in not giving workers much direct consideration.[240] It can be argued that, despite the failure to realise meaningful statutory reforms, there was cultural progress that benefited the interests of labour – for example, with the CBI and industrial leaders acknowledging that workers had a right to a consultative role within company management, as well as the TUC's acceptance of the existing capitalist system to place worker representatives on company boards.[241] These developments cannot, however, be equated with statutory requirements for industrial democracy reforms, and although how the worker, the director and the shareholder were seen and understood changed over the post-war period from 1945 to 1979, the core company laws that regulated their relationships, and the principle of shareholder primacy, remained mostly static.

The convergence of evolving political and social attitudes with the treatment of shareholders and stakeholders was evident in the ongoing debate on corporate democracy, shareholder democracy and industrial democracy, which included promoting the creation of more worker shareholders, giving workers a say in management decisions and recognising the rights of labour to be informed of companies' decisions and plans for the future. Whereas there were attempts to align the interests of shareholders and workers more closely, including (but not limited to) turning workers into shareholders, these were not without concerns about how enforcing these policies might impact the existing system, as was expressed in the *Financial Times*:

> Yet unless we can establish a community of interest so that employees work for and welcome higher profits, there is a danger that, with the present balance of power in our society in favour of labour rather than capital, our version of the capitalist system as practised in the UK will wither and die.[242]

The 'balance of interests' concept of board responsibilities had broad approval from different quarters, and was even supported by some company directors, although how those responsibilities and duties should be addressed, and against what metric company boards should be judged, was by no means obvious.[243]

[240] Moore (2018) 158.
[241] Elliott (1984) 244.
[242] Russell (1975) 17.
[243] Shenfield (1971) 20.

8

Post-1979

Shareholders, Stakeholders and the Companies Act

I. THE END OF THE POST-WAR CONSENSUS

The study of shareholders and stakeholders in the post-war era in the preceding chapters lays the foundation upon which the understanding of the following periods is built, and this chapter, undertaken as a supplement to the preceding examination of the post-war period and, as such, selective in its intention, examines some of the pertinent developments between 1979 and the enactment of the Companies Act (CA) 2006, the legislation that frames current UK company law. This chapter should therefore be considered as an addition to the main body of this work that focuses on the post-war era, examining specific developments that follow on from the discussions on the post-war attempts (and failures) to implement changes to UK company law that reform the treatment of shareholder interests and the relationships amongst stakeholders. How the implications of post-war nationalisations, the movements for shareholder democracy and for industrial democracy, and the systemic changes in the shareholder body were understood at the end of the 1970s following the diminished Bullock Report is very different from subsequent considerations that are tempered by the passage of time, the turning of the political wheel and the resulting economic implications. With the benefit of hindsight and the lessons learnt in the years from Thatcher through to New Labour, the 1980s, 1990s and 2000s, add an important epilogue to the detailed examination of the shareholder in the post-war period.

The post-war era, which was built on a consensus that brought widespread political, economic and social changes to Britain as it rebuilt following the Second World War, experienced the rise of democratisation movements that advanced the interests of various constituents and challenged the establishment, with implications for British industry, industrial relations and financial markets. The breakdown of the post-war settlement and the turmoil of the late 1970s under the Callaghan government, which culminated in the punishing conditions of the 'winter of discontent', led not only to a change in political leadership but also to a new approach to the social contract that guided the decision-making of the post-war decades. With the 1979 election of the Conservatives under the leadership of Margaret Thatcher, there was a pivot away from the attempts at industrial democracy reforms that peaked with the Bullock Committee and towards policies that weakened the trade unions and advanced laissez-faire capitalism. Although it is tempting to interpret the 1979 Conservative electoral victory as the public's acceptance of the Party's policy platform and a move to the right of the political spectrum, the unpopularity of the Labour Party and its programme should not be discounted when examining the British electorate's choice in 1979.[1] By the end of the 1970s, the public attitudes that led to the post-war consensus and the acceptance of the Social Contract had shifted, which was manifested in the British public handing the Conservatives a mandate to pursue their policies, including on industrial relations, privatisations, tax reform, immigration, security and defence, and the post-war welfare state.[2]

A. From the 1970s to the 1980s: Fortifying the Case for Shareholder Primacy and the Friedman Doctrine

The 1970s, the decade that saw the unravelling of the post-war consensus, was a period in which the debate on the responsibilities of corporations, and on how the structure of the existing Anglo-American legal system prioritised shareholder interests, was notably ardent. Milton Friedman's now legendary 1970 *New York Times* article was part of the public discourse addressing these issues on both sides on the Atlantic, even if these often intense deliberations resulted not in change, but in the law's preservation of the prioritisation of the interests of shareholders.[3] By the 1980s, the UK had moved away from the ideologies that had sustained the post-war consensus, leaving behind the legacies of the war and the subsequent period of reconstruction, and turning towards the free-market capitalism of the Thatcher era, which included a Conservative economic agenda that preserved the system based on shareholder primacy. Whereas Thatcher sought to upend the foundations on which the post-war consensus was built, her government did not seek to reform the core laws that governed how companies were run, and which had changed little since the nineteenth century.[4]

Although company law remained mostly unchanged, how the interests of shareholders were understood and viewed was not static. In an environment that embraced Thatcherism, charges of short-termism that were (and still are)

[1] Dorey (1995) 164.
[2] Dorey (1995) 165.
[3] See ch 4, section VII of this volume for a discussion of Friedman. On the US, see Cheffins (2018) 187ff.
[4] Gamble and Kelly (2000) 42.

associated with shareholder primacy were raised, leading to the development of a more inclusive understanding of shareholder value and a more probing understanding of how duties to shareholders could be met. UK company law, and its interpretation in the courts, remained unaltered by the challenges to shareholder primacy, although there was also an acceptance of the premise that stakeholder interests could be aligned with those of shareholders in the longer term, allowing directors to consider stakeholder interests while still acting within the law.[5] As the UK underwent meaningful political, economic and social transformations in the 1980s, there was an intensification of the debate on the treatment of the interests of all stakeholders, drawing on examples from other statutory models, like those in Japan, Germany and elsewhere in the EU, as well as the growing importance of corporate governance to the regulation of companies in the Anglo-American context.[6]

In the 1980s, the Friedman Doctrine, and the position taken by the law and economics school in support of shareholder primacy, was increasingly accepted as a default assumption for corporations, and the pursuit of shareholder profit maximisation became the norm of corporate behaviour.[7] Whereas it suited the narrative of the entrenched players to present shareholder primacy as a legal requirement for companies to maximise short-term shareholder profits while disregarding the interests of any other stakeholders, this position is not found in company law, which allows (or even requires) for the consideration of other interests, albeit within a framework in which priority is given to the interests of the company, which is understood to mean its shareholders. This short-term shareholder-only interpretation of how a company's interests should be understood permeated the thinking of market players and corporate leaders (and their advisors) who, reflecting their own incentives, sought to prioritise short-term profits above all other interests. These incumbents benefited from the widespread assumption that there was a legal requirement to restrict directors' duties to shareholders' interests alone, which occurred alongside a certain level of engagement with the demands to consider wider stakeholder interests, thereby protecting their self-interests while simultaneously signalling virtuous good intentions. This cultivated balance created the semblance of responsiveness that served to deflect from the lack of systemic change.

In the decades since the 1980s, corporate leaders have actively promoted the concept of shareholder value maximisation as they chased quarterly improvements in share prices and attracted investors with growing dividends, even if it came at the expense of employees or other stakeholders.[8] This was not, however, the result of a statutory obligation of company law for short-term shareholder primacy. The confusion between the granting of direct legal rights to shareholders – for example, voting, electing directors, making proposals and the right to

[5] Sealy (1987) 174.
[6] Hutton (1996) 300ff; Gamble and Kelly (2000) 43.
[7] Harper Ho (2010) 74.
[8] Keay and Adamopoulou (2012) 2.

the consideration of interests – has distorted the understanding of directors' responsibilities to shareholders and other stakeholders.[9] Regardless of shareholder primacy, even when interpreted through the most shareholder-centric lens, in order to be a profitable going concern, a company needs to take into consideration the interests of its stakeholders, including employees, customers, creditors, policy-makers and the community; a company that ignores the interests of its customer, for example, will not generate the profits needed for distributions to shareholders.[10]

II. 1979: THE END OF THE POST-WAR SETTLEMENT AND THE ELECTION OF MARGARET THATCHER

The election of Margaret Thatcher in 1979 is often identified with the end point of the post-war consensus and the turning away from the mixed-economy system that underpinned the reconstruction of Britain from 1945. By the time of the 1970s crises that preceded Thatcher's election, Britain was benefiting from the significant post-war rebuilding programmes and the ensuing advantages of modern infrastructure, energy and food self-sufficiency, and modernised nationalised industries, as well as from extensive public housing and a modern welfare state.[11] The principles of the post-war consensus that sustained reconstruction were, however, overwhelmed by industrial strife, with striking workers rejecting the policies of the incumbent Labour government and the British public witnessing the fraying of the Social Contract, leading to the 'winter of discontent'.[12] The existing post-war system was inadequate to meet the challenges that the UK economy faced in the tumultuous 1970s, prompting the British electorate to reject Labour and return the Conservatives to power on a platform that promised to reverse the perceived national decline.[13] In power since 1974, the Labour Party governed over a period of economic crisis and industrial unrest that exposed as false the assumption that Labour alone could work with the trade unions and keep industrial relations calm, whereas the Conservatives in opposition positioned themselves as the party that would regain control of the country and, in a break from the mixed economy of the post-war agreement, pursue a free-market approach.[14]

The Thatcher era began with policy shocks to the British economy intended to address rising inflation and unemployment: the end of exchange controls, higher interest rates, and tax reform.[15] Thatcher's government

[9] Harper Ho (2010) 77.
[10] See ch 4, section II of this volume.
[11] Edgerton (2018) 454ff.
[12] Tinline (2022) 225.
[13] Hall (2013) 134.
[14] Tinline (2022) 229.
[15] Matthijs (2011) 116ff.

rejected the Keynesian principles of the post-war period and introduced fiscal and monetary policies designed to reduce inflation and strengthen the supply side of the economy. These consequential changes in approach were accompanied by acute economic reactions, including rising unemployment, falling output, a shrinking public sector and a much-reduced social safety net, resulting in the UK recession of the early 1980s as the government struggled with mass unemployment and social unrest.[16] The miners' strikes of the mid-1980s exemplify the economic turmoil as well as the social and political changes in British society; although conditions were volatile, the anticipated full-scale class war between capital and labour never emerged and the Thatcherite policies that weakened the trade unions, which had lost widespread public support during the 'winter of discontent', cleared the way for a new Britain of free-market economic growth.[17]

A. Thatcher-Era Denationalisations

The economic conditions in Britain at the time of Thatcher's election were challenging and the new Conservative government introduced an economic programme that was based on an assumption, accepted by much of the British electorate and the media, that there was no credible alternative to the Thatcherite intervention that departed from the policies of the post-war era.[18] Whereas the Conservatives claimed that the economic crisis that they inherited in 1979 was the result of the state intervention of the post-war period, the reforms introduced by Thatcher that signalled the end of the post-war settlement were only possible because of the state's investments and successful post-war reconstruction.[19] Of particular importance to the change in the state's approach to industry was the Thatcher government's denationalisation of British companies that had been nationalised in the post-war period.[20] The Conservative Party saw denationalisations as central to addressing the economic challenges facing Britain, not only countering Labour's promise to nationalise more industries but also pledging to return already-nationalised industries back to private ownership and to sell shares to the public, as well as to improve and to interfere less in the management of those industries that remained under government control.[21] Thatcher supported management decisions to bring public sector companies to profitability; in her first years in

[16] Coutts et al (1981) 81.
[17] Tinline (2022) 245.
[18] Matthijs (2011) 118.
[19] Edgerton (2018) 454.
[20] See ch 2 of this volume on nationalisations.
[21] Conservative Unionist Party (1979); Dale (2000a) 272.

office a number of state-run companies went bankrupt or were significantly downsized – for example, British Leyland and the British Steel Corporation – further decreasing the number of employees in the public sector.[22]

The 1979 Conservative Party manifesto committed to privatising certain nationalised entities (for example, aerospace and shipbuilding), to selling shares to the public and to encouraging employee share ownership.[23] The manifesto went further, pledging to limit state interference in British industry:

> We shall therefore amend the 1975 Industry Act and restrict the powers of the National Enterprise Board solely to the administration of the Government's temporary shareholdings, to be sold off as circumstances permit. We want to see those industries that remain nationalised running more successfully and we will therefore interfere less with their management and set them a clearer financial discipline in which to work.[24]

Throughout the 1980s, after decades of nationalisations under both Conservative and Labour governments, British companies were denationalised as Thatcher's government rationalised industries and returned them to private ownership, contributing to the transformation of the British economy and society.[25] This transformation in ownership led the swell in the number of shareholders as British industries returned to private hands, although not necessarily in the manner envisioned by the post-war promoters of shareholder democracy.[26]

i. Shareholder Democracy and the Privatisation of British Industry

The approaches to shareholder democracy underwent a material change in direction with the election of Margaret Thatcher and the policies of privatisation that were central to her Conservative government. The push for widening individual share ownership and policies supporting a property-owning democracy were important aspects of Thatcher's platform that could not be achieved without the liberalisation of the existing financial system.[27] By the end of the post-war period, the small individual shareholder in British companies was overshadowed by the powerful institutional shareholders, and the institutionalisation of share ownership fundamentally altered the relationships amongst companies, shareholders and other stakeholders. The outdated idea that small shareholders were the stewards of governance and corporate behaviour was a throwback to before the war and to the immediate post-war period, when

[22] Matthijs (2011) 124.
[23] Conservative Unionist Party (1979); Dale (2000a) 272.
[24] Conservative Unionist Party (1979); Dale (2000a) 272.
[25] Edgerton (2018) 455.
[26] See ch 3 of this volume on shareholder democracy.
[27] Oren and Blyth (2019) 608.

individuals directly controlled the majority of shares and ownership was much less dispersed.[28] In most cases, the increasingly powerful institutional investors did not fill the governance void left by the more concentrated and personally connected equity owners that had dominated share registries, leaving other stakeholders vulnerable to the consequences of the prioritisation of shareholder interests. Although activism by institutional investors increased, and continues to grow in influence and prevalence, the purpose of these interventions was (and is) inevitably in the interests of shareholders, whether cloaked in enlightenment or motivated purely by profit; similar to today, most investors, including institutions, are passive and have limited influence on corporate behaviour regardless of the narrative of shareholder activism.[29]

The efforts in the post-war era to dramatically increase small shareholding were unsuccessful, whereas Thatcher's release of British industry from state ownership placed equity shares into the hands of the British public at unprecedented levels. By the end of her three terms in office, over 75 firms were privatised, and after her resignation, John Major, the next Conservative Prime Minister, oversaw the completion of the privatisation programme during his subsequent two terms.[30] In contrast to the Conservative government under Edward Heath of the early 1970s that failed to implement a privatisation policy, and that even brought additional industries under state control, the Conservative governments of the 1980s were successful in returning much of British industry to private ownership.[31] In 1979, the level of nationalised industries in Britain was the highest of any advanced industrial country, representing 9 per cent of British GDP and 11 per cent of investments, which was reduced by 1990 to 3.5 per cent and just over 3 per cent, respectively.[32]

The privatisation policies resulted in a material increase in the number of new shareholders as the equity markets absorbed newly listed companies. During this period, the number of individual shareholders increased from 3 million in 1979 to more than 11 million in 1993, which represented, respectively, 3 per cent and 22 per cent of the adult population of Britain.[33] Furthermore, the employees of the companies being denationalised were participating in the disposal programmes, at rates as high as 90 per cent.[34] Each privatised company had its own scheme and subscription mechanisms, with both individuals and

[28] See ch 3, section II of this volume on the types of shareholders. See Littlewood (1998) 442 on the ownership of UK equities by investor type from 1957 to 1994.

[29] See Harper Ho (2010) for a discussion of ESV and institutional ownership in the US. See also ch 3, section III.C of this volume on post-war shareholder activism.

[30] Florio (2002) 2ff. See also Florio (2002) and Littlewood (1998) for further discussions of privatisation during the Thatcher and Major eras.

[31] Middlemas (1990) 314. On Heath, see ch 2, section X of this volume.

[32] Foreman-Peck and Millward (1994) 319.

[33] Florio (2002) 5.

[34] Florio (2002) 5.

institutions participating; examples include payment plans, loyalty incentives and preferred terms for customers, as well as the offer of free shares for employees.[35] Shareholder democracy, as well as industrial democracy in the form of the worker shareholders, which were ideas promoted and supported by the Conservative Party in the post-war period, were finally being realised on a meaningful scale. Despite the resulting increase in individual share ownership, however, private individuals as a percentage of total UK equity ownership continued to decline, reported by the Central Statistics Office at 66 per cent in 1957, 54 per cent in 1963, 47.4 per cent in 1969, 37.5 per cent in 1975, 28.2 per cent in 1981, 20.6 per cent in 1989, 20.3 per cent in 1994 and 16.5 per cent in 1997.[36]

Although privatisation increased the number of individual shareholders, the post-war trend of institutional investors dominating the equity markets continued. Individuals increasingly owned securities indirectly through the institutional investors, consolidating power in the hands of the financial institutions and not in those of dispersed individual shareholders; shareholder democracy and industrial democracy were impacted by the privatisations and the distributions of shares in previously state-owned companies, yet influence on and control of companies were not directly in the hands of the individual small equity owner. Most individual shareholders often held small number of shares in only one company and of those who acquired shares through the privatisation programmes, the majority sold within a year.[37] Furthermore, the deregulation of the financial markets that occurred alongside the privatisation of British industry resulted in an increase in foreign investors in the UK capital markets, which in the 1980s became the largest single group of equity shareholders.[38] The goal of a shareholder democracy that had individual British shareholders directly owning shares in British companies on a meaningful scale, which would translate into influence and governance oversight, remained elusive and unrealised.

III. THE COMPANIES ACT 1980

With the failure of the Bullock Committee and its recommendations, the immediate threat of systemic reforms to how UK companies were structured and regulated was removed, although the debate on stakeholder interests persisted, perhaps a reflection of a change in corporate attitudes or, alternatively, an effort to pre-empt

[35] Florio (2002) 18.
[36] Littlewood (1998) 442; Florio (2002) 19.
[37] Florio (2002) 19.
[38] Littlewood (1998) 442; Florio (2002) 19.

future changes through proactive decisions and self-regulation.[39] The Bullock Report did not result in the comprehensive statutory reforms that the supporters of post-war industrial democracy envisioned, although there were some changes limited to company law that directly referenced the consideration of workers' interests.[40] These changes serve to highlight the disappointing compromises of the Bullock Report and its aftermath, emphasising the unfulfilled promises of the post-war industrial democracy programme and the withering of what had seemed like an irreversibly robust trajectory.

As in the post-war period, and in particular during the debates in the 1970s that surrounded the Bullock Committee, there were differing views as to how industrial democracy should be achieved and disagreements as to the efficacy of statutory requirements for the inclusion of worker directors on company boards. The requirement for directors to consider the interests of workers was another initiative pursued by the promoters of industrial democracy, which raised some of the same concerns that were mooted in the post-war period about the introduction of worker directors – that is, that they undermined the existing channels for industrial relations, such as collective bargaining and industrial strikes, and left workers with less power and protection. It was argued that the mandatory inclusion of employee interests in directors' duties as defined by company law could have similar unsatisfactory results, that is, creating only the semblance of increased protection for workers that is unenforceable and would serve to give company directors a shield for their decisions. Nonetheless, changes to company law were pursued, encouraged by the state of industrial relations in the 1980s that was testament to the failure of the traditional non-judicial avenues to protect employee interests. When the self-regulatory system fails to balance the conflicting interests of all stakeholders, including workers and shareholders, and to contain the resulting societal economic and social disruptions, the state may take steps to intervene, including legal reform.[41]

The changes introduced in the CA 1980 included only traces of the wholesale reforms that had been envisioned in the post-war period, falling short of introducing modifications that would upset the existing dynamics amongst the various stakeholders and with minimal implications for corporate behaviour. That is not to suggest that the reforms in 1980 were not viewed as progress. Unlike the proposed provisions of the 1973 and 1978 Bills, the 1980 changes became law, giving hope to those pushing for greater reforms that UK company law was evolving in favour of the interests of stakeholders in general and employees in particular; yet, these aspirations for additional statutory changes were unrealised and this legislative path remained unfollowed.

[39] Gamble and Kelly (2000) 44.
[40] See ch 7 of this volume on the Bullock Report.
[41] Xuereb (1988) 171.

A. Section 46: Expanding Directors' Considerations

The CA 1980 preserved the primacy of shareholders, but it also introduced into law the requirement to consider one group of stakeholders in addition to shareholders, in this case the interests of employees.[42] Whereas before the CA 1980 there was no explicit duty for directors to take into consideration the interests of employees, and only what was in the interests of the company (that is, its shareholders), section 46 made the consideration of employee interests a mandatory duty.[43] Even with this change that explicitly identified and elevated employee interests, as well as the ambiguity that it introduced to the interpretations of directors' duties, the requirement for directors to act in the interests of the company remained undisturbed. Directors were to have regard for both employees' interests and shareholders' interests, although the law did not provide any guidance on prioritisation or precedence; yet, because directors were the representatives of the shareholders alone and were not accountable to other stakeholders, including employees, shareholder primacy was maintained even with the introduction of the statutory requirement to consider employee interests.[44]

The specific inclusion of employee interests in the CA 1980 should be viewed within the context of the changes in industrial relations and the policies of the new Thatcher government towards employee rights and labour law.[45] These changes in UK company law did not disrupt the primacy of shareholder interests, whose influence on company decisions was more implicit than explicit, and occurred alongside the weakening of the trade unions and the declining impact of industrial action that were accompanied by developments in employment law in the UK.[46] The introduction of the requirement to consider employee interests in section 46 did modify the status quo, and it can be interpreted as being at least a symbolic gesture to employee interests, even if it did nothing to challenge the position of primacy of the providers of equity capital, the shareholders. In section 46 of the CA 1980, employees were the only non-shareholder stakeholders whose interests were explicitly identified, whereas other groups, like consumers and communities, did not receive the same consideration, even if the value of this statutory change was questionable and its impact limited.

In the 1983 first edition of *Boyle and Birds' Company Law*, section 46 of the CA 1980 is presented as being a 'welcome acknowledgement of the fact that modern management does often take into account the interests of employees'

[42] Companies Act 1980, s 46; Knight (1982) 13; Durham (1982) 568; Prentice (1981). See also ch 4, section VIII of this volume.

[43] Prentice (1981) 2; Boyle and Birds (1983) 576.

[44] Moore (2018) 150.

[45] On labour law in the Thatcher years, see Fredman (1992).

[46] Gelter (2009) 192.

and links this reform to the recommendations of the Bullock Report.[47] Coming not long after the recommendations of the Bullock Committee, section 46's introduction of the consideration of employee interests reflects the idea introduced in the Conservatives' unrealised 1973 Companies Bill that directors could take into consideration the interests of employees, which was further advanced in Labour's Companies Bill of 1978.[48] The 1978 Bill was based on Labour's 1977 White Paper, *The Conduct of Company Directors*, which drew on the findings of the Bullock Report, declaring that: 'The Government also believes that employees should be given legal recognition by company law. The statutory definition of the duty of directors will require directors to take into account the interests of employees as well as of shareholders.'[49]

The 1978 Companies Bill was seen at the time to reflect the existing attitudes towards employee interests and the prevailing conduct of most companies, moving beyond the 1973 Bill's permission for consideration by introducing a statutory requirement. By making it mandatory for directors to take employee interests into account, the law was reflecting what responsible directors (who were the majority) were already doing, while requiring the non-complaint companies to rectify their behaviour.[50] The 1978 Bill failed to become law, however, and although it was the basis for section 46 of the Conservative's CA 1980, the Act reflected the new government's consequential amendments to the Bill – that is, that the director's duty is to the company alone and is not extended to the employees.[51] Although the changes to the CA 1980 did not challenge the existing principle of shareholder primacy, they did nonetheless explicitly acknowledge the requirement to consider the interests of non-shareholder stakeholders – that is, employees – in the law.

Despite the apparent progress made in advancing the cause of industrial democracy and employee interests that occurred with the reforms to the CA 1980, changing directors' consideration of employee interests from an entitlement to a requirement was not accompanied by any other major reforms.[52] Section 46 required the consideration of employee interests, but the primary duty remained to the company's members (that is, the shareholders) and 'ultimately, the employees' interests will be subordinate to those of the shareholders. Directors will be able to say honestly that they have considered the employees' interests but have regretfully come to the conclusion that other criteria must override them'.[53] Although viewed as improving the treatment of employees by imposing a positive duty on directors, the directors were not required to subordinate the interests of shareholders or any other stakeholders

[47] Boyle and Birds (1983) 575.
[48] Feldman and Meisel (1996) 156. See ch 4, section VIII of this volume.
[49] *The Conduct of Company Directors* (Cmnd 7037, 1977) para 5.
[50] Mackenzie (1982) 688–89.
[51] Mackenzie (1982) 690.
[52] Boyle and Mordlsey (1980) 284.
[53] Boyle and Mordlsey (1980) 284.

to those of employees, thereby falling short of introducing a legal requirement that had any real impact on corporate behaviour.[54] Although this change in the law was not symbolically insignificant, and the context of the reform within the development of the industrial democracy movement was important, its effect on corporate behaviour should not be overstated, primarily because even prior to the legal change, there was no prohibition against considering employee interests if they aligned with the interests of shareholders.[55] The entrenched default to shareholder primacy and to the maximisation of shareholder value remained the norm amongst corporate managers, having resisted the calls for change during the height of the industrial democracy movement of the 1970s, and notwithstanding the introduction of the consideration of employee interests in section 46 (and section 309 of the CA 1985).[56] This change in the Companies Act was not a mechanism to obstruct shareholder primacy or to promote corporate social responsibly or industrial democracy, and the protection of stakeholder interests, be it workers or other constituents, was left to other areas of the law.[57]

i. The Law and the Parliamentary Debate

The real impact of the change in law was limited, yet the parliamentary debate on the legislation that would become section 46 of the CA 1980 reflects how supporters of the Bill presented this reform as elevating the interests of employees and of it making a fundamental change to the duties of directors, as argued by Conservative Lord Mackay of Clashfern on 27 March 1980:

> Since 1973 Governments of both parties have attempted to introduce such a provision as this one, but I believe that the formula we have now adopted achieves the right balance between the need to recognise in company law the contribution that employees make and the necessity to avoid saddling directors with confusing or conflicting duties as regards the interests of employees and shareholders … First, we wanted to make sure that the clause stated quite unambiguously that directors have a duty – that is, a mandatory and not a permissive requirement – to consider the interests of employees. Secondly, we consider that this new duty on directors should be seen as part of, not in conflict with, the directors' general fiduciary duties to the company; the new duty is therefore expressed along with the general duty that the directors have to regard the interests of the members.[58]

Even at the time of the debate, however, it was clear that the reforms were not disturbing directors' primary duty to shareholders and that the mandatory

[54] Durham (1982) 568; Boyle and Mordlsey (1980) 284.
[55] Prentice (1980) 137.
[56] Bercusson (1986) 144. See also ch 8, section IV.A of this volume.
[57] Sealy (1987) 176. See also ch 4, n 37 of this volume.
[58] HL Deb 27 March 1980, vol 407, col 1019; Durham (1982) 568. Lord MacKay of Clashfern was a Conservative member of the House of Lords from 1979 and was Lord Chancellor from 1987 to 1997 under Thatcher.

considerations of employee interests were still within the context of what was in the company's interests – that is, in the interests of its members – which might conflict with what was in the interests of workers. Decisions regarding employee layoffs or balancing the choice between the reinvestment or the distribution of profits were just two obvious examples.

In response to Lord Mackay, Labour Lord Mishcon criticised the wording of section 46(2), which he sought to have deleted, not to take away the statutory rights of employees, but to remove the introduction of law behind which directors can shelter. Section 46(2) was:

> [D]eemed to be a shield for the directors and not a spear ... that if a director is criticised, indeed is attacked in the courts, for not having fulfilled duties to the members of the company solely in their interests because he has taken into account the interests of employees, which may slightly or substantially derogate in a certain case from the interests of the members, it shall be taken into account that the director had this statutory duty.[59]

Section 46 was a toothless gesture towards increasing the protection of employee interests, and a distraction from meaningful legal reform, while also diminishing the power of shareholders. The Conservative Lord Mackay responded to Lord Mishcon's proposal to remove section 46(2), arguing that although the interests of shareholders and employees might differ:

> [W]e believe that it is the responsibility of the directors of the company to try to resolve any differences that there may be between these and to do their best to ensure that these interests are pursued both in the interests of the members and of the employees.[60]

Despite the rhetorical appeal to compromise, the requirements of the law clearly prioritised the interests of shareholders, which were themselves weakened in favour of company directors.

Lord Mishcon's concerns about the law being used to provide cover for directors, and to weaken the position of shareholders as opposed to fortifying that of employees, were not unfounded. The silence of section 46 of the CA 1980 on prioritisation or on how to deal with conflicts of interests impeded the enforcement of the law, while providing directors with a defence for their decisions.[61] With the CA 1980, directors were given wider latitude for their actions, requiring them to consider employee interests, but with no obligation to act on those considerations in their duties to the interests of the company.

[59] HL Deb 27 March 1980, vol 407, col 1022. Lord Mishcon was a Labour member of the House of Lords from 1978 to 2006.

[60] HL Deb 27 March 1980, vol 407, col 1025.

[61] Sealy (1987) 176. See also Berle (1932) 1367 on the danger of weakening of shareholder primacy in favour of other stakeholder interests: 'When the fiduciary obligation of the corporate management and "control" to stockholders is weakened or eliminated, the management and "control" become for all practical purpose absolute.'

Despite the semblance of diluting shareholder primacy, the inclusion of employee interests in directors' considerations did not give this stakeholder group any real gains at the expense of shareholder interest, but, rather, provided directors with protection against shareholders who might oppose their decisions.[62]

Furthermore, the wording of the law, 'to have regard', is undefined and imprecise, giving directors room to justify almost any reasonable decision.[63] Section 46(1) provides:

> The matters to which the directors of a company are to have regard in the performance of their functions shall include the interests of the company's employees in general as well as the interests of its members.[64]

It does not, however, give any guidance on how directors should balance the interests of these different stakeholders or how to determine employees' interests.[65] Despite the arguments demonstrating how this statutory change in the CA 1980 was without substance and did not reflect the efforts for industrial democracy reform of the previous decades, it did, nonetheless, recognise the interests of employees, alone amongst non-shareholder stakeholders, and demonstrate the changing attitudes towards stakeholder interests that nudged this development in UK company law.[66]

The statutory requirement to have regard for employee interests reflected what was already happening 'on the ground' in British companies – that is, that directors and managers were considering the needs of numerous stakeholders, be they workers, customers, creditors or other constituents, when making decisions.[67] Whereas section 46 made it a statutory requirement for directors to consider the interests of employees without disrupting the premise that directors' duties are owed to the company and the company alone, it did focus attention on the question as to whether the interests of the company can, or should, mean more than that of its members.[68] Commenting on the new legislation in *The Company Lawyer* in 1980, legal scholars AJ Boyle and Barry Mordlsey observed that: 'It may be useful having something in a statute which reminds directors of their duties towards employees, but in a conflict situation, it is unreal to think that the employees' position can be improved.'[69] Whereas the interests of employees were recognised, the law was silent on how to act in a potential

[62] Villiers (2000) 596.

[63] Although she discusses s 309 of the CA 1985, which has almost identical language to s 46 of the CA 1980, see Villiers (2000) 595.

[64] Companies Act 1980, s 46.

[65] Prentice (1981) 2; Villiers (2000) 595. See also Prentice (1981) on how s 46 potentially impacts directors' actions in takeover situations.

[66] Farrar and Hannigan (1998) 386; Bercusson (1986) 143.

[67] Xuereb (1988) 158.

[68] Companies Act 1980, s 46(2); Bercusson (1986) 144.

[69] Boyle and Mordlsey (1980) 285.

conflict of interests between employees and shareholders.[70] Ultimately, the definition of what was in the company's interest was not altered by this change in the CA 1980, which reinforced the priority of shareholders, who enforced the duties of directors.[71]

ii. Challenges of Enforcement

The inclusion of a specific reference to the interests of employees in addition to those of shareholders in the delineation of directors' duties in the CA 1980 was, despite appearances, a weak attempt at advancing industrial democracy, as section 46 not only lacked clarity but also had no explicit enforcement requirements.[72] Even if the introduction of section 46 is interpreted as altering the definition of a company's interests to include the mandatory requirement to balance the interests of shareholders and employees, it was unenforceable.[73] Section 46(2) makes clear that the duties remained unchanged – that is, that they were owed by directors to the company – and there was no enforcement mechanism to force directors to consider employee interests or to have those considerations reflected in their decisions. Furthermore, if employee interests were not considered, shareholders had no obvious incentives to pursue breaches of section 46, whose enforcement was their responsibility and which would require them to take action that would be against their own interests; of course, worker shareholders could be motivated to prioritise the protection of employee interests over those of shareholders, but, as has been demonstrated, worker shareholding was not widely adopted and did not result in meaningful activism.[74] Attempts to encourage worker shareholding as an effective check on company management were not successful, and the likelihood of workers achieving a majority position amongst all the shareholders in a company was unrealistic.[75] Not only was the balance of interests left to the discretion of directors, but the employees whose interests it was the duty of directors to consider also had no recourse *as employees* to enforce this duty.[76]

Section 46(2) states that the duty is owed by directors 'to the company (and the company alone) and is enforceable in the same way as any other fiduciary duty owed to the company by its directors'.[77] The inclusion of the requirement

[70] Feldman and Meisel (1996) 156.

[71] Bercusson (1986) 144; Boyle and Birds (1983) para 20.3. For an alternative reading of whether s 46/s 309 altered the definition of the interests of the company, see Parkinson (1993) 82ff.

[72] Prentice (1980) 138.

[73] Parkinson (1993) 83.

[74] Prentice (1981) 4. See also ch 5 of this volume on worker shareholders.

[75] Minority shareholders were limited in their ability to act by *Foss v Harbottle* (1843) 2 Hare 461, and this was codified in ss 260–63 of the Companies Act 2006; see Villiers (2000) 596.

[76] Durham (1982) 568.

[77] Companies Act 1980, s 46(2).

to consider employee interests did not change the outcome for the stakeholders as, regardless of whether directors considered the interests of employees or not, there was no recourse; like the shareholders whose interests were in conflict with those of employees, directors acting on behalf of the company were unlikely to deviate from their understanding of their duties to satisfy the demands of employees.[78] Furthermore, the interpretation of what was in the interests of the company is subjective and establishing bad faith by directors is very difficult, as directors only needed to demonstrate that their decisions, which might appear to be against the interests of (certain) employees – for example, closing a factory – were in the interests of the company.[79]

Despite the impression that stakeholder interests were advanced in the CA 1980, the changes belied a lack of real reform. Employees did not have the statutory right to board representation, a main demand of the industrial democracy movement, they had no avenues to enforce section 46 and they had no right to participate in a general meeting that could be called to attempt to enforce this directors' duty.[80] Furthermore, judicial remedies faced the challenge of proving that directors did not 'have regard' for the interests of employees and, even if this was found to be the case, there were no defined remedies to rectify any such breach.[81]

B. Section 74: Reversing *Parke v Daily News*

Section 46 was not the only change in the CA 1980 that addressed stakeholder interests other than those of shareholders. Arguably a more meaningful change for the protection of employee interests was section 74, reversing the decision in *Parke v Daily News*.[82] The *Parke v Daily News* ruling held that payments of compensation to employees on the winding-up of a business, even when ratified at a general meeting, could not be made as they were not in the interests of the company.[83] In Labour's 1977 White Paper, *The Conduct of Company Directors*, which recognised that the proposed changes to company law might not adequately address the specifics of the *Parke v Daily News* decision, the government stated its intention to deal with it specifically through legislation 'to make it lawful for directors to make provisions for employees or former employees when closing down the whole or any part of the business'.[84]

[78] Villiers (2000) 596.
[79] Parkinson (1993) 84.
[80] Feldman and Meisel (1996) 157. See ch 6 of this volume on worker directors.
[81] Prentice (1981) 5.
[82] *Parke v Daily News* [1962] Ch 927; Arden and Eccles (1980) 4, 123. See also ch 4, section IV of this volume.
[83] Moore (2018) 156.
[84] *The Conduct of Company Directors* (Cmnd 7037, 1977) para 7.

Unlike section 46, which addresses directors' duties, the section 74 change impacts directors' powers, giving the company the capacity to act in the interests of stakeholders, in this case employees, both current and former, including those of subsidiaries, and not solely in the interests of shareholders.[85] Section 74 makes explicit the ability of directors to prioritise the interests of employees in these specific circumstances, addressing the issues inherent in section 46 when there is a divergence of interests between shareholders and employees.[86] This proposed change corrects the *Parke v Daily News* ruling, which was considered to be out of step with how companies viewed their responsibilities and how directors were expected to behave, reflecting the evolving attitudes of the 1970s.[87]

Enacted under the new Conservative government, the CA 1980 represented the prevailing attitudes towards the *Parke v Daily News* ruling, which led to the statutory intervention of section 74 that allowed for such 'quasi-redundancy' payments to employees and former employees at the cessation or transfer of a business, establishing that it was not ultra vires for a company to take the interest of employees into consideration in such situations.[88] Section 74 makes it explicit that provisions may be made for employees when a business is being wound down regardless of the interests of shareholders, determining that section 46 applies to this type of situation where there might be a conflict between the interests of shareholders and employees, although, not insignificantly, such a provision still required ratification.[89] When a company ceases to trade it no longer has a direct interest in its employees, therefore it cannot be in the interests of the company to make provisions for employees, a conflict which was addressed by section 74.[90] This power given to directors by section 74 was still limited by the company's shareholders, as any provisions for employees made by directors under section 74 were still subject to the ratification requirements of a company's memorandum or articles.[91] Thus, the shareholders retained the right to exercise corporate power, unless a provision in the company's memorandum or articles explicitly provided for employees.[92] In addition, section 74 required that any payment to employees must be made from funds available for distribution or from the assets available to members when the company was being wound up – that is, it was not to be paid by the creditors.[93]

[85] Prentice (1980) 138.
[86] Durham (1982) 580.
[87] Mackenzie (1982) 688.
[88] Prentice (1980) 138; Alcock (2009) 364.
[89] Durham (1982) 580.
[90] Prentice (1980) 141.
[91] Boyle and Mordlsey (1980) 285.
[92] Boyle and Mordlsey (1980) 285.
[93] Prentice (1980) 142.

IV. THE COMPANIES ACT 1985

The CA 1980 was enacted almost immediately after the election of Thatcher, reflecting the legislative work of the prior Labour government, whereas the CA 1985 became law when the Conservatives had been in power for over five years. The new Act, which consolidated different pieces of legislation and introduced various material changes in terms of how companies were governed, remained consistent on directors' duties to shareholders and stakeholders, that is, section 46 and section 74. The common law tradition of viewing the interests of the company as the same as the interests of the shareholders was preserved, including the changes introduced in the CA 1980 to address the consideration of the interests of employees. These changes, which reflected the broader demands for statutory requirements acknowledging stakeholder interests, including those of the industrial democracy movement seeking greater powers for employees, had little influence on corporate behaviour.[94] Regardless of the legal requirements, the attention of directors in the day-to-day management of companies was on profitability, which required the ongoing balancing of the interests of different stakeholders, including shareholders, creditors, suppliers, employees, consumers and the community, while taking into consideration the size and type of company and the nature of the decisions being made, and was not on the details of the CA.[95]

A. Section 309

Section 309 of the CA 1985 replicates the wording of section 46 of the CA 1980 almost exactly, preserving the statutory requirement:

> The matters to which the directors of a company are to have regard in the performance of their functions include the interests of the company's employees in general, as well as the interests of its members.[96]

The mandatory consideration of employee interests remained a statutory obligation in the CA 1985, and with it the accompanying challenges of enforcement and the questions of its effectiveness as a buttress to shareholder primacy. Section 309, like section 46 of the CA 1980, was ambiguous, although it was typically interpreted to mean that, whereas directors were obliged to have regard for the interests of employees, they were only required to act in the interests of the company – that is, its shareholders. This formulation explicitly acknowledged employee interests in the law, but still failed to adequately reflect their

[94] Bercusson (1986) 144.
[95] Farrar and Hannigan (1998) 387.
[96] Company Act 1985, s 309(1).

central importance to the success of a business and how the interests of all stakeholders, including shareholders and employees, contributed to the creation of shareholder value.[97]

The duty imposed on the directors in section 309(1) 'is owed by them to the company (and the company alone) and is enforceable in the same way as any other fiduciary duty owed to a company by its directors'.[98] The consideration of employee interests did not change the meaning of the 'interests of the company', which preserved the primacy of members/shareholders.[99] As observed by the legal scholar Andrew Keay, section 309 'has been next to useless. The provision has hardly been used and there is very little case law on the section'.[100] Employees still had no standing to enforce the duty to consider their interests and there was little case law; section 309 was viewed as a 'lame duck' provision that was hardly used.[101] As with the CA 1980, the law offered employees little redress, and instead of increasing accountability to their interests, the limited case law saw section 309 used to protect directors, with the courts utilising it as a shield for directors and not, even indirectly, as a positive duty to employees.[102] The weaknesses of section 46 of the CA 1980 and section 309 of the CA 1985 suggest that these reforms were attempts to appear to address the criticisms of an established system that was based on shareholder primacy by including employee interests in the law, yet were no more than pacification exercises that did nothing to empower employees, but instead strengthened the position of directors by providing them with a tool to weaken shareholder claims.[103] Commenting in 1987 that '[a] supposed legal duty which is not matched by a remedy is a nonsense', the legal scholar Len Sealy adroitly concluded that: 'The emptiness of the UK's section 309 is thus exposed. It is either one of the most incompetent or one of the most cynical pieces of drafting on record.'[104]

B. Section 719

The CA 1985 also preserved the other section in the CA 1980 that addressed employee interests in the event of the cessation of a company: section 74. The 1980 statutory challenge to the *Parke v Daily News* decision remained in the CA 1985, although it provided fewer details.[105] Company law required directors to

[97] Kiarie (2006) 338.
[98] Company Act 1985, s 309(2).
[99] Bercusson (1986) 144.
[100] Keay (2007) 607.
[101] Keay (2006) 356; Keay (2007) 593.
[102] Villiers (2000) 597. See also Armour, Deakin and Konzelmann (2003) on s 309 in the context of takeovers.
[103] Feldman and Meisel (1996) 157.
[104] Sealy (1987) 177; Feldman and Meisel (1996) 157.
[105] Arden and Eccles (1980) 123; Joffe and Hochhauser (1980) para 12.106.

make decisions that prioritised the interests of shareholders over employees (or other stakeholders), although section 719, like section 74 of the CA 1980, allowed for the specific exception of the cessation of a business, and this reform to the law would most likely have protected the directors in *Parke v Daily News*.[106] This change in the law, first introduced in the CA 1980, established a specific exception to directors' duties in the interests of the company, which alongside section 309 (which identifies explicitly the interests of employees) can be interpreted as challenging, however weakly, the prior commitment to the primacy of shareholders that made no allowances.[107] The lack of enforcement, however, suggests that these reforms were signals rather than attempts at any sort of genuine rebalancing. Even with the reform of directors' powers to account for employee interests under certain circumstances that was included in company law with section 719 of the CA 1985, as with section 74 of the CA 1980, shareholder consent was still required for any form of consideration that was against the company's interest (unless the articles of association permit otherwise). Although this power was 'exercisable notwithstanding that its exercise is not in the best interest of the company', it was still the shareholders that ratified decisions taken under section 719, making the likelihood of a gratuitous payment to employees unlikely and preserving the established principle of shareholder primacy.[108]

V. THATCHER'S BIG BANG AND THE FINANCIAL SERVICES ACT 1986

The post-war changes to the shareholder body, and the increase in institutional managers shepherding the funds of an expanding pool of indirect capital in the form of pensions, insurance and other vehicles, coincided with the Thatcher government's liberalisation of the financial markets in the Big Bang, which was intended to provide domestic capital with a strong and growing platform for investment.[109] Following the economic hardships of the 1970s and the removal of the Labour Party from power, as well as the liberalisation and modernisations of the financial markets in the US and elsewhere, the UK's self-regulating and restrictive LSE was increasingly uncompetitive.[110] Shareholders invested in listed British companies, most of which were traded on the LSE, faced restrictions, exemplified by the LSE admitting no new companies as members from 1945 to 1986, the prohibition of foreign ownership of listed companies, the limitations on which products financial services firms could offer investors, and the segregation of the functions of financial institutions.[111] Furthermore, post-war

[106] Keay (2012) 121.
[107] Moore (2013) 192.
[108] Parkinson (1993) 87.
[109] Clark and Knight (2009) 265.
[110] Oren and Blyth (2019) 607.
[111] Fishman (1993) 6.

financial markets in Britain were mostly unregulated or self-regulated, functioning on traditional notions of gentlemen's agreements and codes of honour which, inevitably, contributed to underperformance and even scandal in an increasingly globalised financial system that saw exponential growth in share ownership by increasingly sophisticated institutions.[112] These dynamics culminated in Thatcher's Big Bang – that is, the Conservative government's overhaul of the financial services industry that began in 1983 and resulted in the introduction of legislation in 1986 and 1987, which led to London's repositioning as a global financial services leader.[113]

The process of liberalising the LSE began before Thatcher took office, yet it was in the 1980s that the restrictions on ownership, including by foreign institutions, were loosened, fixed commissions were removed, the walls separating different types of financial institutions fell, and the trading systems became increasingly transparent and automated.[114] These steps to transform the British financial markets in the 1980s, alongside the removal of capital constraints and the influx of foreign financial institutions into the UK, attracted investment from around the world, making London a leader in the modernising global economy. The Britain imagined by Thatcher and her government was one of economic efficiency, productivity and capitalist competitiveness, and the post-war UK financial markets that existed when she took office did not embody these traits. The reform of the City was part of the broader Thatcherite trends that included privatisation, deregulation, share and property ownership, public services reform and the general deconstructing of the post-war settlement.[115]

Shareholders in the 1980s were operating in a changed and increasingly sophisticated and impersonal environment, which required them to place their trust in the self-regulating bodies that were expected to provide adequate guardrails in the market conditions that followed Thatcher's Big Bang; the traditional protections that the old system had given investors were weakened by the liberalisation and globalisation of the markets, leaving shareholders vulnerable. Furthermore, this change in the character of the UK financial markets was occurring as the privatisations of British public sector companies placed shares directly in the hands of more small shareholders, as well as indirectly through pension plans and other investment vehicles.[116] Whereas the risks to small shareholders created by Thatcher's reforms of the financial markets were clear to those promoting the systemic changes, the desire to create attractive markets for financial institutions trumped concerns for the individual shareholder; the

[112] Fishman (1993) 6.

[113] The legislative overhaul included the Banking Act of 1987, which strengthened the Bank of England's power and oversight over deposit-taking institutions. A detailed study of the regulatory and legislative nuances of the Big Bang is beyond the scope of this study; see Fishman (1993); Gower (1988).

[114] Oren and Blyth (2019) 609.

[115] Moore (2016) 215.

[116] See section II.A above.

arguments in favour of financial deregulation were accompanied by a broad acceptance of the principle of market efficiencies and of the market's ability to regulate itself.[117]

The end of the era of the City as a closed club, and the liberalisation and modernisation of the UK financial markets, put shareholders and investors at increased risk, and despite Thatcher's inclination towards deregulation, there was a need for a regulatory framework, which led to the Financial Services Act 1986.[118] With the Financial Services Act, the UK's tradition of self-regulating financial markets was disrupted, and laws to protect shareholders and bring the activities of the markets under the purview of determinative state control were introduced.[119] The Big Bang fundamentally changed the structure of UK financial markets and broke down traditional barriers, creating conditions for increased activity and growth; alongside these reforms, the Financial Services Act 1986 introduced detailed statutory requirements, much of which was under the supervision of self-regulatory bodies.[120]

The financialisaton of the UK economy intensified during the Thatcher era, and the associated risks of liberalisation were de-emphasised by both the Conservatives and the New Labour governments that followed. The Big Bang of 1986 brought deep structural change to the City, incubating the conditions that contributed to the financial crash of 1987, Black Wednesday in 1992 and the global financial collapse of 2007–08.[121] In 2022, the resurgence of Thatcherite ideas and the call by recent Conservative governments for a deregulatory post-Brexit 'Big Bang 2.0', promoted as a solution to the current era's sluggish growth and economic malaise and as a way to promote the City's competitiveness, is both hauntingly reminiscent of the Thatcher era and notable in its lack of consideration of the stark differences in economic conditions and of historic context.[122]

VI. NEW LABOUR'S 'THIRD WAY' AND THE COMPANIES ACT

By the beginning of the 1990s, the economic recovery of the Thatcher era was under strain, from the Black Monday market crash in 1987 to the slowing economic growth, decreasing output, increasing unemployment, falling value of the currency and rising inflation of the 1990–92 recession. Yet, despite these unfavourable economic conditions, John Major won the 1992 election with 42 per cent of the vote, more a testament to the British electorate's distrust of

[117] Oren and Blyth (2019) 610.
[118] Moore (2016) 216.
[119] Moore (2013) 199.
[120] Fishman (1993) 84ff.
[121] For a detailed account of the City during these periods, see Kynaston (2001).
[122] For example, Parker, Thomas and Morris (2022); Forrest (2022); Cordon (2022).

the Labour Party as capable economic stewards than an endorsement of the governing Conservatives.[123] In the 1997 election, the Labour Party, under the leadership of Tony Blair and with the marginalisation of the Labour radical left, presented itself as a credible alternative to the party of Thatcher and Major, and promoted concepts of regional economic development and the advancement of the interests of various stakeholders.[124] The Conservatives were voted out of power and were replaced by Labour (which won 43 per cent of the vote), which sought a moderate equilibrium that hewed a centrist line combining free-market principles with social-democratic ideals, bringing many concepts traditionally associated with the Conservatives under the banner of 'New Labour'.[125] The new Labour government presented itself as an appealing alternative to the stale offerings of the Conservatives, promising regulatory reform and seeking the support of business and the City with commitments to fiscal and budgetary responsibility.[126]

Despite the rhetoric of achieving social-democratic objectives while pursuing market flexibility and economic efficiencies, New Labour's 'Third Way' was not a radical departure from many of the existing Conservative policies of the 1990s.[127] The post-war consensus on which the mixed economy was built, based on Keynesian economic theory and a traditional approach to the role of government and the welfare state, was challenged and dismantled by Thatcher's free-market policies, but by the mid-1990s it was clear that the Thatcherite approach also had its failings as Britain faced growing inequalities and increasingly strained public services.[128] To appeal to the British electorate, New Labour took the position that it needed to reflect the neoliberal economic framework introduced by Thatcher, adopting the ideas of a 'Third Way' that rejected the traditional post-war divisions between the political right and left, and accepted the idea that government, including a Labour government, needed to work within the capitalist system.[129] In his drive to reform the party's values and aims, Blair's New Labour finally reformed Clause IV, which advocated for the nationalisation of British industry and had been part of Labour policy since 1918, an undertaking that was not without controversy.[130]

The 'Third Way' was also used to describe the evolving corporate governance norms in the UK, with the concept of ESV presented as a compromise between the American stakeholder-centric wealth-maximisation regime and the EU's emphasis on stakeholder interests.[131] The UK was including stakeholder

[123] Matthijs (2011) 151.
[124] Edgerton (2018) 508.
[125] Edgerton (2018) 503.
[126] Rowbottom and Schroeder (2014) 665.
[127] Matthijs (2011) 2.
[128] Giddens (2010) 186.
[129] See Matthijs (2011) 156ff for a more detailed discussion.
[130] See ch 2, section V.C of this volume on post-war nationalisations and Clause IV; Matthijs (2011) 155.
[131] Williams and Conley (2005) 500. See also ch 4, section II of this volume on ESV.

interests in its governance codes and in the legal definition of directors' duties, leading some contemporary observers to conclude that, driven by the demands of institution investors, there was a move away from traditional shareholder primacy norms. In their 2005 paper 'An Emerging Third Way? The Erosion of the Anglo-American Shareholder Value Construct', Cynthia A Williams and John M Conley wrote that 'shareholder capitalism in the UK is beginning to diverge from its American counterpart and develop its third way: a long-term enlightened shareholder value perspective with strong elements of European stakeholder thinking'.[132]

The shareholder democracy and industrial democracy of the post-war era were precursors to these discussions on stakeholderism and to alternative interpretations of shareholder value. In a 1987 paper on the responsibilities of directors, Sealy argued that company law's concentration on the shareholders was too narrow:

> It is contended on many sides that the law ought to allow, or even require, directors to have regard to other, wider, considerations and interests. There are demands for overt recognition of the claims of the company's workforce, its customers and clientele, its suppliers and creditors, more broadly, the local community, the national interest, exports, welfare, the environment.[133]

These considerations of shareholder primacy and stakeholder interests, although not new, were now occurring in a political environment defined by New Labour that provided a receptive atmosphere for reflections on the established approaches to shareholder value. The acknowledgement of employee interests in the CA 1980 and the CA 1985 reflected these ideas, even if the application of the law remained mostly static, creating the semblance of momentum without disrupting the status quo.

A. The Stakeholder Society

In 1995, the journalist Will Hutton published the best-selling book *The State We're In*, which reflected the mood of the period that brought New Labour into government and the British public's willingness to accept the policies and ideological underpinnings of the 'Third Way'. The final chapter of Hutton's influential book considers the topic of stakeholder capitalism, arguing that the economic problems of Britain should be addressed by reforming the existing system that is based on shareholder primacy and on short-term profits.[134] Hutton's book identifies the empowerment of stakeholders as a way to solve

[132] Williams and Conley (2005) 499.
[133] Sealy (1987) 169.
[134] Hutton (1996) 298.

the problems of the British capitalist system and, like earlier trends of the post-war period that challenged the existing economic and political constructs, the rhetoric of reform (which resonated with the British public) was absorbed into the political narrative of the time; the idea of a stakeholder society was rhetorically useful for New Labour as it promoted new policies and ideas to an electorate aching for change, even if the more radical approach advocated by Hutton was never endorsed.[135]

Hutton promoted his idea of a 'stakeholder society' as an alternative to the existing system and identified many overlapping ideas with Labour's 'Third Way', although his concept of stakeholder capitalism was more radical than the ideological compromises promoted by Blair.[136] Hutton's proposals included dramatic reforms, including initiatives that addressed the republicanisation of the Bank of England, how banks provide credit, the time horizon for shareholders and the market for corporate control.[137] The movement for stakeholder capitalism required legal and cultural changes in terms of how British companies were run, although expressions of support for the consideration of stakeholder interests, which proved popular to some business leaders and politicians, did not necessarily mean approval for systemic change.[138] In comparison, Blair's 'Third Way', although influenced by Hutton, was a diluted interpretation that did not embrace transformative reform of the economy and political systems.[139] Unlike the journalist Hutton, the politician Blair's goal was to win elections, and New Labour sought to give the British electorate confidence that a Labour government would not harm the City, British industry or the existing capitalist system. The discussion of the 'Third Way' and of a stakeholder society was rhetorically effective, but, like the movements that preceded and succeeded it, offered little change to the legal frameworks underpinning the existing system of shareholder primacy, leaving the transformative ideas in the realm of ideological discussions.

As observed in *The Independent* in January 1996, Blair and his Chancellor Gordon Brown were cautious and clear in ruling out changes to corporate legislation, sticking instead to safer areas of reform and distinguishing 'between measures which would trespass on the ownership rights of shareholders, which would be political death, and measures which encourage the representatives of shareholders, whether company managers or investing institutions, to display more long-termist behaviour'.[140] New Labour's stakeholder capitalism was a departure from the traditional Labour policies of the post-war consensus

[135] Morrison (2004) 168.
[136] Driver and Martell (2000) 148.
[137] Hutton (1996) 298ff.
[138] Ireland (1996) 287.
[139] Matthijs (2011) 159. In 2015 Hutton published a second book, *How Good We Can Be*, which revisited the arguments for stakeholder capitalism for the post-global financial crisis generation (Hutton (2015)).
[140] Davies (1996).

that built the modern British welfare state, with echoes of Thatcher's calls for individual responsibility audible in Blair's emphasis on mutual responsibilities, suggesting a new consensus based on shared obligations and not on state support and the redistribution of wealth.[141] The stakeholder society of New Labour was a pivot away from the post-war mixed economy and traditional Labour ideas of state intervention, and a re-alignment to the policies of the Conservative governments that New Labour sought to replace, preserving the existing capitalist system in which company directors have legal obligations to shareholders and where shareholder primacy is untroubled by competing stakeholder interests.

VII. THE COMPANY LAW REVIEW STEERING COMMITTEE

Britain's financial, commercial and industrial spheres continued to evolve alongside the changes in governments, while elements of the laws that regulated the corporate arena remained mostly static, with many legal rules unchanged from the CA 1862, highlighting a disconnect between statute and practice, and leading to the Labour government's commissioning of a comprehensive review.[142] In 1998, the Department of Trade and Industry established the Company Law Review Steering Group (CLRSG) to review UK company law and the purpose of the company, including the consideration of the interests of shareholders and of other stakeholders.[143] The question of in whose interests companies should be run was addressed, examining shareholder primacy as well as options for considering a broader range of stakeholder interests.

The CLRSG was established in an atmosphere of political change and the semblance of shifting priorities as corporate behaviour was scrutinised and entrenched assumptions were questioned; in keeping with this pervading mood, the Hampel Committee on corporate governance, another example of this type of enquiry, which was established in 1995 and was chaired by Sir Ronald Hampel, the Chairman of ICI, published its report in 1998.[144] The CLRSG, established that same year, was made up of experts in company law, academics, business representatives and other interested parties, and delivered a number of interim documents as well as its final report in July 2001.[145] Amongst the questions that the Steering Committee sought to address were those on stakeholder interests and the responsibilities of companies and their directors:

> Companies striving to act responsibly – not only for their shareholders, but also their employees, creditors, trading-partners and the wider community – are uncertain

[141] Macintyre (1999) 125.
[142] Keay (2012) 65.
[143] Keay (2012) 14.
[144] See section VIII.B below. The Final Report of the CLRSG addresses the Combined Code in s 5.42.
[145] Keay (2012) 65.

> where their legal duties lie. And those who make up the wide range of interests to whom any company is accountable are not receiving the information necessary to assess the nature of the company and its business.[146]

The question of directors' duties, and how they should be interpreted and codified, was central to the committee's mandate – that is, what does it mean to act in the interests of the company?

Despite the rhetoric of change and the actions taken to examine alternatives to the established legal norms within which companies functioned, in its 1999 Consultative Document, the first to be issued by the CLRSG in its review of company law and that introduced its strategic framework, the CLRSG lays out two approaches to reforming the existing system based on shareholder primacy – that is, ESV and pluralism.[147] In describing ESV, it states that this approach accepts that 'the ultimate objective of companies as currently enshrined in law – ie to generate maximum value for shareholders – is in principle the best means also of securing overall prosperity and welfare'.[148] The pluralist approach goes further than ESV, arguing for the requirement for companies to consider stakeholder interests beyond those of shareholders and on an equal footing.[149]

The CLRSG explicitly refers to the debate on directors' duties and the responsibilities to shareholders and stakeholders, identifying the conflicting positions of ESV and pluralism.[150] The ESV approach preserves shareholder primacy and positions the interests of other stakeholders within the context of creating shareholder value, whereas the pluralist approach argues for stakeholder interests being considered in their own right, a position that required a change in company law that ESV did not demand.[151] The Consultative Document explains, however, that some supporters of ESV acknowledge that in practice neither maximising shareholder value nor overall prosperity and welfare are realised, based partly on the erroneous belief by some directors that short-term profit is the same as shareholder value: 'Thus the law as currently expressed and understood fails to deliver the necessary inclusive approach.'[152] Nonetheless,

[146] Department of Trade and Industry, *Modern Company Law for a Competitive Economy: Final Report* (2001) Foreword, s 5.

[147] Department of Trade and Industry, *Modern Company Law for a Competitive Economy: Strategic Framework* (1999) s 5.1.12; Collison et al (2011) 5.

[148] Department of Trade and Industry, *Modern Company Law for a Competitive Economy: Strategic Framework* (1999) s 5.1.12; Keay (2012) 29.

[149] Department of Trade and Industry, *Modern Company Law for a Competitive Economy: Strategic Framework* (1999) s 5.1.13.

[150] Department of Trade and Industry, *Modern Company Law for a Competitive Economy: Strategic Framework* (1999) ch 5.1; *The White Paper on Modernising Company Law* (HC 439, 2003) ch 3.

[151] Department of Trade and Industry, *Modern Company Law for a Competitive Economy: Strategic Framework* (1999) ss 5.1.12, 5.1.13; *The White Paper on Modernising Company Law* (HC 439, 2003) ss 14–15.

[152] Department of Trade and Industry, *Modern Company Law for a Competitive Economy: Strategic Framework* (1999) s 5.1.12.

in presenting arguments for and against both ESV and pluralistic approaches to directors' duties and posing questions for consideration by the CLRSG, the report on the strategic framework of company law argues that having companies consider the interests of multiple stakeholders, and not just shareholders (that is, the pluralistic approach), would 'dangerously distract management into a political balancing style at the expense of economic growth and international competitiveness'.[153]

Although the CLRSG debated the value of both the ESV and pluralist approaches, some of those who participated in the process questioned whether there was ever a genuine questioning of the acceptance of the principle of shareholder primacy or whether the whole exercise was designed to support and reaffirm the status quo.[154] A 2011 Association of Chartered Certified Accountants (ACCA) research report examining the work of the CLRSG, which included interviews with participants, concluded that:

> [O]ur own analysis of the arguments advanced in the CLR documentation for and against the 'pluralist' and 'enlightened shareholder value' positions did suggest that they were less than even-handed and implicitly favoured the status quo. This perception is consistent with the position of a number of interviewees regarding the lack of serious consideration given to alternatives to shareholder primacy.[155]

Like the post-war examples of attempts to reform company law, such as the Bullock Committee, the process of deliberation was performative, highly visible and open to accusations of bias, with the recognisable outcome being the lack of meaningful reform.

A. The CLRSG Addresses Section 309

Section 46 of the CA 1980 and section 309 of the CA 1985 introduced changes to directors' duties that explicitly recognised the requirement to consider the interests of employees, although in such a way that preserved the underlying premise of shareholder primacy. In its 1999 report, the CLRSG presented the argument that ESV, which was based on the premise of shareholder primacy, did not require changes to 'the ultimate objective of companies, that is, shareholder wealth maximisation' and that there was no need for a statutory reform of directors' duties, even if the lack of change could lead to short-termism and to ignoring the interests of non-shareholder stakeholders. The report continues, arguing:

> It is on our view clear, as a matter of policy, that in many circumstances directors should adopt the broader and longer-term ('inclusive') view of their role. This is

[153] Department of Trade and Industry, *Modern Company Law for a Competitive Economy: Strategic Framework* (1999) s 5.1.28.

[154] Collison et al (2011) 31.

[155] Collison et al (2011) 42.

> indeed now widely acknowledged. But we do not accept that there is anything in the present law of directors' duties which requires them to take an unduly narrow or short-term view of their functions. Indeed they are obliged honestly to take account of all the considerations which contribute to the success of the enterprise.[156]

The apparent lack of clarity on, and understanding of, the specific requirements for directors in interpreting section 309 of the CA 1985 was apparent to the CLRSG and what, if anything, should be done was a key question for it.[157] The attempt to balance the interests of all stakeholders, be it through ESV or a pluralistic approach, was central to the debate on company law reform in the UK, with examples in Europe, the Commonwealth and the US serving as foils to the UK status quo.[158] The conclusions drawn from these comparisons remained consistent with existing approaches to shareholder and stakeholder interests, with the CLRSG rejecting the European model of directors' duties, claiming it was inconsistent with British values.[159] In its 2001 Final Report, the CLRSG recommended statutory definitions of directors' duties that:

> [G]ive directors a clear authoritative statement of what their duties are; bring the law into line with modern business practice and accepted standards of behaviour; encourage responsible behaviour by making clear that in promoting the success of the company for the benefit of its members as a whole, directors must take account of long- term as well as short-term consequences; and that they must recognise, where relevant, the importance of relations with employees, suppliers, customers and others, the need to maintain a reputation for high standards of business conduct, and the impact of their actions on the community and the environment.[160]

Section 309's requirement for directors to consider the interest of employees only partially satisfied this recommendation.

The duty of directors to shareholders was made explicit by the CLRSG in answering the question of 'scope' – that is, in whose interests should companies be run – in the Final Report:

> [O]ur proposed statement of the duty of loyalty makes clear the obligation of each director to act to serve the purposes of the company as laid down in the constitution and as set for by its members collectively: that is, it sets as the basic goal for directors the success of the company in the collective best interests of shareholders.[161]

[156] Department of Trade and Industry, *Modern Company Law for a Competitive Economy: Strategic Framework* (1999) s 5.1.19.

[157] Department of Trade and Industry, *Modern Company Law for a Competitive Economy: Strategic Framework* (1999) s 5.1.17; p 148.

[158] Department of Trade and Industry, *Modern Company Law for a Competitive Economy: Strategic Framework* (1999) ch 4.

[159] Department of Trade and Industry, *Modern Company Law for a Competitive Economy: Developing the Framework: A Consultation Document* (2000) s 3.35; Keay (2012) 72. See also ch 6, section IV.C of this volume on the European Economic Community.

[160] Department of Trade and Industry, *Modern Company Law for a Competitive Economy: Final Report* (2001) ss 3.5–3.11.

[161] Department of Trade and Industry, *Modern Company Law for a Competitive Economy: Final Report* (2001) s 3.8.

The Final Report continues, however, acknowledging the requirement:

> [T]o recognise, as the circumstances require, the company's need to foster relationships with its employees, customer and suppliers, its need to maintain its business reputation, and its need to consider the company's impact on the community and the working environment.[162]

This acknowledgement of the need to consider stakeholders other than shareholders preserved the shareholder primacy that underpinned the existing system, while also reflecting what business leaders already know – that is, that success depended on engaging with many constituents. The CLRSG emphasised the importance of stakeholders and endorsed the principles of ESV without, however, deviating from the primary goal of creating shareholder value.

The CLRSG confirmed the shareholder primacy interpretation of company interests, endorsing the need for directors to focus on shareholder value, although, consistent with section 309 of the CA 1985's inclusion of employee interests, also requiring directors to take into consideration the interests of other stakeholders.[163] The arguments in favour of shareholder primacy and against a pluralist approach were familiar, including the difficulty for directors to prioritise amongst stakeholders, the challenges of policing and of enforcement, the implications for the courts, the impact on the ability to attract investment, and the blurring of the meaning of loyalty to the company.[164] These arguments, made in support of shareholder primacy when confronted with demands for legal reforms, were similar to those of the post-war period and the debates on industrial democracy, culminating in the Bullock Report, and which also did not lead to a reform of core company law, but rather aided in preserving the existing system.[165] The push for the statutory recognition of stakeholder interests continued in the decades following the post-war period and into the next century, although with similar results and negligible changes. Ultimately, efforts to progress stakeholder capitalism remained subordinate to the perpetuation of shareholder primacy in UK company law.

B. The Operating and Financial Review

The Final Report of the CLRSG also embraced the concept of the Operating and Financial Review (OFR) as part of the disclosure required in a company's

[162] Department of Trade and Industry, *Modern Company Law for a Competitive Economy: Final Report* (2001) s 3.8.

[163] Department of Trade and Industry, *Modern Company Law for a Competitive Economy: Developing the Framework: A Consultation Document* (2000) s 2.22; Keay (2012) 71.

[164] Department of Trade and Industry, *Modern Company Law for a Competitive Economy: Developing the Framework: A Consultation Document* (2000) ss 3.24–3.31; Keay (2012) 72.

[165] See chs 6 and 7 of this volume.

annual report to improve 'the understanding of a business's performance and prospects'.[166] The OFR was proposed as a way to strengthen corporate governance, providing:

> [A] review of the business, its performance, plans and prospects. It would include information on direction, performance, and dynamics (capital projects, risks, etc.) and on all other aspects which the directors judge necessary to an understanding of the business, such as key business relationships with and environmental and community impacts. The requirement to produce an OFR would improve the quality, usefulness and relevance of information available to the markets and to everyone with an interest in the company. As such, we expect it to lead to improved understanding of business performance and prospects, as well as promoting accountability and encouraging responsiveness and high standards of business.[167]

The CLRSG recommended that disclosure requirements of the OFR include three mandatory elements: (i) the company's business, strategy, and principal drivers of performance; (ii) a review of the company's business over the year; and (iii) the dynamics of the business, including events, trends and other factors which may substantially affect future performance.[168]

In addition, acknowledging the importance to the company and its shareholders of the interests of other stakeholders:

> The OFR will also contain much other important information; for example, on corporate governance, relationships with employees, customers, suppliers and others on whom the company success depends, and on environmental, community, social, ethical and reputational issues.[169]

This additional information was for the benefit of shareholders and its purpose should not be understood as a means for increasing stakeholder engagement; furthermore, this disclosure was discretionary and its materiality was determined by a company's directors.[170] The CLRSG's inclusion of the OFR was to support shareholder interests, arguing that this non-financial information impacted share price and financial performance, and therefore should be disclosed.[171]

[166] Department of Trade and Industry, *Modern Company Law for a Competitive Economy: Final Report* (2001) s 3.32. For a European comparison, see Directive 2003/51/EC of the European Parliament and the Council of 18 June 2003 (amending Directives 78/660/EEC, 83/349/EEC, 86/635/EEC and 91/674/EEC on the annual and consolidated accounts of certain types of companies, banks and other financial institutions and insurance undertakings [2003] OJ L178/16) ('the EU Modernisation Directive').

[167] Department of Trade and Industry, *Modern Company Law for a Competitive Economy: Final Report* (2001) s 3.34.

[168] Department of Trade and Industry, *Modern Company Law for a Competitive Economy: Final Report* (2001) s 3.39.

[169] Department of Trade and Industry, *Modern Company Law for a Competitive Economy: Final Report* (2001) s 3.39.

[170] Department of Trade and Industry, *Modern Company Law for a Competitive Economy: Final Report* (2001) s 3.49; Clark and Knight (2009) 273.

[171] Clark and Knight (2009) 274.

The emphasis on the importance of access to information, including material non-financial information, which was often resisted by company directors, was consistent with earlier appeals by shareholders and stakeholders alike.

VIII. SHAREHOLDERS, STAKEHOLDERS AND UK CORPORATE GOVERNANCE

Following the failure of the Bullock Committee to achieve the industrial democracy statutory reforms that were envisioned by the Labour government that had established the Committee, there was growing momentum supporting the need for self-regulating non-mandatory corporate governance codes for British companies and for the increasingly complex and modernising UK financial markets. The various governance codes of the 1990s contributed to the establishment of the 2000 Combined Code of Corporate Governance and its subsequent revisions; the Cadbury Committee was established in 1991 in response to a number of corporate scandals, the Greenbury Committee was established in 1995 to address executive remuneration, and the Hampel Committee was established in 1998 to consider the existing codes and was the last stage before the creation of the Combined Code that amalgamated its predecessors.[172] These codes, which were non-governmental and had no statutory standing, focused on the interests and rights of shareholders and their relationships with directors, with the consideration of stakeholder interests remaining firmly within the context of shareholder value.[173]

The increased support for taking into consideration the interests of non-shareholder stakeholders should not be interpreted as broad-based demands for systemic changes in UK company law, with the issues being further complicated by the blurring of the lines of differentiation between stakeholderism and ESV, with the former requiring statutory change and the latter remaining within the framework of existing law that kept the shareholder firmly in primary position alongside voluntary consideration of other stakeholders.[174] The concepts associated with the stakeholder society that Hutton and Blair brought into the mainstream seeped into the rhetoric of some business leaders who declared their support for a more inclusive approach to how companies were managed, although the lack of accompanying systemic change suggests that these proclamations were more strategic and symbolic than transformational.[175] The exercise of making the right pronouncements about stakeholder interests was a proven and effective deflection strategy, projecting the semblance of change

[172] Parkinson and Kelly (1999) 101.
[173] Parkinson and Kelly (1999) 106.
[174] Gamble and Kelly (2000) 45.
[175] Ireland (1996) 286.

without there being any accompanying statutory reforms disrupting the status quo. Despite public statements of inclusivity and advancement, UK industry was consistent in its resistance to reform and the governance codes remained voluntary, as demonstrated by the 1992 LSE listing requirements that only necessitated companies to disclose how they comply with the Combined Code and, if they did not, to explain.[176] The option to comply or explain remains an important aspect of company disclosure, relying on shareholder pressure, and market expectations, to monitor and enforce corporate governance.

A. The Cadbury Report 1992

The Committee on the Financial Aspects of Corporate Governance, chaired by Lord Adrian Cadbury and known as the Cadbury Committee, was established in 1991 by the Institute of Chartered Accountants in England and Wales (ICAEW), the LSE and the Financial Reporting Council (FRC). The Committee's recommendations were focused on financial reporting and accountability, but also addressed corporate governance more generally, at the heart of which was a Code of Best Practices for obtaining a high standard of corporate behaviour.[177] The Report emphasised the importance of shareholders and their role in pressuring companies to adopt the voluntary code, with an understanding that 'if companies do not back our recommendations it is probable that legislation and external regulation will be sought to deal with some of the underlying problems which the report identifies'.[178] This desire to pre-empt statutory requirements through self-regulation is central to the UK self-regulatory tradition, with more recent deflection strategies mirroring the efforts of previous decades.

In its introduction, the Cadbury Report makes clear the central role of shareholders in the corporate governance system; directors are responsible for governance, the directors are appointed by, and report to, the shareholders, and '[t]he board's actions are subject to laws, regulations and the shareholders in general meeting'.[179] The Committee not only recognised the importance to good governance of the board providing relevant information and adequate disclosure to shareholders, but also that shareholders have a role 'through their willingness

[176] Gamble and Kelly (2000) 45.

[177] *Cadbury Report of the Committee on the Financial Aspects of Corporate Governance (Report with Code of Best Practice)* (1 December 1992) s 1.3. See Cheffins and Reddy (2022) for an argument in favour of ending code-based corporate governance system introduced by the Cadbury Committee. For a response to Cheffins and Reddy (2022) see Marchetti and Passador (2022).

[178] *Cadbury Report of the Committee on the Financial Aspects of Corporate Governance (Report with Code of Best Practice)* (1 December 1992) 1.10.

[179] *Cadbury Report of the Committee on the Financial Aspects of Corporate Governance (Report with Code of Best Practice)* (1 December 1992) s 2.5.

to exercise their responsibilities as owners'.[180] The Report, in describing the relationship between the board of directors and shareholders, states that:

> [T]he shareholders elect the directors, the directors report on their stewardship to the shareholders and the shareholders appoint the auditors to provide an external check on the directors' financial statements. Thus the shareholders as owners of the company elect the directors to run the business on their behalf and hold them accountable for its progress. The issue for corporate governance is how to strengthen the accountability of boards of directors to shareholders.[181]

Despite decades of effort from numerous constituents to elevate the interests of stakeholders other than shareholders, the concept of the equity shareholder as the owner of the company to whom the board reports remained entrenched.[182]

B. The Hampel Report 1998

In 1998, the findings of the Cadbury Committee were reviewed by a new committee led by Sir Ronnie Hampel that addressed the balance between rigid compliance requirements and flexible governance principles, leading to recommendations for reforming the Code that were adopted in the first Combined Code on Corporate Governance in 2000.[183] The Report promoted the idea of a governance structure that met the changing needs of British companies and capital providers, stating that: 'Good corporate governance is not just a matter of prescribing particular corporate structures and complying with a number of hard and fast rules. There is a need for broad principles.'[184] The concept of 'comply or explain' that has become a core aspect of UK corporate governance was part of the Hampel Report's recommendations on how companies should disclose their governance practices, including any departures from best practices, arguing that prescriptive 'box ticking' that did not account for a diversity of experiences of company directors was neither fair nor conducive to good corporate governance.[185]

The Hampel Report, building on the corporate governance principles and self-regulating approach of the Cadbury Report, emphasised the use of

[180] *Cadbury Report of the Committee on the Financial Aspects of Corporate Governance (Report with Code of Best Practice)* (1 December 1992) s 3.4.

[181] *Cadbury Report of the Committee on the Financial Aspects of Corporate Governance (Report with Code of Best Practice)* (1 December 1992) s 6.1.

[182] The term 'stakeholder' does not appear in the Report. Employees are referenced in connection to a board's statutory duty to take their interests into account; *Cadbury Report of the Committee on the Financial Aspects of Corporate Governance (Report with Code of Best Practice)* (1 December 1992) s. 2.7.

[183] Moore and Petrin (2017) 61.

[184] *Hampel Committee on Corporate Governance: Final Report* (January 1998) s 1.11.

[185] *Hampel Committee on Corporate Governance: Final Report* (January 1998) s 1.13.

the AGM as the means by which to hold directors accountable, building on a theory of shareholders' power that is rarely witnessed in actuality; as was the case throughout the post-war period, and continues beyond it, the AGM was typically an expression of shareholders' rational apathy or reticence, with only occasional disruptions that may (or may not) have any impact on corporate behaviour.[186] Whereas the support of the AGM as the mechanism for corporate governance preserved the shareholders centrality to the governance process, as well as bolstering the pretence of shareholder democracy, while also maintaining the established system that served most boards in an environment where shareholders (including most institutional investors) were passive and, except in extreme circumstances, approved directors' decisions. The occasions when shareholders used the AGM, or other public methods, to clash with directors received media attention and interest, were rare, if often fascinating, occurrences.[187]

The Hampel Report acknowledged the central role of shareholders and how this impacted corporate governance, declaring that:

> The single overriding objective shared by all listed companies, whatever their size or type of business, is the preservation and the greatest practicable enhancement over time of their shareholders' investment. All boards have this responsibility and their policies, structure, composition and governing processes should reflect this.[188]

Furthermore, it stated clearly that company directors are accountable to shareholders and not to stakeholders, with any change in directors' duties to include stakeholders would undermine accountability, 'a recipe for neither good governance nor corporate success'.[189] The Hampel Report elaborates, clarifying that this should not be understood as support for short-termism, but for the interests of present and future shareholders, and that long-term success depends on developing and sustaining stakeholder relationships, as well as on considering the broader acceptability of their conduct.

C. The Combined Code on Corporate Governance

The 2000 Combined Code on Corporate Governance that followed the Hampel Report was subsequently revised in 2003 and again in 2006 and 2008. Building on the recommendations of the Hampel Report, the Combined Code advocated for the preservation of shareholder primacy, with the 2003 revised Combined Code emphasising the role of shareholders in corporate governance and encouraging

[186] Barnard (1998) 113; *Hampel Committee on Corporate Governance: Final Report* (January 1998) s 5.

[187] See ch 3, sections I.D and section I.E of this volume for post-war examples of the perceptions of apathetic and uninformed shareholders.

[188] *Hampel Committee on Corporate Governance: Final Report* (January 1998) s 1.16.

[189] *Hampel Committee on Corporate Governance: Final Report* (January 1998) s 1.17.

institutional shareholders to exercise their votes and to communicate actively with company directors.[190] The changes in 2008 to the Combined Code on Corporate Governance included rewording of the Code's preamble to explicitly state that:

> Good corporate governance should contribute to better company performance by helping a board discharge its duties in the best interests of shareholders; if it is ignored, the consequences may well be vulnerability or poor performance. Good governance should facilitate efficient, effective and entrepreneurial management that can deliver shareholder value over the longer term.[191]

Earlier versions of the Code did not emphasise the interests of the shareholders in this way, suggesting either an assumption of the primacy of shareholder interests or, perhaps more likely, the need in 2008 – in an environment of increasing stakeholderism – to emphasise explicitly that good corporate governance contributed to fulfilling directors' duties in the best interests of shareholders.[192] In 2010, after consultation, the UK Corporate Governance Code, as the Combined Code was now called, was published, alongside a Stewardship Code for institutional investors. The UK Corporate Governance Code is regularly updated, most recently in 2018.[193] The debate on the Combined Code continues to evolve, with the current discussion posing the fundamental question of whether the Combined Code has served its purpose and should be abolished.[194]

IX. THE COMPANY LAW REFORM BILL AND THE COMPANIES ACT 2006

It took a number of years for the recommendations of the CLRSG to become law in a protracted process, albeit one that resulted in a reformulation of directors' duties. Following the final report of the CLRSG, a White Paper, *Modernising Company Law*, was presented by the government in July 2002.[195] In March 2005, another White Paper, *Company Law Reform*, was published, and on 1 November 2005 the Company Law Reform Bill was introduced, reflecting many (but not all) of the concepts on directors' duties and shareholder and

[190] *Hampel Committee on Corporate Governance: Final Report* (January 1998) ss 2.13, 2.14; Williams and Conley (2005) 514.

[191] Combined Code on Corporate Governance (2008) Preamble, s 1.

[192] Combined Code on Corporate Governance (2008) Preamble.

[193] Combined Code on Corporate Governance (2018). For a historical timeline of the UK Corporate Governance Code, see the Institute in Chartered Accountants of England and Wales at www.icaew.com/technical/corporate-governance/codes-and-reports/uk-corporate-governance-code/history.

[194] For the current discussion, see Cheffins and Reddy (2022).

[195] *Modernising Company Law Department of Trade and Industry* (Cmnd 5553, 2002). See also *The White Paper on Modernising Company Law* (HC 439, 2003) for the House of Commons inquiry into some of the themes of *Modernising Company Law Department of Trade and Industry* (Cmnd 5553, 2002).

stakeholder interests addressed in the preceding White Papers. The legislative process was long and the discussion of directors' duties was a central issue, also becoming the subject of numerous Private Members' Bills that were introduced during this period in response to a number of high-profile corporate scandals.[196] The push to create a system of increased accountability for directors received support in Parliament as well as by interest groups campaigning for heightened corporate responsibility.[197] The Company Law Reform Bill, which received royal assent in November 2006, became the CA 2006.[198] The Bill and the subsequent Act were presented by the government as a shift in approach and a commitment to ESV as a core principle, based on the recommendations by the CLRSG.[199] Thus, the new CA 2006 solidified the principle of shareholder primacy in UK company law.

A. Directors' Duties and Section 172

The CLRSG's consultation papers and final report recommendations were precursors to the CA 2006's codification of directors' duties to act to promote the success of the company for the benefit of its members (a change from the duty to act in the best interests of the company), while taking into consideration other stakeholders, as expressed in clause 156 of the Company Law Reform Bill of 2005 and the preceding White Papers in 2002 and 2005 (March and October).[200] Section 172(1) of the CA 2006 provides:

> A director of a company must act in the way he considers, in good faith, would be most likely to promote the success of the company for the benefit of its members as a whole, and in doing so have regard (amongst other matters) to—
>
> (a) the likely consequences of any decision in the long term,
> (b) the interests of the company's employees,
> (c) the need to foster the company's business relationships with suppliers, customers and others,
> (d) the impact of the company's operations on the community and the environment,
> (e) the desirability of the company maintaining a reputation for high standards of business conduct, and
> (f) the need to act fairly as between members of the company.[201]

In a gesture that suggests consideration for stakeholders within a shareholder primacy framework, this change in directors' duties introduces an ESV model

[196] Collison et al (2011) 25.
[197] Collison et al (2011) 25.
[198] For a timeline of the post-CLRSG legislative process, see Collison et al (2011) 24.
[199] Loughrey, Keay and Cerioni (2008) 85; *The White Paper on Modernising Company Law* (HC 439, 2003).
[200] Keay (2012) 76.
[201] Companies Act 2006, s 172(1).

for corporate governance that combines shareholder primacy with stakeholder models.[202] The advocates promoting stakeholder interests can point to section 172(1) as progress in breaking down the supremacy of shareholders, although, despite the semblance of material change, the position of the shareholder is not altered; ultimately, the company's interests are those of its members (that is, its shareholders), whose power remains unobstructed, regardless of what other stakeholders are considered. Furthermore, the language introduced in clause 156 of the Company Law Reform Bill and subsequently in section 172 of the CA 2006, is vague, with no definitions of 'success' or clarification of the meaning of 'for the benefits of its members as a whole', introducing uncertainty of interpretation.[203] Once again, the potential for reform that was expressed in the public and political discourses did not result in changes in core company law, with the established shareholder primacy system remaining intact, with only ephemeral gestures towards increased inclusiveness.

The CA 2006, although reflecting the general acceptance of the need for directors to consider of the interests of stakeholders other than shareholders, changed course from the approach of the CA 1980 and the CA 1985. Section 172 of the CA 2006 repealed section 309 of the CA 1985, instead including employees as one of a list of many stakeholders whose interests should be considered, and this consideration is not a requirement.[204] The expansion of directors' duties to include more than just employees reflected the diminishing power of the industrial democracy movement and the consideration of a deeper pool of constituent demands. The CA 2006 reflects the ESV approach supported by the CLRSG, moving away from the post-war focus on industrial democracy and the elevation of employee interests to consider a range of other stakeholders. Whereas section 46 of the CA 1980, on which section 309 of the CA 1985 was based, and which came directly after the apex of the British movement for industrial democracy and the Bullock Report and before the weakening of the trade unions and the change in industrial relations dynamics of the Thatcher era, placed employees as the singular non-shareholder interest to be considered, section 172 of the CA 2006 suggests a different direction in terms of how stakeholders are considered and treated.

Although section 172 was presented as a new approach to directors' duties and a change in the law, touted as embodying the principles of ESV that had gained popular support prior to the CA 2006, it was not understood to have material impacts on how directors behaved.[205] Section 309 was viewed as ineffective at promoting employee interests and was mostly unused, and the effectiveness of its replacement – section 172 – must also be questioned.[206] The statutory

[202] Harper Ho (2010) 78.
[203] Keay (2012) 83.
[204] Keay (2007) 593.
[205] Loughrey, Keay and Cerioni (2008) 90.
[206] Keay (2007) 607.

changes introduced in section 172, although including additional elements to directors' duties and reflecting an ESV perspective, still preserved shareholder primacy, which reflected the tone of the CA 2006 more generally.[207] Section 172 is unambiguous in its requirement for directors to act in the interests of the company for the benefit of its members, with all other considerations, 'amongst other matters', serving that purpose.[208]

As explained by law scholars David Kershaw and Edmund Schuster, the codified duties of directors are to exercise corporate power in good faith for the benefit of the members, that is, a long-term increase in value; section 172(1) and (2) makes it clear that the purpose of a company is to further shareholder interests.[209] Furthermore, for there to be a change to the prioritisation of shareholders in favour of other stakeholders would require the shareholders to amend the articles of association, requiring a super-majority of 75 per cent of votes cast in the general meeting, thereby acting against their self-interests, to change how the company's interests are defined, arguably an improbable scenario for most companies with dispersed ownership.[210] The rhetorical positioning of the changes in the CA 2006 suggests a shift away from shareholder primacy and the short-termism with which it was (and still is) associated, although the interpretation of the law preserved the primary position of shareholders and the duty of directors to prioritise shareholder interests above those of other stakeholders, even when they were required to take those interests into consideration.

As with section 46 of the CA 1980 and section 309 of the CA 1985, section 172 of the CA 2006 does not provide directors with guidance on how to balance the interests of shareholders and other stakeholders when fulfilling their fiduciary duties to the company, which is coupled with enforcement difficulties. Although the list of additional stakeholders to be considered under section 172 expands beyond just employees and shareholders, there are no directions on how the interests of the various constituents should be balanced. Rather than elevating the interests of non-shareholder stakeholders, section 172 served to protect directors from accusations of not fulfilling their duties to members (shareholders). Ultimately, this codification of directors' duties did not alter the prioritisation of these considerations, but made explicit the need to consider them for the protection of shareholder interests and for the long-term success of the company.[211]

B. Section 247

Although section 172 is the focus of most of the discussion on directors' duties, shareholder primacy and stakeholder interests, section 247 of the CA 2006, like

[207] Collison et al (2011) 27.
[208] Companies Act 2006, s 172(1).
[209] Kershaw and Schuster (2019) 6.
[210] Kershaw and Schuster (2019) 6.
[211] Clark and Knight (2009) 278.

its predecessors, section 74 of the CA 1980 and section 719 of the CA 1985, should also be considered. The statutory protections given by section 247 to directors in the case of the cessation of a business that explicitly allows for the elevation of employee interests above those of shareholders remained intact.[212] Whereas the CA 2006 repealed section 309 of the CA 1985, replacing it with a new focus on the consideration of different stakeholders for the benefit of shareholders, section 719 of the CA 1985 is retained in section 247 of the CA 2006, although with changes as to how it can be exercised.[213] In section 74 of the CA 1980, and section 309 of the CA 1985, the company is freed from the ultra vires restriction prohibiting the payment to employees; in section 247 of the CA 2006, the power is given to the directors, who require authorisation to exercise it. Furthermore, in the CA 2006, a directors' resolution, which must be authorised by the company's articles, cannot be used to make a payment to directors, former directors and/or shadow directors.[214] Shareholder approval is still necessary.

C. Disclosure and Stakeholder Considerations: Operating and Financial Review and Section 417

Alongside the changes introduced to directors' duties, section 417 of the CA 2006 identified stakeholders in its requirements for the contents of the business review in the directors' report, whose purpose 'is to inform members of the company and help them assess how the directors have performed their duty under section 172 (duty to promote the success of the company)'.[215] Section 417(5), which deals with the business review requirements for quoted companies, includes 'to the extent necessary for an understanding of the development, performance or position of the company's business':

> (b) information about—
>
> (i) environmental matters (including the impact of the company's business on the environment),
>
> (ii) the company's employees, and
>
> (iii) social and community issues,
>
> including information about any policies of the company in relation to those matters and the effectiveness of those policies.[216]

If, however, the review does not contain this information, the type of information that has been omitted must be stated.[217]

[212] Keay (2012) 121.
[213] Moore (2013) 192, fn 78.
[214] Birds et al (2007) 168, Companies Act 2006, s 247(5).
[215] Companies Act 2006, s 417(2).
[216] Companies Act 2006, s 417(5).
[217] Companies Act 2006, s 417(5).

Similar to the inclusion of stakeholders in the changes in directors' duties, these reporting requirements suggest that as part of a broader push for transparency, there was a shift in company law to require companies to be more inclusive of the interests of non-shareholder stakeholders, in particular the environment, employees, social issues and the community. The disclosure, however, is for the benefit of the shareholders, whose priorities are not necessarily aligned with the stakeholders listed. The interpretation of section 417 as ESV assumes that increased disclosure will lead to heightened considerations for stakeholder interests, although this must still be done within the scope of creating shareholder value. Furthermore, companies are free to exclude this information from the business review and in the event of a company having no policies for the consideration of stakeholder interests, there is nothing to report other than their absence.

i. The Fate of the Operating and Financial Review

This inclusion of stakeholder information in the CA 2006 business review was based on the OFR regulation proposed by the CLRSG to amend the CA 1985. The information required by the OFR was already disclosed voluntarily by most UK-listed companies since the 1990s, becoming a statutory requirement in March 2005.[218] In 2000, the CLRSG formally recommended in a White Paper that statutory OFR be adopted and an OFR Working Group was established in 2002.[219] The new OFR regulation stated that:

> review must include —
>
> (a) information about environmental matters (including the impact of the business of the company on the environment),
> (b) information about the company's employees, and
> (c) information about social and community issues.[220]

In addition:

> (1) The review must, in particular, include —
>
> (a) information about the policies of the company in each area mentioned in sub-paragraph (1), and
> (b) information about the extent to which those policies have been successfully implemented.[221]

Where the information is not included in the review, it must state what information and analysis is excluded.[222] When announced, the OFR was presented

[218] Rowbottom and Schroeder (2014) 661.
[219] Rowbottom and Schroeder (2014) 661; see also at 662 for a statutory timeline of the legislation.
[220] Companies Act 1985 (Operating and Financial Review and Directors' Report etc) Regulations 2005 (SI 2005/1011) s 4(1).
[221] Companies Act 1985 (Operating and Financial Review and Directors' Report etc) Regulations 2005 (SI 2005/1011) s 4(2).
[222] Companies Act 1985 (Operating and Financial Review and Directors' Report etc) Regulations 2005 (SI 2005/1011) s 3(2).

as expanding the information that all quoted companies would disclose to shareholders, building on existing best practices of some large companies and following the recommendation of the independent CLRSG. In a speech made by the Trade and Industry Secretary Patricia Hewitt announcing the OFR, she stated that: 'While prepared for shareholders, the OFR will also be useful to other vital stakeholders such employees, customers and environmental groups.'[223]

Reacting to a changing business environment that was both increasingly complex and scrutinised:

> The Government also argues that directors need to consider the success of the company and should take into account relationships with employees, customers and suppliers and the company's impact on the wider community as well as the company's impact on the environment. The OFR should contain details of all these aspects where they are relevant to an assessment of the company's business.[224]

That this increased transparency might also help stakeholders was rhetorically convenient, although it did not disturb the primacy of shareholder interests. It was the shareholders' needs that determined the content of the OFR, which was made clear in the Accounting Standards Board's (ASB) Reporting Standards, the statutory reporting standards of the OFR, in which shareholder interests superseded any claims of considerations of stakeholder interests.[225] Whereas stakeholder interests, or a subset of them, were important to directors and managers for running successful businesses, the legal requirements for shareholder primacy in the considerations of the best interests of the company were left untouched.

The OFR, within the framework of shareholder primacy, nonetheless made disclosure on stakeholder issues a legal requirement, seeming to advance the cause for elevating employee, community and societal interests; this perceived step forward was fleeting, however, and the law was quickly repealed and replaced. Despite support from the government, the OFR, which met resistance from elements of the business community that did not support the mandatory nature of the disclosure requirements, was ultimately deemed to be too arduous and in November 2005 the Labour Chancellor of the Exchequer, Gordon Brown, made a surprise announcement at the CBI annual conference of its repeal.[226] With that announcement, the OFR, which was central to the CLRSG's proposals, was dropped as part of a broader initiative of deregulation; the repeal legislation passed in January 2006.[227] With the repeal of the OFR, the ASB Reporting Standard lost its statutory power and became a statement of

[223] Department of Trade and Industry, 'Hewitt Announces Plans to Strengthen Corporate Britain' (Press Release, 5 May 2004).

[224] Villiers (2006) 208.

[225] Villiers (2006) 224.

[226] Keay (2012) 154; Rowbottom and Schroeder (2014) 664.

[227] Rowbottom and Schroeder (2014) 664; Collison et al (2011) 27.

'best practices', offering guidance rather than mandatory requirements.[228] This, in turn, opened the door for inconsistent, non-standardised and unclear disclosure by companies, providing shareholders with weaker tools with which to assess, and monitor, investee companies. The repeal decision was criticised by stakeholder groups and faced a legal challenge by Friends of the Earth that sought a legal review; the matter was settled out of court.[229]

Although Brown's repeal was based on the argument that with the OFR the regulators 'were goldplating beyond the demands of the EU rules', as well as a political opportunity to deregulate, the UK still had to comply with the EU disclosure requirements for companies to provide a fair review of business that were introduced with the Modernisation of Accounts Directive adopted in 2003.[230] The government was under pressure to deregulate, in particular where EU laws were seen as obstructive and where EU regulations were convenient scapegoats, and the repeal of the OFR was identified by the Treasury as a way to bolster political support from constituents perceived as being critical of increased regulatory interference in business.[231] The repeal of the OFR was the end of the statutory disclosure requirements, although the expectation for narrative disclosure by listed companies persisted with the introduction of the business review requirements of section 417 of the CA 2006, which were notably less stringent. Whereas the OFR mandated the inclusion of information about the environment, employees, and social and community issues, this is not compulsory under section 417, which only requires that this information be included in the business review 'to the extent necessary for an understanding of the development, performance or position of the company's business'.[232] If the information is not provided in the business review, section 417(5) requires that this be stated, although an explanation for the omission is not obligatory. Even the more demanding OFR requirements left discretion in the hands of directors, allowing them to determine if the non-financial matters and indicators – environmental, employee, social etc – did, or did not, have enough impact to require inclusion in the disclosure.[233]

As compared to the OFR, section 417 was more lenient in its requirements from directors and had a lighter regulatory burden, and whereas the OFR and section 417 both increased transparency and disclosure, thereby strengthening corporate governance, the motivations for these changes in company law were still shareholder-centric – that is, to provide shareholders with information that they need to make informed decisions. The framing of the argument supporting

[228] Aiyegbayo and Villiers (2011) 718.
[229] Rowbottom and Schroeder (2014) 664.
[230] Rowbottom and Schroeder (2014) 656; Aiyegbayo and Villiers (2011) 704.
[231] Rowbottom and Schroeder (2014) 668.
[232] Companies Act 1985 (Operating and Financial Review and Directors' Report etc) Regulations 2005 (SI 2005/1011) s 4(1); Companies Act 2006, s 417(5).
[233] Villiers (2006) 213.

the business review was that, through the tools of narrative reporting, it provided shareholders with additional information on how the company's activities and operations impacted other stakeholders, including the environment, society and the community, and how this might affect future prospects of a business, in the hope that this disclosure obligation would encourage directors and investors to consider both long-term and short-term issues, influencing the company's relationship with not only its shareholders (both existing and future), but also other stakeholders and constituents.[234] In step with the movement advocating for ESV, this enhanced disclosure was for the benefit of shareholders, even if it was framed within the context of broader stakeholder interests. Furthermore, section 417 did not result in increased clarity, but instead led to greater burdens on companies, more complex and difficult-to-compare non-financial reporting, and unclear communication; nonetheless, increased disclosure has generally been viewed positively by shareholders, even if the content did not necessarily serve the intended purpose.[235]

With the demise of the OFR, in what appeared to be a political move to win the support of British business, the Labour government, with the input of the CBI, sought to deliver pro-business deregulation despite objections from other stakeholders, including within Whitehall and Parliament, as well as from institutional investors.[236] Although the CBI supported the OFR's repeal, there was no clear consensus from the broader business community, including professional accounting bodies, many of which saw the benefits of the OFR disclosure requirements for all stakeholders, including shareholders. As explained by Nick Rowbottom and MAS Schroeder in their 2014 article 'The Rise and Fall of the UK Operating and Financial Review', the repeal in general:

> [W]as received negatively by the vast majority of interested parties including those who had not fully supported the statutory OFR but who were disappointed with the timing of its repeal. The only groups publicly supportive of the OFR repeal were the CBI, the British Chambers of Commerce, Deloitte and the London Stock Exchange. Although all four groups are arguably powerful institutions likely to represent the holders of capital, the repeal of the OFR did not appear to win the Government much political support, from elsewhere in the business sector.[237]

The assumption by policy-makers that business interests would unreservedly support deregulation, and by extension the party that implemented it, was flawed; increased transparency and disclosure were viewed by some constituents as positive contributions to decision-making, even if there were associated costs.

[234] Aiyegbayo and Villiers (2011) 705.
[235] Aiyegbayo and Villiers (2011) 709.
[236] Rowbottom and Schroeder (2014) 670.
[237] Rowbottom and Schroeder (2014) 671.

9

Contemporary Corollaries and Concluding Considerations

I. CONTEMPORARY RELEVANCE

THE POST-WAR DEBATES on shareholder and stakeholder rights and interests are once again resonating as the established system is under growing pressure to reform and various constituents seek to address the societal impacts of the global financial scandals, dislocations and disruptions of the first decades of the 2000s. The widespread appeals for action and demands for increased governance and accountability accompanied the declarations for a new era of stakeholder capitalism and corporate purpose that came in the wake of the global financial crisis of 2007–08, followed by the acute economic disruptions of the COVID-19 pandemic and the 2022 escalation of the Russo-Ukrainian war, which are extreme 'stress tests' of the regulatory frameworks within which the financial markets function.[1] The ESG, stakeholderism and corporate purpose campaigns are the most recent expressions of long-standing phenomena that are cyclical in their popularity and stubbornly constant in their seeming inability to achieve core legal reforms.[2] These most recent calls for change and the questioning of the shareholder primacy-based system are part of a broader movement for greater corporate governance, a reaction to what is widely believed to be a systemic failure by what is seen by many as a broken, and mostly unaccountable and unrepentant, financial system.[3] In many ways, the current climate is reminiscent of the historical arch of post-war Britain, an era that also saw political and social upheavals accompanying an economically challenging period of destruction followed by reconstruction, which offered the promise of reform, yet failed to yield statutory changes in company law in favour of the interests of non-shareholder stakeholders.[4]

[1] The scholarship on the corporate governance and the global financial crisis is extensive. See, for example, Alrayes (2019); Sun, Stewart and Pollard (2011); Tomasic and Akinbami (2011); Kirkpatrick (2009); Pajuste and Toniolo (2022).

[2] Kershaw and Schuster (2019) 31; Bavoso (2014) 220.

[3] See Davis (2021) on an iteration of industrial democracy, and possible nationalisations, as a requirement for successful governance.

[4] Pollak (2013) 106.

Driven by grassroots calls for change, as well as political eagerness to appear responsive to swelling popular movements of discontent with the existing system, leaders in industry, finance and politics seek to address publicly what they believe are the concerns of their varied constituents. In a post-crisis environment of widespread hostility towards the global financial system, ignoring the escalating demands for change is not a viable option for the leaders of public companies and financial institutions, who need investors and regulators to perceive them as both suitably reactive and credibly proactive. In addition to the demands for reform generated by the global financial crisis, the more recent economic upheavals and inflationary conditions created by the impact of the COVID-19 pandemic, and worsened by the ongoing Russo-Ukrainian war, are also leading to calls for structural reforms of a system that was saved from collapse not by the pursuit of short-term shareholder value, but by the cooperation between employers and employees, which was the result of the government's fiscal activism that supported public-private partnerships and kept restructuring and nationalisations as possible options for British industry.[5] The tone and tenor of these most recent calls for systemic reforms have distinct similarities to those of the post-war period, demonstrating the same urgency, seeming political commitment, public support and rhetorical flourishes that still fell short of disrupting the entrenched system.

The engagement with the issues of the broader shareholder/stakeholder debate continues to swell as more and more attention is paid to these key questions on the legal nature of the company and the duties of its directors; there is a distinct divide between those who accept as sincere the current enthusiasm for the stakeholder model and others who view the corporate leaders, financial advisors, capital providers, law-makers and thought leaders who endorse the stakeholderism movements as engaging in public relations theatre that creates the semblance of change while preserving the existing shareholder-centric system that serves their entrenched interests.[6] This latest iteration in the discourse on the nature of the company and in whose interests it should be run goes back decades, involving robust debate in legal academic communities, influencing scholars, politicians, and practitioners in the UK, the US and other jurisdictions. Although there are many participants debating the stakeholder/shareholder dilemma, and many ways in which to address it, the ongoing exchange between Professor Colin Mayer (University of Oxford) and Professor Lucian Bebchuk (Harvard University) is at the heart of the current stakeholder capitalism/shareholder capitalism controversy, with the former a representative of the supporters of stakeholderism and the latter of those questioning its effectiveness.[7] The Mayer-Bebchuk 'great debate' serves as an example of

[5] Coulter (2020) 534.

[6] Lipshaw (2021) 347. Lipshaw discusses the US, although the implications from his research are more far-reaching.

[7] Bebchuk and Tallarita (2020a); Bebchuk and Tallarita (2020b); Bebchuk and Tallarita (2021); Mayer (2019); Mayer (2020). Bebchuk's position questioning the movement for stakeholderism and

how the questions of shareholder and stakeholder interests have become one of the 'great controversies in business today', preoccupying the legal and business communities globally, although typically with inadequate reference to, or knowledge of, historical precedents.[8]

A. Rhetoric or Reform?

Following the global financial crisis of 2007–08, a narrative developed that there was now an opportunity to recalibrate the basic principles and assumptions underpinning corporate governance, the purpose of the company and the expectations of corporate behaviour within broader political, economic and social contexts.[9] Reminiscent of the post-war enthusiasm with which the Labour Party launched its nationalisation programme that then led to industrial democracy policies that sought, unsuccessfully, to bring about systemic reforms, this contemporary stance is part of the wider discussion on the responsibilities of industry and the financial sector, following similar patterns of appeasing rhetoric, political positioning, promises of change and very few real changes.[10] Similarly, there are identifiable transitions as corporate leaders adapt to changing expectations and adopt the language of their critics, assimilating the ideas of stakeholderism and corporate purpose into their narratives and letters to shareholders, although typically falling short of altering their corporate governance guidelines.[11]

The debate on governance responsibilities often intensifies in periods of economic or financial volatility, as was seen following the global financial crisis when many institutions countered the criticisms of having been passive share owners during the financial crash by subsequently taking more active positions when dealing with company management of investee companies, bringing challenges on a range of issues and making AGMs more difficult for the directors of UK companies that were unaccustomed to these levels of shareholder engagement.[12] To the powerful institutional investors, reluctant to shoulder the weight of governance but feeling the pressure brought by their beneficiaries for whom they create the impression of responsible engagement, today's corporate

corporate purpose has also drawn fire from prominent corporate lawyer Martin Lipton, who regularly publishes contributions to the debate; see, for example, Lipton and Savitt (2007); and, more recently, https://corpgov.law.harvard.edu/2021/08/24/more-myths-from-lucian-bebchuk. Professor Alex Edmans is another key contributor whose research has reached the mainstream; see Edmans (2020b).

[8] On 'Stakeholder versus Shareholder Capitalism: The Great Debate', see https://www.sbs.ox.ac.uk/oxford-answers/stakeholder-versus-shareholder-capitalism-great-debate.

[9] Greenfield (2014) 749.

[10] Bainbridge (2021) 312; Bebchuk and Tallarita (2020a) 4.

[11] Bainbridge (2021) 312; Lipshaw (2021) 351; Bebchuk and Tallarita (2020a) 4.

[12] Baker (2012) 66. See also Ivanova (2017). For a discussion on institutional investors, agency problems and corporate governance responsibilities, see Bebchuk, Cohen and Hirst (2017).

leaders must appear responsive and committed to looking beyond just short-term shareholder interests (although without sacrificing shareholder value).[13] By making appeasing statements, detached from any statutory reforms, shareholder interests and value are protected; like the post-war statements supporting stakeholder interests and questioning shareholder primacy, or the movements embracing ESV and the 'stakeholder society' in the post-1979 period, the more recent announcements by corporate leaders that are widely applauded for their fresh and progressive approach use similar tones and language.[14] If history is a guide, the public calls for change, and the corporate and political responses to them, lead to impassioned statements and gestures, especially when in the grips of a crisis or scandal, but fall short of core legal reform, a dynamic that follows the evolution of the economic cycle as it moves from crisis and crash to stabilisation and growth.[15]

The post-war lessons are germane for evaluating the current wave of calls for stakeholder rights and a re-evaluation of the role of the company, with an emphasis on the repercussions when rhetoric and intent fall short of achieving statutory reform and legislative progress. The shifting public attitudes towards prioritising multiple interests and away from shareholder primacy represent potential existential challenges and the ability to communicate change whilst preserving the established system is an effective mechanism for survival. For observers of today's 'revolution' of stakeholder rights, these examples from the 1950s, 1960s and 1970s are conspicuously familiar. Attempts to increase the involvement of non-shareholder stakeholders, and workers especially, including through legislative and regulatory means, are not necessarily at odds with the principles of capitalism, often trying to work within the existing system to make it more inclusive, equitable and sustainable or, at least, wanting to appear to be doing so.[16] The rhetoric of stakeholder democracy and stakeholder capitalism is not limited to the political left, with Conservative politicians leveraging the public dissatisfaction with corporate behaviour and growing inequality with promises to fight 'the establishment'. For example, in her 2016 leadership campaign speech, Theresa May pledged to change the system, including the radical reform of introducing employee and consumer representation on company boards, declaring 'if I'm Prime Minister, we're going to change that

[13] Bainbridge (2021) 314.

[14] 'US Business Association Redefines the Purpose of a Corporation' (2019) 360. Stakeholderism and corporate purpose are increasingly tied to value, although often without empirical back-up, further amplifying the fervour for pithy taglines and eye-catching headlines. See, for example, Blackrock's revolving credit agreement with terms tied to diversity and inclusion targets: Turner (2021).

[15] Fairfax (2006) 710. In a similar pattern, commenting on the gains for shareholder democracy in the US following the takeover battles of the 1980s and the possibility for legislation and reform, Professor Jayne W Barnard remarked that 'when the scandals of the moment died down, so did the prospect of substantive reform' (Millman (2003) 46). The example of the 'Shareholder Spring' of 2012, which was specifically aimed at executive pay, is a further example. See Baker (2012) 66; Gerrard (2016); Ringe (2015) 398.

[16] Cressey and MacInnes (1980) 6.

system – and we're going to have not just consumers represented on company boards, but employees as well'.[17] Perhaps unsurprisingly, despite becoming Prime Minister, this campaign promise was never fulfilled. Stakeholderism's popularity as a banner under which politicians can take a stand endures alongside the stickiness of shareholder primacy in UK company law.

These clamorous movements for change appeal to the broader public, and are reflected in the rhetoric of corporate leaders, particularly in times of distress caused by economic challenges and when there is growing emphasis on the implications of socioeconomic differences – for example, post-war reconstruction, the economic crisis of the 1970s, the global financial crisis in 2007–08, and the economic distress caused by the COVID-19 pandemic and the effects of the Russo-Ukrainian war – whereas the bland process of legislative reforms draw far less popular attention, leading to few actual changes.[18] With increasingly vocal critics commenting on the flaws in the existing system and making demands both for more oversight and for reforms of regulations and laws, supported by a largely sympathetic public that has experienced the harsh realities of austerity, muted wage growth and the many byproducts of corporate scandals, economic failures and political dysfunction, the leaders of finance, commerce, industry and government are under increasing pressures to respond. Whether those responses correspond to meaningful, systemic changes is another question – or, as queried in the *Financial Times* in December 2019, 'will this time be different? Are the world's companies really going to mend their ways?'[19]

II. CORPORATE PURPOSE: A NOTE ON CONTEMPORARY PARALLELS

Since the global financial crisis in 2007–08, there have been growing calls to reassess shareholder primacy, with an emphasis on a stakeholder model, and more than at any time since the end of the post-war era, increasing numbers of companies are embracing practices that address the interests of non-shareholder stakeholders, creating the appearance of a growing openness to re-evaluating fundamental questions on the nature of the company, to whom companies owe obligations, and how to consider the company's role and the regulations and legislation that govern them.[20] The question of corporate purpose is again at the centre of the narrative on a company's identity, behaviour and responsibilities, as well as at the forefront of companies' brand representations and corporate communications.[21] The prioritisation of corporate purpose creates an amplifying buzz amongst business, financial and political leaders, as well as those who observe and advise them, leading to an intensification of how companies

[17] See www.ukpol.co.uk/theresa-may-2016-speech-to-launch-leadership-campaign.
[18] Bainbridge (2021) 318.
[19] Skapinker (2019) 9.
[20] Greenfield (2014) 749; Sneirson (2020) 84.
[21] For a recent broad discussion on purpose, see Fisch and Solomon (2021).

seek to promote themselves to investors (both existing and future) and other stakeholders.[22]

The post-war period from 1945 to 1979 and the response to the global financial crisis of 2007–08 both led to calls by politicians for systemic changes that echoed loudly in the public sphere and received significant popular support, although in both cases these proved to be mostly toothless. The political environments of the two eras were, however, markedly different; in the post-war period, the struggle between socialism and capitalism was still very much alive and unresolved, whereas the more recent demands for stakeholder rights and empowerment are occurring within the context of an entrenched and secure capitalist system that has outlasted the collapse of the communist Soviet Union and the fall of the Iron Curtain, as well as the dismantling of socialist regimes across the world and the weakening of UK organised labour domestically.[23] The current movements for corporate change are, for the most part, not viewed as having the potential to overthrow capitalism, but are part of broader currents, built on decades of precedents, calling for more enlightened and purpose-driven approaches within the existing capitalist order, with the focus on the laws, regulations and governmental oversight of that system.[24]

A. The Business Roundtable

In August 2019, the Business Roundtable (BRT), an American organisation representing the leaders of US companies, released a new statement on the purpose of a corporation, endorsed by 181 CEOs, which included a commitment to all stakeholders, identified as customers, employees, suppliers, communities, and shareholders.[25] This widely publicised statement by the CEOs of companies from the world's largest market, which was subsequently endorsed and applauded by an array of institutional investors (themselves the target of criticism for governance failings), was, by putting all stakeholders on an equal footing, perceived by a broad global audience as disrupting the accepted premise of shareholder primacy.[26] In most cases, commentators reacted to the BRT's statement by

[22] See, for example, Fleischer (2021); Fisch and Solomon (2021); Langford (2020); Kershaw and Schuster (2019).

[23] For a summary of the shift to neoliberalism that followed the post-war era, see Shabani et al (2015) 208.

[24] Chen and Hanson (2004) 107. See also Kershaw and Schuster (2019) on corporate purpose and the 2018 Corporate Governance Code.

[25] See businessroundtable.org for statement and signatories; see also 'US Business Association Redefines the Purpose of a Corporation' (2019) 360. This statement by the BRT reiterates similar earlier views in support of stakeholders, such as those expressed in its 1981 Statement of Corporate Responsibility; see Cheffins (2020) 23; Bainbridge (2021) 288ff.

[26] See Harrison, Phillips and Freeman (2020) for an overview of the statement and reactions to it. For a debate on the legal implications of the statement, see Lipshaw (2021); Bainbridge (2021). On institutional investors, see Hertig (2018) 823. For a view on how the BRT's statement was a move against institutional shareholder power, see Pistor (2019) 47.

promoting it as evidence of a new and tangible change in corporate intention; the mere act of these business leaders declaring a self-proclaimed redefinition of the purpose of the corporation was accepted as sufficient for creating a new framework and re-alignment of the parameters within which public companies function.[27] Yet, despite the attention and praise it received, the 2019 statement was not particularly innovative, but was a reiteration and recycling of its own prior public communications on stakeholder rights, which it repackaged to meet the demands of the current environment.[28]

Notwithstanding its public posturing, the BRT has no authority and no enforcement powers. The 2019 statement does not reflect any changes in laws or regulations and it does not give the impression that core legal questions were of particular interest when the BRT took aim at shareholder primacy.[29] On the contrary, these forms of public statements can be seen as deflections that draw attention away from the cause of core legal reform.[30] Furthermore, the decisions to endorsed the BRT statement that were made by the CEO signatories were taken without board-approved resolutions in all but one example, with all the CEO signatories also retaining shareholder-centric corporate-governance policies. As observed by Bebchuk and co-author Roberto Tallarita:

> Notwithstanding statements to the contrary, corporate leaders are generally still focused on shareholder value. They can be expected to protect other stakeholders

[27] Despite the suggestion that the doctrine of shareholder primacy was uncomplicated and fully accepted (see, for example, Hansmann and Kraakman (2001), that '[t]here is no longer any serious competitor to the view that corporate law should principally strive to increase long-term shareholder value'), and that it leads to short-termism and unmitigated shareholder greed at the expense of all other stakeholders, there exists a long and detailed debate of its legal meanings and managerial implications that continues amongst legal scholars today. For the genesis of the debate, see Berle (1932); Dodd (1932). For an overview of the Berle–Dodd debate, see Sommer (1991). For a discussion of the concept of 'the stakeholder', including the coining of the term in 1963 at the Stanford Research Institute to refer to 'those groups without whose support the organization would cease to exist', see Freeman and Reed (1983) 89. For a description and historical survey of corporate rhetoric supporting stakeholder rights in the US and arguments supporting how companies have moved away from the doctrine of shareholder primacy, despite the legal scholarship asserting that shareholder primacy is the victorious model, see Fairfax (2006). Fairfax, however, seems to accept the rhetoric as an indication of change, whereas this thesis posits that the rhetoric deflects attention from the static nature of core law. See also Bavoso (2014).

[28] The BRT's position on stakeholder rights and shareholder primacy has changed over the years, with the most current deceleration returning to the 1981 position, which is also similar to that of 2012, although in 1997 the Roundtable deviated from these positions and embraced the popular stance of shareholder value. For a review of these changes in position, see Mintzberg (2019). See also Bebchuk and Tallarita (2020a).

[29] Whereas the BRT does not engage with the details of the legal debate, within the communities of legal scholars and interested practitioners, there is, of course, a vibrant ongoing discussion on the implications of stakeholder capitalism, corporate purpose, industrial democracy and shareholder democracy, which is mostly ignored by the business and financial players actively engaging with these topics and with the most conspicuous proclamations and calls for change. See Bebchuk and Tallarita (2020a) 4; Bebchuk and Tallarita (2020b) A15; Bebchuk and Tallarita (2021) A17.

[30] Bainbridge (2021) 317.

> only to the extent that doing so would not hurt share value. That conclusion will be greatly disappointing to some and welcome to others. But all should be clear-eyed about what corporate leaders are focused on and what they intend to deliver.[31]

To protect their position and deflect challenges, company boards use appeasing corporate statements and rhetoric as shields to keep law-makers and policy-makers from intervening in their business decisions and operations.[32] Larry Summers, the former US Treasury Secretary, commented in the *Financial Times* in August 2019: 'I'm wary … I worry the Roundtable's rhetorical embrace of stakeholders is in part a strategy for holding off necessary tax and regulatory reform.'[33]

The 2019 BRT's Statement on the Purpose of a Corporation, a crucial waypost on the path of stakeholderism whose impact was felt in the UK and elsewhere outside of the US, was followed by similar proclamations from other organisations seeming to challenge the principles of shareholder primacy. A growing numbers of CEOs, investment managers and thought leaders positioned themselves as the initiators of a bold new approach, causing students of history to have a sense of déjà vu; for the UK followers of this trend, a voyage back to a time before Thatcher's Big Bang reveals that today's movement for corporate purpose and stakeholder capitalism might have modernised its terminology and adjusted its lexicon for a contemporary audience, but the message is far from novel, demonstrating remarkable similarities to the discourses on industrial and corporate democracy, and the calls for systemic legal reforms of the post-war period.[34] The language of the post-war movement for industrial democracy foreshadowed the current discourse on stakeholderism and stakeholder capitalism that is being narrated in starkly similar terms, accompanied by comparable willingness to demote the interests of equity shareholders.[35] Examined through a wider historical lens, the challenges that contemporary corporate leaders face are just the most recent in the cycle of disruptions, and their reactions are both predictable and have historical precedents.

Whereas it may be naïve to expect corporate and financial leaders to know the legal and business history of the issues on which they make definitive public statements, it is fair to claim that informed perspective helps to avoid the inefficiencies of repetition both for those seeking and for those resisting reforms, as well as providing more clarity on the methods used and the barriers encountered. Those who view the current movements for reform as exercises in diversion can point to post-war examples when similar calls for change echoed loudly in the

[31] Bebchuk and Tallarita (2020b) A15. See also Bebchuk and Tallarita (2021) A17. See Martin Lipton's response to these claims at https://corpgov.law.harvard.edu/2021/08/24/more-myths-from-lucian-bebchuk.

[32] Fairfax (2006) 707.

[33] Henderson and Temple-West (2019).

[34] Coulter (2020) 7.

[35] For a brief historical context of the BRT statement, see Harrison, Phillips and Freeman (2020) 1226.

public sphere and received broad popular support and political endorsements, but core company law remained largely static. The test of the current commitments to systemic reform will come when there is a return to stability and growth – will there be a repeat of the retreat like that experienced at the end of the post-war period or will the most recent promises succeed in bringing change to the status quo?

B. Beyond the Business Roundtable

Although the BRT's statement originates in the US, neither the context in which it was made nor the nature of its content is limited to American companies and markets. In the UK, where there might not have been the same headline-grabbing statements by as high-profile a cohort of corporate leaders, there are, nonetheless, parallel developments in the cycle of increasingly vocal demands for changes in a system that is seen to be unfair and unrepresentative.[36] The British Academy's Future of the Corporation initiative, '[a] major research and engagement programme examining the purpose of business and its role in society', published *Reforming Business for the 21st Century: A Framework for the Future of the Corporation*, followed by *Principles for Purposeful Business*, which did not propose specific actions, but introduced eight principles for business leaders and policy-makers.[37] Facing the same political, economic and social disruptions as the BRT in the US, the arguments in support of stakeholderism have gained traction in this most recent iteration of challenges to shareholder primacy, as senior *Financial Times* editor and columnist John Plender reported in 2019:

> No surprise, then, that there is a groundswell at least in the UK in favour of dethroning the shareholder and redefining directors' legal duties to other stakeholders. Investors are also placing more emphasis on environmental, social and governance factors in corporate performance.[38]

[36] For example, the British Academy, which published a report on the future of the corporation in 2018 (British Academy Future of the Corporation Programme (2018)), responded to the BRT: 'We wholeheartedly applaud their initiative and this significant step forward for the corporate world. And, we now challenge the signatories of the Roundtable statement to engage with us and others on the question of how they will follow through to re-organise their businesses around these purposes.'

[37] British Academy Future of the Corporation Programme (2019). See www.thebritishacademy.ac.uk/publications/future-of-the-corporation-principles-for-purposeful-business. The World Economic Forum (WEF), a further example of an organisation adopting this approach, published on the difficult challenge of how to measure stakeholder capitalism and on stakeholder principles in the COVID era (World Economic Forum (2020)). Along similar lines, the founder and executive chairman of the WEF published 'The Davos Manifesto 2020: The Universal Purpose of a Company in the Fourth Industrial Revolution', emphasising the importance of all stakeholders in its quest for a better kind of capitalism (World Economic Forum et al (2020)); see www.weforum.org/reports/measuring-stakeholder-capitalism-towards-common-metrics-and-consistent-reporting-of-sustainable-value-creation; http://www3.weforum.org/docs/WEF_Stakeholder_Principles_COVID_Era.pdf; Schwab (2019).

[38] Plender (2019), 11.

The CA 2006 opened the door to the idea that directors, when promoting the success of the company, should have regard for stakeholder considerations in addition to those of shareholders, and the UK, like the US, has witnessed a shift in the content and tone of public comments made by the investing community on their expectations from company boards in relation to stakeholder demands.[39] The Combined Codes on Corporate Governance of 2003 and 2006 made no mention of stakeholders, but the 2018 revised UK Corporate Governance Code updates the Code's application of Principles and sets higher corporate governance standards, explicitly included the interests of stakeholders other than shareholders in the 'quasi-voluntary' 'comply or explain' code, although still fell short of statutory requirements.[40] The newly revised UK Stewardship Code 2020, which applies to asset owners, asset managers and the service providers that support them, has also aligned itself with the Corporate Governance Code in elevating the importance of stakeholders.[41] Although the prospect of reforming core company law remains remote, the current climate nudges the debate in the direction of raising questions as to the unassailability of shareholder primacy, which ultimately depends on the acceptance by the British public, and suggests that there is a waning of support for preserving the traditional shareholder-centric corporate-governance system as it exists in the UK.[42]

Despite the auguring of the demise of the existing system, a more probing consideration of the signposts of change should be undertaken. The CA 2006 does gesture towards non-shareholder stakeholder interests in the requirements in section 172(1) for promoting the success of the company, although it does so without interfering with the principles of shareholder primacy.[43] The UK Corporate Governance Code's treatment of corporate purpose, which appears to address the deficiencies in the shareholder profit-centric status quo, falls short of its ambitions by virtue of its vague and undefined terminology, its 'comply or explain' nature and the need to be aligned with the requirements of the CA 2006.[44] Whereas those wanting to demonstrate change have ample fodder to meet the rhetorical demands of a dissatisfied public, substantive systemic legal reform is still lacking.

[39] CA 2006, s 172. See Kershaw and Schuster (2019) 6ff; Konzelmann, Chic and Fovargue-Davies (2021) 19. Statements like those by institutional investor Blackrock's CEO Larry Fink in his 2019 open letter to CEOs of the companies in which Blackrock invests, whereby he states that companies must have a 'purpose' and are responsible to all stakeholders, are increasingly prevalent. See www.blackrock.com/corporate/investor-relations/larry-fink-ceo-letter. For examples of studies of UK institutional investors, see Allcock (2018); Becht et al (2010).

[40] CA 2006, s 172(1); Bebchuk and Tallarita (2020a) 15; Combined Code on Corporate Governance 2003; Combined Code on Corporate Governance 2006; UK Corporate Governance Code 2018; Fairfax (2006) 697. See Kershaw (2018a) 870ff on 'comply or explain'. Although compliance with the Code is not mandatory, UK Listing Rules require that companies disclose how they have complied and, if not, to provide an explanation (Armour, Deakin and Konzelmann (2003) 539). See also ch 8, section VIII of this volume.

[41] UK Stewardship Code 2020.

[42] Moore (2013) 31; Moore (2018) 144.

[43] CA 2006, s 172; Fleischer (2021) 173ff; Kershaw and Schuster (2019) 4.

[44] UK Corporate Governance Code 2018; Fleischer (2021) 173; Kershaw and Schuster (2019) 4.

III. CONCLUDING THOUGHTS

In the years of reconstruction following the Second World War and the post-war decades that witnessed consequential political, economic and social changes to Britain, there was a sense of momentum that seemed to be leading to systemic changes to the shareholder primacy principles underpinning UK company law, an assumption revealed by history to be overstated. In the period from 1945 to 1979, the shareholder body evolved dramatically, influencing how equity owners engaged with industry and the financial markets, as well as their relationships with other stakeholders. By the end of the post-war consensus, however, the movements for nationalisations, shareholder democracy and industrial democracy were overtaken by the values espoused by Thatcher's policies of privatisations, deregulation and free-market capitalism as the economic cycle continued to revolve and the 1980s embraced an interpretation of shareholder primacy that fixated on short-term returns and profits. As stated by scholars Tami Oren and Mark Blyth in 2019: 'In fact, given that little has changed institutionally and regulatorily, it is fair to say that despite its near fatal collapse in 2008–2009, the finance-led growth model that the UK erected in the 1980s is still with us today.'[45] Nonetheless, despite the lack of systemic reform, the questions that were prevalent in the post-war period are being revisited with growing urgency, including the fundamental issue of how to balance shareholder and stakeholder interests.[46] In 2023, as the world endures the economic crises caused by the COVID-19 pandemic, the repercussions from the ongoing Russo-Ukrainian war and destabilising decisions by incumbent Conservative governments, the ideas of post-war industrial democracy and stakeholder capitalism are repurposed and presented by reformers as antidotes for the breakdown of capitalism and the failure of shareholder primacy. Nonetheless, those seeking to find corporate solutions to today's challenges continue to work within the existing system, arguing that the new versions of industrial democracy and stakeholderism will drive companies to stay true to their purpose, even when the definition of corporate purpose is itself contentious and under pressure, possibly creating openings, however small and difficult to reach, for more radical systemic change.[47]

The arch that stretches from Clement Attlee's nationalisations to Lord Bullock's Report on industrial democracy in the 1970s spans decades of criticism of the established system based on shareholder primacy, with calls for core legal reform and the reassessment of corporate purpose intensifying with each financial challenge, crisis and scandal. It is in times of flux and disorder that these movements gain momentum and enhance their profiles, only to be pushed to the margins when stability is restored and a sense of security dulls the urgency

[45] Oren and Blyth (2019) 618.
[46] Coulter (2020) 3.
[47] Davis (2021) 903.

of the demands for systemic change.[48] By the mid-1970s, the political and social climate created the illusion that Britain was on the cusp of radical systemic change, similar to the period of the Great Recession of the late 2000s, which followed the global financial crisis of 2007–08; the post-war period did not result in systemic changes or core legal reforms and nor have the more recent global financial crises. It can be imagined that were it not for the changing political, economic and social winds that led first to a weakened Labour Party and then to Thatcher's victory in 1979, the post-war movements for industrial democracy might have led to the promised legislative reforms.[49] A warning, perhaps, to the adversaries of shareholder primacy and the current promoters of stakeholder capitalism of how changes in the political landscape, and the refocusing of social and economic priorities, can result in reversals of what appear to be irrevocable developments in the relationships amongst all stakeholders, including shareholders, and their treatment by industry, policy-makers and law-makers.

[48] See Poole (1982) 193 on cyclical theory and industrial democracy.
[49] Oren and Blyth (2019) 607.

Bibliography

Abbott, S (1973) *Employee Participation* (London, Conservative Research Department).

Ackers, P (2007) 'Collective Bargaining as Industrial Democracy: Hugh Clegg and the Political Foundations of British Industrial Relations Pluralism' *British Journal of Industrial Relations* 45(1), 77–101.

Acton Society Trust (1959), *Wider Shareholding* (London, Acton Society Trust).

Addison, P (1985) *Now the War is Over: A Social History of Britain 1945–51* (London, British Broadcasting Corporation).

Admati, A and Pfleiderer, P (2009) 'The "Wall Street Walk" and Shareholder Activism: Exit as a Form of Voice' *Review of Financial Studies* 22(7), 2645–85.

'Ads & Takeovers' (1973) *The Economist* (24 March) 105.

Aiyegbayo, O and Villiers, C (2011) 'The Enhanced Business Review: Has it Made Corporate Governance More Effective?' *Journal of Business Law* 7(7), 699–724.

Alcock, A (2009) 'An Accidental Change to Directors' Duties?' *Company Lawyer* 30(12), 362–68.

Aldington, T (1959) *Everyman a Capitalist: Some Proposals for the Small Saver in Industry* (London, Conservative Political Centre).

Allcock, D (2018) 'The "Invisible" Hand: Views from UK Institutional Investors' *Corporate Governance* 18(6), 1074–88.

Alrayes, SA (2019) 'Shareholder Empowerment, Steps Forward and Steps Back' *Journal of Financial Regulation and Compliance* 27(2), 169–96.

'An Association of Investors?' (1949a) *Financial Times* (28 February) 4.

'An Association of Investors?' (1949b) *Financial Times* (1 March) 2.

'An Association of Investors?' (1949c) *Financial Times* (2 March) 4.

'An Association of Investors?' (1949d) *Financial Times* (3 March) 2.

Arden, M and Eccles, G (1980) *Companies Act 1980: An Explanatory Guide* (Croydon, Tolley Publishing Company).

Armour, J (2020) 'Shareholder Rights' *Oxford Review of Economic Policy* 36(2), 314–40.

Armour, J, Deakin, S and Konzelmann, SJ (2003) 'Shareholder Primacy and the Trajectory of UK Corporate Governance' *British Journal of Industrial Relations* 41(3), 531–55.

Attenborough, D (2009) 'How Directors Should Act When Owing Duties to the Companies' Shareholders: Why We Need to Stop Greenhalgh' *International Company and Commercial Law Review* 20(10), 339–46.

Avi-Yonah, RS (2005) 'The Cyclical Transformations of the Corporate Form: Historical Perspective on Corporate Social Responsibility' *Delaware Journal of Corporate Law* 30(3), 767–818.

Bainbridge, SM (2021) 'Making Sense of the Business Roundtable's Reversal on Corporate Purpose' *Journal of Corporation Law* 46(2), 285–318.

Baker, N (2012) 'A Closer Look at Britain's "Shareholder Spring"' *Compliance Week* 9(102), 66–67.

Barker, B (1982) 'The Relationship between Public Companies and Their Shareholders' in K Midgely (ed), *Management Accountability and Corporate Governance* (London, Macmillan Press) 85–90.

Barnard, JW (1998) 'The Hampel Committee Report: A Transatlantic Critique' *The Company Lawyer* 19(4), 110–15.

Barratt Brown, M and Coates, K (1975) *Accountability and Industrial Democracy* (Nottingham, Institute for Workers' Control).

Barry, E (1965) *Nationalisation in British Politics: The Historical Background* (London, Jonathan Cape).

Bartlett, S and Chandler, R (1997) 'The Corporate Report and the Private Shareholder: Lee and Tweedie Twenty Years on' *British Accounting Review* 29(3), 245–61.
Batstone, E, Ferner, A and Terry, M (1983) *Unions on the Board: An Experiment in Industrial Democracy* (Oxford, Basil Blackwell).
Bavoso, V (2014) 'The Global Financial Crisis, the Pervasive Resilience of Shareholder Value and the Unfulfilled Promises of Anglo-American Corporate Law' *International Company and Commercial Law Review* 25(6), 213–20.
Bebchuk, L, Cohen, A and Hirst, S (2017) 'The Agency Problems of Institutional Investors' *Journal of Economic Perspectives* 31(3), 89–112.
Bebchuk, L and Tallarita, R (2020a) 'The Illusory Promise of Stakeholder Governance' *Cornell Law Review* 106(1), 91–178.
——. (2020b) '"Stakeholder" Capitalism Seems Mostly for Show' *Wall Street Journal* (Eastern edn, 7 August) A15.
——. (2021) '"Stakeholder" Talk Proves Empty Again' *Wall Street Journal* (Eastern edn, 19 August) A17.
Becht, M, Franks, J, Mayer, C and Rossi, S (2010) 'Returns to Shareholder Activism: Evidence from a Clinical Study of the Hermes UK Focus Fund' *Review of Financial Studies* 23(3), 3093–129.
Beck, W (1962) 'Worker Shareholders' *Financial Times* (14 February) 12.
Beer, S (1982) *Modern British Politics: Parties and Pressure Groups in the Collectivist Age*, 3rd edn (London, Norton).
Benn, T (1989) *Against the Tide: Diaries 1973–1977* (London, Hutchinson).
Benoit, D (2016) 'Don't Make Me Do This: The Rise of the Reluctant Activist' *Wall Street Journal* (18 February) C.1.
Bercusson, B (1986) 'Workers, Corporate Enterprise and the Law' in R Lewis (ed), *Labour Law in Britain* (Oxford, Blackwell) 134–58.
Berle, A (1931) 'Corporate Powers as Powers in Trust' *Harvard Law Review* 44(7), 1049–74.
——. (1932) 'For Whom Corporate Managers Are Trustees: A Note' *Harvard Law Review* 45(8), 1365–72.
Berle, A and Means, GC (1967) *The Modern Corporation and Private Property*, 2nd edn (New York, Harcourt, Brace & Wood).
Bhagat, S and Hubbard, RG (2020, September) 'Should the Modern Corporation Maximize Shareholder Value? *AEI Economic Perspectives*, www.aei.org/wp-content/uploads/2020/09/Should-the-Modern-Corporation-Maximize-Shareholder-Value.pdf?x91208.
Birds, J (1980) 'Making Directors Do Their Duties' *Company Lawyer* 1(2), 67–74.
Birds, J, Boyle, A, Clark, B, MacNeil, I, McCormack, G, Twigg-Flesner, C and Villiers, C (eds) (2007) *Boyle and Birds' Company Law*, 6th edn (Bristol, Jordan).
Black, B (1990) 'Shareholder Passivity Reexamined' *Michigan Law Review* 89(3), 520–608.
Black, B and Coffee, J (1994) 'Hail Britannia? Institutional Investor Behavior under Limited Regulation' *Michigan Law Review* 92(7), 1997–2087.
Blanden, M (1971) 'The Role of the Shareholder' *Financial Times* (11 June) 19.
——. (1973) 'Every Worker a Shareholder' (1973) *Financial Times* (29 February) 17.
——. (1974) 'Shareholders: The Silent Majority' *Financial Times* (30 September) 7.
Blumberg, P (1971) *Industrial Democracy: The Sociology of Participation* (London, Constable).
Bogdanor, V (1970) 'The Labour Party in Opposition, 1951–1964' in V Bogdanor and R Skidelsky (eds), *The Age of Affluence, 1951–1964* (London, Macmillan) 78–116.
——. (1994) 'The Rise and Fall of the Post-War Settlement' *Parliamentary History* 13(3), 351–62.
'Booboisie and Boardoisie' (1966) *The Economist* (1 January) 53.
Bowley, T and Hill, JG (2022) 'The Global ESG Stewardship Ecosystem', European Corporate Governance Institute – Law Working Paper 660/2022.
Boyle, A and Birds, J (eds) (1983) *Boyle and Birds' Company Law* (Bristol, Jordan).
Boyle, AJ and Mordlsey, B (1980) 'The Interests of Employees' *Company Lawyer* 1(6), 284–85.
Brannen, P, Batstone, E, Fatchett, D and White, P (1976) *The Worker Directors: A Sociology of Participation* (London, Hutchinson).

Breckenfelder, J (2020, 17 December) 'Competition among High-Frequency Traders and Market Liquidity' *VoxEu*, https://voxeu.org/article/competition-among-high-frequency-traders-and-market-liquidity.
'Britain Needs Wider Share Ownership' (1960) *Financial Times* (23 February) 12.
British Academy Future of the Corporation Programme (2018) *Reforming Business for the 21st Century: A Framework for the Future of the Corporation* (London, British Academy).
——. (2019) *Principles for a Purposeful Business: How to Deliver the Framework for the Future of the Corporation: An Agenda for Business in the 2020s and Beyond* (London, British Academy).
Bruner, C (2013) *Corporate Governance in the Common-Law World: The Political Foundations of Shareholder Power* (Cambridge, Cambridge University Press).
'Bullock is Dead. Long Live Workers' Participation' (1977) *The Economist* (14 May) 125.
'C & W Ltd 1946 Div' (1946) *Financial Times* (24 December) 1.
Cabrelli, D (2008) 'The Reform of the Law of Directors' Duties in UK Company Law', https://www.pure.ed.ac.uk/ws/portalfiles/portal/13215836/CABRELLI_D_PRESENTATION_FOR_UNIVERSITA_BOCCONI_ON_THE_REFORM_OF_THE_LAW_OF_THE_DIRECTORS_DUTIES_IN_UK_COMPANY_LAW.pdf.
Carr of Hadley, Lord (1982) 'The Function of Ownership and the Role of Institutional Shareholders' in K Midgely (ed), *Management Accountability and Corporate Governance* (London, Macmillan Press) 91–101.
Caste, NJ (1994) 'Corporate Democracy' *Journal of Social Philosophy* 25(2), 168–78.
Cheffins, BR (2008) *Corporate Ownership and Control: British Business Transformed* (Oxford, Oxford University Press).
——. (2015) 'The Rise of Corporate Governance in the UK: When and Why' *Current Legal Problems* 68(1), 387–429.
——. (2018) *The Public Company Transformed* (Oxford, Oxford University Press).
——. (2020) 'Stop Blaming Milton Friedman!' University of Cambridge Faculty of Law Research Paper 9/2020, 1–46.
Cheffins, BR and Black, BS (2006) 'Outside Director Liability across Countries' *Texas Law Review* 84(6), 1385–480.
Cheffins, BR and Reddy, B (2022, 9 June) 'Thirty Years and Done – Time to Abolish the UK Corporate Governance Code', https://ssrn.com/abstract=4132617 or http://dx.doi.org/10.2139/ssrn.4132617.
Chen, R and Hanson, J (2004) 'The Illusion of Law: The Legitimating Schemas of Modern Policy and Corporate Law' *Michigan Law Review* 103(1), 1–149.
Chester, D (1975) *The Nationalisation of British Industry, 1945–51* (London, HMSO).
Chiplin, B, Coyne, J and Sirc, L (1977) *Can Workers Manage? Post-Bullock Essays in the Economics of the Inter-relationships between Ownership, Control and Risk-Taking in Industry, with Special Reference to Participation by Employees* (London, Institute of Economic Affairs).
Churchill, W (1945) *General Election 1945: Mr Churchill's Declaration of Policy to the Electors* (London, SH Benson).
——. (1951) *The Manifesto of the Conservative and Unionist Party, General Election, 1951* (London, Conservative and Unionist Party).
City Company Law Committee (1975) *First Report: Employee Participation* (London).
City Company Law Committee and Great Britain Committee of Inquiry on Industrial Democracy (1977) *A Reply to Bullock* (London).
Clark, GL and Knight, E (2009) 'Implications of the UK Companies Act 2006 for Institutional Investors and the Market for Corporate Social Responsibility' *University of Pennsylvania Journal of Business Law* 11(2), 259–96.
Clarke, T (1977) 'Industrial Democracy: The Institutionalized Suppression of Industrial Conflict?' in T Clarke and Clements (eds), *Trade Unions under Capitalism* (Glasgow, Fontana) 351–82.
Clegg, HA (1951) *Industrial Democracy and Nationalisation: A Study Prepared for the Fabian Society* (Oxford, Basil Blackwell).
——. (1960) *A New Approach to Industrial Democracy* (Oxford, Basil Blackwell).

Clements, L (1977) 'Reference Groups and Trade Union Consciousness' in T Clarke and L Clements (eds), *Trade Unions under Capitalism* (Glasgow, Fontana) 309–32.

Clift, B, Gamble, A and Harris, M (2000) 'The Labour Party and the Company' in J Parkinson, G Kelly and A Gamble (eds), *The Political Economy of the Company* (Oxford, Hart Publishing) 51–81.

Coates, K (ed) (1968) *Can the Workers Run Industry?* (London, Sphere in association with the Institute for Workers' Control).

——. (1995) *Common Ownership: Clause IV and the Labour Party* (Nottingham, Spokesman).

Coates, K and Topham, T (1968a) 'Participation or Control?' in K Coates (ed), *Can the Workers Run Industry?* (London: Sphere in association with the Institute for Workers' Control) 227–40.

——. (1968b) *The Labour Party's Plans for Industrial Democracy* (Nottingham, Institute for Workers' Control).

——. (1975a) *Schools for Democrats: A Book of Readings and Witnesses for Worker's Control* (Nottingham, Spokesman).

——. (1975b) *Shop Stewards and Workers' Control: A Book of Readings and Witnesses for Worker's Control* (Nottingham, Spokesman Books).

——. (1975c) *Industrial Democracy and Nationalization: A Book of Readings and Witnesses for Workers' Control* (Nottingham, Spokesman Books).

——. (1977) *The Shop Steward's Guide to the Bullock Report* (Nottingham, Spokesman Books).

Colchester, N (1978) 'CBI Urges Closer Contact with Shareholders' *Financial Times* (20 February) 34.

Collison, D, Cross, S, Ferguson, J, Power, D and Stevenson, L (2011) *Shareholder Primacy in UK Corporate Law: An Exploration of the Rationale and Evidence.* (London: Certified Accountants Educational Trust).

Confederation of British Industry (1973a) *A New Look at the Responsibilities of the British Public Company: An Interim Report for Discussion* (London, Confederation of British Industry).

——. (1973b) *The Responsibilities of the British Public Company: Final Report of the Company Affairs Committee Endorsed by the CBI Council on 19 September 1973* (London, Confederation of British Industry).

——. (1977) *In Place of Bullock* (London, Confederation of British Industry).

'Conscience Calls' (1975) *The Economist* (23 August) 70.

Conservative Central Office (1950) *This is the Road: The Conservative and Unionist Party's Policy: General Election, 1950* (London, Conservative Central Office).

Conservative Party (1955) *United for Peace and Progress: The Conservative and Unionist Party's Policy, General Election 1955* (London, Conservative Central Office).

——. (1959) *The Next Five Years, General Election 1959* (London, Conservative Central Office).

——. (1964) *Prosperity with a Purpose, General Election 1964* (London, Conservative Central Office).

——. (1966) *Action, Not Words: The New Conservative Programme: Manifesto for the General Election of 1966* (London, Conservative Central Office).

Conservative Trade Unionists (1970) *Participation: A New Way Ahead* (London, CTU).

Conservative Unionist Party (1970) *A Better Tomorrow: The Conservative Programme for the Next 5 Years* (London, Conservative Central Office).

——. (1974a) *Firm Action for a Fair Britain: The Conservative Manifesto, 1974* (London, Conservative Central Office).

——. (1974b) *Putting Britain First: A National Policy from the Conservatives* (London, Conservative Central Office).

——. (1979) *The Conservative Manifesto 1979* (London, Conservative Central Office).

Copeman, G (1958) *The Challenge of Employee Shareholding: How to Close the Gap between Capital and Labour* (London, Business Publications).

——. (1975) *Employee Share Ownership and Industrial Stability* (London, Institute of Personnel Management).

Copeman, G and Rumble, T (1972) *Capital as an Incentive* (London, Leviathan House).

Cordon, G (2022) 'Rishi Sunak Targets Scrapping EU Laws in Fresh Pitch to Brexiteers' *The Independent* (19 July), www.independent.co.uk/news/uk/liz-truss-rishi-sunak-brexit-penny-mordaunt-mps-b2124910.html.

Cornish, W, Banks, S, Mitchell, C, Mitchell, P and Probert, R (2019) *Law and Society in England 1750–1950*, 2nd edn (Oxford, Hart Publishing).

Cottrell, SA (1978) 'Abroad: On "Industrial Democracy"' *Challenge* 20(6), 58–59.

Coulter, S (2020) 'All in it Together? The Unlikely Rebirth of Covid Corporatism' *Political Quarterly* 91(3), 534–41.

Coutts, K, Tarling, R, Ward, T and Wilkinson, F (1981) 'The Economic Consequences of Mrs Thatcher' *Cambridge Journal of Economics* 5(1), 81–93.

Cressey, P and MacInnes, J (1980) 'Voting for Ford: Industrial Democracy and the Control of Labour' *Capital & Class* 4(2), 5–33.

Crosland, CAR (1959) 'What Does the Worker Want?' *Encounter* (February) 10–17.

'Daily News Shareholder Wins £1.12m Action' (1962) *Financial Times* (7 June) 19.

Dale, I (ed) (2000a) *Conservative Party General Election Manifestos, 1900–1997* (London, Routledge).

——. (2000b) *Labour Party General Election Manifestos, 1900–1997* (London, Routledge).

——. (2000c) *Liberal Party General Election Manifestos, 1900–1997* (London, Routledge.

Daniel, W and McIntosh, N (1972) *The Right to Manage? A Study of Leadership and Reform in Employee Relations* (London, Macdonald).

Davenport, N (1961a) 'Wider Share Ownership – I' *The Spectator* (10 March) 341–42.

——. (1961b) 'Wider Share Ownership – II' *The Spectator* (17 March) 376–78.

David, R (1972) 'Distillers' Shareholders in Thalidomide Move' *Financial Times* (16 December) 15.

Davies, A (2017) *The City of London and Social Democracy* (Oxford, Oxford University Press).

——. (2019) 'Pension Funds and the Politics of Ownership in Britain, c. 1970–86' *Twentieth Century British History* 30(1), 81–107.

Davies, G (1996) 'Tony Blair Puts Meat on the Stakeholder Bones' *The Independent* (15 January), www.independent.co.uk/news/business/tony-blair-puts-meat-on-the-stakeholder-bones-1324167.html.

Davies, P (1978) 'The Bullock Report and Employee Participation in Corporate Planning in the UK' *Journal of Comparative Corporate Law and Securities Regulation* 1, 245–72.

——. (1991) 'Institutional Investors: UK View' *Brooklyn Law Review* 57(1), 129–44.

Davies, P (1994) 'Institutional Investors in the United Kingdom' in T Baums, RM Buxbaum and KJ Hopt (eds), *Institutional Investors and Corporate Governance* (Berlin, Walter de Gruyter) 257–85.

——. (2010) *Introduction to Company Law*, 2nd edn (Oxford, Oxford University Press).

——. (2015) 'Shareholders in the United Kingdom' in JG Hill and RS Thomas (eds), *Research Handbook on Shareholder Power* (Cheltenham, Edward Elgar) 355–82.

Davies, P and Lord Wedderburn of Charlton (1977) 'The Land of Industrial Democracy' *Industrial Law Journal* 6(1), 197–211.

Davis, GF (2021) 'Corporate Purpose Needs Democracy' *Journal of Management Studies* 58(3), 902–13.

De Haas, R and van Horen, N (2013) 'Running for the Exit? International Bank Lending During a Financial Crisis' *Review of Financial Studies* 26(1), 244–85.

Deakin, S (2005) 'The Coming Transformation of Shareholder Value' *Corporate Governance: An International Review* 13(1), 11–18.

'Divided We Stand' (1978) *The Economist* (23 September) 125.

Dodd, E (1932) 'For Whom are Corporate Managers Trustees?' *Harvard Law Review* 45(7), 1145–63.

Dorey, P (1995) *British Politics since 1945* (Oxford, Blackwell).

——. (2019) *Comrades in Conflict: Labour, The Trade Unions and 1969's In Place of Strife* (Manchester, Manchester University Press).

Draper, H (1974) 'Marx on Democratic Forms of Government' *Socialist Register* 11, 101–24.

Driver, S and Martell, L (2000) 'Left, Right and the Third Way' *Policy & Politics* 28(2), 147–61.
Du Cann, E (1959) *Investing Simplified: A Guide to Unit Trusts, Investment Clubs and Other Share-Purchase Schemes* (London, Neane).
Durham, MF (1982) 'The Companies Act, 1980: Its Effects on British Corporate Law' *Northwestern Journal of International Law & Business* 4(2), 551–85.
Dutton, D (1997) *British Politics since 1945: The Rise and Fall of Consensus*, 2nd edn (Oxford, Basil Blackwell).
Eatwell, R (1979) *The 1945–1951 Labour Governments* (London, Batsford).
Edgerton, D (2018) *The Rise and Fall of the British Nation: A Twentieth-Century History* (London, Penguin Books).
Edmans, A (2020a) 'Company Purpose and Profit Need Not Be in Conflict if We "Grow the Pie"' *Economic Affairs (Harlow)* 40(2), 287–94.
——. (2020b) *Grow the Pie* (Cambridge, Cambridge University Press).
Edwards, A (2016) '"Manufacturing Capitalists": The Wider Share Ownership Council and the Problem of "Popular Capitalism", 1958–92' *20th Century British History* 27(1), 100–23.
Edwards, RB (1970) 'BLMC Workers as Shareholders' *Financial Times* (13 August) 2.
Elliott, J (1978) 'Only Shareholder Should Choose Board, Urges CBI' *Financial Times* (16 June) 7.
——. (1984) *Conflict or Cooperation? The Growth of Industrial Democracy*, 2nd edn (London, Kogan Page).
'Equity Investment and its Responsibilities' (1964) *The Economist* (4 July) 75.
Evershed, A (1968) 'Use Pay Rises to Foster Employee Shareholders' *Financial Times* (9 April) 6.
Fairfax, LM (2006) 'The Rhetoric of Corporate Law: The Impact of Stakeholder Rhetoric on Corporate Norms' *Journal of Corporation Law* 31(3), 675–718.
——. (2019) 'From Apathy to Activism: The Emergence, Impact, and Future of Shareholder Activism as the New Corporate Governance Norm' *Boston University Law Review* 99(3), 1301–46.
Fama, EF (1980) 'Agency Problems and the Theory of the Firm' *Journal of Political Economy* 88(2), 288–307.
Fama, EF and Jensen, MC (1983) 'Separation of Ownership and Control' *Journal of Law Economics* 26(2), 301–26.
Farrar, JH and Hannigan, BM (1998) *Farrar's Company Law*, 4th edn (London, Butterworths).
Fatchett, D (1977) 'Industrial Democracy: Prospects after Bullock' University of Leeds Occasional Papers in Industrial Relations 2.
Feldman, D and Meisel, F (1996) *Corporate and Commercial Law: Modern Developments* (London, Lloyds of London).
Financial Times Reporter (1968) 'Shareholders to Vote on £5,000 Gift to Tories' *Financial Times* (31 December) 2.
Fisch, JE and Solomon, SD (2021) 'Should Corporations Have a Purpose?' *Solomon Texas Law Review* 99(7), 1309–46.
Fisher, A (1979) 'Britain's New Breed of Shareholders' *Financial Times* (31 October) 31.
Fishman, J (1993) *The Transformation of Threadneedle Street: The Deregulation and Reregulation of Britain's Financial Services* (Durham, NC, Carolina Academic Press).
Fleischer, H (2021) 'Corporate Purpose: A Management Concept and its Implications for Company Law' *European Company and Financial Law Review* 18(2), 161–89.
Fleming, S (1975) 'Institutional Muscle Flexing to Test Shareholder Power' *Financial Times* (21 February) 16.
——. (1976) 'For Shareholder Democracy' *Financial Times* (23 January) 7.
Florio, M (2002) 'A State without Ownership: The Welfare Impact of British Privatisations 1979–1997' Università Degli Studi di Milano Dipartimento di Economia Politica e Aziendale Working Paper 24/2002.
Foote, G (1986) *The Labour Party's Political Thought: A History*, 2nd edn (London, Croom Helm).
'For the Shareholders to Decide' (1973) *The Economist* (12 May) 96.
Foreman-Peck, J and Millward, R (1994) *Public and Private Ownership of British Industry 1820–1990* (Oxford, Oxford University Press).

Forrest, A (2022) 'Chancellor Promises Post-Brexit "Big Bang" for City in Move to Ditch EU Finance Laws' *The Independent* (19 July).

Fox, A (1985) *History and Heritage: The Social Origins of the British Industrial Relations Systems* (London, Allen & Unwin).

——. (2017) 'Corporatism and Industrial Democracy: The Social Origins of Present Forms and Methods in Britain and Germany (1977)' *Historical Studies in Industrial Relations* 38, 171–219.

Francis, M (2012) '"A Crusade to Enfranchise the Many": Thatcherism and the "Property-Owning Democracy"' *Twentieth Century British History* 23(2), 275–97.

Franks, J, Mayer, C and Rossi, S (2004) *Spending Less Time with the Family: The Decline of Family Ownership in the UK* (Cambridge, National Bureau of Economic Research, Inc).

——. (2009) 'Ownership: Evolution and Regulation' *The Review of Financial Studies* 22(10), 4009–56.

Fredman, S (1992) 'The New Rights: Labour Law and Ideology in the Thatcher Years' *Oxford Journal of Legal Studies* 12(1), 24–44.

Freeman, RE (1994) 'The Politics of Stakeholder Theory: Some Future Directions' *Business Ethics Quarterly* 4(4), 409–21.

Freeman, RE and Liedtka, J (1997) 'Stakeholder Capitalism and the Value Chain' *European Management Journal* 15(3), 286–96.

Freeman, RE and Reed, DL (1983) 'Stockholders and Stakeholders: A New Perspective on Corporate Governance' *California Management Review* 25(3), 88.

Frege, CM (2003) 'Industrial Relations in Continental Europe' in P Ackers and A Wilkinson (eds), *Understanding Work and Employment: Industrial Relations in Transition* (Oxford, Oxford University Press) 242–62.

Friedman, M (1962) *Capitalism and Freedom* (Chicago, University of Chicago Press).

——. (1970) 'A Friedman Doctrine – The Social Responsibility of Business is to Increase its Profits' *New York Times* (13 September) SM17.

Furlong, JC (1977) *Labor in the Boardroom: The Peaceful Revolution* (Princeton, NJ, Dow Jones Books).

'Future of Henry Briggs Son & Co' (1946) *Financial Times* (22 August) 1.

Gamble, A and Kelly, G (2000) 'The Politics of the Company' in J Parkinson, G Kelly and A Gamble (eds), *The Political Economy of the Company* (Oxford, Hart Publishing) 21–49.

——. (2001) 'Shareholder Value and the Stakeholder Debate in the UK' *Corporate Governance: An International Review* 9(2), 110–17.

Garrard, J (2001) *Democratisation in Britain: Elites, Civil Society and Reform since 1800* (New York, Palgrave).

Garrett, R (1956–1957) 'Attitudes on Corporate Democracy: A Critical Analysis' *Northwestern University Law Review* 51(3), 310–36.

Gatti, M and Ondersma, C (2020) 'Can Broader Corporate Purpose Redress Inequality? The Stakeholder Approach Chimera' *Journal of Corporation Law* 46(1), 1–74.

——. (2021, February 26) 'Stakeholder Syndrome: Does Stakeholderism Derail Effective Protections for Weaker Constituencies?' Rutgers Law School Research Paper No Forthcoming.

Gelter, M (2009) 'Dark Side of Shareholder Influence: Managerial Autonomy and Stakeholder Orientation in Comparative Corporate Governance' *Harvard International Law Journal* 50(1), 129–94.

Gerrard, B (2016) 'Shareholder Spring Shows No Sign of Abating' *Investors Chronicle* (5 May).

Giddens, A (2010) 'Tony Blair, 1997–2007' in V Bogdanor (ed), *From New Jerusalem to New Labour: British Prime Ministers from Attlee to Blair* (Basingstoke, Palgrave Macmillan) 184–201.

Gilson, R and Gordon, J (2013) 'The Agency Costs of Agency Capitalism: Activist Investors and the Revaluation of Governance Rights' *Columbia Law Review* 113(4), 863–927.

Gindis, D (2020) 'On the Origins, Meaning and Influence of Jensen and Meckling's Definition of the Firm' *Oxford Economic Papers* 72(4), 966–84.

Gleeson, A (1981) *People and Their Money: 50 Years of Private Investment* (London, M & G Group).

Golumbia, D (2013) 'High-Frequency Trading: Networks of Wealth and the Concentration of Power' *Social Semiotics* 23(2), 278–99.
Goss, J (1973) *Employee Participation in British Companies: An Examination of All Levels of Employee Participation in Industry* (London, Bow Publications Ltd).
Gould, W (1972) 'Taft-Hartley Comes to Great Britain: Observations on the Industrial Relations Act of 1971' *Yale Law Journal* 81(8), 1421–86.
Gower, LCB (1988) '"Big Bang" and City Regulation' *Modern Law Review* 51(1), 1–22.
Greenfield, K (2014) 'The Third Way' *Seattle University Law Review* 37(2), 749–74.
Grey, W (1978) 'Workers as Shareholders' *Financial Times* (21 September) 19.
Grout, P (1987a) 'The Wider Share Ownership Programme' *Fiscal Studies* 8(3), 59–74.
——. (1987b) 'Wider Share Ownership and Economic Performance' *Oxford Review of Economic Policy* 3(4), 13–29.
Gumbrell-McCormick, R and Hyman, R (2019) 'Democracy in Trade Unions, Democracy through Trade Unions?' *Economic and Industrial Democracy* 40(1), 91–110.
Hague, D and Wilkinson, G (1983) *The IRC: An Experiment in Industrial Intervention: A History of the Industrial Reorganisation Corporation* (London, Allen & Unwin).
Hailsham of St Marylebone, Lord (1958) *Prospect for Capitalism: Strength and Stress* (London, Conservative Political Centre).
Hall, PA (2013) 'The Political Origins of Our Economic Discontents: Contemporary Adjustment Problems in Historical Perspective' in M Kahler and DA Lake (eds), *Politics in New Hard Times: The Great Recession in Comparative Perspective* (Ithaca, NY, Cornell University Press) 129–49.
Hansmann, H and Kraakman, R (2001) 'The End of History for Corporate Law' *Georgetown Law Journal* 89(2), 439–68.
Hanson, C and Rathkey, P (1984) 'Industrial Democracy: A Post-Bullock Shopfloor View' *British Journal of Industrial Relations* 22(2), 154–68.
Harman, AAJ (1974) 'Shareholder Control' *Financial Times* (11 July) 2.
Harper Ho, VE (2010) '"Enlightened Shareholder Value": Corporate Governance Beyond the Shareholder-Stakeholder Divide' *Journal of Corporation Law* 36(1), 59–112.
Harris, K (1995) *Attlee*, new and revised edn (London, Weidenfeld & Nicolson).
Harrison, JS, Phillips, RA and Freeman, RE (2020) 'On the 2019 Business Roundtable "Statement on the Purpose of a Corporation"' *Journal of Management* 46(7), 1223–37.
Head, FD (1945) 'Powers of the Board' *Financial Times* (17 October) 3.
Heller, F (1979) *What Do the British Want from Participation and Industrial Democracy?* (London, Anglo-German Foundation for the Study of Industrial Society).
Henderson, J (1977) *A Guide to the Bullock Report* (London, Industrial Society).
Henderson, R and Temple-West, P (2019) 'Group of US Corporate Leaders Ditches Shareholder-First Mantra' *FT.com* (19 August).
Hennessy, P (2007) *Having it So Good: Britain in the Fifties* (London, Penguin).
Hertig, G (2018) 'Governance by Institutional Investors in a Stakeholder World' in JN Gordon and W-G Ringe (eds), *The Oxford Handbook of Corporate Law and Governance* (Oxford, Oxford University Press) 821–38.
Hill, JG (2015) 'Images of the Shareholder: Shareholder Power and Shareholder Powerlessness' in JG Hill and RS Thomas (eds), *Research Handbook on Shareholder Power* (Cheltenham, Edward Elgar) 53–73.
Höchstädter, A and Scheck, B (2015) 'What's in a Name: An Analysis of Impact Investing Understandings by Academics and Practitioners' *Journal of Business Ethics* 132(2), 449–75.
Horn, L (2012) 'Company Law in the European Union: From Industrial to Shareholder Democracy?' in L Horn (ed), *Regulating Corporate Governance in the EU* (London, Palgrave Macmillan) 80–103.
Horner, J (1974) *Studies in Industrial Democracy* (London, Gollancz).
Hutton, W (1996) *The State We're In* (London, Vintage).
——. (2015) *How Good We Can Be: Ending the Mercenary Society and Building a Great Country* (London, Little, Brown Book Group).

'Institute of Chartered Accountants' (1954) *Financial Times* (6 May) 2.

Ireland, P (1996) 'Corporate Governance, Stakeholding, and the Company: Towards a Less Degenerate Capitalism?' *Journal of Law and Society* 23(3), 287–320.

——. (1999) 'Company Law and the Myth of Shareholder Ownership' *Modern Law Review* 62(1), 32–57.

Ivanova, MR (2017) 'Institutional Investors as Stewards of the Corporation: Exploring the Challenges to the Monitoring Hypothesis' *Business Ethics* 26(2), 175–88.

Jackson, B (2005) 'Revisionism Reconsidered: "Property-Owning Democracy" and Egalitarian Strategy in Post-War Britain' *Twentieth Century British History* 16(4), 416–40.

Jackson, JBH (1982) 'Board Structures' in K Midgely (ed), *Management Accountability and Corporate Governance* (London, Macmillan Press) 15–26.

Jefferys, K (2007) *Politics and the People: A History of British Democracy since 1918* (London, Atlantic).

Jensen, M (2001) 'Value Maximisation, Stakeholder Theory, and the Corporate Objective Function' *European Financial Management* 7(3), 297–317.

Jensen, MC and Meckling, WH (1976) 'Theory of the Firm: Managerial Behavior, Agency Costs and Ownership Structure' *Journal of Financial Economics* 3(4), 305–60.

Jervis, F (1966) *The Company, the Shareholder and Growth* (London, Institute of Economic Affairs).

Jobson, R (2013) '"Waving the Banners of a Bygone Age", Nostalgia and Labour's Clause IV Controversy, 1959–60' *Contemporary British History* 27(2), 123–44.

Joffe, V and Hochhauser, A (1980) *The Companies Act 1980: A Practical Guide* (London, Oyez Publishing Ltd).

'Johnson & Phillips, Limited (Cable Makers, Electrical & General Engineers & Contractors)' (1956) *Financial Times* (18 May) 4.

Johnston, A (2020) 'Market-Led Sustainability through Information Disclosure' in B Sjåfjell and CM Bruner (eds), *The Cambridge Handbook of Corporate Law, Corporate Governance and Sustainability* (Cambridge, Cambridge University Press) 204–17.

Jordan, AG, Richardson, JJ and Kimber, RH (1977), 'The Origins of the Water Act of 1973' *Public Administration* 55(3), 317–34.

Jung, J and Dobbin, F (2012) 'Finance and Institutional Investors' in K Cetina and A Preda (eds), *The Oxford Handbook of the Sociology of Finance* (Oxford, Oxford University Press) 52–74.

Kahn-Freund, O (1946) 'Company Law Reform: A Review of the Report of the Committee on Company Law Amendment' *Modern Law Review* 9(3), 235–56.

——. (1977) 'Industrial Democracy' *Industrial Law Journal* 6(1), 65–84.

Kavanagh, D (1992) 'The Postwar Consensus' *Twentieth Century British History* 3(2), 175–90.

Kavanagh, D and Morris, P (1989) *Consensus Politics from Attlee to Major*, 2nd edn (Oxford, Blackwell).

Keay, A (2006) 'Enlightened Shareholder Value, the Reform of the Duties of Company Directors and the Corporate Objective' *Lloyd's Maritime and Commercial Law Quarterly* 3, 335–61.

——. (2007) 'Tackling the Issue of the Corporate Objective: An Analysis of the United Kingdom's Enlightened Shareholder Value Approach' *Sydney Law Review* 29(4), 577–612.

——. (2010) 'Shareholder Primacy in Corporate Law: Can it Survive? Should it Survive?' *European Company and Financial Law Review* 7(3), 369–413.

——. (2012) *The Enlightened Shareholder Value Principle and Corporate Governance* (London, Taylor & Francis).

Keay, A and Adamopoulou, R (2012) 'Shareholder Value and UK Companies: A Positivist Inquiry' *European Business Organization Law Review* 13(1), 1–29.

Keim, G, Baysinger, B and Meiners, R (1981) 'The Corporate Democracy Act: Would the Majority Rule?' *Business Horizons* 24(2), 30–35.

Kelf-Cohen, R (1958) *Nationalisation in Britain: The End of a Dogma* (London, Macmillan).

Kellett, R (1962) *Ordinary Shares for Ordinary Savers* (London, Institute of Economic Affairs).

Kershaw, D (2012) *Company Law in Context*, 2nd edn (Oxford, Oxford University Press).

Kershaw, D (2018a) 'Corporate Law and Self-Regulation' in JN Gordon and W-G Ringe (eds), *The Oxford Handbook of Corporate Law and Governance* (Oxford, Oxford University Press) 869–905.

——. (2018b) *The Foundations of Anglo-American Corporate Fiduciary Law* (Cambridge, Cambridge University Press).

Kershaw, D and Schuster, E-P (2019) 'The Purposive Transformation of Company Law' LSE Legal Studies Working Paper 4/2019.

Keynes, J (1936). *The General Theory of Employment, Interest and Money* (London, Macmillan).

Kiarie, S (2006) 'At Crossroads: Shareholder Value, Stakeholder Value and Enlightened Shareholder Value: Which Road Should the United Kingdom Take?' *International Company and Commercial Law Review* 17(11), 329–43.

Kirkpatrick, G (2009) 'Corporate Governance Lessons from the Financial Crisis' *OECD Journal: Financial Market Trends* 2009(1), 61–87.

Knight, Sir A (1982) 'The Aims and Objectives of Corporate Bodies' in K Midgely (ed), *Management Accountability and Corporate Governance* (London, Macmillan Press) 3–14.

Kolb, R (2008) *Encyclopedia of Business Ethics and Society* (Los Angeles, SAGE).

Konzelmann, SJ, Chic, V and Fovargue-Davies, M (2020) 'Shareholder Value or Public Purpose? From John Maynard Keynes and Adolf Berle to the Modern Debate' Centre for Business Research, University of Cambridge – Law Working Paper 520.

——. (2021) 'Keynes, Capitalism and Public Purpose' *Cambridge Journal of Economics* 45(3), 591–612.

Konzelmann, SJ, Deakin, SF, Fovargue-Davies, M and Wilkinson, F (2018) *Labour, Finance and Inequality: The Insecurity Cycle in British Public Policy* (London, Routledge).

Kynaston, D (1999) *The City of London*, vol III: *Illusions of Gold, 1914–1945* (London, Chatto & Windus).

——. (2001) *The City of London*, vol IV: *A Club No More, 1945–2000* (London, Chatto & Windus).

——. (2007) *Austerity Britain: 1945–51* (London, Bloomsbury).

Labour Editor (1976) 'Tory Trade Unionists Reject Call for Worker-Directors' *The Times* (5 July) 3.

Labour Party (1945) *Let Us Face the Future: The Labour Party Manifesto 1945* (London, Labour Party).

——. (1950) *Let Us Win Through Together: A Declaration of Labour Policy for the Consideration of the Nation* (London, Labour Party).

——. (1955) *Forward with Labour: Labour's Policy for the Consideration of the Nation, 1955* (London, Labour Party).

——. (1956) *Towards Equality: Labour's Policy for Social Justice* (London, Labour Party).

——. (1957) *Industry and Society: Labour's Policy on Future Public Ownership* (London, Labour Party).

——. (1959) *Britain Belongs to You: The Labour Party's Policy for Consideration by the British People, General Election, Thursday 8 October 1959* (London, Labour Party).

——. (1964) *Let's Go with Labour for the New Britain: The Labour Party's Manifesto for the 1964 General Election* (London, Labour Party).

——. (1966) *Time for Decision: Manifesto of the Labour Party, General Election, 1966* (London, Labour Party).

——. (1967) *Report of the Labour Party Working Party on Industrial Democracy* (London, Labour Party).

——. (1970). *Now Britain's Strong – Let's Make it Great to Live in: The Labour Party's Manifesto for the 1970 General Election* (London, Labour Party).

——. (1974a) *Let Us Work Together: Labour's Way Out of the Crisis: Labour Party Manifesto, February 1974* (London, Labour Party).

——. (1974b) *Britain Will Win with Labour: Labour Party Manifesto, October 1974* (London, Labour Party).

——. (1976) *Labour's Programme for Britain: Annual Conference 1976* (London, Labour Party).

——. (1979) *The Labour Way is the Better Way: The Labour Party Manifesto, 1979* (London, Labour Party).
——. (2017) *For the Many Not the Few: The Labour Party Manifesto 2017* (London, Labour Party).
——. (2019) *It's Time for Real Change: For the Many Not the Few: The Labour Party Manifesto 2019* (London, Labour Party).
Labour Party National Executive Committee (1953) *Challenge to Britain: A Programme of Action for the Next Labour Government* (London, Labour Party).
——. (1975) *Labour and Industry: The Next Steps: A Statement by the NEC Presented to the Labour Party Annual Conference, Blackpool, 1975* (London, Labour Party).
Langevoort, D (2020) 'The Effects of Shareholder Primacy, Publicness, and "Privateness" on Corporate Cultures' *Seattle University Law Review* 43(2), 377.
Langford, R (2020) 'Purpose-Based Governance: A New Paradigm' *University of New South Wales Law Journal* 43(3), 954–76.
'Laporte' (1974) *The Economist* (5 October) 48.
Laufer, W (2003) 'Social Accountability and Corporate Greenwashing' *Journal of Business Ethics* 43(3) 253–61.
Lee, T and Tweedie, DP (1977) *The Private Shareholder and the Corporate Report: A Report to the Research Committee of the Institute of Chartered Accountants in England and Wales* (London, Institute of Chartered Accountants in England and Wales).
Leslie, N (1977) 'A Cordial Way of Shelling out Facts to Shareholders' *Financial Times* (2 December) 21.
Lewis, R and Clark, J (1977) 'The Bullock Report' *Modern Law Review* 40(3), 323–38.
Lex (1947) 'Apathetic Shareholders' *Financial Times* (4 June) 1.
——. (1968) 'Plotting How Shareholders React to Bids' *Financial Times* (8 April) 1.
Liberal Party (1959) *People Count: The Liberal Manifesto 1959* (London, Liberal Party).
Licht, AN (2019) 'Stakeholder Impartiality: A New Classic Approach for the Objectives of the Corporation' European Corporate Governance Institute – Law Working Paper 476/2019 (13 September).
Lines, WM (1970) 'Lines Bros Ltd' *The Economist* (5 September) 96.
Lipshaw, JM (2021) 'The False Dichotomy of Corporate Governance Platitudes' *Journal of Corporation Law* 46(2), 345–84.
Lipton, M and Savitt, W (2007) 'The Many Myths of Lucian Bebchuk' *Virginia Law Review* 93(3), 733–58.
Littlewood, J (1998) *The Stock Market: 50 Years of Capitalism at Work* (London, Financial Times Management).
'Look Who the Owners are' (1977) *The Economist* (29 January) 82.
Loughrey, J, Keay, A and Cerioni, L (2008) 'Legal Practitioners, Enlightened Shareholder Value and the Shaping of Corporate Governance' *Journal of Corporate Law Studies* 8(1), 79–111.
Lowe, R (1990) 'The Second World War, Consensus, and the Foundation of the Welfare State' *Twentieth Century British History* 1(2), 152–82.
Lund, DS (2020) 'Corporate Finance for Social Good', USC CLASS Research Paper No CLASS20-3, USC Law Legal Studies Paper No 20-3, *Columbia Law Review* 121.
Mace, CA (1961) 'The Faceless Ones' *Financial Times* (1 May) 8.
Macintyre, C (1999) 'The Stakeholder Society and the Welfare State: Forward to the Past!' *Contemporary Politics* 5(2), 121–35.
Mackenzie, AL (1982) 'The Employee and the Company Director' *New Law Journal* 132(2), 688–90.
MacNeil, I (2010) 'Activism and Collaboration among Shareholders in UK Listed Companies' *Capital Markets Law Journal* 5(4), 419–38.
Maltby, J and Wilkinson, R (1997) 'UK Corporate Governance in Historical Perspective' *Global Economic Review* 26(3), 37–58.
Manne, HG (1962) 'The "Higher Criticism" of the Modern Corporation' *Columbia Law Review* 62(3), 399–432.

——. (2007) 'The "Corporate Democracy" Oxymoron' *Wall Street Journal* (2 January) A.23.
Marchetti, P and Passador, ML (2022) 'Thirty Years and Far from Being Done: Is it Truly Time to Abolish the UK Corporate Governance Code?' Bocconi Legal Studies Research Paper No 4269661.
Martin, R (2003) 'Politics and Industrial Relations' in P Ackers and A Wilkinson (eds), *Understanding Work and Employment: Industrial Relations in Transition* (Oxford, Oxford University Press) 161–75.
Matthews, D (1989) 'The British Experience of Profit-Sharing' *Economic History Review* 42(4), 439–64.
Matthijs, M (2011) *Ideas and Economic Crises in Britain from Attlee to Blair (1945–2005)* (Abingdon, Routledge).
Mayer, C (2019) *Prosperity: Better Business Makes the Greater Good* (Oxford, Oxford University Press).
——. (2020, 3 June) 'Shareholderism versus Stakeholderism – A Misconceived Contradiction: A Comment on "The Illusory Promise of Stakeholder Governance" by Lucian Bebchuk and Roberto Tallarita' European Corporate Governance Institute – Law Working Paper 522/2020.
McDonald, A (1978) 'Can British Leyland Survive?' *New Statesman* (27 January) 95, 108.
McLachlan, S (1972) 'Pressure on Distillers Mounts from Shareholders and Unions' *Financial Times* (23 December) 24.
'Meeting the Shareholders' (1964) *The Economist* (15 February) 646.
Melling, J (2003) 'Managing the White-Collar Union: Salaried Staff, Trade-Union Leadership, and the Politics of Organized Labour in Postwar Britain, c. 1950–1968' *International Review of Social History* 48(2), 245–71.
Middlemas, K (1979) *Politics in Industrial Society: The Experience of the British System since 1911* (London, Deutsch).
——. (1986) *Power, Competition and the State*, vol 1: *Britain in Search of a Balance, 1940–61* (Basingstoke, Macmillan).
——. (1990) *Power, Competition and the State*, vol 2: *Threats to the Postwar Settlement: Britain, 1961–74* (Basingstoke: Macmillan).
——. (1991) *Power, Competition and the State*, vol 3: *The End of the Postwar Era: Britain since 1974* (Basingstoke, Macmillan).
Millman, GJ (2003) 'Shareholder Democracy' *Chief Executive* (1 October), 44–47.
Millon, D (2013) 'Radical Shareholder Primacy' *University of St Thomas Law Journal* 10(4), 1013–44.
Mintzberg, H (2019, 16 November) 'Round and Round Goes the Business Roundtable', https://mintzberg.org/blog/round-and-round-goes-the-business-roundtable.
'The Modern Shareholder' (1949) *The Economist* (30 July) 256.
Moore, C (2016) *Margaret Thatcher: The Authorized Biography*, vol 2 (London, Penguin Books).
Moore, M (2013) *Corporate Governance in the Shadow of the State* (Oxford, Hart Publishing).
——. (2018) 'Shareholder Primacy, Labour and UK Company Law' in H Wells (ed), *Research Handbook on the History of Corporate and Company Law* (Cheltenham, Edward Elgar) 142–69.
Moore, M and Petrin, M (2017) *Corporate Governance: Law, Regulation and Theory* (London, Palgrave Macmillan).
Moran, M (2001) 'The Rise of the Regulatory State in Britain' *Parliamentary Affairs* 54(1), 19–34.
Morgan, EV and Thomas, WA (1962) *The Stock Exchange: Its History and Functions* (London, Elek Books).
Morgan, KO (1992) *The People's Peace* (Oxford, Oxford University Press).
——. (2010) 'James Callaghan, 1976–1979' in V Bogdanor (ed), *From New Jerusalem to New Labour: British Prime Ministers from Attlee to Blair* (Basingstoke, Palgrave Macmillan) 123–43.
Morrison, D (2004) 'New Labour, Citizenship and the Discourse of the Third Way' in S Hale, W Leggett and L Martell (eds), *The Third Way and Beyond: Criticisms, Futures and Alternatives* (Manchester, Manchester University Press).
Moss, J, Clarke, N, Jenning, W and Stoker, G (2016) 'Golden Age, Apathy or Stealth? Democratic Engagement in Britain, 1945–1950' *Contemporary British History* 30(4), 441–62.

Moyle, J (1971) *The Pattern of Ordinary Share Ownership, 1957–1970* (Cambridge, Cambridge University Press).
Mukwiri, J (2013) 'Myth of Shareholder Primacy in English Law' *European Business Law Review* 24(2), 217–41.
Munro, C (2012) 'The Fiscal Politics of Savings and Share Ownership in Britain, 1970–1980' *Historical Journal* 55(3), 757–78.
Naylor, G (1960) *Company Law for Shareholders* (London, Institute of Economic Affairs).
Naylor, G for the Wider Share Ownership Council (1968) *Sharing the Profits: An Inquiry into the Habits, Attitudes and Problems of Employees' Shareholdings Schemes* (London, Garnstone Press).
Nelson, E (2009) 'Milton Friedman and UK Economic Policy: 1938–1979' *Federal Reserve Bank of St Louis Review* 91(5), 465–506.
——. (2017) 'Reaffirming the Influence of Milton Friedman on UK Economic Policy' *Finance and Economics Discussion Series 2017-096* (Washington DC, Board of Governors of the Federal Reserve System).
'New Basis for Markets?' (1951) *The Economist* (29 September) 758.
Nolan, R (2006) 'The Continuing Evolution of Shareholder Governance' *Cambridge Law Journal* 65(1), 92–127.
Ogden, S (1982) 'Trade Unions, Industrial Democracy and Collective Bargaining' *Sociology* 16(4), 544–63.
Oren, T and Blyth, M (2019) 'From Big Bang to Big Crash: The Early Origins of the UK's Finance-Led Growth Model and the Persistence of Bad Policy Ideas' *New Political Economy* 24(5), 605–22.
Owen, G (1977) 'Fade-out Time for Shareholders' *Financial Times* (17 May) 2.
——. (2021) *The Case for Shareholder-Based Capitalism* (London, Policy Exchange).
Owen, N (1973) 'Reform Plans "Must Protect Shareholders"' *Financial Times* (27 November) 28.
Pajuste, A and Toniolo, A (2022) 'Corporate Response to the War in Ukraine: Stakeholder Governance or Stakeholder Pressure?' European Corporate Governance Institute – Finance Working Paper No 839/2022.
Palmer, TJ (1982) 'Social Responsibility and the Institutional Investor' in K Midgely (ed), *Management Accountability and Corporate Governance* (London, Macmillan Press) 102–13.
Parker, G, Thomas, D and Morris, S (2022) 'New UK Chancellor Kwasi Kwarteng Promises "Big Bang 2.0" for City of London' *Financial Times* (7 September), www.ft.com/content/fdf43b25-cafb-4049-8a72-d386c8ea4fdf.
Parkinson, J (1993) *Corporate Power and Responsibility: Issues in the Theory of Company Law* (Oxford, Clarendon Press).
Parkinson, J and Kelly, G (1999) 'The Combined Code on Corporate Governance' *Political Quarterly* 70(1), 101–07.
Peech, AJ (1966) 'The United Steel Companies Limited' *The Economist* (8 January) 133.
——. (1967) 'The United Steel Companies Limited' *The Economist* (28 January) 359.
Pickard, J (2019) 'Labour Would Cost UK Companies £300bn by Shifting Shares to Staff' *Financial Times* (2 September) 1.
Pint, E (1990) 'Nationalization and Privatization: A Rational-Choice Perspective on Efficiency' *Journal of Public Policy* 10(3), 267–98.
Pinto-Duschinsky, M (1970) 'Bread and Circuses? The Conservatives in Office, 1951–1964' in V Bogdanor and R Skidelsky (eds), *The Age of Affluence, 1951–1964* (London, Macmillan) 55–77.
Pistor, K (2019) 'Why America's CEOs Have Turned against Their Shareholders' *Australian Financial Review* (28 August) 47.
Plender, J (1982) *That's the Way the Money Goes: The Financial Institutions and the Nation's Savings* (London, Deutsch).
——. (2019) 'Shareholders are Being Dethroned as Rulers of Value' *Financial Times* (3 January) 11.
Pollak, L (2013) 'Labour's Kryptonite? The Lessons of the Bullock Commission on Industrial Democracy' *Renewal* 21(2–3), 105–09.

Pollard, S (1992) *The Development of the British Economy: 1914–1990*, 4th edn (London, Edward Arnold).
Poole, M (1982) 'Theories of Industrial Democracy: The Emerging Synthesis' *Sociological Review* 30(2), 181–207.
——. (1986) *Towards a New Industrial Democracy: Workers' Participation in Industry* (London, Routledge & Kegan Paul).
Prentice, DD (1980) *Companies Act 1980* (London, Butterworths).
——. (1981) 'A Company and its Employees: The Companies Act 1980' *Industrial Law Journal* 10(1), 1–9.
'Privileged Shareholders' (1957) *The Economist* (29 June) 1183.
'Profile of the Small Investor' (1959) *The Guardian* (14 December) 8.
Radice, G (1974) *Working Power: Policies for Industrial Democracy* (London, Fabian Society).
Radice, G and Lewis, R (1976) *Workers in the Boardroom* (London, Fabian Society).
Ramsay, H (1977) 'Cycles of Control: Worker Participation in Sociological and Historical Perspective' *Sociology* 11(3), 481–506.
Readhead, P (1971) 'Aunty Mabel's View of Bids' *Financial Times* (26 November) 19.
Ream, B (1978) *A Guide to the White Paper on Industrial Democracy* (London, Industrial Society).
'Recent Developments' (1974) *Harvard International Law Journal* 15(3), 541–54.
Reddish, Sir H (1960) 'Rugby Portland Cement' *The Economist* (30 April) 470.
'Reforming Company Law' (1960) *Political Quarterly* 31(2), 142–50.
Regan, RL (1962a) 'Worker-Shareholders' *Financial Times* (12 February) 6.
——. (1962b) 'Worker-Shareholder' *Financial Times* (27 February) 8.
'Report & Accounts' (1977) *The Economist* (2 April) 130.
'Reports and Awards: Industrial Democracy' (1975) *Industrial Law Journal* 4(4), 249–53.
Riddell, P (1977) 'Decline of Small Shareholder Continues' *Financial Times* (23 April) 11.
——. (1997) 'The End of Clause IV, 1994–95' *Contemporary British History* 11(2), 24–49.
Rideout, RW (1971) 'The Industrial Relations Act 1971' *Modern Law Review* 34(6), 655–75.
Ringe, W-G (2015) 'Shareholder Activism: A Renaissance' in JN Gordon and W-G Ringe (eds), *The Oxford Handbook of Corporate Law and Governance* (Oxford, Oxford University Press) 387–424.
Rissman, P and Kearney, D (2019) 'Rise of the Shadow ESG Regulators: Investment Advisers, Sustainability Accounting, and their Effects on Corporate Social Responsibility' *Environmental Law Reporter News & Analysis* 49(2), 10155–87.
Robertson, N and Sams, KI (1972), 'The New Legal Framework for Britain's Industrial Relations' *Monthly Labor Review* 95(3), 48–52.
Roe, MJ (2001) 'The Shareholder Wealth Maximization Norm and Industrial Organization' *University of Pennsylvania Law Review* 149(6), 2063–81.
——. (2021) 'Corporate Purpose and Corporate Competition' European Corporate Governance Institute – Law Working Paper 601/2021.
Rose, S (1989) *The Shareholder: The Truth about Wider Share Ownership* (London, Mercury).
Rowbottom, N and Schroeder, M (2014) 'The Rise and Fall of the UK Operating and Financial Review' *Accounting, Auditing & Accountability Journal* 27(4), 655–85.
'RTZ' (1974) *The Economist* (25 May) 42.
Rubner, A (1966) *The Ensnared Shareholder: Directors and the Modern Corporation* (Harmondsworth, Penguin)
'Rugby Portland Cement' (1952) *Financial Times* (31 March) 2.
Runciman, W (1966) *Relative Deprivation and Social Justice: A Study of Attitudes to Social Inequality in Twentieth-Century England* (London, Routledge & Kegan Paul).
Russell, GR (1975) 'Fair Play for Shareholders' *Financial Times* (4 June) 17.
Rutterford, J (2012) 'The Shareholder Voice: British and American Accents, 1890–1965' *Enterprise & Society* 13(1), 120–53.
Rutterford, J and Sotiropoulos, D (2017) 'The Rise of the Small Investor in the United States and United Kingdom, 1895 to 1970' *Enterprise & Society* 18(3), 485–535.

'S.E. Chairman's Call for 5m Shareholders' (1956) *Financial Times* (16 March) 9.
Sampson, A (1965) *Anatomy of Britain* (London, Hodder & Stoughton).
——. (1971) *The New Anatomy of Britain* (London, Hodder & Stoughton).
Sánchez Serrano, A (2020) 'High-Frequency Trading and Systemic Risk: A Structured Review of Findings and Policies' *Review of Economics* 71(3), 169–95.
Scarlett, AM (2011) 'Imitation or Improvement? The Evolution of Shareholder Derivative Litigation in the United States, United Kingdom, Canada, and Australia' *Arizona Journal of International and Comparative Law* 28(3), 569–628.
Schons, L and Steinmeier, M (2016) 'Walk the Talk? How Symbolic and Substantive CSR Actions Affect Firm Performance Depending on Stakeholder Proximity' *Corporate Social Responsibility & Environmental Management* 23(6), 358–72.
Schwab, K (2019, 2 December) 'Davos Manifesto 2020: The Universal Purpose of a Company in the Fourth Industrial Revolution', Davos: World Economic Forum, www.weforum.org/agenda/2019/12/davos-manifesto-2020-the-universal-purpose-of-a-company-in-the-fourth-industrial-revolution.
Sealy, LS (1987) 'Directors' Wider Responsibilities Problems Conceptual, Practical and Procedural' *Monash University Law Review* 13(3), 164–88.
Seldon, A (1994a) 'Consensus: A Debate Too Long?' *Parliamentary Affairs* 47(4), 501–14.
——. (1994b) 'The Rise and Fall (and Rise Again?) of the Post-war Consensus' in B Jones (ed), *Politics UK*, 2nd edn (Hemel Hempstead, Harvester Wheatsheaf) 42–59.
Shabani, M, Tyson, J, Toporowski, J and McKinley, T (2015) 'The Financial System in the UK' FESSUD Working Paper No 14.
Shackleton, JR (1977) 'Bullock on Industrial Democracy' *Political Quarterly* 48(2), 228–33.
'Shades of the Prison House' (1973) *The Economist* (22 December) 87.
'Shareholder Pressure' (1973) *Financial Times* (5 January) 18.
'Shareholders and Directors' (1959) *The Economist* (14 February) 612.
'Shareholders and Dividend Restraint' (1951) *Financial Times* (21 December) 4.
'Shareholders on the Rack' (1975) *Financial Times* (24 January) 38.
'Shareholders Oppose State Steel' (1958) *Financial Times* (31 January) 8.
'Shareholders: Why So Few?' (1966) *The Economist* (2 July) 52.
Shenfield, B (1971) *Company Boards: Their Responsibilities to Shareholders, Employees, and the Community* (London, Allen & Unwin).
Shleifer, A and Vishny, R (1997) 'A Survey of Corporate Governance' *Journal of Finance* 52(2), 737–83.
Shonfield, A (1958) *British Economic Policy since the War* (Harmondsworth, Penguin Books).
'Shorter Note' (1965) *The Economist* (11 September) 1029.
'Should British Leyland Have More Worker-Shareholders?' (1974) *The Economist* (21 December) 91.
'Silent Shareholders' (1963) *The Economist* (27 July) 385.
Singer, A and Ron, A (2018) 'Models of Shareholder Democracy: A Transnational Approach' *Global Constitutionalism* 7(3), 422–46.
Singer, MW (1950) 'Small Investors and Dividend Limitation' *Financial Times* (7 July) 4.
Skapinker, M (2019) 'Responsible Business: Is This Time Different?' *Financial Times* (17 December) 9.
'Small Mercies' (1974) *The Economist* (27 July) 80.
Smith, D (1998) 'The Shareholder Primacy Norm' *Journal of Corporation Law* 23(2), 277–324.
Sneirson, JF (2020) 'The History of Shareholder Primacy, from Adam Smith through the Rise of Financialism' in B Sjåfjell and CM Bruner (eds), *The Cambridge Handbook of Corporate Law, Corporate Governance and Sustainability* (Cambridge, Cambridge University Press) 73–85.
Sommer, A (1991) 'Whom Should the Corporation Serve? The Berle-Dodd Debate Revisited Sixty Years Later' *Delaware Journal of Corporate Law* 16(1), 33–56.
Soohun, K and Yoon, A (2020, 17 March) 'Analyzing Active Managers' Commitment to ESG: Evidence from United Nations Principles for Responsible Investment', https://ssrn.com/abstract=3555984 or http://dx.doi.org/10.2139/ssrn.3555984.

'Sorry, We Slept' (1979) *The Economist* (12 May) 122.
'Speaker's Worker Shareholders' (1974) *Financial Times* (16 January) 20.
Spiegelberg, R (1973) *The City: Power without Accountability* (London, Blond and Briggs).
Stapledon, GP (1996) *Institutional Shareholders and Corporate* Governance (Oxford, Clarendon Press).
'The State as Shareholder' (1978) *The Economist* (4 March) 93.
'Steady as She Sinks' (1976) *The Economist* (9 October) 47.
Stewart, F (2011) 'Berle's Conception of Shareholder Primacy: Forgotten Perspective for Reconsideration during the Rise of Finance' *Seattle University Law Review* 34(4), 1457–500.
'Stewarts and Lloyds, Limited' (1958) *Financial Times* (29 January) 10.
'Stewarts and Lloyds Ltd' (1960) *The Economist* (13 February) 660.
Stone, O (Director) (1987) *Wall Street* (American Entertainment Partners; Amercent Films).
Sun, W, Stewart, J and Pollard, D (eds) (2011) *Corporate Governance and the Global Financial Crisis: International Perspectives* (Cambridge, Cambridge University Press).
Sunday Times of London Insight Team (1979) *Suffer the Children: The Story of Thalidomide* (London, Deutsch).
Swift, DB and Fagan, HA (1959) 'Shareholders and Directors' *The Economist* (21 February) 680.
'Takeover without Tears?' (1965) *The Economist* (27 March) 1426.
'Tate & Lyle, Limited' (1949) *Financial Times* (16 September) 6.
Taylor, P (1977) 'Shareholders' Rights' *Financial Times* (15 February) 15.
'The Thalidomide Issue' (1973) *The Economist* (6 January) 9.
'That Old Black Magic' (1973) *The Economist* (2 June) 103.
Thomson, AW (1977) 'New Focus on Industrial Democracy in Britain' *Annals of the American Academy of Political and Social Science* 431(1), 32–43.
Tinline, P (2022) *The Death of Consensus 100 Years of British Political Nightmares* (London, Hurst).
Titmuss, R (1960) *The Irresponsible Society* (London, Fabian Society).
Tomasic, R and Akinbami, F (2011) 'Towards a New Corporate Governance after the Global Financial Crisis' *International Company and Commercial Law Review* 22(8), 237–49.
Trades Union Congress (1944) *Post-War Reconstruction: Interim Report* (London, Trades Union Congress).
——. (1973) *Industrial Democracy: Interim Report by the TUC General Council* (London, Trade Union Congress).
——. (1974) *Industrial Democracy: A Statement of Policy by the Trade Union* Congress (London, Trade Union Congress).
Trades Union Congress and Great Britain Committee of Inquiry on Industrial Democracy (1977) *TUC Guide to the Bullock Report on Industrial Democracy* (London, Trade Union Congress).
Trafford, J (1974) 'Why Fisons Examines its Shareholders' *Financial Times* (17 July) 17.
'The TUC Goes for Parity' (1976) *The Economist* (4 September) 79.
Turner, M (2021) 'BlackRock Signs ESG "Milestone" Loan Tied to Employee Equality' *Global Capital* (8 April).
'Two Diamonds' (1975) *The Economist* (2 August) 12.
'US Business Association Redefines the Purpose of a Corporation' (2019) *Company Lawyer* 40(11), 360.
Vernon, R, Middleton, M, and Harper, DG (1973) *Who Owns the Blue Chips? A Study of Shareholding in a Leading Company* (Epping, Gower Press).
'Very Interesting' (1974) *The Economist* (1 June) 96.
Villiers, C (2000) 'Section 309 of the Companies Act 1985: Is it Time for a Reappraisal?' in H Collins, P Davies and R Rideout (eds), *Legal Regulation of the Employment Relation* (London, Kluwer Law International) 593–614.
——. (2006) *Corporate Reporting and Company Law* (Cambridge, Cambridge University Press).
'Vote for Reform' (1966) *The Economist* (19 March) 1170.

Wall Street Journal London Bureau (1946) 'Bank of England's Fate under Nationalization "Up to Administrators"' *Wall Street Journal* (Eastern edn, 23 January) 4.

Warner, S (2019) '(Re)politicising "the Governmental": Resisting the Industrial Relations Act 1971' *British Journal of Politics & International Relations* 21(3), 541–58.

Webb, S (1918) *The New Constitution of the Labour Party: A Party of Handworkers and Brainworkers, etc* (London, Cooperative Printing Society).

Webb, S and Webb, B (1897) *Industrial Democracy* (London, Longmans Green & Co).

Wedderburn, B (1977) 'Industrial Democracy Revisited' *New Statesman* (29 July) 94, 137.

Wedderburn, KW (1977) 'Industrial Democracy and Company Law' in R Benedictus, CJ Bourn and AC Neal (eds), *Industrial Democracy, the Implications of the Bullock Report: Proceedings of a Conference Held at the University of Leicester, 4–5 April 1977* (Leicester, Department of Adult Education, University of Leicester).

Wells, C (2002) 'Cycles of Corporate Social Responsibility: An Historical Retrospective for the Twenty-First Century' *University of Kansas Law Review* 51(1), 77–140.

Wheeler, H (2008) 'A New Frontier for Labor' *Labor Studies Journal* 33(2), 163–78.

Whiting, R (2004) 'The City and Democratic Capitalism 1950–1970' in R Michie and P Williamson (eds) *The British Government and the City of London in the Twentieth Century* (Cambridge, Cambridge University Press) 96–114.

'Who is the Small Investor?' (1959) *Financial Times* (14 December) 6.

'Who Owns What?' (1972) *The Economist* (8 January) 73.

'Who Owns What?' (1976) *The Economist* (13 November) 22.

Williams, CA (2018) 'Corporate Social Responsibility and Corporate Governance' in JN Gordon and W-G Ringe (eds), *The Oxford Handbook of Corporate Law and Governance* (Oxford, Oxford University Press) 634–78.

Williams, CA and Conley, JM (2005) 'An Emerging Third Way? The Erosion of the Anglo-American Shareholder Value Construct' *Cornell International Law Journal* 38(2), 493–552.

Williamson, A (2016) 'The Bullock Report on Industrial Democracy and the Post-War Consensus' *Contemporary British History* 30(1), 119–49.

Wilson, H (1973) *Democracy in Industry: A Speech Delivered at the N.W. Regional Conference of the Labour Party*, 17 March (Edinburgh Series of Policy Speeches No 3) (London, Labour Party).

Wincott, H (1967) 'Role of the Shareholder' *Financial Times* (10 November) 14.

——. (1968) 'How Not to Make Workers Shareholders' *Financial Times* (30 July) 12.

'With a Quaint Device, the Banquet Vanishes' (1972) *The Economist* (29 April) 102.

World Economic Forum (2020) *Stakeholder Principles in the COVID Era*, World Economic Forum (April), www3.weforum.org/docs/WEF_Stakeholder_Principles_COVID_Era.pdf.

World Economic Forum, Deloitte, EY, KPMG and PwC (2020) *Measuring Stakeholder Capitalism: Towards Common Metrics and Consistent Reporting of Sustainable Value Creation* (September), www.weforum.org/reports/measuring-stakeholder-capitalism-towards-common-metrics-and-consistent-reporting-of-sustainable-value-creation.

Xuereb, PG (1988) 'The Juridification of Industrial Relations through Company Law Reform' *Modern Law Review* 51(2), 156–72.

Yeung, K (2010) 'The Regulatory State' in R Baldwin, M Cave and M Lodge (eds), *The Oxford Handbook of Regulation* (Oxford, Oxford University Press) 64–83.

Zweig, F (1961) *The Worker in an Affluent Society: Family Life and Industry* (New York, Free Press of Glencoe).

'Zzzzz' (1976) *The Economist* (13 November) 138.

Index

www.ingramcontent.com/pod-product-compliance
Ingram Content Group UK Ltd.
Pitfield, Milton Keynes, MK11 3LW, UK
UKHW020239290926
15470UKWH00002B/634

9 781509 966806